One Thousand Years of Philosophy

One Thousand Years of Philosophy

From Rāmānuja to Wittgenstein

ROM HARRÉ

BLACKWELL
Publishers

First published 2000

2 4 6 8 10 9 7 5 3 1

Blackwell Publishers Inc.
350 Main Street
Malden, Massachusetts 02148
USA

Blackwell Publishers Ltd
108 Cowley Road
Oxford OX4 1JF
UK

Library of Congress Cataloging-in-Publication Data

Harré, Rom.
    One thousand years of philosophy : from Ramanuja to Wittgenstein / by Rom Harré.
        p.   cm.
    Includes bibliographical references and index.
        ISBN 0-631-21900-5 (alk. paper) – ISBN 0-631-21901-3 (pb : alk. paper)
        1. Philosophy – History.   I. Title.
    B72 H317   2001
    109 – dc21
                                                                00-033743

British Library Cataloguing in Publication Data
A CIP catalogue record for this book is available from the British Library.

Typeset in 11 on 13 pt Bembo
by Best-set Typesetter Ltd., Hong Kong
Printed in Great Britain by MPG Books Ltd., Bodmin, Cornwall

This book is printed on acid-free paper.

Contents

Preface

Why is philosophy still important enough to make such a study as this a worth while undertaking? Philosophy is, above all, a critical examination of human ways of life. Every human practice, be it intellectual or practical, presupposes all sorts of beliefs and attitudes, most of which are not consciously formulated by the practitioners. The role of the philosopher is to bring at least some of these pre-suppositions to light. Once we are made aware of them we can bring our critical faculties to bear upon them. Some presuppositions will survive our examination. Others will not. Of course, this analytical and critical practice that is philosophy has its own presuppositions, which, in their turn, can become legitimate topics for philosophical enquiry.

In making such a survey as this, one becomes aware of changes and continuities in the content and the methods of philosophical reflections that have occurred in the thousand years since the turn of the first millennium. In India about this time philosophers shifted their attention from an examination of the presuppositions of the means for escaping from selfhood into a selfless fusion with the cosmos, to a project for reshaping traditional concepts to make sense of personal salvation, even after death. Chinese philosophers have continued to reflect mainly on practical matters, retaining much of the point of view of Confucius and the Confucians for two millennia. Their interests took them toward the foundations of political philosophy, even though Buddhism, with its emphasis on the means of escaping from this world, had become well established in China by the end of the first Christian millennium. The problems thrown up by reflection on the presuppositions of religion dominated the philosophical interests of both Islamic and Christian philosophers during the first half of the

second millennium. This was to give way in the European West to the
study of the foundations of the claims of science to give a definitive
account of the cosmos and the human beings that inhabit a small
corner of it.

In attempting this project I have tried to avoid the superficialities
of a mere survey by being very selective in the topics I have chosen
to discuss. I have tried to highlight certain themes that seem to me to
have been important during the last thousand years of philosophical reflection. Thematic choices have strongly influenced the philosophies and philosophers that I have drawn upon. By arranging the
material thematically I have aimed at presenting the reader with a
certain amount of detail in the exposition of arguments and analyses.
This study has no pretensions to be an encyclopedia. I hope enough
detail has been given to allow the reader to follow the arguments, as
well as appreciate the conclusions. My aim in narrowing the number
of topics and authors has been to prevent the book from slipping into
a mere catalogue of the opinions of the famous and the influential.
I have tried to show, often in the words of the philosopher in question, how these opinions have been reached and how they have been
disputed.

Millennia and their constituent centuries provide no more than a
convenient scaffolding for telling a complicated story. Other ways of
marking epochs are scarcely less arbitrary. The "Renaissance" and the
"Enlightenment" will appear occasionally as rough guides to a certain
style of thinking, but I do not see them as rigidly demarcated moments
in the history of philosophy.

Philosophy has its own vocabularies of established terms. For those
trained in the discipline, there is always an echo of the implications
and nuances of philosophical terminologies that are not second nature
to the layperson. With the help of my friends I have made a serious
effort to present every philosophical argument and its constituent and
background concepts in a way that will be intelligible for those for
whom philosophy has not been a specialist field of study. I am sure
that I have not succeeded in every case. But I hope that the attempt
has been successful enough for readers without a formal background in philosophy to get some of the pleasure that comes from
appreciating a subtle analysis and a telling argument.

What of the insights of a thousand years of intellectual effort? As
we shall see, many of the presuppositions of the past are to be found

in the practices of the present. Patterns of thought emerge, fade, and reappear. The most potent of the philosophical stances of the millennial moment is relativism. This is the thesis that morality, knowledge, and meaning are relative each to their own moments in the history of humankind, and dependent for their authenticity on local contexts and cultural forms. In our time relativism has been promoted with enthusiasm and supported with some plausible arguments. But it has been proposed more than once in the long history of philosophy. Of course, philosophers in our day have come to relativist views somewhat differently from the paths followed in the past.

However, there is one line of development in contemporary philosophy that does seem to have no obvious antecedents, nor does it seem to echo anything in the past of other cultures. This is the turn from a study of what is expressed to the investigation of the means of its expression. This has been called the "linguistic turn." Some influential philosophers have had the bold intention of demonstrating that most of the puzzling philosophical problems of the past have not been genuine problems at all. From a search for solutions, we have moved to demonstrations of dissolutions. Many perennial philosophical problems are declared to be nothing but the surface appearances of deep-laid conceptual confusions.

Projecting from the past history of a discipline to its possible future is a hazardous enterprise. It is likely that many of the issues that seem to have been resolved will reappear in new guises. However, it would be very surprising if the critical stance to the very existence of philosophical problems were to be abandoned. No doubt new problems will appear. But, if I am right, they too will eventually yield to the techniques of dissolution.

Browsing through the philosophy collection in some major university library, where one happily has access to the stacks, and can sample here and there, one is struck by the breadth and excellence of what is available in surveys and histories. Few, however, attempt to cover philosophical thought in both the Orient and the Occident. This is generally left to the encyclopedias. Excellent though they are, the specialist articles are not generally addressed to a lay readership. A notable exception is Ninian Smart's massive and readable *World Philosophies* (1999). In the bibliography I have highlighted one or two comprehensive histories for each of my four cultural centers. Each important philosopher is represented by one or more major works in the bibliographies for each section, and by a short biography in the text.

Some philosophers of stature have led very dull lives. Kant springs to mind as the leader of this category, though the Indian recluse Aurobindo, despite a somewhat stormy youth, retired early from the world. Others have had perhaps more variety than they would have wished, for instance, John Locke had more than one profession and suffered political exile, as did Maimonides. Yet others, such as Confucius and St Bernard of Clairvaux, actively sought political influence. I would have liked to describe these lives in more detail, but that is a task for another time and a more ample space.

Acknowledgments

I owe many debts to friends and colleagues. The quality of the text has benefited immeasurably from criticisms by Fathali Moghaddam and Bede Rundle. I owe a considerable debt to Kathleen Buc, who painstakingly worked through successive drafts at several stages of the composition of this book, with her red pencil at the ready not only to highlight infelicities of style, but also to point to those places where one's "contract" with the reader to make it all clear had been broken. Finally to my colleague and friend, Dan Robinson, I owe a host of valuable suggestions, generously given and gratefully taken up which have done much to sharpen and balance the treatment of topics throughout the text.

The University of Illinois at Champagne-Urbana gave me splendid hospitality as George A. Miller Professor in the fall of 1999. Not only did I benefit from the erudition of colleagues but I had the privilege of making use of the one the world's great university libraries where there is unrivalled access to the collections. Such scholarship as this study displays owes a great deal to that opportunity.

Some of the thoughts and opinions I have expressed in what follows have been presented elsewhere, but in other ways and different forms. This text is new minted for the occasion.

Rom Harré,
Oxford, Georgetown, and the American University
March 2000.

Events Timeline

Historical Chart

900

960: Founding of Sung Dynasty

970: University founded in Cairo

996: Al-hakim becomes Fatimid Caliph

980: Ibn Sina (Avicenna)

1000

1017: Rāmānuja
1032: Ch'eng Hao
1033: Ch'eng I
1033: St Anselm

1054: Schism of Eastern and Western Christianity

1058: al-Ghazālī

1066: Norman Conquest of England

1079: Abelard

1085: Reconquest of Toledo
1088: University of Bologna founded

1091: St Bernard of Clairvaux

1100

1126: Ibn Rushd (Averroes)
1130: Chu Hsi
1139: Lu Hsiang-shan

1160: University of Paris
  founded
1170: University of Oxford
  founded
1175: Muslim conquest of
  Western India
  completed

1200

1207: Jalāl al-Dīn Rūmī
1225: St Thomas Aquinas
1227: Tokijori

1249: Conversion of Finland
  completes the
  Christianizing of Europe

1262: Ibn Taymiyah

1279: Fall of Sung Dynasty
1280: Reconquest of Cordoba
1280: Mongol rule in China
  established.

1285: William of Ockham

1300

1310: Fall of Chola Empire in
  India
1347: The Black Death
1368: Ming Dynasty founded

1400

1492: Columbus crosses the
  Atlantic

1500

1517: Luther's 95 theses
      published
1541: Copernicus heliocentric
      theory published
1542: Portuguese arrive in
      Japan
1555: Mogul Empire
      established in India

1561: Francis Bacon
1564: Galileo Galilei
1588: Thomas Hobbes
1596: René Descartes

1600

1613: Ku Yen-wu

1615: Shogunate regime
      founded in Japan

1627: Robert Boyle

1628: Harvey announces
      circulation of the blood

1632: John Locke
1632: Benedict de Spinoza

1638: Galileo's *Two New
      Sciences* published

1642: Isaac Newton

1643: Accession of Louis XIV
1644: Manchu dynasty
      founded

1646: Gottfried Leibniz
1668: Giambattista Vico
1685: George Berkeley

1687: Newton's *Principia
      Mathematica* published

1700

	1709: J. O. de La Mettrie
	1710: Thomas Reid
	1711: David Hume
	1712: Jean-Jacques Rousseau
	1724: Immanuel Kant
	1742: James Wilson
1770: Industrial Revolution begins in England	1770: G. W. F. Hegel
1776: American Independence	
1789: French Revolution	
	1794: William Whewell
	1798: Auguste Comte

1800

1804: Napoleon becomes Emperor	
1805: Herschel's galactic model of the universe published	
	1806: John Stuart Mill
	1813: Søren Kierkegaard
	1818: Karl Marx
	1838: Ernst Mach
	1839: Charles Sanders Peirce
1842: Treaty of Nanking opens China to foreigners	1842: William James
	1846: F. H. Bradley
	1848: Gottlob Frege
1853: Opening of Japan to foreigners	
	1854: Henri Poincaré
	1856: Sigmund Freud
1859: Darwin's *Origin of Species* published	1859: Edmund Husserl
1871: Unification of Germany completed	

1872: Bertrand Russell
1872: Aurobindo
1873: George Henry Moore
1882: Moritz Schlick

1886: Mendel's gene theory
of inheritance

1888: Radhakrishnan
1889: Ludwig Wittgenstein
1895: Fung Yu-lan

1900

1900: Boxer Rebellion in
China
1900: Planck's quantum
theory published
1901: Death of Queen
Victoria
1905: Einstein's Special Theory
of Relativity published

1911: Rutherford's discovery
of the nuclear atom

1914: Outbreak of First
World War
1917: Russian Revolution

1939: Outbreak of Second
World War
1947: First modern computer
constructed
1949: Communist regime
established in China
1951: Watson and Crick
publish structure of
DNA
1965: Chinese "Cultural
Revolution"
1988: Fall of Russian
Communism

1900: Gilbert Ryle

1905: Jean-Paul Sartre

1908: W. van Ormond Quine
1911: John Austin

1912: Alan Turing

1922: Thomas S. Kuhn

1

What is Philosophy?

Whence comes the perennial urge to reflect not only on our lives but on how we reflect on our lives? Those of a philosophical temperament have engaged in systematic and persistent struggles to forge ways of life appropriate to their vision of humanity's possibilities and the cosmos we live in. Prophets, reformers, religious leaders, and many others have been engaged in the same project. What is it that differentiates the philosophers from the rest? It is their willingness not only to reflect on the human situation, but to reflect on those reflections. For the most part, to be a philosopher just is to engage in this second-order reflection. Why might anyone think this activity to be important enough to devote their lives to it? The word "philosophy" is used both for reflections on life and for reflections on reflections on life. In looking at philosophy in the second millennium we will be following the transition in history from the one level of reflection to the other.

Whatever else people might be they are embodied in a fragile fleshly form. They live in tribes and families. They encounter the world from a narrowly constrained point of view, the here and now. Their growing cognitive powers some time in the past were turned upon themselves. What did they perceive? Everyone dies, whether they want to or not. The strongest and the most cunning get the better of the weaker and the more foolish. The wisest are woefully narrow in what they know about their world. People are ignorant, exploitative, and mortal.

The origins of the philosophical stance

What did this growing awareness of the place of humanity in the cosmos lead to? Though the earliest written records of ancient life are mostly bureaucratic, we soon find very complex speculative accounts of the universe that go far beyond what anyone might observe in the world around them. Perhaps personal being did not end with the death of the body. Perhaps there is some transcendent power that can compensate for human inequalities. Perhaps we can imagine a hidden realm of things and processes that explains the mysterious regularities in the world as we encounter it. Speculations of the grander sort that emerge from reflection on the predicaments of human life have traditionally been called "philosophy." In popular parlance they still are.

There is also reflection on the concepts and assertions that are involved in these attempts to resolve the predicaments that self-conscious reflection reveals to be integral to human life. This is also traditionally called "philosophy." If we are only material mechanisms then dissolution of the body is also the death of the person. Are we just material mechanisms? We will see that this is not a question to which science can provide an unequivocal answer. We must reflect on whether psychological concepts can be exhaustively replaced by material concepts. How do we strike a balance between personal liberty and social equity? It depends in part on how we understand the concepts of "liberty" and "equity."

In the last thousand years philosophy in both forms has found an important place in the heart of four great cultures: that of India, of China, of Islam, and of the European West.

The studies that follow are meant to open up the history of philosophy in the millennium in all four centers to many kinds of readers, some of whom will be meeting philosophy for the first time. How should this complex and seemingly esoteric activity be introduced?

Philosophy and religion

For many people philosophy and religion are intimately related. Both are expressions of insights into some of the big but vague questions that trouble us. Human life is an erratic and sometimes seemingly inexplicable and irrational mixture of the wonderful and the horrible. Dreadful diseases, even now, attack people who have lived lives of service and virtue. Disagreeable and even wicked people are sometimes spared this kind of suffering. People betray one another for reasons that seem to others contemptible or trivial, yet we can be fairly sure that in lots of cases the betrayers feel as righteous in their hearts as the betrayed. We now see ourselves, albeit reluctantly, as kin to the animals, in a universe of unimaginable vastness, in which we seem to have no place, except this little earth. From the first records of human reflection on the situation of the species, the omnipresence and the eventual certainty of bodily death has been a spur to the imagination. Can this fate be outflanked in some way? Can the shortcomings of this life be compensated somehow? Not all cultures have seen the solution in personal survival of death, though, as we shall see, all have eventually come to hope and even plan for it.

At the same time another aspect of human life has grown to some level of maturity, the development of critical intelligence. Paleoarchaeologists have suggested that the capacity to apply standards of correctness in judgment on what one has done oneself and what others have done can be first identified in Stone Age quarries in which imperfectly worked flints seem to have been cast aside. Criteria of perfection make no sense unless the hominids in question could reflect upon the quality of their performances and the products thereof. No doubt the capacity for critical commentary, for assessment according to criteria of good and bad work, was, even then, applied to all sorts of human productions including the cognitive ones. By the time we have substantial records of such reflections there are works like the Book of Job in which even God is brought to judgment. Philosophy is not only the expression of intuitions concerning our place in the universe and our manner of life, but also the product of the exercise of critical intelligence on these intuitions and on the presuppositions that underlie them.

The story of philosophy in the second millennium discloses a complex interweaving of cosmic intuitions and critical insights. As the intellectual and imaginative life of the millennium unfolded the balance between intuition and critical insight shifted. Now, philosophy is predominantly a critical intellectual endeavor, though even 150 or more years ago both Thomas Carlyle and Søren Kierkegaard would have been called philosophers. Yet, for the most part, they wrote in almost a preaching tone on life and its vicissitudes.

In this survey I have tried to bring out how, from the earliest recorded reflections on our life and its place in the universe, in the ancient sources of Indian and Chinese philosophy particularly, the two aspects of philosophizing were interwoven. Mencius delved into the presuppositions of the political insights of Confucius. Rāmānuja subjected the traditional relationship between *Atman*, the spiritual core of human beings, and *Brahman*, the essence of the universe, to critical analysis. When we turn to the Occident, to Islamic and Christian philosophy in the Middle Ages, we find that they share with Judaism, their common ancestor, the presupposition that revealed religion is the best source for ideas about how human life is to be lived. Not only that, but it is also taken as the source of our understanding of our place in the cosmos. Are these claims justified? Philosophers began to question whether revelation was enough. By the turn of the millennium the role of philosophy in Islam had already shifted toward the examination and the defence of the fundamental presuppositions of revealed religion. In the second half of the millennium, until very recently, religion still occupied a dominant place as a source of answers to the big questions. Only in the nineteenth century does it begin to lose its place with the most thoughtful and articulate members of the Western intelligentsia. For example, here is Hegel's lament:

> *God has died — God is dead* — this is the most frightful of all thoughts, that everything eternal and true *is not*, that negation itself is found in God. The deepest anguish, the feeling of complete irretrievability, the annulling of everything that is elevated, are bound up with this thought. However the process does not come to a halt at this point; rather a reversal takes place: God, that is to say, maintains himself in this process, and the latter is only the death of death. God rises again to life and things are reversed. (quoted in A. N. Wilson, 1999)

There is no doubt that God as Allah has risen again to life in Islamic fundamentalism, but the temper of the European West is profoundly irreligious. Who knows, though, what the new millennium will hold?

THE TRADITIONAL DISCIPLINES OF PHILOSOPHY

Traditionally philosophy as commentary and criticism has been divided broadly into metaphysics, epistemology, ethics, and logic. Allied with these are narrower fields of study such as political and legal philosophy, philosophy of science, philosophy of mind, philosophical problems of space and time, and so on. Coupled with all three major fields, logic has been an integral part of philosophy since Aristotle first gave the principles of correct reasoning explicit expression. For our purposes the traditional divisions make a useful starting point to collect our thoughts. Let us first consult a very well-known encyclopedia of philosophy (Edwards, 1967) for brief characterizations of these disciplines.

Metaphysics

Metaphysicians have . . . aspired to say what there is in the world . . . [they have been] preoccupied with the concepts of existence and reality.

[Metaphysics is] the most fundamental and comprehensive of enquiries.

[Scientists] work under assumptions which it is the business of philosophers to uncover and correct. (Walsh in Edwards, 1967: vol. 5, 301)

Metaphysics is concerned with the fundamental presuppositions of every sort of enquiry, particularly where these express the content of concepts and their relations, rather than putative matters of fact. For instance, we frequently make a distinction between coincidences, pairings of events which seem to have no relation to one another, and happenings which have discernible causes. To be able to make the distinction we need to have some concept of causation to hand by means of which we can single out patterns of events that are truly connected. We seem to make use of two concepts of causal production. In many of the affairs of life we take persons and things to be the efficacious sources that bring things about. However, we also make use of the concept of efficacious events. Could one of these concepts be shown to be more fundamental than the other? Metaphysicians debate such questions. In so doing they try to bring out much that is presupposed in the very distinction between events as causes and material things and persons as causes.

Epistemology

Epistemology, or theory of knowledge, is that branch of philosophy which is concerned with the nature and scope of knowledge, its presuppositions and basis, and the general reliability of claims to knowledge. (Hamlyn in Edwards, 1967: vol. 3, 7–8)

Epistemology is not concerned with matters of fact but with the concepts and criteria by which putative matters of fact are expressed, for example, the concept of "knowledge." How stringently we make demands of what we would be willing to accept as knowledge affects our confidence in the many ways we have for finding out about the world and other people. If only that of which we are absolutely certain can rank as knowledge and all our claims to know about the natural world are fallible, neither common observation nor scientific investigations could ever give us true *knowledge*. There is much that goes along with the accolade "knowledge." States of mind like "certainty" and "confidence" are prominent. Skepticism looms. The only genuine knowledge we could have, it would seem, would be of the relations between concepts. The relations between the concepts do not seem to rely on fallible perception, since they are something we ourselves create. Are there, then, two kinds of knowledge? This is the kind of issue that we find discussed in epistemological enquiries.

Ethics

[Traditionally] moral philosophy had a practical purpose . . . [it consisted of] practical knowledge as to how we ought to live . . . What distinguishes a specifically philosophical account of morality is its generality, its systematic nature and its attempts to prove its claims. (Nielsen in Edwards, 1967: vol. 3, 117)

For the purposes of this millennial survey I propose to treat ethics, political philosophy, and philosophy of law as departments of a coherent field of studies: What is the best way to live and how could any such claim be made intelligible, and if intelligible, be justified?

The philosophical study of right behavior involves bringing out the concepts used for describing and discussing the moral life. At the same time philosophers engage in a critical examination of arguments for and against accepting the most general moral principles that are among the presuppositions of moral discourse. For example, if we are considering the utilitarian principle that we should seek the greatest good of the greatest number, and we assume that human good is tied up with happiness, we must face the problem of how the happiness of individuals could be added up into the happiness of all. Group happiness and personal happiness seem to be quite different concepts. This is the sort of issue that one finds in ethics.

Logic

Logic has a history, from its first beginnings in the writings of Aristotle through many extensions and elaborations in the Middle Ages, to its astonishing development in the last century. In its beginnings logic was the study of the principles of correct and incorrect inferences. What was the shape of a valid argument, in which a conclusion followed *logically* from the given premises? "Following logically" meant by virtue of the form of the argument, and not its content.

> Like its predecessors modern logic is most widely studied as a means of testing the validity of arguments – specifically *deductive* arguments. (Blumberg in Edwards, 1967: vol. 5, 13)

Aristotle set out the principles of a common form of reasoning that would be applicable whatever the subject matter.

Medieval logicians inherited the Aristotelian system, but turned their attention to patterns of reasoning in which "modal" concepts were important, that is, concepts like "necessity" and "possibility." Other "specialist" logics have been developed, for example,

> the logic of obligation, is that area of thought in which are we formulate and systematize such principles as that nothing can be obligatory and forbidden at once. (Prior in Edwards, 1967: vol. 4, 509)

In the twentieth century the study of logic burgeoned, with many specialized logics being developed. But its role in philosophy did not become central until the beginning of the twentieth century.

At that time the extraction of logical form, once a prerequisite for examining the validity of a pattern of reasoning, was thought to be the key not only to right reasoning, but to all philosophy. Why? Because the study of logical form was supposed to reveal not only the structure of patterns of reasoning, but also the real structure of propositions of all kinds. It was thought that once the "true" structure of a puzzling proposition was revealed the philosophical problems it seemed to create would disappear. For example, if we agree that the proposition "Unicorns are white" is meaningful, and that it is true that unicorns are white, must there not be a realm in which there are, after all, some unicorns for this proposition to be about? Logical analysis might reveal that the troubling proposition is of a different form from, say, "Elephants are grey," a form that does not call for the postulation of a realm of nonexistent beings. This was among the many problems discussed by logicians in the last century of the second millennium.

THE METHODS OF PHILOSOPHY

Philosophical reflection is aimed at bringing to light the hidden presuppositions and assumptions implicit in all sorts of discourses and practices. Concepts and their interrelations come into focus. For example, reflecting on the seemingly irreversible direction of time, from past to future, the close connection between causal and temporal concepts might be exposed. The work of philosophy is not only analytical but also critical. The presuppositions that have been revealed by philosophical analysis can be examined, and if found wanting, will be criticized for various vices and failings, such as inconsistency, paradox, and other inadequacies. Implicit patterns of thought can be revealed and assessed by reference to established standards of correct reasoning. These standards might themselves come under scrutiny to become the focus of another level of critical philosophical appraisal.

Making Presuppositions Manifest

Philosophy is the work of extraction, analysis, and critical discussion of the presuppositions of all sorts of human practices. For the most part philosophers seem to rely on experience and intuition in discerning presuppositions and abstracting relevant conceptual relations implicit in discourses. There does not seem to be any universal recipe for debating moral issues. The search for the presuppositions of knowledge-garnering practices, such as the use of experiments in the sciences, involves both experience of the work of a scientific community and a keen intuition for what makes the practice successful.

There have been suggestions for more systematic methods of enquiry than reliance on intuition. The philosopher Collingwood (1940), reflecting on these matters, proposed a technique for revealing the "absolute" presuppositions of some human practice. They are reached, he thought, by considering the conditions or presuppositions that must hold for there to be answers to each of a sequence of probing questions. At each step the set of presuppositions, so far revealed, prompts further questions, the answers to which depend on yet further presuppositions until the chain of questions and presuppositions ends in a level of absolute presuppositions.

We can express this idea quite generally. As a philosopher one should keep on asking oneself "What would I have to believe for some claim I or someone else has made to make sense, to be assessable for truth or falsity, to be?" That belief itself can be treated as a claim, the meaningfulness of which depends on yet another level of belief, and so on. Notice, and this is of the utmost importance, that the question is not whether a claim is true, that is, a question for observation and experiment, but whether it makes sense. For example, the claim that locally obtained experimental evidence supports belief in a universally applicable law of nature makes sense if we believe that natural processes are the same everywhere, and at all times. Clearly this belief could not be tested experimentally! How would we know whether the same causal processes occurred at all places and at all times? We could suspend our judgment on the matter for practical reasons. What would we have to believe for that claim to make sense? And so on. Perhaps it cannot be shown to "make sense." However, this would lead to skepticism about the original step of inferring universal laws of nature from local evidence obtained on earth in this millennium. We might instead take a belief in the uniformity of nature, that the here and now is a fair sample of what happens everywhere and at all times, as an absolute presupposition of the rationality of experimental science.

Not only scientific beliefs and methods but also every religion and philosophy of life has its repertoire of sense-making presuppositions. Of course, being human productions, we will not be surprised to find that in some cases the presuppositions have not been coherent or, even if coherent, defensible. The claims to which they are relevant perhaps do make sense, after all. This is where philosophizing as commentary and criticism begins to play its part.

The Critical Examination of Presuppositions

A philosophical thesis, critical of the validity, meaningfulness, or applicability of some concept, can be disputed in various ways. Presuppositions are thus subjected to critical examination in a pattern of argument, in which criticisms are themselves subject to criticism.

The use of imagined cases

There is a long-running debate in the philosophy of psychology about the meaning and viability of the concept of "free will." Some have argued that there is no such thing as an action which is freely chosen since all actions are determined, if not by observable causes then by unobservable ones. This is the thesis of determinism. Does it make sense? We must bring out what would be presupposed if it did. The nub of the matter is this: It is presupposed that there are a pair of concepts, "being free" and "being determined," which mutually define each other. To be free is not to be determined and to be determined is not to be free. The arguments of determinists are supposed to show that only the latter has any application in reality.

But if there is no free will then all actions are coerced, so it must be presupposed that the distinction between acting freely and acting under coercion is empty. The philosopher A. G. N. Flew (1965) drew attention to the sorts of cases in which the concept "acting freely" gets its meaning. Even to reject it we must understand what it is we are rejecting. Compare, he asks, two situations. In one the bridegroom stands sullenly at the altar while behind him stands the father of the bride with a loaded shotgun. In the other all is smiles and the bridegroom stands happily at the altar *of his own free will*. This is a *paradigm case* of free action. Since it is the sort of case in which the meaning of "acting freely" is established it cannot be reconstrued as a case of hidden "determination." We have no trouble seeing the difference between the two situations. What seems to be a presupposition of the determinist claim, that there is *really* no difference between the cases, is challenged.

Here we have a typical "argument." Its function is to highlight a conceptual issue, one which had been overlooked when the determinist was making the dramatic claim that no actions were really free. Of course, the issue of the correct account to be given of the role of molecular processes in the genesis of action is not preempted by this argument. It simply shows that across-the-board dogmatic pronouncements on such matters should be very closely examined to see whether they are internally coherent, self-defeating, or suffering from other shortcomings. We can do this by bringing out and scrutinizing presuppositions. It is worth remarking that the presupposition upon which all this pattern of argument and counterargument rests has not been shared by every philosopher who has thought about the possibility of free action in a world of causes. Aristotle distinguished between three categories, voluntary action, nonvoluntary action, and involuntary action.

The display of a self-defeating paradox

Another case of an across-the-board argument that seems to come to a dramatic conclusion is the reasoning that leads some philosophers to declare that there are no universal moral principles by which we can judge the actions of people of cultures and epochs other than our own (Rorty, 1989). This claim can be challenged by the use of another kind of critical argument. We could try to show that among the presuppositions of the meaningfulness of the claim is one which contradicts that very claim.

Moral relativism has a long history. In recent times it has been given a new impetus from anthropology and history. The argument starts by pointing out that different peoples at different times have adopted very different moral principles. It has been suggested that for every moral principle we hold dear there are or have been people who either did not share it or rejected it. Nevertheless such people lived coherent and fulfilling lives. For example, we hold infanticide to be a great evil. In Ancient Greece it was thought not only not wrong but praiseworthy to leave unwanted or sickly infants out on the hillside to die. Not so long ago it was thought immoral for women and working people to be educated. We now take the opposite view, that everyone has a right to an education. And so on. On the positive side this argument is meant to open up the public domain of debate and discussion to voices that are seldom if ever heard, those of the obscure, the downtrodden, and others on the fringes of society. But the cost in enfranchising the unheard in this way is heavy. It seems that we must allow the voices of the authors of the holocaust, of the perpetrators of the killing fields, and so on to be heard as well. Each represents a local culture, which is not our own. How can we presume to criticize them?

Surely we want to say that genocide, whosoever perpetrates it, however sincere their beliefs in the political or biological basis of the practice, is evil. Some philosophers, for example, Richard Rorty, have argued that all it can mean to say that the genocide Hitler's anti-semitism inspired is evil is that if it had been done by people in our community it would have been a great wrong. It seems to follow from Rorty's reasoning that we would have no rational basis for judging any-thing that was done in Nazi Germany other than by a comparison between how *we* would feel about these matters had we had the oppor-tunity to live in Germany in the 1930s with how we would feel about what we are accustomed to do at home in our liberal democracies. But this is just to import our moral standards into a cultural complex defined by others. And that we cannot legitimately do, so it is argued. The denial that there are any defensible universal principles of good character and right action is "radical moral relativism."

However, among the presuppositions of the radical relativist claim is one which contradicts it. The author of such a claim has written it down or made it verbally in a lecture. To do that language must be used. The efforts to persuade us of the correctness of moral relativism make sense only if the relativist believes that we will understand what has been written or said in defense of the claim. Indeed, it is also nec-essary that the very author of the claim will understand it too. All this presupposes that the general conditions for the possibility of there being a language with which to make these relativistic pronouncements are met. Some of these conditions are moral. For example, no one could learn a language if everyone who seemed to be making articu-lated sounds never meant what they seemed to mean, that is, they were systematically lying or trying to deceive their listeners. A generation of deceivers could never pass on their language to the next generation. There simply would not be a language to pass on. Whatever these people were doing when they made articulated sounds it was not meaningful speech. Thus, in order to advocate moral relativism, a philosopher must accept as universal at least those moral principles the sharing of which makes language possible.

Here we have a paradox. The moral position that is being advocated, radical moral relativism, can only be put forward under conditions which include the denial of that moral position. We will come across other examples of paradoxes like this when we look more closely at some dramatic philosophical claims in later chapters.

I have set out examples of two styles of argument critical of claims for a radical revision of our concepts, and found counterarguments that show that both are wanting. A successful philosophical claim – say, that there could be no rational proof of the existence of God – would need to be based on defensible presuppositions. This would mean that neither paradoxes nor counterexamples have been found, so far!

Exposing misleading grammatical analogies

When scientists study materials, in the disciplines of chemistry and metallurgy, among the presuppositions or tacit principles that guide their work is one which expresses the idea of "essence," the properties that a substance must have to be counted as a genuine sample. An essence is simply the set of properties that are necessary and sufficient for identifying something as a being of a certain kind. For something to count as silver it must have certain properties, such as being metallic, being a certain colour when in the solid state, having a certain specific gravity, a certain atomic number, and so on. In chemistry such properties are ranked into two sets. There are those which are observable, and used to pick out silver items in practical contexts. Philosophers have called this set the "nominal essence." Then there are those which are theoretical or unobservable, such as the structure of the atoms of the substance in question, which are used to explain the grouping of the properties expressed in nominal essences. This has been called the "real essence." For example, the atomic structure of silver atoms accounts for the electrical and chemical properties of the metal. So everything that is rightly called "silver" has both a nominal and a real essence. Sometimes the same substance can have more than one nominal essence, that is, appear in different guises to observers. For example, carbon appears as combustible coal, as admantine diamond, and as slippery graphite. In each case the stuff has the same real essence, namely the atomic constituents of coal, diamond, and graphite have the same structure, though their molecular structures differ.

We are tempted to think that because the same word is used in a variety of cases and contexts there must be something common to all these cases that explains the use of the same word in each of them, a common essence. The "grammar" of chemistry might serve as a model for understanding the terminologies of other sciences, for example, psychology. If everything that is called "gold" has a common atomic structure, perhaps everything that is called "belief" has a common essence.

One might think that this useful pattern of organizing knowledge could be applied everywhere. Should we work with the presupposition that when we find the same word used in a number of seemingly different situations there *must* be something in common in all these cases? Let us look a little further into the case of "belief." We find the words "belief," "believe," "believing," and so on being used by people in a wide variety of contexts and in many ways. One might be tempted to think that because the same word is used there must be something common to all these uses and contexts, if only we could find it. It might be very deep or it might be very abstract or both. However, when we carefully describe the different uses of these closely related words we can see that there is no single common feature which ties them all together. They are related by a network of similarities and differences. We can see that the phrase "I believe . . ." has at least two very different uses. In one sort of context, for example, in religious services and discussions, it expresses the speaker's commitment to something. For example, the Christian Creed begins "I believe in God the Father . . .". But sometimes the same phrase is used to express doubt, uncertainty, and lack of commitment, as when we prefix "I believe" to some assertion of which we are not sure. For instance, having given a stranger a street direction, say to Manor Place, we might weaken the force of what we have said by inserting "I believe": thus, "I believe Manor Place is somewhere off 37th Street" whereby we draw back from commitment to the sure and certain veracity of what we have said. It seems implausible to propose that there is a common essence to all cases in which the word "belief" or any of its cognates is used. Of course, there may be a perfectly good historical explanation of the range of family resemblances in the meanings of some key expression. The point is not to assert dogmatically that there can never be a common essence to a range of seemingly different uses of a word or expression. Rather it is to alert us to the possibility that there may not be one, and that we should be very cautious in assuming that there must be.

I have chosen these examples to illustrate some of the methods to be employed in reflecting critically on the presuppositions that lie buried in scientific research, moral debates, and other human practices.

The Dynamics of Philosophical Traditions

In the surveys to follow we will be concerned with the growth and development of long-standing philosophical traditions in each major center where philosophy has flourished: India, China, Islam, and Christendom. What is the driving force that sets philosophers to work, engaging in the analytical and critical studies that are characteristic of philosophy? In each case we will find that there has come into being a well-established position or positions on the major topics of concern to people. At a certain point these positions are no longer taken for granted and come under philosophical scrutiny. Abstracting the concepts implicit in such positions leaves a residue of matters of fact, which may or may not stand up to scientific examination. But the philosopher's attention is on the conceptual system in use and particularly its linguistic expression. In India and China philosophers were mostly concerned with how people should manage their lives. There were no divine revelations in these cultures. There were texts that told heroic tales or offered illustrative anecdotes. *Brahman*, not being in any sense a person, did not dictate the *Upanishads*. The author of the *Analects*, Confucius, was very much a man. In Christianity and Islam there was a revealed religion with a code of living ordained by God, and revealed in the sacred Scriptures.

Philosophy as the critical interpretation of texts

Philosophy as a commentary upon the presuppositions of the discourses and material practices of a culture seems to have developed in response to the problem of interpreting obscure or metaphorical sacred or established texts, and of finding justifications for these interpretations. In India the texts that attracted the attention of philosophers were the *Upanishads* and the *Bhagavad-gita*, two sets of abstracts from an extensive religious literature. In China the secular writings of Confucius came to have a role similar to those of religious texts in India and the West. There is no doubt that a major impetus to philosophizing in the lands bordering the Mediterranean was the need to interpret the sacred texts of Judaism, Christianity, and Islam. In all three cases the same technique of philosophical reflection was adopted. Ancient Greek philosophy supplied the tools for philosophical analysis and criticism. This is hardly surprising, since philosophers from all three religious communities became acquainted with Greek philosophy through translations into Arabic of the writings of Aristotle and other ancient philosophers, which, mainly in Muslim Spain, were rendered into Hebrew and Latin. Later, original sources became available.

Philosophy as the defence of science

Though the sciences, as important and often idealized human enterprises, have attracted the attention of philosophers since antiquity, in the modern era, that is, since about 1500, they have been the focus of intense philosophical scrutiny. They have played much the same role as religion did in medieval Christendom. The upshot of 500 years of reflection on the metaphysics and methodologies of our human attempts to come to an understanding of the world around us, and of ourselves as fit subjects for science, has been three main schools of thought.

In a later chapter we will examine them in greater detail but for the moment we need describe them only in outline.

POSITIVISM: Science is a project aimed at making a comprehensive and ordered catalogue of well established correlations between phenomena given to us by our sense organs. Theories are merely means of ordering observational generalizations and facilitating the making of predictions.

CONVENTIONALISM: Science is a project aimed at creating a comprehensive interpretative scheme for categorizing the whole gamut of human experience. The laws of nature are not inductive generalizations from experience, but conceptual constructions developed to make sense of experience. What the world reveals to us is determined, at least in part, by the conceptual systems we use to make sense of our experience.

REALISM: Science is a project aimed at penetrating behind the world of common experience to attain an understanding of unobserved mechanisms and processes. Theories describe real processes, structures, and entities, even though these can not generally be observed by means of the human senses, but their nature and existence have to be inferred indirectly.

Each standpoint has had its advocates. We will investigate the presuppositions of these rival interpretations of the natural sciences. They have been the focus of debate since the sixteenth century, when they emerged as rival ways of making sense of the many astronomical models that were invented at that time. Each of the three major ways of interpreting the sciences condenses a diffuse array of presuppositions that are needed to make the claims of the sciences intelligible and warrantable.

The shift of focus from the philosophical problems of religion to those of science did not mean that the problem of interpreting religious discourses had been abandoned. Religion did not disappear in the Renaissance! A great deal of subsequent philosophy has been concerned with finding and critically examining ways of reconciling science and religion, as seemingly incompatible ways of comprehending the universe.

In none of the other three centers did philosophy shift from its prime focus on religion or something religion-like to science. This shift is, I believe, largely responsible for the characteristic style of philosophy in the European West since about 1500.

THE PRODUCTS OF PHILOSOPHY

Having looked deep into human practices to discern their absolute presuppositions and to bring to light their taken-for-granted conceptual resources, what do we have for our pains? We have discovered and examined the concepts presupposed by the ways we frame and order our perceptions, our judgments, and our discourses. We have brought to light some of the interrelations between them. All this must be expressed in propositions in order that a philosopher may share insights and arguments with other people. These propositions express some of the presuppositions of the ways in which we think and act. Just what sort of propositions are they? Are they reports of rather recondite matters of fact? Are they rules for the guidance of the perplexed? Are they necessary truths, of the same stature as the laws of arithmetic?

Two kinds of propositions

Aspects of the world are represented by human beings to human beings with the help of symbolic systems. Shapes are represented geometrically, quantities are represented numerically, types are represented taxonomically, thoughts are represented linguistically, material surroundings are represented pictorially, and so on. The means of representation seem to have a degree of independence from that which they are used to represent. All sorts of different aspects of the world can be represented with the same representational devices. Geometrical figures are shapes, and pictures are perceptible. But numerals are not multiplicities, nor are words thoughts and feelings.

There are many ways that representations and what is represented can be related. Each of these genres of representation mentioned above can be presented as a system in which elementary symbols are related to one another according to rules of formation. The theorems of geometry are an axiomatic system, made famous by Euclid. They govern the ways that lines, planes can be arranged in a certain kind of two- and three-dimensional space. Taxonomies of plants and animals are type-hierarchies organized by species: *Canis familiaris*, the dog, *is a* carnivore, *is a* mammal, *is an* animal, and so on. Words are ordered by semantic and syntactical conventions. The term "grammar" is now commonly used in philosophical circles for both sorts of conventions. This usage follows Wittgenstein's (1953) practice in his later philosophy of extending the scope of the word from the expression of the standards of syntactical correctness to all the normative undergirding of language.

Many philosophers have tried to give accounts of the ways that symbolic systems and that which they symbolize differ. If a symbol system is independent of that which it is used to symbolize, then there is no surety that a *well-formed* complex of symbols will *truly* represent anything in its relevant domain. Traditionally this insight has been expressed in the principle that there are two kinds of truths. There are the sets of rules for the proper construction of complex symbols, such as the rules of arithmetic, that two and two make four. These are grammars, in the wider use of that word. Then there are statements, using these expressions, that purport correctly to represent some matter of fact in the relevant domain, such as the statement that there are two pairs of sheep that have not yet been shorn, making four to go before the end of the day.

As we have seen, the business of philosophers is with the abstraction and critical examination of the propositional expression of the meanings and interrelations of concepts. Scientists are supposed to busy themselves with matters of fact. Of course, philosophers do draw on their knowledge of the way the world is, and scientists devote considerable effort to the refining of definitions and other conceptual matters.

Associated with this roughly drawn distinction are a number of other dichotomies that have been topics of intense philosophical discussion. For example, there is the distinction between necessary and contingent truths. The former are supposed to be independent of matters of fact while the truth of the latter is taken to depend on what is the case. The link to conceptual structure has been highlighted in the distinction between analytical and synthetic statements. The former express the results of the analysis of concepts, for example, that parents have children. The latter express correlations of concepts that reflect experience of the common world, for instance, that there are four children under ten years of age in the Jones family.

We can learn a good deal by following the accounts of the distinction between conceptual truths and matters of fact offered by four Occidental philosophers, Leibniz (1646–1716), Reid (1710–96), Kant (1724–1804), and Wittgenstein (1890–1952). I have chosen these authors, all from the European region and from the Western tradition. Unlike the philosophers of India, China, and Islam, they made explicit studies of the nature and status of the propositional expression of the presuppositional bases of human thought and practice. In other traditions the status of presuppositions was more or less taken for granted by even the most subtle authors.

Where do clusters of presuppositions come from?

Leibniz finds his distinction between *truths of reason* and *truths of fact*
in the difference between the limited intellectual capacities of human
beings and the unlimited intellectual capacities of God. Reid finds the
source of the *general principles of common sense* in a divinely ordained
original human nature. Kant finds the origin of *synthetic a priori propositions* in the general conditions for the possibility of experience.
Wittgenstein finds the grounding of *grammars* in the interplay between
the general conditions of human life and the history and traditions of
human associations. Though their terminologies differ in significant
ways all four philosophers are homing in on the same issue: What is
the nature of the propositions that express the ways we frame our
thoughts and perceptions, the presuppositions of our practices? Through
this progression from Leibniz's views to Wittgenstein's, we can see both
the humanizing and the domesticating of the sources of the deep
frames of our ways of thinking and living.

Leibniz: the truths of reason/truths of fact distinction

Leibniz thought that all linguistic representations must take the
subject–predicate form. For instance, "The Horse is quadrupedal" and
"Alexander's horse was called Bucephalus" are both of that form, the
subject being the species *Equus caballus* in the one case and a particular member of the species in the other. The former states one of
the defining characteristics of the species, and so serves to specify part
of the meaning of the word "horse." A definition through which
human beings expressed the meaning of a species or kind word could
involve only a finite number of predicates, otherwise we could never
be sure whether we had identified a specimen of the type or species
in question. But any statement about an individual could be elaborated
indefinitely. Indeed Leibniz thought that propositions which would
fully specify any concrete and particular being would involve infinitely
many predicates, since there are infinitely many ways that one individual can differ from another. There are clearly two kinds of propositions looked at from the point of view of the intellectual capacities
of human beings. Expositions of the characteristics of species are truths
of reason, while statements about particular beings are truths of fact.

   The "finite/infinite" distinction is not relevant for God, so from His
point of view there is only one kind of proposition. In all subject–

predicate propositions the properties of the subject are included in the content of the predicate. For human beings, propositions expressing some aspect of the defining characteristics of a species or type can be known to be true by anyone who reflects on the meaning of the relevant words. No one can be sure that he or she has the whole truth about any particular being. God does.

It looks as if we have the glimmering of a possible test for whether a statement is about the world or expresses some feature of the symbolic system we use to make statements about the world. It also seems as if we could know the truth of a statement used as part of the procedure for setting up a symbolic system, for example, "Horses are herbivorous," without examining horses. We use statements like this to pick them out in the first place. To know whether the racehorse Phar Lap had staying power we would have to study him.

However, further reflection undermines the possibility of using Leibniz's logical insight to systematically sort propositions into those that delineate the frame and those that describe the picture. How would one know, other than by some kind of pragmatic test, whether the finite set of properties one was using in accordance with the relevant "truth of reason" was really closed? And how would one know that the set of predicates that one had begun to assemble to describe an individual did indeed go on for ever? Might it not terminate after only one or two additions? It seems as if one could only make use of the Leibnizean distinction if one already had a way of telling whether an expression was to be used for a type or for an individual, as part of the frame or as part of the picture.

Reid: the principles of "common sense"

Reid used the notion of the principles of common sense to pick out propositions that played an *a priori* role, delineating the conceptual frame presupposed in all our particular thoughts and perceptions. By "common sense" he did not mean folk wisdom, but rather what was common to all human activities. It would not be anachronistic to say that his point was rather modern. The discourses of human kind were not explicable wholly by reference to experience. They were managed and supported by the principles of common sense, an array of absolute presuppositions. Some of these, such as the ethological foundations of language, the natural expressive gestures on which true linguistic practices were founded, were features of human biology, and were found in other species as well. Others had a more clearly discursive role as the principles of all shared and reasonable congress between intelligent, language-using beings.

Reid introduces his common principles as follows:

> There are, therefore, common principles, which are the foundation of all reasoning, and of all science. Such common principles seldom admit of direct proof; nor do they need it. Men need not to be taught them; for they are such as all men of common understanding know; or such, at least, as they give ready assent to, as soon as they are proposed and understood. (Reid, 1788, [1969]: 31)

The distinction is of the greatest importance and again Reid catches a modern note. He says:

> very ingenious men . . . have lost much labour, by not distinguishing things, which, though they may admit of illustration, yet being self evident, do not admit of proof. (p. 33)

> It may, however, be observed, that the first principles of natural philosophy are of quite a different nature from the mathematical axioms. They have not the same kind of evidence, nor are they necessary truths. They are such as these: that similar effects proceed from the same or similar causes . . . These are principles, which, though they have not the same kind of evidence that mathematical axioms have, yet have such evidence, that every man of common understanding readily assents to them, and finds it absolutely necessary to conduct his actions and opinions by them, in the ordinary affairs of life. (pp. 32–3)

In the end all proofs of the seemingly self-evident principles of common sense must depend on one universal principle, the law of contradiction, that nothing can be at one and the same moment both A and not-A.

Kant: the synthetic a priori

The world appears to beings like us as a flux of events and an array of things ordered by spatial and temporal relations. Things can be above and below one another, in front or behind, and so on. Events can be before or after one another, or past, present, and future with respect to the present moment. We perceive and act in and on a world of endur-

ing and changing material things, among which we must count ourselves as embodied persons. According to Kant, this organization is not
found in the world and then reflected or reproduced in our thought.
It is the product of the synthetic activity of the thinker shaping up a
stream of sensory impressions. The result is an empirical world on the
one hand, and our minds as we are aware of them on the other. While
things are organized in space and time, thoughts and feelings are organized in time only. The *a priori* intuitions of space and time are the
logically necessary conditions for there to be any experience at all.
Philosophers do not discover them by doing a little anthropology
or biology, on the side, so to speak. They are "discovered" by philosophical analysis of the presuppositions of the very idea of sentient
experience.

The first level of order in our experience comes about by the imposition of the structures of space and time on the flux of sensations. The
second level of order comes about by the synthesis of the spatially and
temporally ordered flux into a world of causally active, relatively permanent things. In revealing the rules by which this level of synthesis
is accomplished we reach the absolute presuppositions of all human
knowledge and experience, according to Kant. So the *possibility of
experience* that gives objective reality to all our *a priori* modes of knowledge "rests on the synthetic unity of appearances, that is, on a synthesis according to the concept of an object of appearance in general"
(Kant, 1787 [1996]: B196).

Kant's synthetic *a priori* propositions express the laws to which experience must conform, since they express the schemata or rules by which
that experience is shaped. It is important to understand the significance
of the unfamiliar expression, "synthetic *a priori.*" By this famous phrase
Kant means that these propositions are not derived from experience,
though they are exemplified in experience. For reasons that it would
take us too far afield to discuss at this stage of our studies, Kant thought
that there were a fixed and limited number of synthesizing rules, which
were constrained by the limited variety of judgments a rational being
could make. These limitations have been much disputed.

Wittgenstein: the autonomy of "grammars"

By a "grammar" Wittgenstein meant an open set of rules for the correct
use of a loosely bounded symbolic system, the most important, though

not the only one, being the open system of language. The application
of rules can be either explicit, as when a rule is followed consciously
as an instruction, or implicit, as when a person acts habitually in accordance with a rule that may have been long forgotten. Grammars are
independent of the world they are used to manage, that is, they are
not derived from it by induction, in the way that scientists are said to
discover laws of nature. However, the world cannot be ignored altogether. Some grammars are better adapted to the world they are being
used to understand and manage than others.

But this ought not to encourage us to think that grammars are
chosen from a list of candidates, all fully formed and up and running
to be looked over and taken up or abandoned.

> Thus the truth of our necessary truths is not a matter of our having
> *chosen* or agreed to linguistic conventions, for choice presupposes that
> we can envisage and understand alternatives from which to choose.
> (Wittgenstein, 1956: § 149)

Of course grammars do change. Some rules, for example, those for
determining who is a witch, fade away. Others, for example, those for
the diatonic scale, come into use. But these changes do not come
about, Wittgenstein insists, by the deliberate consideration of alternatives. Grammatical rules are expressed as propositions. And so are the
substantive things we use grammars to say. The open set of grammatical propositions Wittgenstein likens to a frame, and the propositions that are about some feature of the world he likens to the picture
in the frame. It is of the utmost importance not to mistake the status
of some proposition that seems to us to be of importance. Is it part of
the frame or part of the picture? One of Wittgenstein's enduring contributions to philosophy was the invention of a way by which frame
or grammatical propositions could be distinguished from picture or
substantive propositions in many cases.

Suppose someone were to declare that nothing can be loud and soft
at the same time. Is this a report about sounds or a grammatical rule
for the use of the words "loud" and "soft"? The way to tell is to consider the negation of the proposition in question. What are we to make
of "Something is both loud and soft at the same time"?[1] Is it false? It
might seem at first glance that while the original claim is incontestable
and looks like a truth, its negation must be false. However, further

reflection shows us that the trouble with the negation of a grammatical proposition is not falsity. For a proposition to be false there must be a real or imagined situation in which it would be true. There are no situations to which the negations of grammatical propositions would apply. Such a proposition is not false, but empty or meaningless. This gives us a general rule for picking out grammatical propositions. Their affirmations have the air of truth; we willingly assent to them. But their negations are meaningless, having no conceivable applications.

What is the origin of a grammar? The answer is history, the natural history of humankind and the traditions that are inherent in this or that form of life.

The changing bases of our thought ways

There is an obvious similarity between Wittgensteinian grammatical propositions and Kantian synthetic *a priori* propositions. Yet there are also differences. Wittgenstein remarks that the everyday uses of language can and do change, though at different rates. The Kantian repertoire of synthetic *a priori* propositions was meant to be a universal system for all rational beings. Wittgenstein makes the point in many places and by the use of a variety of metaphors:

> the river-bed of thoughts may shift. But I distinguish between the movement of the waters on the river-bed and the shift of the bed itself, though there is no sharp division of the one from the other. (Wittgenstein, 1969: §99)

The frame may enter into the picture and parts of the picture can become a frame. Definitions can become descriptions and descriptions definitions.

How do "frames" and "grammars" change? We cannot, ahead of time, think the new, nevertheless in concert with the adoption of new practices, new language games with old resources, and so on, we find ourselves in a new grammatical universe.

Recently the same point has been made by Shweder (1998). In describing the foundations of life in Orissa (India) he points out that there are local principles or "contingent universals" around which life is organized, for example, the ways that funeral practices are managed. Much of this unattended background to the Orissa "form of life" is expressed in religious stories as well as in local practices. Commenting on the power of such stories Shweder says:

> Such is the work of the collective creative imagination in producing cultural frameworks of interpretation for structuring our psychological life and filling in that discretionary space in between the necessary truths of logic and the rather bare facts of experience. (Shweder, 1998: 17)

Contingent universal propositions are locally binding, having the force of necessity in their own "place." The rules of games, for instance, have this character. It is clear that Shweder's repertoires of contingent universals are none other than Wittgenstein's grammars.

The most startling consequence of this way of looking at the foundations of our relations with the world and one another is the realization that *the kind of thing* that is readily and as a matter of course available to human experience at any time or place is to a greater or lesser extent determined in advance by the content and structure of the symbolic system with which our activities in the world, including perception and manipulation, are managed and ordered. Unless I can recognize a persimmon it is no good sending me out to pick some. This point must be stated rather carefully. I do not mean that a person cannot see something for which he or she has no word. Rather the point is that what is salient for any culture is usually expressed in the vocabulary and practices of that culture in a more elaborated and refined way than that which is peripheral to local interests. We scarcely notice the inedible fruits of our own forest trees. That much is obvious. But is it also true that the very spatiotemporal structure of the world in which I perceive and act is imposed through the application of pre-existing categories to an inchoate sensory experience?

Whether it is Leibniz's distinction between truths of reason and truths of fact, or Reid's distinction between principles of common sense and ordinary discourse, or Kant's between analytic propositions and the synthetic *a priori*, or Wittgenstein's between the frame and the picture, all four agree that we do not experience the world as if our minds were soft wax to be shaped by the impress of a seal. Our world comes into being for us through active intervention and exploration.

What there is or could be for us is not determined by simple sensations caused by our surroundings, nor by our reflections on these.

Nor is what we believe just the shadow cast upon the world by our presuppositions.

Grammars and the disciplines of philosophy

I began this chapter with a brief survey of the four fields of enquiry that have traditionally been cultivated by philosophers. I described the work of philosophy as the bringing to light of at least some of the presuppositions of our ways of thinking and acting. What do we have when the products of philosophical enquiry are presented to us? Not matters of fact, nor the formal instructions for the successful or proper performance of a task. We have the principles, rules, and so on that are implicit in the means for recognizing and expressing matters of fact, and for setting out intelligible and coherent instructions for a practice. Philosophers of law do not examine and assess the quality of particular items of evidence, but reflect on the concept of "evidence" in relation to the practices of the law. Metaphysicians examine possible conceptual systems, expressing the categories for some picture of what there might be. Scientists, presupposing some such system of categories, can set about examining aspects of the world their presuppositions make available to them. What metaphysicians examine and scientists presuppose are grammars, systems of synthetic *a priori* propositions, principles of common sense and truths of reason.

Conclusion

In this chapter I have tried to make clear what it is that philosophers are doing by sketching some of the characteristic tasks that philosophers undertake. I have summarized some of the techniques for bringing out for examination the underlying presuppositions upon which much that we think and do ultimately rests. Once these have been brought to light we looked at three ways, and there are others, by which they can be subject to criticism. There are thought experiments by which the meaningfulness of a presupposition that seems to express some thrilling philosophical claim can be tested. Then there is the technique of bringing to light a presupposition among the conditions for holding some view that contradicts that very view or opinion. Then there is the subtle technique of detecting and examining grammatical analogies that covertly mislead us. Finally we looked at four well-known ways of distinguishing the presuppositions that frame our practices from those that express matters of fact.

The examples I have used in this chapter are exclusively drawn from Western philosophy of the second half of the second millennium. I could have drawn on material from Islam, India, or China. But in order for that material to help in this exposition of what it is to do philosophy a huge amount of scene-setting would have been needed. I have been drawing on certain common assumptions of Western thought, shared by all of us, whether or not we are philosophers. We shall find that the exposition of "philosophy" in this chapter will be readily applicable to the philosophical writings of the other traditions, at that point at which they shift from presenting the virtues of a way of life to a critical examination of what would be presupposed both in realizing it and in commenting upon it.

NOTES

1   Al Mosley pointed out that the example only works if the words "loud" and "soft" are taken to be determinates of the same determinable, namely sound. Otherwise, if one were sound and the other texture, a puppy could be loud and soft at the same time.

PART I

Philosophy in the East

---- 2 ----

India: The Traditions

Sometime in or about the year 579 B.C. a youngish man was out driving about the town in his chariot. He was awaiting the birth of his first child. As he drove around he passed a very old man, a very sick man, and a corpse, on its way to be cremated at the burning *ghat*. Up till this moment he had not been a person much given to reflection, but these encounters disturbed him. The next person he passed was a holy man. Perhaps, he thought, there was something in the religious life that would resolve his unease. Just then a servant arrived to tell him of the birth of a son. Here indeed was a newly forged tie to bind him to his home and family. As he was driving back a young woman, Kisagotami, looked out from her balcony and saw him pass. She was so struck by his cool and dignified bearing that she burst into song, the theme of which was the nobility of his demeanor. Reflecting later about these events, he was pleased by the song and the attribution to him of detachment and calmness of mind. So he sent the singer a pearl necklace. She took this as a declaration of love. Disgusted with the complexity of his life the young man, who was then 29 years of age, set off on a journey, renouncing home, family, and all personal attachments. This journey was to occupy the rest of his long life. The young man's name was Siddhatta Gautama, though we have all come to know him as the Buddha.

The disgust with life and the search for deliverance by transcending the everyday, which loomed so large in the life of the Buddha, has always been at the heart of Indian philosophical and religious thought.

THE SCOPE OF PHILOSOPHY IN INDIA

The Indian Philosophical Tradition

Philosophy in India displays that double aspect I have emphasized in chapter 1. On the one hand it is directed toward building a comprehensive cosmology within which the outlines of the "best" life can be discerned. On the other hand it is directed to the extraction and skilful examination of the presuppositions of the cosmologies and the associated conceptions of the proper forms of life.

The main lines of Indian thought were established by about A.D. 500. Thereafter new schools of philosophy developed as refinements and clarifications of what was already well articulated.[1] Reference to and the reworking of the ancient philosophical sources has continued to dominate Indian philosophy right through the second millennium, even to the present day. In the writings of the years after A.D. 1000 we can always discern the outlines of classical Indian philosophy. Historians remark on the way in which the systems that emerged from the last few hundred years of the first millennium, and took their final form in the first half of the second millennium thereafter, hardly changed (Frauwallner, 1973: 14–17). Contemporary Indian philosophy, at the end of the second millennium, displays a variety of mixes of surviving classical thought with the well-established traditions of Western philosophy.

Who were the philosophers in ancient and classical India? It is evident that there was a considerable density of the kinds of activity that we would now call "doing philosophy." The pattern of the teacher and the student, who then in turn becomes a teacher, is found throughout Indian history. Teachers expounded their positions, at the heart of which were prescriptions of ways of life, including techniques for achieving enlightenment. These were buttressed by conceptual analyses, metaphysical arguments, epistemological discussions, and so on in a manner any Western philosopher would recognize as philosophical in the critical sense – the search for presuppositions and their assessment. Disciples and rivals disputed and debated the teachings of the master. Winning and losing public debates is a central theme in stories of the lives of the great teachers. The practice also existed of a teacher finding his way into a royal court and debating with and sometimes converting the ruler to a new way of life. Of course, this involved the exposition of the philosophical doctrines that went with it. Sometimes the ruler might abandon his court and set up as a teacher himself. But what is so striking in the histories of Indian philosophy is how many such people there were. In describing the eleventh-century school of Rāmānuja, Dasgupta (1940: 100–13) cites page after page of names of people who were in contact with or influenced by the sage. Schools of philosophy emerged very early in India, and with them hundreds of minute variations on the main philosophical traditions.

The Evolution of Indian Philosophy: from A-theism to Theism

It has been said that India is a country that has never distinguished philosophy from religion (Prabhavanda, 1963: 7). Be that as it may, Indian philosophy has been dominated for millennia by the *Vedas*, a body of diverse sacred writings having its origins so deep in antiquity that its authors are unknown. Most formal Indian philosophy has consisted of commentaries on the *Upanishads*, which are respectively the last of the four parts of each of the four Vedas. Two great schools of Indian critical and analytic philosophy emerged in ancient times from the Vedantic sources, the *Sāmkhya* and the *Yoga*. Though both evolved from the Vedas, they differed greatly in the role that each assigned to a personal god. A third, the complex of moral exhortation and philosophical depth that grew out of the teachings of Gautama, Buddhism, appeared along with the philosophical schools of the Vedanta. Looked at from the perspective of world history, perhaps it has been of greater importance than either *Sāmkhya* or *Yoga*.

By the beginning of the Christian era the ancient philosophical systems had emerged as fully systematic expositions of integrated ontological and moral positions from the religious background in the Vedic writings. For the most part the sources were the *Upanishads* and the *Bhagavad-gītā*. Historians discern an early system-building stage that was followed by a shift of emphasis toward epistemological topics, in which discussions of the status of knowledge of the more problematic features of the Hindu worldview predominate.

One could say that, despite the rich pantheism of "gods," ancient Indian thought was a-theistic, in the sense that the spiritual essence of the world was not personified. However, the systems of the period of the second Christian millennium are theistic, and coalesced around religious movements. The philosophical schools of the second millennia were supportive of ideas of a personal God, who appeared in diverse forms such as Shiva and Vishnu. These Lords of the World were not rival deities but, like everything else, aspects of *Brahman*, the spiritual ground of all being. In a sense they were the same deity. Rather as philosophy in the European Middle Ages was dominated by problems that had their origins in the intellectual puzzles of Christianity, so the schools of later Indian philosophy were driven by these new theistic interests. The theistic doctrines were derived from the sacred writings of the religious traditions. However, paradoxically, they were worked out with philosophical ideas almost wholly drawn from the ancient schools in which the idea of a personal god, *Iśvara*, had no place. Far from serving as a brake on philosophical thought, the new theism of the first half of the second millennium provoked a short period of vigorous and diverse activity (Frauwallner, 1973: 15).

In India the thrust of the classical philosophy of the era was toward ways of deliverance from the cycle of rebirths which brought a person back and back into this miserable world, not necessarily in human form. The transmigration of "souls" from life to life did not terminate in a personal escape, but in the complete dissolution of selfhood. *Atman*, the self, becomes assimilated into *Brahman*, the spiritual reality of the universe. Gautama himself, *the* Buddha of all buddhas, introduced the principle of sudden enlightenment, by which *Nirvāna*, the selfless state of absorption of *Atman* into *Brahman*, the particular into the universal, could be instantly achieved. Later Buddhist sects developed, at least in part, out of critical examination of the morality of this idea. Surely it is grossly selfish to leap in a trice into *Nirvāna* while all the rest of humankind continues to suffer in this imperfect world?

Around the turn of the first millennium Indian philosophy was transformed in substance, though not in style, by the appearance of the idea of personal immortality, salvation rather than deliverance. Philosophers found themselves with the task of reworking a tradition which had been firmly grounded for 1,500 years in the sacred texts, particularly the *Upanishads*.

How might the transition, from an a-theistic scheme in which *Brahman* is the impersonal ground of all being to a theistic scheme in which

Īśvara is a personal God, be explained? One might venture on a sketch of an "externalist" explanation. Here is one suggestion. Indian political and cultural history is a story of successive invasions and conquests from the north. Aryan invaders overran but did not eliminate the Dravidian cultures of truly ancient India. Coming from the north, the invaders created and recreated a strong and persisting distinction between the northwestern areas of the subcontinent and the southern parts. The penultimate arrivals, the Muslim invaders who set up the Moghul Empire, dominated the northwest, and indeed still do, since that region is now a distinct political entity, Pakistan. Finally the British created their own Raj, the influence of which is predominant in much of everyday life in the whole subcontinent even in the present day. Throughout these successive impositions of layer upon layer of alien patterns of life and thought on the indigenous population, there remained an Indianness, the persistence of Hindu life-ways that subtly exerted their influences on all those who arrived, whatever their religion. It has been suggested that the new philosophies that developed around the religious cults of Shiva and Vishnu should be seen as the emergence of the underlying and persisting theistic Hinduism of India, breaking through the abstractions of the Aryan overlay. The Muslim conquest was not complete until the seventeenth century, about the time that the European powers began to take an interest in India, though, at first, this was only in a commercial way. So the second millennium displays the Aryan superstructure being subtly subverted by a persisting Hindu tradition that had been submerged but not destroyed. At the same time, certain new ideas, it seems to me of a much more Western cast, and we must include Islam among the Western influences, appeared in the philosophical writings that took their stance from the Vedanta.

The three centuries preceding the establishment of Islamic rule in most of India in the twelfth century were a time of incessant petty warfare and dynastic squabbles. Kingdoms rose and fell with great rapidity. During this time the states that emerged for a while in the northern plains and the more settled and stable kingdoms of the Deccan, the Indian peninsula, had little to do with one another, except for occasional southern military adventures into the northern states. This period is described by Smith (1924) as "never-ending dynastic wars and revolutions . . . [each state] governed in the old-fashioned way by despotic Rajas, each of whom, could do as he pleased, so long as his power lasted, unless he suffered his will to be controlled by *Brahman* or other religious guides" (Smith, 1924: 181).

Social chaos and personal insecurity are likely, one supposes, to turn one's mind towards escape, but it cannot be in this world. This is the familiar Indian theme. Surely the Muslim conquest of substantial areas of the subcontinent would have brought not only Islamic styles of civil administration, but at least some inkling of the highly personalized Islamic conception of the afterlife. So far as I know there is no textual evidence to support this intuition. Yet it seems too great a coincidence that ideas of personal immortality, salvation rather than deliverance, appeared at just this time and became the focus of the philosophical work of one of the greatest Indian philosophers, Rāmānuja.

Efforts at creating an eclectic union of ancient tradition and imported philosophies have always been a feature of Indian life. However, only rarely, if ever, have these imports succeeded in radically modifying the indigenous tradition. Islam did not become integrated with Hindu philosophy and religion. There was and is a deep separation between Hindu and Muslim culture in the subcontinent. Some of the antagonism can be put down to the contrast between the bleak monotheism of Islam which stands so starkly over against the lush pantheon of lesser Indian gods. The complexity of unsophisticated Hindu religious life contrasts with the simplicity of the basic principles of the sophisticated abstractions of the Vedic philosophical schools.

In the last two centuries Western philosophy was rapidly absorbed into Indian thought, but it did not displace the doctrines of the great classic schools any more than Islam had done. In the period of British dominance one can identify little that is new or original in Indian thought, until the last 100 years or so when the influence of Western philosophy began to be felt. Even then, the weight of tradition is the dominant influence. As we shall see, neither Aurobindo nor Radhakrishnan offer us more than a mild Western spin on an essentially traditional philosophical outlook.

The Vedic Tradition

The main philosophical schools evolved from Vedanta, *Sāmkhya, Yoga,* and Buddhism share a great deal of their basic outlook.[2] It would not be incorrect to see them as varieties of response to the cosmic ontology that has dominated Indian thought since antiquity. Though it would be misleading to characterize classical Indian philosophy in terms of the Western contrast between the spiritual and the material, all three major schools were focused on subjective patterns and techniques of thinking, rather than on action in the material world. However, there were other movements and philosophical schools that stood outside this mainstream, particularly materialists of several stripes. The most influential was the school of Cārvāka, presenting itself in deliberate opposition to the immaterialist philosophies that arose out of the Vedas. There was the school of *Vaisesika*, which developed an atomistic materialism according to which the world and all that existed was construed as a shifting structure of material corpuscles. In the eleventh-century transition from an impersonal to a personal cosmology materialist metaphysics vanished completely.

Indian thought has a remarkable stability and continuity though it presents a continuously changing and developing appearance. In no small measure this is due to the existence of revered texts. Though these are for most part epics, heroic stories, they do embody philosophical doctrines. The Vedic texts have survived for millennia. Heroes take occasion to deliver advice, homilies, lectures, and useful instruction in the course of the adventures and wars that are the main topics of the Vedanta. The ancient philosophical doctrines are presented in these speeches. We shall draw on two such collections or compilations of texts, to establish the basic knowledge that we need to appreciate those doctrines I have called "classical Indian philosophy."

The thought of the Vedic culture of the Aryans, who dominated northwestern India from well before the birth of Christ, has been preserved in the *Upanishads*. I shall begin with a selection of texts that highlight the major concepts that recur again and again in Indian thought. These concepts are by no means straightforward. Their exegesis has always been both pressing and controversial, the ideal soil for a rich and varied crop of philosophy. Nevertheless, the flavor of Vedic philosophy that we get from a taste of the *Upanishads* is perennial.

Vedic metaphysics has much the same role as metaphysics does in Western thought: namely, the exposition of very general concepts through which the detail of the world as we know it can be comprehended in a systematic fashion. Then, as now, there was a seamless web of concepts of which some can be recognized as proto-scientific, others as abstractly metaphysical and ethical.

Cosmology

The first step in our exploration of Indian philosophy, in both its role as a guide to life and as critical commentaries, will be to sketch the sources of the major cosmic and moral doctrines in the sacred texts.

The identity of Atman and Brahman

The ground of the world, the essence of pure being, is *Brahman*. But we human beings live as individual selves. The pure, real, or essential self that is realized in each human being is *Atman*. *Atman* is not to be confused with the Western concept of the soul. Each human being has his or her own soul, but *Atman* is everywhere the same. Here, from the Kena *Upanishad* (Radhakrishnan and Moore, 1957: 45–6) is an extended account of the *Atman* in relation to *Brahman*.

> The wise one is not born, nor dies. This one has not come from any-where, has not become anyone. Unborn, constant, eternal, primeval, this one is not slain when the body is slain.
>
> More minute that the minute, greater than the great, is the Self that is set in the heart of the creature here. One who is without the active will beholds him, and becomes freed from sorrow.
>
> Know thou the *Atman* as riding in a chariot. The body as the chariot. Know thou the intellect *buddhi*, as the chariot driver and the mind as the reins . . . He who has not understanding . . . reaches not the goal . . . He, however, who has understanding, who is mindful and ever pure reaches the goal from which he is born no more.
>
> He who is awake in those that sleep, the Person who fashions desire after desire, that indeed is the Pure. That is *Brahman* . . . On it all the worlds do rest.
>
> The Inner Self of all things, the One controller, who makes his one form manifold – the wise who perceive Him as standing in oneself, they, and no others, have eternal happiness.

Thus *Atman* and *Brahman* are the same. The innermost self of each creature is also the ground of all being. That is indeed a difficult idea, and its exegesis was the driving force of much of the critical, analytical philosophy that bridged the first and second millennia. The *Upanishads* also make it very clear that coming to know anything about *Brahman* is impossible by an empirical or even a conceptual enquiry. None of the attributes of the world as we know them either belong or do not belong to *Brahman*. They can neither be affirmed nor denied of It. From the same *Upanishad* we have:

> Not by speech, not by mind, not by sight can He be apprehended. How can He be comprehended otherwise than by one's saying "He is."

This theme is further elaborated in the Mundukya *Upanishad* (Radhakrishnan and Moore, 1957: 56) as the content of the fourth state of consciousness.

> This is the lord of all. This is the all-knowing. This is the inner controller. This is the source of all for this is the origin and the end of all beings. Not inwardly cognitive, not outwardly cognitive, not both-wise cognitive, not a cognition mass, not cognitive, not non-cognitive, unseen, with which there can be no dealing, ungraspable, having no distinct mark, non-thinkable, that cannot be designated, the essence of the assurance of which is the state of being one with the Self *(Atman)*, the cessation of development, tranquil, benign, without a second. He is the Self *(Atman)*. He should be discerned.

It seems that these passages can only mean that by seeking *Atman*, the core of one's own being, one finds *Brahman*, the ground of all being. They are the same, yet not the same. The resolution of this paradox will lead to the characteristically complex Indian concept of *māyā*, how human beings know the world imperfectly. Finally there is a passage from the Chanogya *Upanishad* (Radhakrishnan and Moore, 1957: 65), which expresses the identity thesis explicitly.

> Containing all works, containing all desires, containing all odours, containing all tastes, encompassing this whole world, the unspeaking, the unconcerned – this is the Self of mine within the heart, this is *Brahman*. Into him I shall enter on departing hence.

The cosmic cycles

The cycle of birth and rebirth, *samsāra*, repeated returns to life in a
material world, is implicit in the background to these passages, since
that is the fate that following the way to *Brahman* allows one to escape.
The earlier *Upanishads* are dominated by cyclical principles, perhaps
abstracted from the natural cycles which were prominent in very
ancient Indian cosmology. The cycle of *samsāra* is vividly described in
the Maitri *Upanishad* in the following passage:

> In this body, which is inflicted with desire, anger . . . delusion . . .
> hunger, senility . . . what is the good of enjoyment of desires? In this
> sort of cycle of existence (*samsāra*) what is the good of enjoyment of
> desires, when after a man has fed on them there is seen repeatedly his
> return here on earth. Be pleased to deliver me. In this cycle of exist-
> ence I am like a waterless well. [Only he knows the true nature of the
> *Atman*] you are our way of escape. (Radhakrishnan and Moore, 1957:
> 93–4)

It seems that the idea of natural cycles had emerged very early in
Indian thought. The material universe, including the human beings
within it, is the result of, and in itself nothing but, three major cycles,
that of water, that of breath, and that of fire. It has been suggested that
the ultimate source of these concepts is to be found in the cyclical
biological pattern of human organic life. Procreated in a liquid
medium, surviving while breathing, and in dying growing cold, we see
the manifestation of these generic cycles. A cosmic connection is forged
between the Moon as the source of water and the Sun as the source
of fire. The later doctrine of *samsāra* seems to be a final abstraction of
the underlying cycle that defines the overall characteristics of human
life.

Classical Indian Philosophy

Here were a cluster of powerful dogmas and insights, drawn from
ancient writings and supported by traditions. What did they presuppose and could they be rationally grounded by reflection on their presuppositions? The generalization of the idea of life cycles to forge a

cosmology required two major problems to be solved. There was an ethical problem: What are the criteria by which the kind of life into which a person is to be reborn is to be determined? Then there was a metaphysical problem: What was the bearer of personal identity through the cycles of rebirth?

Ethics

Ethics must take account of the cyclical but progressive character of the cosmos and the place of human beings in it. From the earliest texts we have, Indian thought embraced the fateful doctrine of cycles of birth–death–rebirth–death and so on. What one must do in the life in which one is currently engaged to move towards deliverance?

Generally the *Upanishads* agree that it is a matter of the balance of good and bad "works" that one achieved in the life just over. What would close or end the cycle? This is provided for only in the barest outline, so far as I know, in the collection of texts that define ancient Indian philosophy, the *Upanishads* and the *Bhagavad-gītā*. For example, again from the Maitri *Upanishad* we have the following advice:

> study of the knowledge of the Veda, and pursuit of one's regular duty. Pursuit of one's regular duty in one's own stage of the religious life. (Radhakrishnan and Moore, 1957: 95)

Which is not saying much more than "be diligent and be good!" It is not surprising that for later generations of philosophers, as we shall see, the details became a matter of consequence for ethical discussion.

The simple, early cosmology took the fire-aspect of each person to be manifested as knowledge. In the end it is knowledge that is required for deliverance (*Mokṣa*) from the cycle of rebirths, but the delivering knowledge is none other than the realization that *Brahman* and *Atman* are identical. Some sages believed that this knowledge was also manifested as a "subtle body" that passes from one corporeal manifestation to another. In Indian psychology the material body is intimately engaged with another body, more subtle in nature. I am not sure that the ontological question of the bearer of personal identity from one incarnation to another could be decided from the texts of the *Upanishads* alone. We shall come across it as one of the most thoroughly examined conceptual issues in later Indian critical philosophy.

The hugely popular Indian epic, the *Mahābhārata*, like the *Upanishads*, includes passages that express moral and cosmic insights. These have been singled out as the *Mokṣa-śāstras*, the treatises of deliverance. There are those which seem to belong to the ancient era, and others which are later accretions. Summarizing the "ancient" texts, presented particularly as a dialogue between Manu and Brhaspati, we have a fairly clear-cut metaphysical scheme, and an outline answer to the question of the nature of the continuity from birth to rebirth and finally to deliverance.

The highest entity in the hierarchical organization of a person is *Atman*. It is imperceptible and unthinkable, yet it exists. *Atman* passes through the cycles of rebirth. Manifesting itself as an embodied person, it opens itself up in three aspects. There is knowledge (*buddhi*). Then there is a capacity for thought, or perhaps one could say a mental organ of thought (*manas*). Finally there are the five sense organs (*indriyas*). Thus *Atman* is, in a sense, the ground of the material world. But this is not Idealism, that is, *Atman* in opening itself up does not constitute that world, but opens itself to it. In consequence the good and bad actions of life in the world (*karma*) become attached to the psychic structure of *buddhi*, knowledge; *manas*, intellect; and *indriyas*, the senses, and as we shall see, thereby play a role in the cycle of rebirths.

But given all this, how is a person to attain to delivering knowledge? The five senses cannot supply it, since they tie the psychic structure to the material world into which rebirths must occur. So how is it to be attained? By *manas*, the organ of thought, attending deliberately not to the deliverances of the senses, that is disattending *indriyas*. One systematically and willfully turns one's attention away from the world as one perceives it. At this moment, if the disattention can be fully achieved, the whole psychological structure of the individual embodied person collapses back into *Atman*, and the cycle ends. With the collapse of the structure its attachments too dissolve, so *karma* can no longer play a fatal role.

Metaphysics

The fundamental cosmological principles recur in various forms and guises through the whole history of classical Indian thought. The world emanates from *Brahman*; people misunderstand their own natures. They fail to grasp that the core self of every person is *Atman*, which must be an aspect of *Brahman*. The belief that the world is wholly material, *māyā*, binds them in *samsāra*, the material world with its cycle of birth and rebirth. Deliverance is accomplished by coming to a correct knowledge of the nature of people and the cosmos. The core of this knowledge is the realization of the true relation between *Atman* and *Brahman*: namely identity.

What of the presuppositions of this vision? This was where deep divisions of view appeared in Vedanta studies as the second millennium began. If *Atman* and *Brahman* are identical, then after escaping the cycle of rebirth the individual person as a distinct self-consciousness would merge into the unity of *Brahman* and thus disappear. Nor is *Brahman* anything like a personal God. By A.D. 1000 these issues had become the focus of some very sophisticated analytical and critical philosophy. If Indian philosophy as a prescription of a way of life was to make sense, Indian philosophy as a critical discipline must ensure it. In particular, a paradox must be resolved. What passes on from life to life? The self, immersed in *māyā*, a mistaken but only too natural assumption about the materiality of the world, would conceive it as personal survival. But once one sees that the self is *Atman* one loses one's selfhood. To put it epigrammatically: "Once you get it, you lose it."

THE VEDIC PHILOSOPHIES

We have seen just how central a place is occupied by the problem of deliverance in all Indian thought. Metaphysics and ethics in one way or another revolve around the various ways that deliverance might be accomplished. It is worth remarking how persistent has been the willingness of Indian thinkers to take the problem as if the background assumptions were a given. What if there was no cycle of rebirth? Would there then be no problem of deliverance? This would be a stance quite alien to Indian thought.

The ultimate aim in this chapter is to follow the development of the philosophical traditions that preceded the appearance of philosophical arguments to support the "insertion" of a personal God, *Īśvara*, into the impersonal cosmos of *Atman* and *Brahman*. The very first of the major second-millennium philosophers, Rāmānuja, was an advocate of a personalized cosmology and, on a domestic scale, an adherent of the God Vishnu, enthusiastically supporting his cult. The *Sāmkhya* philosophical tradition, developing out of the *Upanishads*, served as the major source of philosophical concepts for the philosophers of the second millennium to use in their critical developments of a very different cosmology, since the concept of a personal god was explicitly rejected by the *Sāmkhya* school.

There seems to have been no place for the personal in the metaphysics of the *Sāmkhya* school, while their ethics is simply a justification for the means to transcend it. *Yoga*, the second of the great classical philosophies, developed a very different means for reaching deliverance. While for *Sāmkhya* and, for Buddhism, the act of deliverance was intellectual, achieving a certain level of knowledge, in the *Yoga* tradition it was phenomenological, an act of deliberately turning one's attention away from whatever one perceives, achieved in skilful meditation.

Sāmkhya

The balance between matter and spirit

We can distinguish philosophical discussions of the nature and source of releasing knowledge, the means of deliverance, from the practices that are undertaken to achieve this knowledge. *Sāmkhya* was philosophical, and the path to releasing knowledge is shaped by logic. *Yoga* was practical, and the path to releasing knowledge was by meditation.

The striking difference between *Sāmkhya* as a philosophical movement and the Vedic thought from which it developed, was the balance that was newly struck between the material and the immaterial. One finds the words "soul" and "matter" used by commentators on this development, but I will try to avoid them since they carry for most Western readers too heavy a burden of the traditions of European and particularly Christian thought. In the doctrine of *Sāmkhya* the five material elements are introduced explicitly as existing in a way quite different from *Atman*. The five elements are *akāśa* (the most refined material stuff), *agni* (fire), *vāyu* (wind), *āpas* (water), and *prthivī* (earth). Each element is associated with a sensory modality, for example, *akāśa* with sound. *Manas* and *buddhi* do not originate from *Atman* as a kind of unfolding, but come from the arrangements and structures of the material elements.

There are two key notions in this metaphysics. *Prakrti* is primordial matter but in an active or potential sense. *Purusa* is the empirical self, the core of the person as manifested in this world. Beings, as they are manifest in this world, are characterized by three attributes or constituent qualities. These are the three *gunas*. *Sattva* is boyant and illuminating, and is potential consciousness. *Rajas* is exciting and mobile and is potential activity. Finally *Tamas* is sluggish and enveloping, and is potential resistance. Whichever one of these qualities is in play, so to say, it dominated the others. However, the operation of any one depends on the cooperation of the others. They are jointly effective and could not exist independently. *Prakrti* is the state of equilibrium between them. From it evolves intellect and *buddhi*, active mind. *Prakrti* is not only the source of all things, but also that which is known by *purusa*, the self as knower. The three *gunas* have psychological aspects, as pleasure, pain, and boredom respectively.

How do we achieve deliverance? One must bear in mind that deliverance is not salvation. It is an *end* to selfhood. It is by *Atman* coming to an awareness of its true nature, which is not material. That is, it becomes aware that pleasure, pain and boredom do not belong to it, but belong to matter. Just this insight is the crucial step to deliverance. This is a logical or philosophical route to deliverance since it involves a consideration of the nature of the senses, the organs of thought and perception, and so on. By reflection on what this tells us about that which is imperceptible, we indirectly grasp *Atman*. But *Atman* must be immaterial if it is imperceptible. So it can not be intimately involved with matter.

What of the candidate for a personal God, *Īśvara*? In the *Sāmkhya-Pravacana* Sutra there are several explicit repudiations of the possibility of a personal God. For example, we find the following text:

1.95: The sacred texts which speak of *Īśvara* are either glorifications of the free self or homages paid to the perfect ones. (Radhakrishnan and Moore, 1957: 448)

1.98: The superintendence [of the world] is through proximity to *prakrti*, as in the case of the loadstone. (Radhakrishnan and Moore, 1957: 448)

Finally we have this very firm statement:

> III, 57: 10: On account of the non-existence of the evidence there is
> no proof of an eternal *Īśvara*. (Radhakrishnan and Moore, 1957: 451)

In *Sāmkaya*, *Īśvara* emerges. It is not eternal.

Pancasikha: the resolution of the contradictions

The greatest Indian philosopher of the period we are discussing, and one who prepared the way for the adoption of many of these ideas by the religiously oriented philosophers of the second millennium, was Pancasikha. He realized that *Sāmkhya* was radically dualistic and presented a seeming contradiction. How could a material system bind an immaterial *Atman* into the cycle of rebirth? How could the senses create a state of affairs from which we must seek deliverance? And how could *Atman* in self-reflection accomplish an unbinding from material states of affairs?

Given his conviction that this must be so — after all, the outlines were given in the *Upanishads* — he offered two metaphors that have served Indian thought ever since. The most dramatic is that of the blind man who cannot direct action (the material organs) and the lame man who cannot act (*Atman*). The lame man rides on the back of the blind man and together they make their way. The second image, one that has shaped Indian thought very deeply, was that of the female principle (*prakrti*), material and creative, and the male principle (*purusa*), knowing and directing. This generic distinction appeared and reappeared in many guises. In *Sāmkhya* "*prakrti* and its products include mind stuff, the senses, the body, and so forth . . . *Purusa* is the unchanging principle of consciousness" (Prabhavananda, 1963: 221).

Yoga

The metaphysical scheme based on *prakrti* and *purusa* is shared by *Yoga*. The distinctive character of *Yoga* comes from the critical analysis of *Sāmkhya* credited to an ancient teacher, Patañjali (ca. 150 B.C.) and set out in the *Yoga Aphorisms*. The *Yoga* metaphysics is a-theistic, so the root meaning of "*yoga*," that is, "union," refers to the union with God.

We are in familiar Hindu territory here, in that by grasping that our selves are *Atman* we achieve union with *Brahman*.

The word "*yoga*" also refers to the practices by which that union is achieved. These boil down to a sequence of steps by which the mind is transformed. The structure of the mind as it presents itself to us is not its real structure. Perception sets thought in motion and that thought is ordered with respect to a self, expressed, for example, in the first person. This self is affected in pleasant and unpleasant ways by thoughts. The real self, the *purusa*, is unchanging and unaffected by the character of ordinary thoughts. Tranquility of mind can be achieved only if the *purusa* can be reached. *Yogas*, as practices of inward mind control, are aimed at reaching the *purusa*.

There are some matters of philosophical interest in this account. The thoughts of the everyday life of the mind cannot just be disattended. Every thought leaves behind a trace or latent form, the *samskāra*, which continue to exert a covert influence on all we do and think. The revamping of the whole mind reaching for the *purusa* must include steps to deal with the huge deposit of *samskāras* left by this and all previous lives. The details of *yoga* practices are not of philosophical interest except in so far as they include the important principle that though painful thoughts must first be displaced by pleasant ones, in the end the pleasant ones must also be abandoned.

Buddhism

The doctrine of sudden enlightenment

The third great philosophical school of the ancient era, the influence of which pervades the philosophy of the second millennium, is Buddhism. While I think it is true to say that the various schools of Hinduism we have been examining in this chapter so far remained, with some exceptions, the source of predominantly Indian philosophical developments in the second millennium, Buddhism spread rapidly into other parts of Asia, namely Sri Lanka and China, and to Japan. It has remained a force in India until the present day, and so must have its place in this survey. To grasp its role in the larger picture of the philosophical trends of the second millennium, we must eventually follow the development of Buddhism on the international stage.

Buddhist teachings derive from the preaching of a single individual, Siddhattha Gautama. Born about 560 B.C., the son of the ruler of a small state, he grew up in the normal pattern for such a person. We have already heard one story of how he came to be a religions leader. After studying with two different teachers, with both of whom he was dissatisfied, he decided to follow the traditional path toward enlightenment, meditation within an austere way of life. But this proved unsatisfying to him. Finally, meditating under a tree, famed from then on as the Tree of Enlightenment, he arose to declare that he had become Buddha, and had already passed beyond the cycle of rebirth. He had achieved deliverance, and had found the releasing knowledge. This enlightenment was evidently sudden! How to pass on this great insight to others? Later, in China, the Buddhist movement was to split over the issue as to whether indeed enlightenment was sudden or gradual.

It has been remarked that the original simplicity of Buddhist teaching is to be explained by the way in which the Buddha himself focused all his attention on the problem of deliverance. Gautama often asserted that no doubt much else could be said, but deliverance was all that mattered. Nothing else could be of such importance for human beings.

However, in his efforts to make clear to his disciples the nature of the Buddhist moment of enlightenment, Gautama introduced a profound metaphysical principle, the principle of causality. If the cycle of *samsāra* is to be broken one must understand how it is caused in the first place. Existence, he declared, is the effect of desire. Thus, eliminate desire, and with the cause deleted from the universe, so the effect will be. His insight and the psychological state that accompanied it under the Tree of Enlightenment was simply the cessation of desire, *of every kind*. Desire was comprised of all those hankerings that beset one in the ordinary course of life, and especially for life itself. Practising celibacy, austerity, and goodness to others, the adept reached *Nirvāna*, *Brahman* under another name, and ceased to exist in the way that the unenlightened people of this world exist, namely as individual, conscious, and suffering selves.

From the point of view of our second-millennium focus, it is the developed forms of Buddhism that spread to China and Japan and are still with us on which I shall concentrate. Again our interest is in Buddhism as philosophy in both its popular senses, as philosophy of life and as a system of metaphysics and ethics. Buddhism incorporates both reflections on and advice about a way of living, and reflections on the philosophical, especially metaphysical assumptions that sustain these life practices and are presupposed by them.

Here are some quotations from the traditional literature that purport to report the very words of Gautama himself:

> Now this, O monks, is the noble truth of the cause of pain: that craving which leads to rebirth, combined with pleasure and lust, finding pleasure here and there, namely, the craving for passion, the craving for existence, the craving for non-existence.

> Now this, O monks, is the noble truth of the cessation of pain: the cessation without a remainder of that craving, abandonment, forsaking, release, non-attachment. (Radhkrishnan and Moore, 1957: 274)

This is entirely consistent with the general Indian philosophical tradition. But the nihilism of *Nirvāna* is profound. And here the Buddhist seems to offer something very different from the fusion of self with the cosmos, and the notion that *Atman* is *Brahman*. In a discussion with a disciple, Vaccha, Gautama sums up a lengthy exposition as follows:

> All consciousness by which one could predicate the existence of the saint [someone meditating and engaging in a virtuous life], all that consciousness has been abandoned, uprooted, pulled out of the ground like a palmyra-tree and become non-existent, and not liable to spring up again in the future. The said, O Vaccha, who has been released from what is styled consciousness, is deep, immeasurable, unfathomable, like the mighty ocean. To say that he is reborn would not fit the case. To say that he is not reborn would not fit the case. To say that he is neither reborn and not reborn would not fit the case. To say that he is neither reborn nor not reborn would not fit the case. (Radhakrishnan and Moore, 1957: 292)

The advent of the Bodhisattva

Buddhism quickly evolved into two major schools, the original form being Hinayana Buddhism, the "lesser vehicle." The point of life is to achieve *Nirvāna*, in which the person as individual self is lost. *Everyone* should seek deliverance. However, if that is taken as a general prescription of a philosophy of life, who will be left to offer the kind of help that the troubled of this world, still in *samsāra*, are deserving? This question is the source of the Mahayana school, or the Great Vehicle. According to this prescription the truly good person, by postponing ultimate enlightenment and the step to *Nirvāna*, becomes a *Bodhisattva*, one who is devoted to the amelioration of the lives of others. It opens up another question. If we postpone *Nirvāna* for whatever reason, what fills the gap between life and deliverance? Into this vacuum the Buddhists inserted all sorts of heavens and hells, purgatories added to the millions of earthly lives that a person could lead between now and the moment of enlightenment.

The distinction has been nicely summarized by Nan Huai-chin (1995: 52): "The philosophy of the *Mahayana bodhisattva* path opens up the Hinayana philosophy of detachment into a spirit of active entry into the world."

The Buddhist "movement" seems to have been particularly prolific in sectarianism. The *Mahayana* school of Buddhism soon divided into the *Mādhyamika* and the *Yogācāra* school. These were the dominant forms of Buddhist thought that were influential in China and Japan, though it is a moot point whether we should see them as sources of the various schools of Zen. However, the common element among the schools was the Mahayana doctrine of the six ways of transcendence. The six stages form a ladder of ascent. At the summit is the stage of *prajnā* wisdom. The first way is giving, the second discipline, the third tolerance, the fourth diligence, and the fifth concentration (in meditation). The sixth way is *prajnā*, a kind of summation of the virtues acquired in the practice of the five ways. But there is a major difference between this moral philosophy and those we are familiar with. It is a way of transcendence. The distinctions between the virtues and vices at each level must be *transcended*. That means that enlightenment comes by abandoning the distinction between, say, giving and keeping. Again to quote Nan Huai-chin (1995: 52), "by having no idea of tolerance in the inner mind, only then does it count as tolerance."

The nature of the Buddha

The metaphysical issues that led to the various schools of Buddhist thought are simple to set out, but not so easy to see one's way through. Essentially the issue was the nature of Buddha, "the enlightened one," in the person of Gautama. Was he just a man? He himself seems to have denied this, though equivocally. In claiming to have eradicated craving he would have ceased to be a being of the kind that craves, and that is a man. Rather he is a buddha, an enlightened one. The ambiguity was enough perhaps to encourage the development of a transcendental account of Gautama's mode of being, in the doctrine of the plurality of Buddhas "leading to a transcendentalist monism as represented by terms like *tathāta* (objectivity) and *dharmakāya* (*dharma-body*) in the later *Mahāyana* texts" (Kalupahan, 1976: 118). Thus Gautama was himself a plurality of earthly appearances, each time as a buddha, and indeed there would be other such serial buddhas as well, infinitely many of them. At the same time, as I have described it above, the *Prajñāparamita-sutra* taught a quite specific procedure for attaining the status of a *bodhisattva*, a being aspiring to enlightenment. The aspirant learned to transcend a sequence of false oppositions, such as "rich/poor" and in the end even "enlightened/unenlightened," so obtaining deliverance from *samsāra*, the cycle of rebirth. A *bodhisattva* could pass to *Nirvāna*, having attained the level of "knowledge," but chooses not to do so. Again there seems to be a paradox: If, to put the point in classical Indian terms, one knows that *Atman* is *Brahman*, should not that automatically achieve deliverance?

This is set out in the *Diamond Sutra* in the form of instructive stories, but it does not conceal very deeply a profound paradox in the *Prajñāparamita* teachings. To be able to help others, and to have risen thus far in the scale of enlightenment to that of the *bodhisattva*, one must be in *samsāra*, the material world of the cycle of rebirth. Only there can such a person help others toward *Nirvāna* by eliminating ignorance (*avidjā*), craving (*tanhā*), and grasping (*upādāna*), and thus be released from *samsāra*. But just in achieving this, the aspiring one will become not a *bodhisattva* but a buddha and so will be released from *samsāra*. So released, the person will be delivered from the world wherein there are people in need of the wisdom and succour of the *bodhisattva*. Thus the conditions for virtuous action make virtuous action impossible. The *bodhisattva* sacrifices deliverance for the opportunity to save any and all sentient beings.

Some of this sort of difficulty was swept aside by the *Mādhyamika* school, who roundly denied that concepts could denote reality. Discursive thought stands between us and reality. So the paradoxical character of the *bodhisattva* is not surprising when we formulate the path to enlightenment *conceptually*. For Gautama himself, the only rule was just to act. As we shall see the "just do it" school began to dominate the forms of Buddhism that took root in China and Japan, and flourished in the second millennium.

In passing it is perhaps worth repeating, though the point is not strictly speaking philosophical, that the time from now to *Nirvāna* is not necessarily occupied with rebirths into *samsāra*. There developed an elaborate scheme of heavens and hells, purgatories, and other points of temporary stasis as the person sought enlightenment and thus achieved deliverance. There could be millions of these lives!

A Radical "Refusal"

We have been following one line of thought through various changes and refinements, but in all its long history the *Atman/Brahman* concept complex has been immaterialist. In order to grasp the force of the Śankaran philosophy that became the starting point for the philosophy that dominated the second millennium in India, we must pay some attention to a movement that was radically and even aggressively materialist, Cāvarkā. In the next chapter we will look at the contrast between materialism and immaterialism. The victory of the latter determined the form of Indian philosophy for the millennium to come.

Logic in Indian Thought

One of the glories of philosophy in Ancient Greece was the invention and cultivation of the study of logic – the formal principles of correct reasoning. This field of study was extended into an examination of fallacies and sophisms. The former were arguments based on faulty principles, while the latter were the result of verbal tricks and ambiguities. It also came to include the study of systems of categories and methods of classification. In the writings of Aristotle it reached a particular maturity. Logic was still being taught from textbooks based on Aristotle well into the twentieth century.

The central focus of Greek logic was the principles and patterns of correct or valid deductive arguments. Other forms of reasoning were studied but they remained peripheral. Indian logic was not only developed independently of the logical tradition of the Greeks, but was primarily a study of the principles and methods best adapted to reach new knowledge. Deductive logic brought out the implications of what was already known. In modern terminology, Indian logic was inductive.

It is easy to see why. The route to deliverance was through the acquisition of knowledge, and particularly knowledge that one did not have before the moment of enlightenment. Inductive reasoning covers the rules and criteria for acquiring new knowledge. Indian logicians did discover and comment on the syllogism, but deductive logic took a decidedly second place to a logic of discovery.

Buddhists developed a sophisticated inductive logic, building on the aphorisms of a certain Gautama, from the same tribe as the Buddha himself. It grew out of the rules for the proper conduct of a public debate. The first major treatise on syllogistic reasoning, *Naya-śāstra*, was the *Naya-sutra*, composed about A.D. 400. A syllogism, or argument-form in which a conclusion is drawn from two premises, has the general form

$$A \text{ are } B$$
$$\underline{B \text{ are } C}$$
$$A \text{ are } C$$

These propositions may be variously qualified, and so give rise to a variety of formal structures.

Extended to the realm of empirical inference, Buddhist logicians introduced something very like the Western Principle of Sufficient Reason. To infer what there is on a hill from the observation of smoke, one uses an intermediary, namely that fire is a sufficient reason for smoke (Vidyabhusana, 1971: Section II).

However, the most important book on logic in the Indian philosophical tradition is the Tattva-cintāmani, composed in the twelfth century A.D. Despite the anachronism of placing a discussion of it in this chapter, it seems appropriate to have some understanding of its doctrines in what follows. It is, of course, a development of themes that reach back into the first millennium, so that its placement at this point is appropriate.

There are four main topics, to each of which a section of the treatise is devoted.

1. The topic of perception covers the grounds of knowledge obtained by means of the senses. Does consciousness of the validity of a claim to knowledge come along with that claim? Surely not. How do we assess validity? The answer has a strikingly modern ring.

> This knowledge is valid because it is conducive to activity which is fruitful; whatever is not conducive to activity which is fruitful, is not knowledge. (quoted in Vidyabhusana, 1971: 409)

Coherence turns out to be the mark of fruitfulness.

2. Inference has the general character of mediated reasoning discussed above under the topic of syllogism. The crucial element is the proposition serving as a sufficient reason why the conclusion follows from the premise. The full development of an argument requires a kind of analysis, in which step by step the presuppositions of the propositions are made evident.

3. The doctrine of "comparison" concerns the subsumption of particulars under universals. Knowledge of general words requires a cognitive act that is different from inference, and also from perception. This is the act of comparison. It requires judgment, since there are infinitely many ways in which any two things are the same and different.

4. The final section deals with the conditions under which a verbal report conveys knowledge. The innovatory aspect of this part of the treatise is the author's distinction between speech which reports perception and speech which reports recollections of things. Both are valid sources of knowledge.

Somehow through these means the enlightened one comes to *know* that *Atman* is *Brahman*.

Conclusion

Though ancient Indian thought is represented by the *Upanishads* and other texts, and developed into three main and distinct traditions, there remained a great deal in common between them. Each recognized the horror of the tie to material existence, *samsāra*. Each emphasized the need for deliverance, *mokṣa*, necessary to escape the cycle of rebirth. Each was based on a metaphysical scheme with which a technique for deliverance could be rationally grounded. To realize that *Atman is Brahman* is the moment of enlightenment. To achieve that stage of sophistication one must disattend from all that belongs to the material world as it is perceived, and as it manifests itself in desires. Then the sense of individual selfhood will vanish. *Atman* has become *Brahman*.

NOTES

1 For a comprehensive survey of classical Indian philosophy, one cannot do better than consult Ninian Smart's *World Philosophies* (1999), chapter 2.

2 In calling these the "main schools" of classical Indian philosophy I am selecting from a much richer array of philosophers and philosophies.

3

Indian Philosophy in the Second Millennium

In or about the year 1150 one might have seen a small group of men making their way through some rough wooded country near the small town of Tamil Nada. The leader urged on those near him and gradually the main party drew ahead of a slower-paced straggler. Eventually he was lost to view. The others did not turn back, since they had hoped to lose him, and indeed that he might perish in the jungle. However, after some time the man who had been left behind encountered a hunter and his wife, who led him out of the wilderness to the vicinity of a temple. Asked to fetch some water from the well, when our hero returned the couple had vanished. The man they saved was none other than Rāmānuja. The attempted murder had been instigated by Yadavaprakāŕa, a sage with whom Rāmānuja had had the temerity to disagree.

From tradition we have two fixed points in the conceptual geography of Indian philosophy. On a cosmic scale there is *Brahman*, the unchanging essence of the world that unfolded itself into the multiplicity of material reality without ceasing to be *Brahman*, the ultimate singularity that is the essence of all being. On the personal scale there is *Atman*, the unchanging essence of the self. How are they related? According to the classical point of view they are identical. There can be no ultimate survival of personhood. Personal being, as an individual, is maintained only in so far as the being in question is trapped in *māyā*, a mistaken view of things. While that persists the person is enmeshed in the cycle of *samsāra*, endless rebirth. Once the cosmos is seen aright, deliverance from selfhood, and so from existence as an individual consciousness, is accomplished.

In the last part of the first millennium the philosophy of the *Upanishads* was given definitive form by Śankara (788–820). He provided an elegant interpretation which preserved the main outline of the Vedic tradition of the *Upanishads*. However, he contrived to do that within a framework of concepts and arguments that we would have no difficulty in recognizing as philosophy in the analytical and critical sense.[1]

The break that initiated the style of philosophy that was to dominate most of the second millennium does not occur so conveniently as to highlight the year A.D. 1000. The key transition had come about in the ninth century. Śankara's idealism overwhelmed the indigenous skeptical materialism that had played a major part in Indian thought from antiquity. In the second millennium Hindu philosophy is through and through idealist. The influence of Śankara was lasting and profound.

It has been suggested that the story of Indian philosophy in the tenth and eleventh centuries can be seen as the result of a resurgence of an indigenous religious tradition, favoring personal gods, in reaction to the "academic" analytical style of philosophy of the Aryan north, with its abstract and intellectually demanding concepts of *Brahman* and *Atman*. Just as we could not appreciate the mode of philosophizing adopted by the Christian later Middle Ages without some attention to Aristotle as a source of philosophical insights, so we have had to become acquainted with the "ancient" Indian philosophical tradition in order to appreciate the borrowings that provided a philosophical grounding for the religious movements that developed around the gods Vishnu and Shiva. It is to these that we now turn.

At the same time, a major philosopher, Śankara, set about establishing a wholly idealist metaphysics, which seems to have coincided with the disappearance of popular materialisms. This was to be followed shortly by the first and, as it turned out, the more or less final version of a cosmic scheme that allowed for personal immortality. In the work of Rāmānuja, the personalized character of popular religion was fused with the tradition of a highly sophisticated philosophy.

To understand the force of the idealism of Śankara we need to look quite closely at the materialism (*Lokāyata*) which it displaced once and for all.

INDIAN MATERIALISM

Materialists were generally thought of as the followers of Cārvāka, one of the dimly visible sages of deep antiquity. This atheistic and skeptical materialism is known to us now only through the presentations of Cārvākan doctrines in the writings of opponents. There are two pillars to the edifice, one antireligious and the other antirational.

The Materialist Doctrines

In Māblava's book, *Sarvadarśanasamagraha*, some very aggressive Cārvākan doctrines are presented.

> In this school the four elements . . . are the original principles; from these alone, when transformed into the body, intelligence is produced, just as the inebriating power is developed from the mixing of certain ingredients; when these are destroyed intelligence at once perishes . . . there is no evidence for any self distinct from the body. (Radhakrishnan and Moore, 1957: 229)

Statement like "I am thin" make sense in the materialist scheme since material attributes and "self-consciousness reside in the same subject (the body)."

Śankara summed up the materialism he wished to combat in the following succinct way:

> There is no world other than this; there is no heaven and no hell. The realm of Śiva and like regions are invented by stupid imposters.

> The pain of hell lies in the troubles that arise from enemies . . . while liberation [deliverance] (*mokṣa*) is death which is the cessation of life breath. (Radhakrishnan and Moore, 1957: 235)

These strong opinions were not the result of intuitions, but of a firmly based and well argued skepticism. The philosopher Jayarāśi set out the Cārvākan views on the limitations of inductive means for gaining knowledge. Perception does not reveal anything beyond what we actually see. Causality is simply unintelligible. "Nothing determines a cause to be necessarily a cause." Nor can we make use of the order or regularity of cognition to decide which is cause and which effect; anything is. We perceive the horns of a cow in a certain succession but the one first seen is not the cause of the one seen later. Induction is dismissed with the observation that we perceive only particulars, so we cannot infer a universal proposition without another inductive argument, and so on, ending in the stultification of an infinite regress.

This was all strong stuff. It was popular in the somewhat discontented times of the ninth century. The purveyors of religion and of the search for deliverance were thought by many to be rogues. It was to the refutation and extirpation of skepticism and the materialism resulted from it that Śankara directed his teaching.

THE ANALYSIS OF JUDGMENTS

Śankara was born in 788. He produced most of his major work when he was very young. Most of his short life was spent in travels during which he promulgated his antimaterialist point of view. But his efforts to strengthen religion were also practical in that he is said to have been responsible for the building of temples and the setting up of religious communities. He died in 820, close to one of the temples that he had founded. He is regarded by many Indian scholars as the foremost philosopher India has ever produced. His work is recognizably "philosophical" in the analytical sense that we are now very familiar with. His technique is to look deeply into the logical and conceptual presuppositions of doctrine, and examine the fundamental patterns of reasoning herein.

The Logical and Epistemological Foundations

The concept of sublation

The main logical concept developed by Śankara is sublation. This is the process of correcting errors or mistakes. A judgment is sublated when, for some reason, we can see that it is false or misleading, and in so doing we must be substituting another and better one. Judgments about the perceived material world and about our own natures can be sublated, so that the world and those natures must be appearances, not constituents of reality. Thus we have a "logical chain of being." Anything which can be sublated is of lesser reality than that which sublates it. It is easy to see that this leads very nicely to the conclusion that the material and experiential world is less real than the universe, which is at once *Brahman* and *Atman*. Reality cannot be sublated by anything. Unreality can be neither sublated nor not be sublated.

In practice, since appearance is the mode of knowing that is framed in the subject/object distinction, a thing (object) appears in such and such a way to a person (subject); transcending that distinction will lead to the sublation of appearances in general. In this way we will arrive at the knowledge that *Brahman* and *Atman* are one. But we can have no discursive understanding of it. The deep unity has no place in appearances. This allows only for a formal proof of the identity of *Brahman* and *Atman*, of the ground of all being with the ground of individual human existence. "One experiences *Brahman* as the sole unsublatable reality when one transcends all distinctions, in particular that between subject and object, so that subject and object coalesce" (Pulingandla, 1975: 222–3). That coalescence is the experience of *Atman*. *Brahman* is both experienced and not experienced.

Appearances

The main epistemological concept in Śankara's system is *māyā*. Pulingandla (1975: 216–17) argues pretty convincingly that the common translation of *māyā* as "illusion" is thoroughly misleading. Śankara uses it to include at least the following: a "persistent tendency to regard appearances as reality"; "our ignorance of the difference between appearance and reality"; and finally, "the creative power of *Brahman* by virtue of which the world of variety and multiplicity comes into existence." The material world is not illusory in the sense of nonexistent. It is an appearance but rooted in the reality that is *Brahman*.

The System at Work

The main ontological concept in this scheme is a triad of subconcepts: reality, appearance, and unreality. It should be clear now that the members of this triad are logically related to the concept of the sublatable. The perceived world is *Brahman* as it appears to us under the superimposition of names and forms, so our *māyā* experience of it can be corrected. This material world exists, but it is neither real nor unreal. Only *Brahman* is real, and only that which could not exist is unreal. Unlike the material world, that which could not exist, the unreal, cannot be sublated. Our knowledge of what does not exist could hardly be improved upon. It can only suffer logical transformations.

This is recognizably critical philosophy, that is, a study of the variety and interconnection of concepts and conceptual systems. It is not an exposition of the life philosophy or philosophies which such concepts are used to prescribe. Śankara has brought the presuppositions of the *Atman/Brahman* doctrine to the fore, and used his concept of sublation to subject them to critical analysis.

The truths about *Brahman* and *Atman* are higher-order truths, involving the concept of "deliverance," *mokṣa*. This is achieved, as all Indian philosophers of the classical period held, through the realization that the cosmos is a thoroughgoing unity, that *Brahman and Atman are one*. There seem to be many selves but in reality there is only one self. This is the meaning of the popular text "That thou art." However, Śankara allowed for lower truths, the truths of everyday life and common sense. At that level it is true that there are many selves, but most significantly, in the context of everyday life it is a lower truth that *Brahman* is *Iśvara*, the personal god. It was on this foundation that Rāmānuja, the most important philosopher of the second millennium, built his philosophy, partly in reaction to the uneasy combination of deep unity with superficial diversity that seemed to characterize the philosophy of Śankara.

FROM DELIVERANCE TO SALVATION

The school of philosophy founded by Rāmānuja lies across the turn of the millennium. As we will see, the basic structure of Indian thought, laid down in the previous millennium, is inherited more or less unchanged. But the interpretation of the system is the matter at issue. The rival to which we should see Rāmānuja's critical conceptual analysis opposed is the work of Śankara. The two concepts under scrutiny are the real core of personhood, *Atman*, and the ground of all being, *Brahman*. Is *Atman* a soul which could carry personal identity through deliverance, and is *Brahman* a personal God for which a different name, *Īśvara*, is required? There can be little doubt that Śankara would have replied in the negative to both questions. Rāmānuja is generally regarded as one of India's most important philosophers, not least because he set about a critical demolition of Śankara's conceptual scheme. He brought the somewhat austere cosmic grandeur of classical Hindu philosophy down to earth, making way for the elevation of a personal God to the very un-Indian role of Supreme Being.

Rāmānuja was born in 1017 in Tamil Nada, in South India. He came of an orthodox Brahmin family and was educated at home, to acquire the usual competence in ritual. However, his maternal grandfather had been a disciple of Yāmunā, a well-known and critical teacher. After completing his formal education, Rāmānuja married, content for a while to fulfill the duties of his class and caste. However, something of his grandfather had come down to him, and he began to study with Yadavaprakāra. Even at this stage of his development Rāmānuja was dissatisfied with the contemplative idea of a life of meditation as the life of virtue. His quarrel with his teacher nearly cost him his life. Following his grandfather's example, he set off to study with Yāmunā, but when he arrived the old man had just died. Unwilling to follow the strict Brahmin code, he took up with a teacher from an "inferior" caste, Kāncīpūrna. Social troubles beset their relationship at first. In the meantime Rāmānuja had gone on a mission to Kashmir on behalf of another teacher, who, incidentally, had been grievously insulted by Rāmānuja's snobbish wife, to examine the work of Bhadarā, really to try to work out how far the new interpretation of orthodoxy could be reconciled with the ancient texts and the *Samkhyan* tradition. This journey freed him from all further self-imposed constraints and shortly thereafter he wrote his great work, *Śrī Bhāsya*. In that and other works he turned Indian philosophy toward this world. His advocacy of a morality of public service rather than one based on the virtue of withdrawal was particularly important. He died in 1127. These dates give him a life span of 120 years. The authorities I have consulted seem to regard this report of an extraordinary longevity as authentic. (For further details of the life of this remarkable man see Lakshamma, 1990.)

What is Brahman?

The Indian cosmos is nothing else but *Brahman*, the permanent and the unknowable which is both the source and the essence of everything. Schools of philosophy agree on the basics, so to say, but differ very deeply in their account of the *"Brahman"* concept. Rāmānuja argues that *Brahman*, in its essence, could not have transformed itself into the world and remained undifferentiated. In this he was challenging a view that we have seen was almost universally held by all but the strict materialists. How does he approach the topic? Very much as an analytical philosopher. In his treatment of the problem he uses one of the techniques we have come across in chapter 1. He looks for a contradiction in the presuppositions of the position he opposes. It is easy to find. If *Brahman* did indeed become the material world it would be subject to the defilement and decay that is characteristic of that world. And this is a contradiction of the essence of *Brahman*. It cannot be both perfect and unchanging *and* defiled and decaying. It follows that *Brahman* can only engender the material world of *samsāra* as a body distinct from its essence. *Īśvara*, the personal God, cannot be an aspect of the *Brahman* essence. It too must be ontologically distinct. *Māyā*, if I have understood this doctrine aright, is not a false view of the cosmos, against which one might juxtapose a true view. It is the only view that limited human powers can have of it. It is transcended by the knowledge that *Brahman* and *Atman* are one, but not, one might say, dispelled by the acquisition of that knowledge. To the enlightened and the unenlightened alike the cosmos will continue to manifest itself as the familiar material world.

Given this conclusion, we must assign a basic causality to the material world. Maintaining the distinction between appearance and reality, now relativized to the world of *māyā*, Rāmānuja argues that the world does not have the ordinary material perceptible qualities (*gunas*) in itself. They must arise psychologically from the triad of basic mental states with which we are already familiar from the ancient philosophical repertoire, *sattva*, *rajas*, and *tamas*, respectively pleasure, passion, and darkness. I think these should be read as personal psychological powers or dispositions, since the whole of this doctrine is expressed in the framework of a general active natural causality. The material world causes people to experience it through the ordinary perceptible qualities of everyday perception.

Rāmānuja's view of logic, as the principles that govern the inference of particular truths from general inductively grounded premises, plays an important part in the system. Since "God" is beyond the senses, no inductions from experience can be found from which inferences to the character or even existence of the God can be made. Furthermore, unlike some philosophers of the period who advocated a dualism within the *Brahman* nature, *Brahman* as pure, formless being and also as the material world, Rāmānuja insists that there cannot be both unity and difference in the same entity. The properties of a being are that very being, and not different from it. As Dasgupta remarks, this amounts to declaring that the predicates are always in the subject, a logical doctrine that is familiar to Western philosophers, famously expounded by Leibniz. The world that *Brahman* engenders is something other than itself.

What are People in this System?

The individuality of the soul

There had been schools of philosophy in earlier periods in India which had argued that the person was wholly body, and others who denied that there were a multitude of individual souls "in reality."[2] That there seemed to be a multitude of "souls" was just another aspect of *māyā*, the ubiquity of appearances. Rāmānuja, and those who thought along similar lines, insisted that there are many self-conscious beings, ensouled. The soul is located in the body, but pervades it as the light of a lamp pervades a room. The light emitted by the soul is knowledge.

The problem of freedom of action

But how can there be free action in a world that is in reality the body of *Īśvara*? To anyone looking toward Indian thought from the vantage point of Western Europe, the philosophy offered by Rāmānuja in about A.D. 1070 is remarkably similar to that proposed by Malebranche and other occasionalists in the seventeenth century. *Īśvara* gives the individual "soul" freedom to formulate desires, wants, and so on, and so arranges the material world that they are realized.

Techniques of deliverance

In Rāmānuja's philosophy the bar to deliverance is still ignorance, *avidya*. It is something positive though, since it is at least as much a complex of worldly desires as it is a lack of insight. It comes about because the self is in contact with matter. Deliverance is possible, according to Rāmānuja, not just by an intellectual insight, getting a correct understanding of the world, but requires observances as well as self-control and good works. Philosophy is melded with religion as a repertoire of practices.

Personal identity

Though Rāmānuja did not actually study under Yāmunā, the initiator of the critical stance to traditional Vedanta, nevertheless he is said to have learned a great deal of his anti-Śankaran opinions from him (Dasgupta, 1940: 101–2). Under this influence Rāmānuja planned a systematic philosophical development of Vedanta that would lead through critical conceptual analysis to the conclusion that the Veda is compatible with the existence of a personal God, *Īśvara*. It must also be compatible with the belief in the survival of personal identity after deliverance. After release from the cycle of rebirth, and thus from the relation of the self to material being, personal identity must survive. The self does not dissipate into formless and unchanging *Brahman*.

The question Rāmānuja asks sets the style for the second millennium in Indian philosophy. It does make our seemingly arbitrary division into millennia meaningful, since no one seems to have asked quite this question before. Why should we go through all the effort and self-denial to achieve deliverance if there is no personal identity in fusion with *Brahman*?

To maintain that the consciousness of the "I" does not persist in the state of final release is again altogether inappropriate. It, in fact, amounts to the doctrine – only expressed in somewhat different words – that final release is the annihilation of the self . . . no sensible person exerts himself under the influence of the idea that after he himself has perished there will remain some entity termed "pure light." (Rāmānuja in Radhakrishnan and Moore, 1957: 547)

Thus we are presented with a fundamental philosophical problem: If the self of each human being, as *Atman*, is somehow also *Brahman*, the ground of all being, and if after release from *samsāra*, the self or soul returns from whence it came, how could personal identity be maintained through this transformation? Closely allied with this is another question which is central to *samsāra* itself, namely, what is the *ground* of the maintenance of personal identity through the cycle of rebirths? If the answer is the self as *Atman*, and *Atman* is *Brahman* the "unchanging," we are faced with the other question Rāmānuja tackled: If the human self and *Brahman* are identical how can the unchanging be related to the changing? Fortunately for us, the texts of Rāmānuja's philosophical arguments are presented in detail by Radhakrishnan and Moore.

The Principle of Difference

Rāmānuja argues that *all* cognition is subject to the principle of difference, that nothing could be cognized except in so far as it differed from something else, or from itself at some other stage of its existence.

Should anyone . . . assert the theory of a substance free from all difference is immediately established by one's own consciousness, we reply that he is . . . refuted by the fact . . . that all consciousness implies difference. (Radhakrishnan and Moore, 1957: 543)

Even to think that something is not subject to difference requires *that* thought to be differentiated from some other thought. Rāmānuja goes on to argue that words make sense only by being differentiated by root and content, so that they could not be a means for gaining knowledge of something devoid of difference. *Brahman*, if undifferentiated, could not be an object of knowledge. But it is just this knowledge that we need for deliverance. And so too for perception, for that requires that the thing perceived, be it as a type or as a particular, is differentiated from everything else. The same holds for inference. It seems then that indeed all cognition rests on the recognition, and thus the fact of difference, in anything that could be thought.

The startling and inescapable conclusion is that perception could not reveal mere Being. Empirical, factual statements would be meaningless unless we acknowledged difference. Why would a man searching for a horse not be satisfied with a buffalo? And if perception was of only one thing, in the absence of difference, everything would be apprehended in one act of cognition. But we know that does not happen. Furthermore, by the same line of reasoning, plurality is not unreal. It is easy to see how what seems contradictory can be resolved by the principle of sublation, in that when a faulty judgment has been sublated by a better one, the former just ceases to be.

Rāmānuja's radical conclusion is that mere Being does not alone constitute reality. Or as he puts it in some places, *Brahman* is not devoid of all difference. Indeed Rāmānuja argues that while *Brahman* is devoid of the imperfections of ordinary selves, and of the matter in which they are embodied, which is that of the material world, the bondage of *samsāra* is bondage to the body of *Brahman*. *Brahman* does carry plurality in itself, since, as the manifestation of its power, the material world is real, but its true nature is cloaked by appearance.

Saving the Self

Since consciousness is an attribute of the self we can see that "the subject of consciousness . . . is permanent . . . while its attribute, that is consciousness, not differing herein from joy, grief and the like . . . comes to an end" (Radhakrishnan and Moore, 1957: 546). The conscious subject as that which has the attribute "consciousness" is real. Furthermore, and here we reach another radical conclusion, "the 'I' is not a mere attribute of the self . . . but it constitutes the very nature of the self" (Radhakrishnan and Moore, 1957: 547). So that *it persists in the state of release or deliverance from samsāra*. Deliverance has become salvation.

Ignorance too is not as it has been supposed. *Māyā* cannot be the explanation of the plurality of existence, as if that came about simply by the superimposition of names and differentiating descriptions on some undifferentiated reality. How then is deliverance to be achieved? The formula worked out in antiquity was quite clear: by overcoming or transcending ignorance, that is, by coming to realize that *Brahman* is the Universal Self, *Atman*. Not so, declares Rāmānuja. Release requires an active intervention by "the highest Self pleased by the devout meditation of the worshipper" (Radhakrishnan and Moore, 1957: 552), or as Christianity has it, by divine grace.

Little development of the Rāmānuja style of analytical philosophy took place even in the hundreds of years following his death. However, his "invention" of a personal God did make a huge impact. He actively promoted the cause of the personal God, seeing to the building of a number of temples to Vishnu and promulgating the cult of the worship of Vishnu as the realization of *Īśvara*.

I think it fair to say that for the next 900 years Indian thought revolved around the teaching and preservation of its deepest insights, and the leisurely debate between the followers of Śankara and his version of Vedanta and the more theistic and personalized version argued for by Rāmānuja. Nothing was resolved. As the tides of Islam borne by the Moghul conquerors arriving from the northwest and of Christianity brought by the British Raj swept across the continent after the ban on missions was rescinded, it seems to me that Indian thought turned in on itself. It was more intent to survive than to enter into any kind of dialogue that might have rekindled the critical and analytical spirit of philosophy.

The Influence of the West

Almost a thousand years of the millennium passed without any deep and fundamental changes to either the root structure and repertoire of concepts or the problems that they were applied to. We have seen the pattern set in deep antiquity, with a relatively small group of key concepts, *Brahman*, *Atman*, *māyā*, *samsāra*, *prakrti*, *purusa*, and deliverance through knowledge. A variety of schools of philosophy appeared, flourished, and faded in this millennium (see Pravhavanda, 1963, Book 5). We have taken a very restricted sample of them, but I hope that it has been enough to illustrate how over more than two millennia Indian philosophers have refined, polished, differentiated, transformed, and continually revised the basic system, as different aspects of it struck people as problematic, vague, or contradictory. During the first millennium the Vedic philosophy of life acquired an analytical justification. At the same time, it diversified beyond the range of the analytical style of philosophy which supported it and which we have seen fully realized in the work of Śankara. Yoga is clearly less a version of Vedanta, more a refinement of the Vedic way of life. It is not predominantly the result of philosophical analysis of concepts. From the point of view of the story of Indian thought in both levels of philosophy, the only development that exerts an influence beyond the boundaries of India[3] and in the world at large, at the end of the second millennium, is Buddhism. We shall look at the extraordinary transformation that Buddhism underwent in China in the next chapter.

The Muslim influence on Indian philosophy is generally thought to be slight, though it seems to me that the new ideas about personal Gods that we find in the second millennium, from the writings and controversies of Rāmānuja onwards, might have come to India from the West, though, to the best of my knowledge, no such influence can be documented by direct quotation or reference. However, the British Raj, more or less fully established by the beginning of the nineteenth century and maintaining its cultural influence even after its dissolution in 1947, wrought very great changes in the patterns of Indian thought. Even if Christianity was not the direct origin of the doctrines of a personal God and the survival of personal identity in *Brahman* after deliverance, it can hardly have failed to have served as some sort of confirmation of the propriety of this development.

The two most important philosophers of the twentieth century in India were Sri Aurobindo (Ghose) (1872–1950) and S. Radhakrishnan (1888–1975). Each, in his own way, sought a union between the long-standing traditions of Indian thought as I have outlined them, and the Western philosophical tradition, as it reached India through British influences. Knowledge of that tradition was also acquired by many Indians who attended British universities in the nineteen and twentieth centuries. Nevertheless, I am sure that the reader who follows the thought of the two most prominent Indian philosophers in the next two sections will see them much more as re-presenting the ancient patterns than synthesizing East with West in any fundamental way. Aurobindo's evolutionism and Radhakrishnan's idealism are absorbed into an essentially traditional philosophical framework.

The Evolution of Consciousness

Destined originally for the Indian civil service, Aurobindo Ghose was educated in England, as were many of his class and time. However, on returning to India, he was very active in the nascent independence movement. Unlike those who imported Western liberal ideas as the foundation of nationalist claims, Aurobindo set about developing a political framework that drew deeply on the Indian mystical tradition, particularly a mystical version of the Indian past. The success of his movement inevitably brought him into conflict with the Raj. However, again in a way that is traditionally Indian, he withdrew from the hurly-burly of political activity to spend the rest of his life in meditation and writing. From this retreat came the books for which he is honored as a philosopher. His work embodies both levels at which philosophy has been practiced. He advocated a certain way of life, the way of contemplation and retreat. At the same time, he developed the conceptual framework which underpinned its unity with the hurly-burly of the everyday world and its political turmoil.

The problem that Aurobindo takes as the province of philosophy is to find a way to unify "two things, the fundamental truth of existence and the forms in which existence presents itself to our experience . . . [the former] is the truth of the spirit; the other is the truth of life" (Aurobindo, 1918: 764).[4] However, West and East have each emphasized a different pole. Aurobindo argues that the antinomy is an unreal one. "Spirit being the fundamental truth of existence, life can be only its manifestation . . . but the forms of life as they appear to us are at once [Spirits] disguises and its instruments of self-manifestation" (Aurobindo, 1918: 765). The way is "to grow in knowledge until these cease to be disguises."

But how can we establish this cosmic vision? It must be by more than a reminder of the *Upanishads*. "To the ordinary material intellect which takes its present organisation of consciousness for the limit of its possibilities," argues Aurobindo (1947: 4), "the direct contradiction of the unrealised ideals with the realised fact is a final argument against their validity." Equally, one might say, the contradiction could be the source of a profound skepticism and despair. But Aurobindo assures us that we can reach both a conception and knowledge of divine existence by getting beyond the physical mind. We do not see this because we have separated ourselves from the cosmic reality by uncritically adopting the distinction between ourselves as subject and the rest as object. We have to develop ways of cognizing directly without the use of sense organs. There is no inevitable necessity in the current limits to the powers of our sense organs. Only thus can we transcend the subject/object distinction.

The most startling claim that Aurobindo makes is that reason is not the instrument by which to arrive at the needful knowledge, since for truths reached by reason the organism must already possess a means for their verification. But we are evolving towards something he calls the "Superconscient," the master word for which is Light, just as Life is the master word for the ordinary intellect, the "Subconscient." The final step in the evolution of consciousness is unblushingly mystical. It comes from the realization, set forth in the *Upanishads*, that we must reconcile in *Brahman* both *vidya* (knowledge of oneness) and *avidya* (knowledge of multiplicity and diversity). Because the One is the reality, the Many is *not* an illusion. *Māyā* does not mean "illusion." To what does this consciousness belong? To an individual person.

The idea of an evolution of consciousness is central to Aurobindo's thought. *Brahman* does not evolve but "it expresses itself in many successive forms of consciousness." However far we ascend we must retain that from which we came, but transfigured. And echoing the Rāmānuja insight, Aurobindo claims that the individual is not transcended in coming to have right knowledge. Individuality of self is necessitated by the whole system. "The conscious manifestation of the transcendent in the individual is the means by which the collective, the universal, is also to become conscious of itself" (Aurobindo, 1947: 350).

Here, in summary, is the position:

The Transcendent, the Supra cosmic is absolute and free in Itself beyond time and space and beyond the conceptual opposites of finite and infinite. But in cosmos it uses Its liberty of self-formation, Its *māyā*, to make a scheme of itself in the complementary terms of unity and multiplicity ... [the] limitation of the universal "I" in the divided ego-sense constitutes our imperfect individualised personality. (Aurobindo, 1947: 40)

But why should we take any of this seriously? Here the analytic philosopher appears to support the sage. We see the inextricable mix of frustration and misery with knowledge and happiness as the current state of things. Is this state of affairs permanent? If it is not evolving toward the higher we have two possible hypotheses. The universe is the product of a flux of "inconscient" energy, or it is the work of an arbitrary creator intent on providing the conditions in which his creatures will learn the inconstancy of the world. Both alternatives can be rejected according to Aurobindo, because neither could account for "the immense and enduring phenomenon of this complex universe." However, this is just what the mathematical cosmologists and evolutionary biologists are trying to show. But Aurobindo has a further argument. There is an ascending series of substances, including one "subtle and flexible enough to . . . to have shapes directly imposed upon it by mind" (Aurobindo, 1947: 237). So we have reason to think that the cosmos is evolving in the direction of the emergence of Gnostic Beings taking up the earthly matter ready for this novelty, just as the emergence of mental beings took up all the earthly matter that was ready for that change. Why should we believe that this higher stage is not only possible but inevitable? Because the evolution in material nature that has led to consciousness and life must tend to the fullness of consciousness and life. Why should it cease to be operative now?

In this way the Western concept of evolution, and especially the evolution of organic and sentient life is woven into the metaphysics of Śankara and Rāmānuja and ultimately with that of the *Upanishads*. The universe evolves, everything returning to and emanating from *Brahman* but not in simple unchanging cycles.

To simplify a little crudely, according to Aurobindo, there is no mind/body problem. It arises, he believed, from the presupposition that matter and spirit are exclusive opposites. According to traditional Indian thought, every seemingly diverse thing is unified through its origin in *Brahman*, and is thus spirit. Thus the evolution of higher forms of consciousness from simpler organic forms and in turn from material stuff does not present a conceptual or philosophical problem since there is no incomparability of the apparently disparate concepts at each level of evolution. Each form of being is at one with *Brahman*.[5]

In the true Indian tradition, Aurobindo insists that human beings can become more than they are. Though they find themselves trapped in materiality, by the practice of meditation, of detachment from the senses, they can transcend bodily existence. In the tradition of the *Upanishads*, it is achieved by attaining a form of consciousness that transcends the empirical-rational and the sensory-intellectual way of living that human beings currently have adopted. That is the appropriate form of life for beings at our stage of development. But we can aspire to something higher, to being in *Brahman*, to the very highest. So we have seen Aurobindo synthesizing the Western idea of an evolving universe with the Indian idea of a universe emanating from *Brahman*. By absorbing the concept of evolution he offers a rational way to establish the human possibility of transcending the existing entrapment in materiality. The world of *māyā* is evolving. As it evolves the creatures in it become more fit to reach an apprehension of *Brahman*.

A Touch of Absolute Idealism

Unlike Aurobindo Ghose, Radhakrishnan was educated in India, but he found a second home in Oxford as Spalding Professor of Eastern Religions. Widely regarded as India's foremost philosopher, he was also active in the grander reaches of political life, becoming President of India in 1962.

His philosophical contribution was not so much a synthesis of Indian and European traditions as a consistent effort to remove some of the more radical misunderstandings of Indian classical thought, especially Vedanta, that had taken root in the West. I have already emphasized that the very important concept of *māyā*, as used in the *Upanishads* to characterize the status of the material world both existentially as an emanation of Brahma and epistemologically as an object of knowledge, is not properly rendered as "illusion." *Māyā* as appearance is not the true and final showing of how the world is. However, it is not an illusion in the sense that it does not exist while something else does. So to perceive an appearance is to know things in a way and at a level that can be sublated, refined, and corrected. In realizing that we live in the world as appearance and that in the end the world is, if sublated, intuitable as *Brahman*, does not dispel an illusion, but allows us to "see things clearly that we saw only cloudily before." Puligandla comments that Radhakrishnan's philosophical position is essentially that of Śankara, in the exposition of which we came across this issue about *māyā*, even toward the end of the first millennium. Radhakrishnan worked to correct a false impression of *māyā* that had persisted until the end of the second millennium.

The ontology of the Radhakrishnan cosmos is dynamic. *Brahma*n is active. However, its activity does not consist in producing an independent material world. This is not the dualism of Rāmānuja. The everyday world just is its activity. In the same way the multitudinous selves of embodied persons are also aspects of the activity of *Brahman*. But Radhakrishnan distinguishes a "higher self," that which can be apprehended only through mystical experience, and is therefore *Atman-Brahman*. This aspect of his thought is reminiscent of Rāmānuja rather than Śankara, since he holds that the self is not annihilated in the transformation wrought by mystical experience. Though *mokṣa*, the knowledge that ensures deliverance, succeeds *māyā*, appearance, the self as *Atman* is man in a superhuman state. Radhakrishnan uses the same traditional expression for this as did Aurobindo, *saccidananda*, Pure Being/Pure Consciousness/Pure Bliss.

Indian classical philosophy never fully analyzed the ontological status of the cosmos as it presented it. However, Radhakrishnan, drawing on Western philosophy, took the Absolute Idealism developed towards the end of the nineteenth century, and known to him through the writings of his Oxford colleague, F. H. Bradley, as a starting point. Accepting the Mind/Body distinction as a representation of the two possibilities for ways of being, the Idealists assimilated material reality to thought. Thought is subject to such categories as consistency, truth, and so on. If the cosmos is essentially thought, then perfect truth and coherence must characterize it. This is the Absolute of the most radical of the Idealist schools in the West. Expressing the matter in a rhetoric of religion, Radhakrishnan says:

> When we consider the abstract and impersonal aspect of the Supreme, we call it the Absolute; when we consider the Supreme as self-aware and self-blissful being, we get God. The real is beyond all conceptions of personality and impersonality. We call it the "Absolute" to show our sense of the inadequacy of all terms and definitions. We call it "God" to show that it is the basis of all that exists and the goal of all. (Radhakrishnan, 1929)

How can we pass from a limited view of ourselves as embodied and limited beings to an apprehension of the real? In the long-standing tradition of Hindu thought, Radhakrishnan tells us that

Meditation is the way to self-discovery [that is, to the discovery that *Atman is Brahman*]. By it we turn our mind homeward and establish contact with the creative centre.

Asking himself the question that seems to the Western reader of Indian thought to be always pressing, Radhakrishnan wonders why, "if the universe is essentially spirit, how do we account for its appearance as non-spirit?" Is the material appearance an illusion? Once again turning to correct persistent Western errors in interpreting *māyā*, he remarks that "we can work up the harmony [of the Absolute] if we remember that the world of ordinary experience is a feeble representation of the perfect world . . . the hasty logic which declares because the one is the real the many are an illusion, is corrected in the view that the one reveals itself in the many." And yet to the Western reader, such as myself, this seems to leave the question unanswered. Why should the real reveal itself as a multiplicity, when that multitude includes millions of miserable people hoping for a way of deliverance from their multiplicity? I am afraid that not even in the writings of Radhakrishnan do we get a hint of an answer.

Conclusion

Indian philosophy was well set in style and substance long before the second millennium began. But it was quite devoid of the idea of an ultimate and eternal personal God. The Gods, depicted so vividly in the bronzes with which everyone is familiar, such as Kali and other many-armed and animal-headed deities, are creatures too of *māyā*. In the outer courtyard of an Indian temple there are many images of animals and plants. In the first inner area the personified Gods appear as highly coloured bas-reliefs and statues. There one can see images of Vishnu, of Krishna and Shiva. At the centre of the building is an empty room, perhaps painted a uniform grey, and sitting there one may see a *sadhu* lost to this world, seeking union with *Brahman* by pursuing the *Atman* within himself.

That peculiar integration of religion and philosophy that is so characteristically Indian has only been exported in one of its many forms, namely Buddhism. While we look in vain for Hinduism much beyond the borders of the Indian subcontinent, in a thousand years of philosophy in China and Japan we will find Buddhism to be a ubiquitous presence.

Perhaps things are changing. Not so long ago, in the 1960s and seventies, one saw little groups of young Americans, dressed in saffron robes, particularly in the waiting areas of airports, offering Buddhism to the unenlightened. They seem to have gone. However, the enthusiasm for setting up ashrams in remote parts of Western countries, where gurus from the East enlighten the many in search of the One, does not seem to have been exhausted. *Brahman* and *Atman* have taken root, though not yet on a large scale, in the thought of the West.

Why has Hinduism been so little represented in the West? It is a deeply engrained and plainly permanent and historically resistant feature of the Indian world. Islam and Christianity washed over it, with almost no discernible effect. Both Aurobindo and Radhakrishnan sip from the cup of the West but do not take deep drafts, despite their thorough grasp of what is on offer.

NOTES

1   I shall follow an excellent account of the work of this philosopher by Puligandla (1975), as well as drawing on the original texts.
2   The texts and commentaries I have used in working up this chapter are written in English, most by distinguished Indian scholars. The usual word for individual self-consciousness, used by these authors, is "soul." The Indian word for "pure consciousness" is *Atman*, as I have used it in the exposition of some of the "ancient" philosophies of India, the Vedantic and the *Samkhya*.
3   Hinduism has a place among the religions of the predominantly Muslim Indonesia.
4   These quotations are drawn from those collected in Radhakrishnan and Moore (1947), chapter XVI.
5   I owe to D. N. Robinson the observation that the Hegelian flavour of Aurobindo's evolutionary ideas may owe something to his English education at a time when there were some influential English Hegelians.

China: Ancient Sources

One day Chang Chu and Chieh Ni were at work together in the fields when Confucius came that way and sent Tzŭ Lu to inquire about the ford there. Chang Chu asked Tzŭ Lu for whom he was acting as driver. He replied that it was Confucius. "What! Confucius of Lu state?" "Yes," said Tzŭ Lu, to which the other replied "He knows where the ford is."[1] Then Chieh Ni said "Who are you?" "I am Tzŭ Lu." "Are you a disciple of Confucius?" He replied, "I am." "The whole Empire," said Chieh Ni, "is rushing headlong to destruction, and who is there will reform it? As for you, instead of following a man who withdraws from prince after prince in succession, would it not be better to follow a man who has withdrawn from the world altogether?" And he went on hoeing without pause. Tzŭ Lu went back and reported these remarks. Whereupon Confucius looked surprised and said "We cannot join the company of birds and beasts. If I am not to associate with men of the ruling class with whom am I to associate? If right principles prevailed in the Empire, then indeed there would be no need for me to reform it" (*Analects*, xviii: 6).

The pattern of philosophical thought over the second millennium in China and Japan has certain similarities to that we have followed in India. A sophisticated and powerful philosophical tradition had been established before the birth of Christ. It was elaborated and developed through the first millennium, becoming stable and established in the second millennium. Not all was of indigenous origin. Buddhism had come into China from India during the first half of the first millennium. It proved attractive to the Chinese, perhaps because some of the tenets of Buddhism had marked similarities to those of Taoism. It became one of the dominant ways of life. It had a supporting philosophy, the result of a long succession of critical examinations of the presuppositions implicit in its conception of people and their relationships. However, it too stabilized in the course of the second millennium. It was never without opposition from Confucians and Taoists. But despite, or even because of the long isolation of China and Japan from Western Europe, by the mid-nineteenth century European philosophies were eagerly taken up by many intellectuals in the region. At the same time, as we shall see, there were many who rejected these influences, and looked back into China's past for an anchorage.

Histories of Chinese philosophies, such as the great work of Fung Yu-lan (1937), reveal a rich and complex pattern of schools and debates. The strong literary tradition in China meant that a good deal was written down and is available to the scholars of our time. In a study such as this, only the main lines of thought and the highlights of long-running debates can be included.

In discussing philosophy in China and Japan we need, more than in most of the domains in which philosophy has taken root, the distinction between philosophy as prescriptions of ways of life, and philosophy as critical examination of the concepts employed in these prescriptions and the presuppositions upon which they rest. This distinction can be exemplified in each era of Chinese intellectual history. Confucius was a philosopher mainly of the "way of life" sort. Mencius, setting about the task of constructing a foundation for Confucian political and moral philosophy, reflecting on concepts and presuppositions of Confucian thought, developed arguments in support of a certain way of conceiving of human nature, and the manner of life which would fulfil its potential. The major import of modern times, Marxism, has exerted such an attraction on the Chinese mind, partly because of its strong practical side, coupled with a seemingly authoritative analysis of human life. Here is how to live, and this is why it is the only right way.

Looked at thematically, Chinese philosophy is dominated by the central problems of the political life. Philosophers were not so much concerned with metaphysics or ethics on a cosmic scale, as these studies were undertaken in India and the West, but with the relations between human beings and the state. This might be discussed in the context of a full engagement of citizens and administrators, as it is in the writings of Confucius. It might be discussed only in relation to ways of disengaging the person from civil and urban life, as it is the writings of the early Taoists.

More than in any other part of this book, I will be presenting Chinese thought under headings that pick out specific authors. In China, as in Japan, the relation of "teacher" and "pupil" or disciple is of enormous importance to this day. The Japanese word for "teacher" is *sensei*, but it means a great deal more than just the one who instructs. One's *sensei* is deeply honored and the respect for one's teacher carries over into such matters as obtaining advice on the choice of a spouse. Chinese sages were honoured as teachers in a far more direct way than the great thinkers of the Christian and Islamic worlds have been. About two and a half millennia separate Confucius from Mao Tse-tung, but the deferential attitude to the "great teacher" seems, from what we know about both of them, to have been very much the same.

CONFUCIUS AND THE CONFUCIANS

Though he was born 200 years before Aristotle, in 551 B.C., we can be tolerably sure that the writings attributed to Confucius are authentic. However, as Creel (1969: 25) remarks, both admirers and detractors of Confucius endeavored to distort the sage's life and thought in various ways. Admirers have tried to provide him with a royal pedigree, while his detractors have reinterpreted his sayings to make them appear less attractive and reasonable. Though he longed to try out his insights in active political life and from a position of genuine executive power, Confucius never attained more than a sinecure. His enormous influence came through his pupils. His teaching practice gradually took on the form of a school, and we know that he exercised considerable discretion in the pupils he admitted, talent outweighing wealth or family.

By the time of Confucius the perennial pattern of Chinese society had already crystallized. The division of society into landlords and peasants, and of the landlord class into soldiers and administrators, provided the background against which the teachings of Confucius must be understood. As in other regions of the world, these *social, economic,* and *pragmatic* divisions became associated with family, and so with the idea of "being of good birth." To be *chün tzŭ*, that is, a gentleman, one had to be born as one. It seems that the upper classes had become deeply corrupted by the time Confucius came to reflect on the possibilities for the betterment of human life. A sense of duty had given way to arrogance and pride in breeding, with a corresponding neglect of what should have been the obligations that came from social position. Seeing the need for both soldiers and administrators, his project was to find ways to create new kinds of people to fill these roles. This was the point of the training he gave in his school. He died in 479 B.C., but was he a success or a failure? He had spent a decade traveling all over China trying to find a ruler who could be persuaded to adopt the Confucian Way, to staff his civil service with men of education, rather than mere functionaries. It is said that the only one who did listen to the great teacher was so corrupt in the management of his state that Confucius left the court in disgust. At the time of his death one would have said that his project had come to nothing. Two and half millennia later we must take a quite different view. His influence in China grew steadily after his death and has never wholly faded.

Confucian Thought

At first reading the *Analects* strike one as anecdotal and didactic. It is a book that is mainly a manual of instructions in how to live, illustrated with commentaries on the characters of particular people known to Confucius and his companions. But that would be a superficial impression. The Confucian conception of life is not an unsupported dogma. It is grounded in analyses of the nature of human beings and of their possible modes of association. It depends on an anti-individualist conception of knowledge. Though it had to wait until the work of Mencius for a systematic critical foundation, it was developed through a combination of conceptual analysis and empirical observations. The ideal Confucian world is also a possible world. Since it is grounded in reflections of the nature of human beings as they show themselves to be, the political ideals expressed in the book suggest ideal forms of association that are within the power of the citizens to bring about. At least we can be sure that Confucius thought so. Ordinary decency rather than saintly virtue is all that is required of those who might construct such a world. After almost two and half millennia this insight remains no less true and seemingly no less impossible of achievement.

The analysis of human nature

The two poles of Confucius' analysis of the conditions for the ideal civic life are human individuals on the one hand and the societies they create on the other. Both are real but the latter, society, is a product of the joint and collective actions of the people who comprise it. Yet those very people are shaped, at least in part, by the society in which they grow up and of which they are themselves the creators. They could not exist other than as social beings. However, a society does not exist, in any sense, prior to or independent of its members. It is by reflection on human nature that the leading Confucian concepts get their content.

Three leading Confucian concepts

The content of Confucius' teaching can be expressed in three main concepts.

CHÜN TZŬ   This expression refers to a person of quality. It had something of the implications of our word "gentleman."

> The Master said: "A noble minded man is not an implement." *(Analects,* II: 12)

> The Master said: "The noble minded are all encompassing, not stuck in doctrines. Little people are stuck in doctrines." *(Analects,* II: 14)

It was in this concept that Confucius' writings, and the instructions offered by his disciples, wrought the most profound change in Chinese patterns of thought. Originally *chün tzŭ* meant a person of good family, just as it was understood until very recently in the West. But, according to Confucius, the term should be reserved for those who, from whatever origin, displayed the right qualities of conduct and character. What were these qualities? This brings us to the second leading Confucian concept.

L I   According to Confucius we live best when our actions are framed within a complex of conventions, rules, and social practices, including especially the customary courtesies. This thesis was not only a general axiom of practical psychology (how to get on with people), but also a moral principle. The root meaning of *li* was sacrifice, in particular sacrifice to one's ancestors. This could be looked on as the starting point for an accretion and elaboration of ways of good conduct that would eventually reach the complexity and sophistication of the behavior of a gentleman.

> "In life serve them [parents] according to Ritual" replied the Master. "In death serve them according to Ritual. And make offerings to them according to Ritual." *(Analects* II: 6)

The rituals of family life provide the model for the rituals of public life. To whom should our respect be directed?

As we have already seen, anyone competent in *li* is truly a gentleman. People of noble birth who fail to live in the customary framework do not merit that standing and the respect that goes along with it. If they perform the proper rituals these are empty forms.

However, conforming to whatever happen to be the local conventions does not necessarily suffice for establishing the good life. "The done thing" is subject to moral scrutiny. There is surely some circularity at the heart of Confucius' thought, since the basis of moral scrutiny is fulfillment of the local conventions. *Li* seems to be both the source and the product of moral intuitions, which, on close inspection, look to be more pragmatic than principled.

T A O   This concept took so many forms in subsequent Chinese thought that there is a temptation to read back later versions and nuances into the writings of Confucius. Creel suggests that we should give a quite mundane interpretation of *tao* in Confucius' own thought. It is just the Way that things should be done.

> Just as *li* comprehended both courtesy and morality, so the Way included, on the one hand, the ethical code of the individual, and, on the other, the pattern of government that should bring about the fullest possible measure of well-being and self-realisation for every human being. (Creel, 1969: 33)

The Confucian Way defined a kind of absolute in human conduct. Adherence to the Way overrode all other loyalties and obligations, especially those of the feudal system. This meant that a Confucian had the moral duty to stand up against unjust and exploitative rulers, to criticize them and to call for them to change their ways. This could have unpleasant, even fatal consequences for the critic.

> The Master said: "Love learning and trust it deeply. Guard the Way of virtue and benevolence unto death. Never enter a dangerous country, and never inhabit a country in turmoil.
> When all beneath Heaven abides in the Way, make yourself known; and when the Way is lost, stay hidden. When the Way rules in your country, there's shame in poverty and obscurity; and when the Way is lost in your country, there's shame in wealth and renown." (*Analects*, VIII: 13)

These potent words have continued to find a place in Chinese thought, though as we shall see, with some remarkable changes of meaning.

Though the meaning of the three leading concepts is tolerably clear, there is no common foundation to be found in the writings of Confucius. They were not integrated into a conceptual unity. Their interrelations were pragmatic, ways of contributing to the well-lived life. It was left to Mencius, writing and teaching some two centuries after Confucius, to develop a critical and integrated Confucian philosophy.

Mencius

If Confucius was the "father" of the movement that bears his name, Mencius was its "philosopher." It was he who worked through the conceptual necessities that are required to express the main themes, *chün tzǔ*, *li*, and *tao*. He was born about 372 B.C. and died in 289 B.C. Seeking office even more assiduously than Confucius, Mencius lived for much of his life in the courts of the petty fiefdoms of the political mosaic that was the China of his day. He did find posts and he was taken seriously as an adviser to some of the rulers of Chinese states.

Philosophical style

In his very well-known book *Mencius on the Mind*, I. A. Richards (1932) gives several characteristic features of the way Mencius presented his arguments.

> (a) They are dominated by a suasive purpose. (b) The purpose of eliciting the point of difference [with his adversaries] is absent. (c) The form of the opponent's argument is noticed, in the sense of *being used* in the rebuttal, but not examined so that the flaw, if any, may be found. (Richards, 1932: 55)

Part of what Mencius argued for was a certain view of the fundamental moral distinctions that shape or should shape our lives. He distinguished between the nobility of Heaven and the nobility of men. The latter is an endowment of worldly power, rank, and influence. The former is a matter of character: "benevolent, just, high-principled, and faithful, and taking an unwearying joy in being good" (Mencius in Legge, 1895: 6(1), 16.1). Creel suggests that "this exaltation of the scholar was not purely a matter of abstract principle. It had to do, very definitely, with the struggle for power and influence that was going on between the scholars and the aristocrats" (Creel, 1969: 77).

Ethics

Mencius' ethics is tied to two extra-ethical issues. He argued that the standard of living of the people is closely tied up with the possibility for virtue. The starving do not have much thought for the right way. But economic adequacy is not a sufficient condition for the acquisition and display of the virtues. These must be taught. Furthermore he seems to have held that actions pursued wholly for profit are likely to be both morally and practically self-defeating.

The second strand is respect for tradition. He looked to historical precedents for models of right living. This seems to have been connected with his thesis that human nature is everywhere the same and capable of good. If one finds the Way one's natural endowment of goodness will flourish.

General philosophy

There is no better guide to the thought of Mencius than I. A. Richards, and I shall follow his exposition closely. Just as in the task of explaining the thought of Confucius, so with that of Mencius, the best way to get the flavor of his teachings seems to be to explain the major concepts he employed and commented on. The interrelated pattern of these concepts is his philosophy. With them he gives the Confucian moral philosophy its rational foundation in the nature of human beings.

HSING   This word refers to that which every human being has in common in so far as it is mental. It distinguishes human beings from animals. It includes not only intellectual skills and capacities, but also impulsions towards action. These can be manifested in good and right acts or bad and incorrect ones. Whether *hsing* gives rise to virtuous or vicious behavior depends on external circumstances, especially the economic situation and the edicts and practices of government.

These impulsions are manifested in native and universal tendencies to "pity, shame, reverence, and the sense of right and wrong" (Richards, 1932: 67). As yet these are not virtues. They are the necessary psychological preconditions for the development of virtues, morally qualified dispositions of mature human beings. These primitive tendencies, according to Mencius, are universal. So proper education in the right social circumstances should lead to universal development of the associated virtues, since they are derived from universal features of human psychology. These derivations run along the following lines.

From the native tendency to pity, with training, we can develop the virtue of *Jen*. This means something like disinterested platonic love. It is not so much an emotion as a moral tendency to favor certain kinds of action sympathetic to other people, particularly in regard to how they might feel. According to Richards it covers "the source of honour . . . with effort to strive for mutuality." It is clearly supportive of the Confucian injunction to serve one's parents, and to use that duty as a model for duties in general.

From the native tendency to shame we can develop the virtue of *Y.* This means something more focused than shame in general. It has to do with the moral uneasiness one would feel at having failed in one's duties, especially one's social duties.

The native tendency to reverence develops into the virtue of *Li*. This means good manners and competence in ritual observances. It also comprehends knowing one's proper place in the social world, and what is correct behavior for one in such a place. Richards remarks (1932: 70) that "Mencius uses *two* pairs of characters: 'the mind of deference-respect' and 'the mind of refusing-yielding'." These add up to a quite complex pattern of social usages and the virtues they express.

The native sense of right and wrong develops into *Chih*. This virtue is shown in judgment and discrimination, especially in social and moral matters.

According to Richards, the goodness of the mind, considered as the four virtues, or social and moral tendencies, just is the tendency of the mind towards self-development. Since it is the development of the social virtues that is in question it is not self-development in the Western sense of 'self-actualization.' To grow in virtue in this dispositional sense is a natural activity, though it needs a guide. It is not the result of a calculation of advantage based on knowledge. We do not acquire the social virtues for any utilitarian reason.

CH'I This is something like the "vital spirits," an all-pervasive "vapor" or "breath" that is the very nature of a human being. It "fills up the body." How is it related to the executive aspect of being human, a capacity that Richards translates as "will"? He notes that it is used almost synonymously with *Hsing* (mind). There is reciprocal action between *hsing* and *ch'i*. In some circumstances Richards says that the will or mind is dominant and in others *ch'i*. Finally there is a hint of a parallel with the important Indian concept of *karma* since one accumulates *ch'i* by right living.

Mencius' conception of the structure of the human character seems to be based on the general idea of a pattern of native dispositions which are refined by education and experience into the civic virtues. The totality of a person's dispositions and capacities are comprehended under *hsing*. But dispositions must be grounded in something nondispositional, something enduring in the person. This is *ch'i*. To take a modern instance, the skill to play a musical instrument must be grounded in a permanent state of the body, acquired during practice.

Diagrammatically presented, the mind/character of the mature person has some such structure as the following:

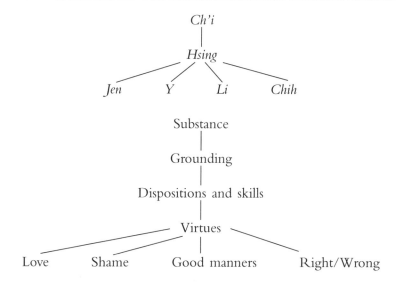

Here we have a moral philosophy that is presented as the ground of a social and political point of view, rooted in a psychology which is itself rooted in a metaphysical or general prescription of the nature of human beings. *Ch'i* grounds *Hsing* which grounds the virtues.

Unlike Confucius, who takes his psychology from common observations and builds the Confucian view of the well-ordered political life from a plateau of taken-for-granted principles, Mencius tries to extract the Confucian political philosophy from first principles. His scheme is not only a psychology, but also a critically analyzed conceptual scheme.

TAOISM

In China, as in India, scholars tell us of the myriad versions, schools, and schismatic heresies that are revealed in the writings of the first millennium and before. This pattern of divergence is particularly true, it seems, of Taoism. Not only were there sects and schools, but the writings in which Taoism comes down to us are sufficiently cryptic to leave room for queries about both translation and interpretation. My strategy will be try to present Taoism in both its mainstream and sectarian forms, but in a way which highlights those aspects of this cluster of philosophies which differentiate it from Confucianism and Buddhism, and from those elements in Western philosophy with which we might be tempted to compare it.

There are two Taoist classics dating from the two centuries after the death of Confucius. The book of Lao Tsŭ was compiled at a later date, but the author of the sayings is thought to have lived around 400 B.C., if he existed at all. The other great work, the book of Chuang Tzŭ, was written by a real historical person, thought to have died about 300 B.C. Chuang Tsŭ is known to have held a minor administrative post in one of the small states. He is well known for having refused a munificent offer of high office from the ruler of Ch'u. This indeed would be in accordance with one of the ways that Taoism is reflected in political philosophy. According to historians of the period, the text of *The Book of Chuang Tsŭ* seems also to have been a compilation.

The Basic Concepts of Taoism

Tao

The key to understanding what I shall call "root-Taoism," lies in the meaning that the expression "Tao" came to acquire in the classical Taoist compilations. In Confucian writings "Tao" means "The Way," the proper forms of conduct for individuals and for the management of governments. The concept is both broader and deeper in Taoism. Not only is Tao a method or a practice, something which one can have or lack. It is also the very being of the universe. According to Ch'en Ku-ying (1977) there are three clearly distinguishable but interlinked meanings of Tao that appear in the classic books. It is a metaphysical reality. It is a kind of natural law. And it is a kind of principle or pattern for human life. If all are aspects of the one, then harmony prevails.

We can see examples of the first sense in these quotations from Lao Tsŭ:

> How unfathomable is the Tao! It seems to be the ancestral progenitor of all things (Lao Tsŭ, ~600 [1937]: 19).

The mightiest manifestations of active force flow from the Tao. (ibid.: 20)

Tao· produces all things. (ibid.: 22)

The root ideas of Taoism include the idea of Tao as the universal substance or ground of every natural thing. This raises the question of whether this ground is as fixed as it is universal. It seems that cyclical change is also fundamental.

> The Tao has no beginning or end. Things die and are born, never resting in their culmination . . . Decay is followed by growth, and fullness by emptiness; when there is an end, there is also a beginning . . . The existence of all creatures is like the galloping of a horse. With every movement there is alteration; at every moment they are undergoing change. (Chuang Tsŭ, ca. 300 B.C.: 6.11a)

Not only is there perpetual change but the change is cyclical.

> All the various species of things transform into one another by the process of variation in form. Their beginning and ending is like an unbroken ring, of which it is impossible to discover the principle. (ibid.: 9.7b)

So we seem to have a coherent doctrine with metaphysical roots, including a firmly expressed skepticism as to the possibility of obtaining knowledge of the deepest reality.

Tao not only includes all actual things of whatever kind, in their genesis, change, and decay. As the substrate of everything, Tao is an indivisible, unchanging whole. Human beings are aspects or parts of Tao. Once this point has been grasped the problematic aspects of human life, especially death and dissolution, need not trouble us in the least.

> In the universe all things are one. For him who can but realise his indissoluble unity with the whole, the parts of his body mean no more than so much dust and dirt, and death and life, end and beginning, are no more to him than the succession of day and night. They are powerless to disturb his tranquillity. (Chuang Tsŭ, 7.18b)

It is not implausible to identify Tao with Nature in general, since some of the advice of Taoist sages could be interpreted as "Turn your back on the artificial works of man and contemplate Nature." However, this is not a simple identity, since the Tao is unknowable in itself, by anyone, however enlightened and informed.

> Tao in its unchanging aspect has no name . . . As soon as Tao creates order, it becomes nameable. (Lao Tsŭ, ca. 600 B.C. [1937]: 21)

The root-Tao attitude to death is derived directly from the doctrine of unity. Repeating the attitude expressed in the passage quoted we find the following in the *Book of Chuang Tsŭ*:

> When life comes, it is because it is time for it to do so. When life goes, this is the natural sequence of events. To accept with tranquillity all things that happen in the fullness of their time, and to abide in peace with the natural sequence of events is to be beyond the reach of either sorrow or joy. This is the state of those whom the ancients called "released from bondage." (ibid.: I, 248)

> The sage man roams with light heart through the universe, in which nothing can ever be lost because all is preserved. (ibid.: 242–3)

Here we have Tao as natural law.

What moral philosophy does this entail? It seems that early Taoism was quietist and relativist. For the one who has understood Tao, since oppositions are irrelevant, the moral stance must be relativistic. "For each individual there is a different 'true' and a different 'false'. So it is for moral oppositions like Right and Wrong, Good and Evil" (Creel, 1982: 3).

Wu-wei

From this principle it is a short step to the doctrine of *wu-wei*: if you do nothing, everything will be accomplished. The following passage vividly expresses the root-Tao moral philosophy, which is more or less the advocacy of *wu-wei* as the ultimate and indeed the only virtue.

> The small man sacrifices himself in the pursuit of gain, the superior man devotes his whole existence to the struggle for fame. Their reasons for

relinquishing the normal feelings of men and warping their natures are quite different, but in that they abandon the proper human course and give over their whole lives to a strange and unnatural endeavour they are exactly the same. Therefore it is said: "Do not be a small man, thus to destroy the very essence of your being. And do not try to be a superior man, either. Follow the natural course. No matter whether crooked or straight, look at all things in the light of the great power of nature that resides within you. Look around you! Attune yourself to the rhythm of the seasons. What difference whether it is called 'right' or 'wrong'? Hold fast to the unfettered wholeness that is yours, carry out your own ideas, bend only with the *tao*." (Chuang Tsŭ: 9.23a)

Here is a clearly defined quietist moral philosophy, sharply opposed to the busybody reformist tendency of Confucianism. The follower of Tao does not scurry about seeking the ear of rulers, with an aim to taking on the task of ruling for himself. He prefers to fish and cultivate vegetables.

At the centre of root-Tao moral philosophy is the concept of *wu-wei*. The man who chooses to fish rather than to rule has chosen to do nothing. But is he thereby accomplishing nothing? Not according to the Taoists. *Wu-wei* is the seeming paradoxical principle that by "By doing nothing there is nothing that is not done." Much scholarly ink has been expended on the exegesis of *wu-wei*, particularly when it is interpreted in the political sphere. How does one do *wu-wei*? One cannot exactly do absolutely nothing. Furthermore, the relativist strand in Tao does not permit the establishment of definite opinions of what to do for the best. The answer seems to me to be in the dynamic character of the Tao as the ground of all things. If there is continual process of change, and "there are ten thousand transformations that are equally good" as the particular one which some human being strives to realize, then Tao will take care of itself. Whatever happens will realize the Way.

The Political Application of Taoism

The virtue of inaction

In a famous passage in *The Book of Lao-tzŭ* it is said that the wise ruler "practices inaction and as a consequence there is nothing that is not properly governed." This seems to me to be significant in two ways. One is as a warning of the folly of interfering in affairs that have some established rightness since they are already going on. This advice is captured in an aphorism which should be engraved on the hearts of all administrators: "If it ain't broke, don't fix it." The other significance is something like "Have faith in Tao." The Tao is permanent but changing in ways of which no individual human has any but the dimmest grasp. This thought might be captured in another useful aphorism: "Left to themselves things will work out." The skeptical aspect of Tao is obvious. "How is Tao obscured that there should be a distinction between true and false? How is speech obscured that there should be a distinction between right and wrong?" (quoted from Fung Yu-lan, 1923, by Creel [1982: 53]). If there is no distinction between right and wrong in Tao, then there is no process of really making a wise decision in favour of right! One may think one has, and so go about interfering in affairs like the Confucians. It is best to do nothing.

> Be sparing of speech and things will come right of themselves. Tao is eternally inactive, and yet it leaves nothing undone. (Lao Tsŭ, 600 B.C. [1937]: 30)
>
> Leave all things to take their natural course and do not interfere. (ibid.: 32)

The paradox of humility

However, while the Taoist advice to refrain from unnecessary action strikes one as coherent with the ontology and epistemology of root-Tao it does not follow from it of necessity. It is possible to start from the same basis and reach the opposite moral position. There are routes to both withdrawal and domination implicit in Tao. And thus we find the emergence of what Creel calls "purposive Tao."

The use of the quietist philosophy of Tao as a recipe for obtaining absolute control over people and states is already to be found in the writings ascribed to Lao Tsŭ. The qualities of character and detachment afforded by Tao are just those that are needed to gain ascendancy over other men. For example, if you are trying to obtain a post, if you do not put yourself forward in a thrusting and aggressive manner, then you are more likely in the end to be chosen.

He who wishes to be above the people must speak as though he were
below them . . . It is just because he does not contend that no one in
the world is able to contend with him. (Lao Tsŭ, chapter 66; quoted in
Creel, 1982: 5)

It seems that some particularly ruthless rulers found their way to power
through adherence to the somewhat slippery doctrine of purposive Tao.

The *I Ching*

Closely related to Tao and indeed, lending Taoism and Confucianism
some basic concepts, was a cosmology which took its start from a book
of divination of very great antiquity, the *I Ching*. The book consists of
a series of diagrams, with associated aphorisms. The cosmology, or *T'ai
Chi*, was based on the balance of two forces or principles, *yin*, the principle of cold and light, and *yang*, the principle of heat and darkness.
These forces were not only changing the pattern of their interactions,
but also changing one into the other. Several cosmological theories
were developed from the *I Ching*, for example, that of Shao Yung
(1011–1077) (Fung Yu-lan, 1937: 382–95). It can hardly be said that
the *I Ching* was the source of an important philosophical movement
in itself. Nevertheless, the dualism of forces was taken up by the major
philosophical schools in China as an integral part of their cosmologies.

THE ISSUE OF IMMORTALITY

Historians of Chinese religious thought emphasize the finitist conception of life that seems to be characteristic both of Confucianism and
of root-Taoism. Death, which is the end of human consciousness,
should be regarded as a natural event, and inevitable at that. The only
possible attitude for a wise person is to take it calmly. Patently this attitude of resignation did not please everyone. Buddhism required a fundamental dualism, since successive lives in *saṃsāra*, the cycle of rebirths,
made sense only if personhood and a particular short-term material
embodiment were quite distinct.

The Immortality Debates

Philosophical issues

About the time of the birth of Christ the spread of Buddhism in China provoked a long-running debate between Buddhists on the one hand and Confucians and Taoists on the other. The issue was the question of the possibility of personal survival after death, a concept essential to Buddhism. The more recondite question of personal immortality in the very long run, which, according to traditional Indian philosophy, would not survive deliverance, was not the issue. The debate was philosophical in that the arguments developed around the nature of the human being as a person.

Fung Yu-lan (1937), in his summary of the texts, offers two main lines of argument that were typical of the Confucian and Taoist opposition to Buddhist survivalism.

In a sense the person did survive, but not as a soul. A person does live on after death in their descendants. This is an important foundation for the ceremonials directed towards one's ancestors. In a similar way one lives on in one's reputation, one's fame. For this to be achieved one's name must be known after one's death.

The more aggressive opposition came from those such as Fan Chen (450–515), who produced a range of arguments to show that whatever is mental about a person is a function of their embodied state. He insisted that the body *is* the soul. Toward the end of the Han dynasty the movement that Fung Yu-lan (1937, vol. II: 425) calls "religious Taoism" appeared. Their doctrines were taken from some of the sayings of Lao Tsǔ, particularly those in which he seems to be identifying "immortality" with a long life, presumably on this earth.

This schism in Chinese thought was never resolved. The temper of philosophy in China has always been pragmatic and materialist. The idea of this world immortality in some form keeps returning in the history of Chinese thought.

Saving the body

About the beginning of the first Christian millennium and for the next four or five centuries an elaborate cult of immortality evolved within the materialist framework established in the philosophical debates on the nature of the person. The advocates of a technology of bodily preservation made use of Taoist aphorisms, at least as a "trademark." As far as I can understand what the historians quote, the practices of this cult were directed not to the sustaining of the immortal soul, if there was one, but to the management of the body's tendency to decay. There was a search for a drug or elixir of immortality. This and other alchemical projects were popular. These projects were funded by governments since the rulers, one presumes, hoped to benefit from them. The opposition, as it had been hundreds of years earlier, was Buddhism.

It seems that at least some of the descriptions of immortalizing practices in Taoist writings are ironical and mocking. Just as early Taoists ridiculed the Confucians for their almost desperate search for placement, preferment, and office, so later Taoists seem to have treated the immortality cults with a similar ridicule. Whatever the actual relation between Taoist thought and the search for immortality, it seems that the association was well established by the first centuries of the first Christian millennium.

BUDDHISM: FROM MAHAYANA TO ZEN

The many correspondences between Buddhism and the philosophical theses of root-Tao seem to me, from what I have read, to have led more to the reworking of Buddhism, when it appeared in China in the first millennium, than to any profound changes in the doctrines of Tao. By the sixth century A.D. the Buddhist philosophy of life was well established in China. In India Buddhism quickly split into two branches, the Hinayana and the Mahayana, the issue being the appropriateness of following the path to enlightenment in a purely personal way. In China too, Buddhism proved to be equally schismatic. The variant that seems to have been most widespread is the one we call "Zen."

Though imported earlier, Buddhism spread very widely through China and Japan at the time of the T'ang dynasty around 700–800 A.D. At this time the two major Zen schools, the Southern, the school of sudden enlightenment, and the Northern, the school of gradual enlightenment, spread their influence widely. The monastic system as a major aspect of the Buddhist way of life was founded in the period and it too became popular. This led to some conflict within the generally tolerant frame of Chinese religious philosophies. The Confucians were highly critical of the monastic system. It took people away from the two sources of order recognized by Confucius, the family and the state.

Like all stories of development of philosophies as ways of life, the story of Zen is complex. For my purposes I need only bring out in what way the Buddhism of India took on the form of Zen when it crossed the Himalayas into China.

The Road to Enlightenment

It is characteristic of oriental philosophical writing to eschew the discussion of ideas in the abstract for parables and anecdotes. This is particularly evident in Buddhist writings, though we have seen it already in the style of the *Analects* of Confucius.

What is the proper way to live? Here is one way to present it. A poor boy, Hui-neng, happened to hear a recitation of the *Diamond Sutra*. He began to reach toward enlightenment at the moment of hearing the verse: "One should enliven the mind without dwelling on anything." Determined to follow the path of enlightenment, he sought out the Fifth Patriarch and entered his monastery. The time came to find a Sixth Patriarch. To show the level of his grasp of the Buddhist way the leading candidate wrote up the verse

> The body is the tree of enlightenment,
> The mind is like a clear mirror on a stand.
> Diligently wipe it off now and again,
> Don't let it gather dust.

for all to see. During the night Hui-neng, working at some menial task, got someone to write up this verse:

> Enlightenment basically has no tree,
> And the clear mirror has no stand;
> Originally there is not a single thing;
> Where can dust gather?

Enlightenment did not come quickly though. On the basis of this verse, the Fifth Patriarch called for Hui-neng. The young man is reported as having recited a standard list of the *Atman/Brahman* foundational doctrine, that our intrinsic nature is identical with all things, and unborn, undying, complete, and immovable. After many years of further meditation on this and similar doctrines, Hui-neng himself became the Sixth Patriarch.

How is enlightenment achieved? By reciting and meditating on the *Diamond Sutra*, the import of which is advice to clear the mind and realize its essential nature. It is very difficult to grasp any essential differences between Zen and other Buddhist schools on larger cosmic questions. Nor are the daily practices that embody the best life very different. The emphasis in all the variants is on quiet meditation and on the attainment of wisdom. However, there is a marked split in the ethical presuppositions. Zen is without the focus on the Bodhisattva role that was central to *Mahayana* Buddhism. Good works play a very much more peripheral role in the Zen life than they do in the ethical prescriptions of the *Mahayana* sect.

How does enlightenment come? Suddenly at a moment of realization or gradually through the rigorous practice of guided meditation to clear the mind? The Southern school of Zen held the former and the Northern the latter. But from the viewpoint of philosophy this distinction is not important. Whatever the technique the principle is the same. It derives directly, though at a far remove in time and place, from the fundamental metaphysics of ancient Indian thought.

The Divisions of Mind

However, there is one aspect of Zen philosophy which is worth noting, and which distinguishes Zen from its Indian ancestors. The meditation practices recommended by the Zen masters presuppose a tripartite division of "mind" into three, past mind, present mind, and future mind. These divisions are among the thought contents of consciousness, and so in a sense are all present thoughts. These contents are available to inner observation. The effort is to focus attention on the immediate present, which, ideally, should become empty. To think what I will think is a present thought. To think what I did think is also a present thought. To think what I am thinking is a present thought. So meditation to "clear the mind" must attend to the immediate present. In that way past, present and future will be disposed of.

Philosophers might well ask: "What is the nature of mind, of thought, and of consciousness?" But to answer that question there would have to be something other than mind in contrast to which that nature could be described. The ultimate source of Buddhist metaphysics in the *Atman/Brahman* account of "everything" leaves the question stranded. To realize that it makes no sense is to grasp the truth that nothing is apart from our essential nature, that *Atman is Brahman.* That insight is at least a part of enlightenment.

For hundreds of years Buddhism coexisted with Confucianism and Taoism. At times the relationship between the indigenous philosophies and the import were hostile. At other times it seemed that much of what Buddhism had to offer was included in variations on the basic themes of Confucianism and Taoism, which themselves were far from doctrinally independent, despite their radically different attitudes to how *li* was to be played out, in public service or private withdrawal.

Conclusion

Just as in India, the philosophy of the second Christian millennium in China was very largely a matter of the reworking of the fund of intellectual capital established before A.D. 1000. In summary we can see the history of Chinese philosophy as a dialectic between Confucians and anti-Confucians. Both Confucius and Mencius were propounding doctrines and insights in what we readily recognize as moral and political philosophy. At the same time they were working at different levels of discourse. For the most part Confucius was expounding the Way, while Mencius was engaged in reflecting on the Way. Mencius began the philosophical enterprise of deriving the main configurations of the Confucian conception of the proper life, as he saw it, from the nature of the human beings who are to live this life. If Confucius reflected at that level of generality about morality and political philosophy, we do not find any explicit expositions of this manner of thought in the *Analects.*

The anti-Confucians seemed to be legion, proliferating, Creel (1969) suggests, as much due to rivalry for the ear of rulers competitively engaged in the great project of uniting China as by intellectually moti-

vated disagreements. However, the Taoists were surely the real opponents of the Confucians. Their doctrine of withdrawal was in direct
opposition to the Confucian doctrine of engagement. Their focus on
unity with Nature was at odds with the Confucian attention to such
metropolitan matters as the education and organization of a civil
service and the right character for a minister. The influx of the
Buddhist version of the Indian philosophies of life added another
ingredient, but for the most part Buddhism and Taoism were not
thought to be antithetical, and were often practiced together. Generally speaking, the atmosphere in China among the practitioners of the
various philosophies of life was eclectic tolerance. It was possible to
give a Confucian turn to Tao and even to Buddhism.

Here, then, is the legacy of the indigenous philosophies of the past
millennium and a half that reaches into the second millennium in
China. And just as in the case of Indian thought, and despite the arbitrary moment that the year A.D. 1000 represents, we can discern a shift
at about that time. It was during the Sung dynasty (960–1279) that a
neo-Confucian philosophy appeared and flourished, achieving a role
in government that Confucius had aspired to but never achieved. To
this mixture Buddhism must be added, a legacy that reached China
long before the second millennium, and which had already begun its
evolution into specific Chinese forms before the second millennium
begins.

Political events seem to have had a profound and immediate effect
on the philosophical atmosphere of China. The waxing and waning of
the dominance of one of the three philosophies of life, which in good
times seem to have coexisted almost syncretically, seems to have been
very sensitive to economic and political forces. Nan Hiai-chin (1995:
6) remarks that "Whenever disorder or rebellion arose, it has always
been necessary to use the guidance of Taoist learning to restore peace.
When peace returned to the land, the governing strategy was to use
Taoism inwardly while making an outward show of the arts of
Confucianism."

NOTES

1   I think that we are invited to hear the comments of Chieh Ni as ironi-
    cal throughout this anecdote.

5

Chinese and Japanese Philosophy in the Second Millennium

On an early summer day about the year 1170 Chu Hsi and Lu Hsian-shan, distinguished philosophers and friendly rivals, met at the Goose Lake Temple. Lu wrote afterwards:

> My elder brother Fu Chai said to me "Tsu-ch'ien has invited Chu Hsi to meet us particularly because we differ from him in doctrine." Chu Hsi was debating with my brother. I said "On the way I wrote a poem . . . Work that is simple and easy will in the end be lasting and great / Understanding that is devoted to fragmentary and isolated details will end up in aimless drifting." When I recited my poem up to these lines, Chu Hsi's face turned pale.

However, we know that Chu Hsi had the last laugh. It was his work that was adopted among the set texts for the civil service examinations and dominated Chinese thought for hundreds of years.

In these days resistance to Whiggish attitudes to history is, in effect, an expression of an injunction against treating history as an anticipation of or a source for our contemporary preoccupations. We must not only acknowledge the influence that the social and political character of an era will surely have on the patterns of thought popular in that era, but we must make an effort to present the philosophy, science, and other intellectual discourses of the past in the terms that they would then have been understood. The Sung dynasty straddled the turning point of the second millennium in a way that is convenient for someone setting out a history of the world in which that millennium is the time frame of the story. Something of importance occurred in the social and political life of China in that era, and in the same short period the most influential Chinese philosopher of the second millennium brought the work of reviving and revitalizing Confucianism to a culmination.

The character of the Sung dynasty

The transitions and developments of all aspects of life, but especially the economic one, that occurred in China at or around the end of the first millennium need to be related to the political situation at the time. Chinese political history is more or less the history of dynasties, or at least that is how we have come to see it. We need to look closely at the major characteristics of the Sung dynasty that seem relevant to the flourishing of philosophical reflection and the way political philosophy was tackled in the beginning of the second millennium.

The advent of the Sung dynasty brought to an end the long period of internecine warfare between small states contending for hegemony over the whole of China. For more than a century none had achieved so great an advantage over its rivals as to gain control of the whole country. By annexing several southern states and by paying tribute to the coalition of northern states, the Sung dynasty was able to secure peace at home and neutralize any threat from abroad.

The newly stable state of affairs seems to have favored philosophical interests, but particularly the cult of immortality. If life is at last offering some earthly satisfactions, surely it makes sense to look for a way of prolonging them after death. As we have seen, in following the debates about personal immortality in the previous millennium, the traditional Chinese conception of the technology of immortality was influenced by the lack of any concept of a "detachable" soul. Mummification, much in the manner of the Egyptian technology of the dead, was developed during the Sung dynasty. This made perfectly good sense if the person's survival was connected with the preservation of the body. But the most striking aspect of the first two centuries of the second millennium in China was the rise and ultimate triumph of neo-Confucianism. This was brought about by the work of a group of innovative philosophers, the most prominent of whom was Chu Hsi (1130–1200).

NEO-CONFUCIANISM

At this time Confucians were everywhere faced by the success of Buddhism, and especially the Zen version, which was indigenous to China and Japan. Their response was once again, as it had been in the early centuries of the first millennium, to try to match the Buddhists in all aspects of doctrine. This meant the development of a powerful metaphysics, a conceptual system adequate to the comprehension of the world and the place of people in it, which, at the same time, would yield a moral philosophy that could rival that of the Buddhists. They began to develop a philosophical style that was unlike the down-to-earth common-sense preaching that Confucius had adopted. He had not made use of arguments in our modern sense, nor had he elaborated an abstract system of concepts as a "grammar" by means of which the diversity of the material world and the moral life of human beings could be made intelligible. Part of the charm of the *Analects* is the conversational tone and the everyday anecdotes which greatly enrich it, not only as philosophy but as literature. Neo-Confucian discussions often developed out of critical commentaries on the sayings of other philosophers. In their own way these authors developed a way of doing philosophy that came to look very like the argumentative style so characteristic of the West.

What had to be established by the neo-Confucians that was lacking in the thought of the Master? First it had to be shown that Confucianism did have a cosmology, a world picture that was more explanatory than that offered by the Buddhists. It also had to be shown how the Confucian morality of custom and proper social behavior could be the source of or even the very meaning of moral virtue. These two aspects, in a unified philosophy, had to be demonstrated to be intimately related to one another. There had to be something in the cosmic order that grounded human morality as the foundation of the order of the human world.

The beginnings of the neo-Confucian movement can be found in the thought of the brothers Ch'eng, Ch'eng Hao (1032–85), and Ch'eng I (1033–1107). Each emphasized a different aspect of a revised Confucianism.

The main contribution of the brothers to philosophy, a contribution that set in motion the whole neo-Confucian movement, was a revival and radical revision of the concept of *li*, or principle. It is both the principle of the unity of all particulars in one world, and it is also the principle of the diversity of all individuals, both material and human. Ch'eng I said "The principle of one thing is one with the principle of all things. The course of one day is one with the course of the year" (Wing-tsit Chan, 1963: 551). Historically, the importance of the Ch'eng brothers lies as much in their explicit repudiation of Buddhist doctrine as in their contribution to metaphysics. Ch'eng I took issue with the Buddhists over three main points. In true Confucian fashion, he rejected their renunciation of family and family ties and obligations. The Buddhist metaphysical thesis of permanence, remaining in the same state through time, he also rejected. Everything is changing all the time. The deepest issue of all concerns something absolutely fundamental to Buddhism, that when one has understood "principle," *li*, attachment to that principle now becomes an obstacle on the path to enlightenment, the *prajñāparamitra*, and must itself be transcended. Ch'eng I argues that there is only one *li*, and it cannot be an obstruction, for if it were there would be a dichotomy between the self which is engaged in the work of transcending the principle and the principle which alone gives the self being.

The historian and translator, Wing-tsit Chan, sees the brothers Ch'eng as differing along a dimension that initiated two schools of neo-Confucianism, which he calls, using Western philosophical terminology, the rational and the idealist. The rationalists, such as Ch'eng I and Chu Hsi, built their system on the basis of *li*, principle, holding that it had an objective being more fundamental than its realization in any mind. The idealists, such as Ch'eng Hao and Lu Hsiang-shan, centered their system on the mind, as permeating all things. *Li* existed only mentally. Whichever route was taken, the opposition to Buddhism was clear.

The Teachings of Chu Hsi

Chu Hsi was born in 1130, into a family that greatly valued education and the pursuit of literary interests. Like Rāmānuja in India, Chu

Hsi produced the definitive version of the greatest classical philosophical school of China, in a form that survived for most of the second millennium. His life was marked by the occupation of a succession of troubled government posts intermingled with periods of tranquil scholastic withdrawal when his intransigent and critical stance to official policy or to corruption had led to his dismissal. He even served for a short while as a provincial governor before demotion to the less demanding role of temple guardian, where he could carry on his scholarly work. Despite all the rumpus in his life, he produced a body of philosophical work that brought together the main themes of what had till then seemed to be divergent and irreconcilable Confucian sectarian schools. The source of his ideas, historians agree, was the complementary teachings of the Ch'eng brothers. So influential did Chu Hsi's eclectic Confucianism become that the subsequent thousand years of Chinese philosophy is perhaps best thought of as a thousand years of the influence of his writings. His work has been described as the "Great Synthesis" by the historian Wing-tsit Chan. Perhaps for this reason his selection of Confucian literature, the Four Great Books, the Confucian *Analects*, the book of Mencius, together with two of his own works, the *Great Learning* concerning metaphysics and epistemology, and the *Doctrine of the Mean*, a treatise on moral philosophy, were the basic texts for the civil service examinations for 700 years. He died in 1200, turning down the offer of a government post on his deathbed!

The generalization of the concept of "li"

His metaphysical innovations were built around the refinement and generalization of the concept with which we have become very familiar, *li*. I will continue to follow the practice of rendering this concept into English as "principle." However, it attains a more cosmic scope than it had in traditional usages. One is tempted to try to explain this new version of the concept in terms drawn from European alchemy, but that would be to explain the inexplicable in terms of the unintelligible. *Li* is explicated by Chu Hsi in the work called *Moral Cultivation* (Wing-tsit Chan, 1963: 614) in relation to two other major concepts, the Way, *Tao*, and "nature." Commenting on a saying of Ch'eng I, that "The nature is the same as principle," Chu Hsi explains the double-sidedness of the concept.

In relation to the mind it is called the nature. In relation to events, it is called principle. The principle of life is called the nature. (Wing-tsit Chang, 1963: 614)

Thus *li* seems to mean, roughly, the source of the distinguishing characters of things.

Chu Hsi and the other neo-Confucians seem to have been confronted with much the same deep metaphysical puzzle as troubled the Indian philosophers of antiquity. How is the diversity of material things and the individuality of people to be reconciled with the unity of the Great Ultimate? Since *li* is what differentiates one individual from another, *li* itself must be differentiated. "The [world of] nature consists of innumerable principles created by heaven," says Chu Hsi.

How is mind and materiality to be brought into concord? The solution strikes me as remarkably subtle, if I have understood the translation correctly. Nature has no physical form, and

is nothing but this very principle. In man, humanity, righteousness, propriety and wisdom are his nature, but what physical form or shape have they? All they have are the principles of humanity, righteousness, propriety and wisdom. As they possess these principles, many deeds are carried out, and man is enabled to have the feelings of commiseration, shame, deference and compliance, and right and wrong. (Wing-tsit Chan, 1963: 615)

Chu Hsi explicates this account with the analogy of the powers of drugs in which the effect does not exist as a physical state in the material but is manifested in the drug's action. This seems to me to make *li*, at whatever level in the hierarchy of differentiating principles we meet it, as the nature of things and people, a dispositional concept. Principles are dispositions to display this or that manifestation.

The universalization of "Ch'i"

Yet another concept is required, in that nature must be realized in something. Like forms which preexist the matter that realizes them in a substantial way, the *li* of something is *logically* related to the material in which it is realized. Realization may not always be seen as properties of individual material substances. Relational properties too are or have their *li*. I used the word "material" in the previous sentence to explain how *li* and its realizations are related. But this is a misleading expression. The Chinese concept is *ch'i*. *Ch'i* is in everything, and what differentiates one thing from another is its instantiation of *li*.

However, these principles are not really differentiated in a deep sense. They are all part of something grander, also *li*, the ultimate, perhaps the principle of principles. Thus *li* as ultimate is unchanging. So what is the source of change? It must be the only other generic something in the universe: namely, *ch'i*. Wing-Tsit Chan translates *ch'i* not as stuff or matter, in the Western sense, but as "material force." This is another dispositional concept. It seems clear that it would be a serious mistake to interpret the doctrine of *li* and *ch'i* as if it were merely an Oriental version of the Platonic form and matter metaphysics, which has become almost second nature to the Western point of view. The complementary mundane forces of *yin* and *yang* complete a system which is dynamic and activity-based throughout.

The impetus to a revival and an elaboration and development of Confucian philosophy seems to have come from a deliberate intention to resist the growing popularity of Buddhism. It is not surprising to find that the metaphysics of diversity in unity expounded by Chu Hsi in the doctrine of *li* and *ch'i* should have a similar "feel" to Buddhist metaphysics, and its Indian-derived concepts of *saṃsāra* and *Brahman*.

Human nature and the ethical principle

A theory of human nature emerges simply by combining the assertion that the *li* of everyone must be the same, since it is one with the ultimate, with the thesis that differences between people must come from their *ch'i* alone. But *ch'i* can be differentiated in another way: in quality. Those who have defective *ch'i* are weak in both intellect and character. How can this be?

> The nature [*li*] of all men is good, and yet there are those that are good from birth and those who are evil from birth. This is because of the difference in material force [*ch'i*] with which they are endowed . . . If the sun and moon are clear and bright . . . the man born at such a time and endowed with such a material force . . . should be a good man. But if the sun and moon are darkened and gloomy . . . all this is evidence

of violent material force. There is no doubt that if a man is endowed with such material force he will be a bad man. (Wing-tsit Chan, 1963: 625)

We must now return to consider how the main Confucian moral concept, *jen*, what is proper to humanity, fits in to the general metaphysics we have now outlined. Chu Hsi carefully differentiates *jen* from the moral qualities, possession of which realizes that which is truly human nature.

When selfish desires can be entirely eliminated and the Principle of Nature freely operates, that is *jen* . . . *Jen* is the principle (*li*) originally inherent in man's mind. With impartiality, there is *jen* . . . But impartiality as such should not be equated with *jen*. (Wing-tsit Chan, 1963: 633)

The Buddhist echoes are strong here too. Another neo-Confucian put it very clearly: "If one could but realise that it is human desire that obscures his true nature, he would be enlightened" (Chu Tsu Yu Lei 1.3a). And this is more or less what we have heard before, on the very lips of Gautama! But how is this moral philosophy to be reconciled with the metaphysical thesis above, which links moral character deterministically with the accident of the state of the weather at one's birth? The answer lies in the difference between the two "components" of being, *li* and *ch'i*. In so far as the nature of human beings is a realization of *li*, people are one with the Great Ultimate. Chu Hsi quotes Cheng I again to emphasize that by enlarging the mind one can enter into all things in the world. This is given both a material and a moral interpretation, when he remarks that "selfishness obscures and obstructs" leading one to leave out something of the world, one's family, for instance. And so one's nature falls short of the *li* of the Cosmos. Just as there are the *yin* and *yang* of material forces, so too there are the *yin* and *yang* of spiritual forces, which show up in the sudden inexplicable changes from augmentation to diminution and so on. The study of material things is as much an enlargement of the mind as a reflection on moral issues.

The historical dominance of Chu Hsi's version of neo-Confucianism was preceded by one of the great controversies of the history of philosophy, the debate with Lu Hsiang-shan.

The Teachings of Lu Hsiang-shan

A near contemporary of Chu Hsi was Lu Hsiang-shan (1139–93). His neo-Confucianism was, like that of Chu Hsi, embedded in a general metaphysics. It differed from the dualism of Chu Hsi, in that instead of a universe in which "*li*" shapes a substance-like "*ch'i*," there was only *li*. This led to a profound difference in epistemology. Chu Hsi, taking the concreteness of things as deriving from both "substance" and "principle/form," advocated empirical investigations of the world in order to understand *li*. Since there was no stuff, Lu Hsiang-shan argued that all one required was a careful contemplation of one's own mind, the ultimate *li*. Lu said "the universe is my mind; my mind is the universe" (quoted in Creel, 1982: 213). Not only did this metaphysical difference lead to differences in how the two neo-Confucians conceived the route to knowledge, but it affected their ethical doctrines in a similar way. Evil, for Chu Hsi, came from *ch'i*, whereas for Lu, since people were originally good, the source of evil must be contamination by the desire for material things. This is so much closer to Zen Buddhism and to Indian thought generally than the moral philosophy of Chu Hsi that it is not surprising that Lu was criticized for advocating a meditative way of life that was almost identical to that of the Buddhists.

The upshot of this twelfth-century debate (and it was a real debate, in that the two philosophers corresponded about philosophical matters) was settled by the choice of some of the works of Chu Hsi as texts for the official government examinations in 1313. Not only did this settle the debate, in a way, but it should be remarked that the amazing persistence of philosophical positions through hundreds of years, and the relative stasis of thought until the modern era in China, is due, in large part, to the conserving power of the texts chosen for the state examinations. However, there was a reaction, and it has to do with the character of the political regime that existed in the fourteenth century, under the unpopular Mongol dynasty.

Neo-Confucianism after Chu Hsi

The Buddhist connection

The official philosophers and their neo-Confucianism came under vigorous attack in the Ch'ing dynasty. The target was more Lu

Hsiang-shan than Chu Hsi. And the *casus belli* (the root of the disagreement) was suspicion of Zen Buddhism. Why was that anathema?
Because it encouraged or even enjoined withdrawal from civic affairs
into a life of contemplation. The leading figure in the reaction was Ku
Yen-wu (1613–82). Perhaps his attitude is not so remarkable since he
played a role in defending China against the Manchu invaders, and later
took to business with some success and, it seems, enthusiasm. Such a
man of affairs could hardly be satisfied with a philosophy which
enjoined the wise to absent themselves from the struggle for justice
and welfare.

A stream of such men came to prominence in China up until the
eighteenth century, criticising this or that aspect of the philosophy
of the neo-Confucians. In the end the differences were deeply
moral – the wrongness of the life of contemplation in the light of the
state of the world. Yet, it must be said that the persistence of neo-
Confucianism as the background to their complaints was in itself a
victory for the Confucians. Whatever else was occupying the mind of
Chinese thinkers in the second millennium, at least until the middle
of the twentieth century, the Confucian point of view provided the
perennial context.

Neo-Confucianism in the twentieth century

I shall be describing the radical break with the past that was brought
about by the importation of Marxism by the Communist Party, and
the writings of MaoTse-tung as philosopher. However, until that point
in the 1960s a new wave of neo-Confucian philosophy had been initiated by Fung Yu-lan.[1] He was born in 1895, and was educated in
classical Chinese philosophy in Peking and in the West, to which he
has been a frequent visitor. Western influence shows in the systematic
and formal development of his version of neo-Confucianism, in contrast to the method of commentary and anecdote characteristic of the
writings and sayings of Chu Hsi and Lu in the twelfth and thirteenth
centuries.

The neo-Confucians of the twelfth century were constructing a
system of concepts with which to comprehend the universe, but they
arrived at it at least partly inductively. Here is how the world of things
and people seems to us to be – what do we need to develop to make
it comprehensible? Fung Yu-lan's approach is, at least in intention,
abstract and *a priori*.

Roughly speaking, he works from the general methodological principle that concepts are prior to objects.

> What makes a thing square is the square . . . the square can be real but not actual . . . In our system we can still say [with Chu Hsi] that "the principle is one but its manifestations are many." But when we say so, the principle we are talking about is still the principle when we discuss it as such . . . [this discussion] does not make any affirmations about reality. (Wing-tsit Chan, 1963: 756)

In a similar way Fung Yu-lan arrives at the concept of *ch'i*, material force, but his version seems to echo the substantivalist thought of the West. Thus he distinguishes between absolute *ch'i* and relative *ch'i*. Abstracting the specific nature from bricks and tiles, and then from the earth of which they are made, and so on, we can continue until we reach absolute *ch'i*, at which point we seem to have arrived at Aristotelian prime matter. Again this concept is prior to anything real, which comes into being only by the combination of *li* and *ch'i*.

Like his predecessors, Fung Yu-lan generalizes the processes of the universe into the Great Ultimate, "the totality of all principles," and the Non-ultimate, which are yet a unity and at the same time *Tao*, the Way. In Western terms, it seems to me that he is presenting a view of how actual things come to be by the realization of potentiality into actuality, as *li* is instantiated through *ch'i*.

The fourth element in the scheme is the tie to morality. The key is the necessity to fulfill the nature of "man" as the realization of a perfection. Fung Yu-lan quotes Mencius to the effect that the model for achieving this is the sage whose conduct is "the ultimate standard of human relations."

The reader will appreciate, I am sure, that there is little in this updated version of neo-Confucianism that is new, or indeed an advance on the thought of Chu Hsi. The flavor, however, is different, at least as it comes through in translation. One seems to detect a whiff of Western, and particularly Aristotelian philosophy of form, matter, and the potential/actual distinction subtly shading the thoroughgoing dispositionalist presentation of *li* and *ch'i* by Chu Hsi.

Historians of Chinese philosophy, such as Creel (1969) and Wing-tsit Chan (1963), leave us in little doubt that in the second millennium the dominant force in Chinese thought was neo-

Confucianism, and specifically the version developed by Chu Hsi. Unlike the situation in the first millennium, in which around the third and fourth centuries A.D. a strong neo-Taoist movement sprang up, so far as I understand the matter, neo-Confucianism in the second millennium opened out into numerous versions and varieties, but suffered no serious and fundamental challenge. That had to wait for the Communist revolution.

CHINESE PHILOSOPHY ABROAD

Chinese philosophy drew from India and itself exported philosophical views, doctrines, and conceptions of life to its neighbors, particularly Japan. There was also a later influence in the West, first in the eighteenth century, when the works of Confucius became known to those also interested in the reform of the state, and in the twentieth century in California, where some versions of Buddhism took root.

Philosophical Exports to Japan

To a really remarkable extent, the history of Japanese culture is the history of imports. This is as true for philosophy as it has been for writing systems, for industry, for clothing, and much else. The traditional and ancient Japanese conception of the universe was shaped by a proliferation of personifications of natural forces, and haunted by the souls of the dead, raised to the status of minor divinities. So far as I know there was no tradition of critical discussion or commentary on this cluster of cosmological fragments.

However, the Japanese began actively to look for all sorts of cultural "goods" from their neighbor, China, from the third century of the first Christian millennium. Official expeditions were sent to China with the specific purpose of acquiring knowledge and techniques, including writing. The period of the most vigorous importation of Chinese thought to Japan coincided with the rising tide of Buddhism, which we have seen. Not surprisingly, the philosophical imports were dominated by Buddhism, and particularly the Zen version. The indigenous cosmology, now called Shinto, absorbed a great deal of Buddhist thought and practice.

Buddhism in Japanese forms

Perhaps the most interesting and seemingly paradoxical of the ways Buddhism was absorbed into Japanese culture was the formal link established with military matters and particularly swordsmanship. How could it be that a quietist philosophy of withdrawal into meditation and the abandonment of all links to the material world, was taken in as the very heart of the greatest military art?

The answer is in the idea of the "empty mind." Just as the Buddhist adept clears the mind of everything material, so the Zen swordsman is so wholly at one with his art, and the instruments of it, that all conscious reflective thought is eliminated. This is particularly important for the thought of death or worry about the outcome. The historical connection between Zen and the military mind and character was established in the thirteenth century when the Hojo family's austere and militaristic regime converted to Buddhism. The first of this family to become a Buddhist was Tokijori (1227–63). The Buddhist concepts of *munen* (no-thought-ness) and *mushin* (no-mind-ness), formulated in Japanese, had direct application to the military arts. The art of swordsmanship is not only a way of killing but leads to the Way, to *Tao*. It has a great advantage over book learning in that error is immediately evident in the outcome of the bout (Suzuki, 1958: 132).

Neo-Confucianism in the Shogunate

However, the political climate in Japan stabilized, and a central government was established by the Tokugawa Shogunate in the seventeenth century. The Shoguns took complete control of the administration of the country, virtually sequestering the Emperor, who was confined to a merely decorative role. Again it is not surprising that during the Tokugawa period another import from China should begin to dominate Japanese political philosophy, namely Confucianism. This was the philosophy of the enlightened bureaucrat. By this time in China, the neo-Confucians were dominant in political philosophy, particularly owing to the well publicized and circulated writings of Chu Hsi.

The effect of this new transplant is well summed up in the following passage:

> in China the emphasis of Confucianism is laid on the duty of filial piety, while in Japan the primary emphasis is on loyalty. (Ho, 1992: 171)

The long period of stability and relative prosperity of the Tokugawas provided just the right conditions for philosophical discussion to become popular. Since the Japanese bureaucracy took much the same form as the idealized Confucian one, with scholars at the right hand of administrators, the popularity of Chu Hsi's writings is not to be wondered at.

Interesting too is the line of recruitment of enthusiasts to the neo-Confucian cause. In several cases prominent neo-Confucians had been Zen monks and had tired of or become disillusioned with the endless search for a state of unthought. Many of these apostates turned in their later years to the task of creating a synthesis of Confucianism and Shinto, as their predecessors had tried to marry Shinto with Buddhism. For example, Yamazaki Ansai (1618–82) followed this pattern, from Zen monk to neo-Confucian tutor to the regent Hoshina Masayuki, and finally to the blending of that philosophy with Shinto. He is said to have declared that Shinto was "the native faith of the land farthest to the east [Japan], the land where the sun rises." His synthesis of Confucian ethics and Japanese nationalism came to be called Suika Shinto.

To this day the religion of Japan is predominantly Shinto, with some substantial numbers of Christians and Buddhists. I think it true to say that no indigenous tradition of political or general philosophy has ever emerged in Japan.

The Influence on the West

Confucius and political thought

It is sometimes said that, in addition to the interest roused in Europe by the Jesuit Matteo Ricci's description of the Chinese writing system, the writings of Confucius or at least reports of them were influential in eighteenth-century Europe among the *philosophes* of the Enlightenment. Though the influence of concept representation, the method of the ideograms, on the efforts by Leibniz and others to develop a form of writing that was independent of local languages and tied directly to reality, is well documented, it has proved difficult to substantiate the claim for a Confucian influence on political thought. The group of political thinkers, nicknamed "the primitivists," not only imagined a primeval social paradise inhabited by the "noble savage," glimpsed by voyagers to the South Seas, but also revered Chinese political philosophers, and particularly Confucius, as the repositories of an unrivalled standard of civic virtue. However, neither the works of Voltaire nor Diderot, heroes of the enlightenment, show any influence, as far as I can see, of the thoughts of the Chinese sage.

There have been numerous English translations of the Confucian *Analects*; the earliest listed in the Bodleian Library catalogue is 1691. For English speakers the most famous is surely the 1938 translation by Arthur Waley. There is therefore no doubt that some version of Confucian thought was available in the West from the seventeenth century, when details of Chinese thought were first made available in the reports by the returning Jesuits. For instance, G. Ghirardini published in Paris a book with "Lettre à M. ** touchant les honneurs que les Chinois rendent au philosophe Confucius & à leurs ancêtres" ("Letter to Monsieur** about the honor the Chinese give to Confucius and their ancestors") in the title.

Zen Buddhism in the mid-twentieth century

The existence of Buddhism was known in Western Europe at least from the sixteenth century. However, the possibility of its becoming established as a way of life and thought in the West was not realized until this century. There have been two important moments in its appearance in the Europe and the United States.

In the 1950s many people were introduced to Buddhism through the popular writings of Christmas Humphreys (1955). A Buddhist Society was founded. Though one could say that there was considerable public interest, Buddhism remained a curiosity in Britain.

The heady atmosphere of mysticism and revolt that spread from California to the rest of the United States and elsewhere in the 1960s and seventies was conducive to an interest in "Orientalism." In particular, the concepts and practices of Buddhism took root, though, in hindsight, it seems that they were largely misunderstood by the majority of the "flower children." It was the Zen version of Buddhism that appealed, a version which had found literary expression in the writings of Allan Watts (1936). His account of Buddhism was a far cry from the mystical extravaganza of Haight-Ashbury and the dharma-bums.

> Zen masters refer to their realization in terms of the most ordinary affairs, for their object is to show Zen as something perfectly natural, as intimately related to everyday life, while the Buddha is just "the old man in all his homeliness"; he has been there all the time, for his home is ordinary life, but no one recognizes him. (Watts, 1936: 81)

The way this pattern of thought was taken up bore more resemblance to Taoism, in its *wu wei* doctrine, than to Buddhism proper. The classic *Zen and the Art of Motorcycle Maintenance* (Persig, 1975) seems to me to have expressed a great deal more Taoist "cool" than the strenuous though meditative search for the moment of instant enlightenment.

THE INFLUENCE OF THE WEST

Paradoxically the overwhelming influence of the West on Chinese philosophical thought was a consequence of the supreme self-confidence and even arrogance of the Chinese view of their place in the world and their attitude to the barbarians who inhabited it. The near colonial status to which China had fallen after the Sino-British war of 1842 was not only a loss of national power, but extraordinarily galling to a people who had, for 3,000 years, regarded themselves as the only truly civilized culture on earth. In a very short time there were foreigners operating the customs service, the railways, and the post office. These were very shortly followed by a flood of missionaries organizing hospitals and schools.

Creel (1969: 237) gives a vivid account of the variety of responses of the Chinese to these humiliations.

> Some [Chinese] have insisted that China's traditional patterns of life and thought are superior to all others, and that the Chinese have found themselves in difficulty not because they have been too conservative but

because they have not lived up to the traditional ideas; if they did so China would be so strong that her troubles would vanish. Others have taken a more moderate view; while they believed that Chinese culture provided the soundest basis for China's development, they wished to modify it to meet the conditions of the modern world, and to take over such Western techniques as appeared to be advantageous. A third group has insisted that China's entire traditional pattern of political, social, and economic organisation is unsuited to the world of today, and that the whole manner of life and thought must be revolutionised.

The transition to Communism as the overarching philosophical and political stance of the ruling elite was preceded by a serious attempt to create a democracy on British lines, with more than a dash of the enthusiasm of the French Revolution added. Their democracy would be republican and not the constitutional monarchy of the other European tradition.

It does not seem unreasonable to say that the Japanese invasion in 1936 made the establishment of a stable, self-renewing, republican democracy virtually impossible. The necessities of war, and the economic havoc wrought by the invaders, reduced China to a terrible condition of poverty and chaos. It is not surprising to see the same attraction to simplistic Marxist explanations of the situation as had attracted young Russians in the similar situation in Russia toward the end of the First World War.

And so we have the famous Long March, and the conquest of all of China by the Red Army. From that moment the shift in China's intellectual focus seemed to have been determined.

Marxism

Marxism is more a point of view than a fully interpreted and coherent system. The most striking feature of Marxism as a philosophy, in the context of China, was the form it took in the writings of Mao Tse-tung. The political and economic arrangements, the excesses of the period of the Red Guards, and the subsequent turn to a form of capitalism within an authoritarian political framework are fortunately only peripheral to my concern. I turn to an analysis of Mao's writings as philosophy.

Mao Tse-tung was born in 1893. He came to Peking in 1918 as an assistant librarian. Through his work he joined the Society for the Study of Marxism. From 1920 he was a primary school teacher in Chang-sha. In that year he married Yang K'hai-hui. She was executed by the Nationalists in 1930. Mao later married Chiang Ch'ing. In 1927 he led a Communist putsch which failed. His retreat to Kiangsi province gave him the chance to develop his ideas of a peasant-led revolution. Eventually he and his men began the Long March. During the year 1934–5, they travelled 6,000 miles to Shensi province. During the Japanese invasion of 1937–45 the Communists made common cause with the Kuomintang Nationalists, but immediately afterward a civil war broke out. The Communists were in complete control of China by 1949. Mao's influence was profound but his projects met with little success. The economic reforms of the Great Leap Forward of 1956–9 failed, and the Cultural Revolution of 1967 was a disaster. Mao died in 1976.

In his early writings Mao presented those orthodox Marxist-Leninist philosophical theses that were particularly relevant to China. The distinction between absolute and relative truth is clearly highly relevant to developing a revolutionary movement in a country the social and economic character of which is quite different from Marx's Europe.

A Marxist recognises that the development of the total process of the universe is absolute, whereas the development of each particular process in this total process is relative. Hence in the great river of absolute truth, man's knowledge of a particular process in each given stage of development is only relatively true. Absolute truth is compounded of a sum-total of relative truths. (Mao Tse-tung, 1961: I, 284; quoted in Cohen, 1964: 11)

This leads Mao to the important observation that successful revolutionary leaders must be ready to change ideas and attitudes in relation to the situation they find themselves in.

The emphasis on flexibility and the uniqueness of the Chinese situation is everywhere implicit in Mao's later writings. The practical question of the role of the bourgeoisie in the revolutionary situation is tied in closely with the theoretical question of the nature of opposition in dialectical contradiction. If both classes are to play a part in the New China, there must be an emphasis on the unity of opposites in a theoretical analysis of contradiction, since the working class and the bourgeoisie are in contradictory opposition. The way that each pole of a contradiction requires its opposite was an important principle of Hegel's dialectic, and we shall encounter it in the discussion of Hegel in a later chapter. Again Mao expresses the thesis of the unity of opposites in a quite orthodox way.

> First, two aspects of every contradiction in the process of development of a thing find the presupposition of their existence each in its opposite aspect and both coexist in an entity. Second, the two contradictory aspects according to given conditions, tend to transform themselves each into its opposite aspect. (Mao Tse-tung: 1961: I, 315)

So there are antagonistic and nonantagonistic contradictions. In China it becomes theoretically possible for the working class and the bourgeoisie to coexist in a socialist state.

In China the process of revolution must be geared to local conditions. That is an obvious practical insight that any political leader hoping for success must have. We have seen already that Mao's emphasis on the relativity of truth to context opens the way for a distinction between the universality of the scientific laws of historical development and the particularity of their form in any concrete historical context. That is all very well, but in what does the particularity consist? In discussing this Mao introduced a novel idea into Marxist-Leninism, the idea that the poles of a contradiction are not symmetrical. There is a principal pole and a secondary pole. Thus the same general pattern of opposition between contradictory poles can take different concrete forms as the balance between principal and secondary changes. It also follows that the contributions of each pole to the totality of which they are the components will not, in general, be equal. The principal aspect will contribute more to the overall quality of the thing than the secondary. So the source of change too will not be symmetrical. It is changes in the principal aspect that are most efficacious in the production of change in the whole.

Which aspect of the possible social contradictions will be the principal one in a country like China? In discussing this question Mao was able to look around, as it were, to find the dynamic core of revolution. He found it in the peasants, the overwhelming majority of those whose lives had been the focus of millennia of exploitation by rural landlords. It would have been impossible to stage a revolution basing it only upon the urban proletariat, which was hardly large enough to man an armed struggle.

> This leadership of the poor peasants is absolutely necessary. Without the poor peasants there can be no revolution. To reject them is to reject the revolution. To attack them is to attack the revolution. The general direction they have taken in the revolution has never been wrong. (Mao Tse-tung, 1961: I, 21)

Once again Mao fitted theory to practice.

As a philosopher Mao adapted the central thesis of Marxist dialectic to his own purposes. Though his work has been presented, especially during his lifetime, as if it had been philosophy first and practice second, it seems in retrospect that in Mao as philosopher we are witnessing a political and military leader with a clear grasp of the state of his own country, who then provides, *ex post facto*, an *a priori* theoretical analysis that makes his practical insights and acts inevitable. This can hardly be regarded as a fatal flaw. Political philosophy has that character. Thomas Hobbes' *Leviathan* (1657) presents a view of the nature of the state that is well adjusted to the need for a sovereign on the pattern of Charles II, who reigned after the Restoration of the monarchy in 1660.

Conclusion

The development of Chinese philosophy in the second millennium follows two main lines. There is the continual readjustment of Confucian philosophy to fit the changing conditions of life, and to cope with the perennial quietist alternatives, Tao and Buddhism. The terminology may have been the same as that used by Confucius himself, but the two most prominent neo-Confucian philosophers gave their own differing interpretations to both *li* and *ch'i*, the one using these concepts to develop a thoroughgoing dualism and the other, by denying the existence of *ch'i*, to create an equally throughgoing monism.

It seems to me that the dominance of Chinese philosophical thought by the discussion and advocacy of attitudes to the state, be they in favour of joining in or against it, meant that the only kind of Western philosophy likely to take root would be political. Marxism seems to have been ideally suited to step into the place of the Confucian tradition in the chaotic conditions of the aftermath of the Japanese invasion. I have already remarked that philosophy in China is predominantly, though not wholly, political philosophy. More than 2,000 years separate Confucius and Mao Tse-tung, but their ways of thinking are remarkably similar. The Confucian philosopher has the prime duty of entering in to the government of the state, bringing his hard-gained wisdom. Mao may have been a revolutionary first and a philosopher second, but his presentation of his version of Marxist-Leninism is in the Confucian spirit. The philosopher brings his wisdom to the management of the state, and thus makes possible the transformation of the lives of the citizens. We have no reason to think that Mao's Confucian style was insincere. It was profoundly Chinese.

So there has been a kind of trade, with Buddhism in its Zen variety finding a place, though not so prominently now, in the social revolution of the 1960s. While China has taken up the most materialist philosophy of the Occident, the West has taken up the most immaterial philosophy of China and the Orient, Zen.

NOTES

1   I had the privilege of meeting him on a visit to China some years ago. He was still held in high regard by the younger philosophers who, after the period of the Red Guards, had reinstituted the study of analytical philosophy.

PART II

Philosophy in the West

Medieval Philosophy

6

Islamic Philosophy

In the spring of the year 1075, a caravan was returning from Gurgan, on the Caspian Sea, to the inland city of Tūs, when it was attacked by a band of robbers. They stripped the travelers of everything. There was a young student among the group. He was devastated by the loss of his notebooks, representing the months of study he had done in Gurgan. Ignoring the advice of the others, he rushed off after the robbers. When he caught up with them he pleaded with the robber chief to return the books. "That cannot be very important knowledge if it can be taken away from you easily!" the chief replied. However, he gave the notebooks back. The youth, 17 at the time, took the comment to heart and thereafter memorized every bit of knowledge he had acquired. To this perhaps we ascribe the prodigious scholarly resources of al-Ghazālī, the greatest Islamic philosopher, for the determined youth was he.

Just as we found with Chinese and Indian philosophy, the second Christian millennium does usher in a distinctive set of issues for philosophers in the West. The history which will unfold shows how very closely intertwined were the traditions of philosophy that developed in the Mediterranean region, including the near East. Islamic, Jewish, and Christian philosophers not only drew on a common monotheistic tradition but faced similar problems in their attempts to provide each revealed religion with a rational foundation. Influenced by the turning of the great Islamic philosophers to Ancient Greece for the tools of rational analysis, Jewish and Christian philosophers in medieval times followed the same program.

We must begin our account of Islamic philosophy by a résumé of the intellectual capital and troubling problems with which the developments of the second millennium began. Though the span of years, from the inauguration of a serious and recognizably philosophical tradition until the turn of the first millennium, was much less in Arabia than in the Orient, thematic threads that persisted well into the second millennium had been well established before A.D. 1000.

The general principle upon which our understanding of Islamic philosophy must be based is that Arab, and then Islamic philosophy in general, begins with the absorption of classical Greek material into Arabic culture. From about the year 700 under the Caliph al-Mansur, Greek texts were translated into Arabic. At first these were medical and astronomical/astrological. The skills in translation thus acquired made possible the commissioning of translations of other Greek works. By about 830 Plato's *Timaeus* and several works of Aristotle, including the *De Anima* and the *Prior Analytics*, were available in Arabic.

The genesis of Islamic philosophy

A rush of further Greek translations began about 830 with the work of Hunain bin Istaq. Not only were these translations commissioned by the state, in the person of the Caliph, but several rich families vied with the court in patronage, and indeed also in learning. By about 900 all the available works of Aristotle had been translated, as well as the philosophical treatises of Galen. Here then was a kit of tools for the rational analysis of the religious texts. Not only was the meaning of the Koran at issue but also the proper interpretation of a large body of apocryphal material that had been collected around the Koranic writings in the centuries since Mahomet's death.

The true beginning of Islamic philosophy can be dated to the emergence of a problem that we will find much to the fore in the European Middle Ages: namely, how to reconcile Greek philosophical categories and the discipline of reason with religious dogma. The Koran is written in an aphoristic and metaphorical style, leaving a great deal of room for different and conflicting readings. In general the declarations of revealed religion are treated as a stable given, since they are presented in immutable texts. Greek philosophy provided the tools for interpretation and exegesis.

From that time until the present day philosophical attitudes in the Islamic world seem to be polarized around two conflicting stances toward exegetical and critical studies. On the one hand there are those who welcomed the reign of reason as the touchstone of faith. On the other hand there were many who resisted anything other than a literalist reading of the sacred texts. Since the language of the Koran is highly metaphorical and anthropomorphic, neither side could offer a definitive reading that would have settled the matter. The doctrine of the Koran is an austere monotheism. The effort to ground it with the help of the powers of reason invites accusations of heresy. Willingness to take the metaphorical and aphoristic declarations literally invited accusations of ignorance and superstition. This polarization in Islamic thought has never been resolved. We find echoes of it to this day.

The themes

Three major problems defined the themes of debates that have lasted for centuries in Islam. The Koran declares that God, who is an unchanging, unknowable unity, created this changing and diverse world. How is it possible for the Imperfect Many to emanate from the Perfect One? This has been called "the problem of emanation." It has a metaphysical side. How can there be multiplicity in unity? It has a moral side. How can the goodness of God be reconciled with the evil in the world?

The Koran also declares that God is wholly in command of the world. How then is it possible to make sense of the thesis that human beings are capable of freely choosing their actions and so subject to moral culpability? We can call this "the problem of free action."

How is the conduct of a person to ensure that his (or nowadays also her) individual soul can be preserved and judged favorably after the death of the body? Is it by establishing direct contact with God, and merging oneself finally with the One? Or is it by meticulous observance of the Law? I shall call this "the problem of salvation."

The Koran as sacred text together with later collections of doctrine, the *Traditions of Mahomet*, formed a stable point around which discussions of the problematic themes – emanation, free will, and salvation – have turned. There was no question of what were the words. There was endless debate on how they were to be interpreted.

However, to follow the development of the philosophical treatment of these three themes from around the turn of the first millennium, we must have some grasp of three essential components already established in Islamic thought. There was Aristotle's *Metaphysics* and the Neoplatonism of Plotinus. There was the doctrine of creation and human action set out in the Koran. In the absence of authoritative editions of the Greek sources, a mixture of Aristotelian and Neoplatonic ideas was absorbed by Islamic philosophers as the "Greek philosophy." At the beginning of this development everything of Greek origin was usually attributed to Aristotle. Getting clear about the sources is an essential preliminary to an understanding of Islamic philosophy.

Two of the most important philosophers who set about tackling the problematic themes of emanation, salvation, and freedom were enthusiasts for the "Greek philosophy." These were al-Fārābī (ca. 890–950) and Ibn Sīnā (980–1037). The latter was very well known to the philosophers of the Latin West as Avicenna. Their most famous critic, al-Ghazālī (1058–1111), disputed their interpretations of Koranic texts and their responses to the three great issues, by disputing the Greek philosophical authority from which these interpretations had come. Fundamentalists and literalists had also disputed the right of philosophers to offer interpretations. Later, "Averroes," Ibn Rushd (1126–98), restored the Aristotelian influence. By meticulous attention to the writings of Aristotle, he severed genuine Aristotelian thought from the Neoplatonism with which the earlier translators of "Greek" philosophy had contaminated it. Ibn Rushd's "Greek" interpretations of the sacred texts were, therefore, very different from those of al-Fārābī and Ibn Sīnā. This did not necessarily endear them to the literalists. In his turn Ibn Rushd directed a good deal of his criticism to the works of al-Ghazālī, reinterpreting Aristotle's doctrines to make them perfectly in accord with the Koran. The traditional dogmas were the basis of the life of ordinary people, and it was no business of philosophers to destroy confidence in them.

THREE SOURCES OF ISLAMIC PHILOSOPHY

Aristotle's *Metaphysics*

The section of the *Metaphysics* that was most heavily drawn on by the Islamic philosophers in whom we have a special interest was concerned with God. There are two passages which bring out the relevant Aristotelian doctrine.

The first lays out the relation between potentiality and actuality, in the context of the genesis of motion. An immobile because unchanging God must be responsible for motion and change, since he is responsible for everything. How can this be?

> It will not be enough even if it does function [as the source of motion] if its essence is potentiality; for there will not be eternal motion, since that which exists potentially may not exist. Therefore there must be a principle of this [divine] kind whose essence is actuality. Furthermore these substances [the sources of motion] must be immaterial; for they must be eternal if anything is. (*Metaphysics*, Lambda, 1071b)

Whatever is the source of motion must be both actual and immaterial, hence its essence includes its existence. What does that mean? At its simplest it means that the divine principle cannot but exist. To be at all it is necessary that it exist. It is not a matter of fact that the divine principle exists. This is one of the most difficult conceptual moves to be found in the whole of Islamic and Christian philosophy. We will find ourselves returning to it again and again.

The second passage links this insight to the idea of God as, in some sense, a person, or at least having attributes analogous to those of a person.

> Such, then is the first principle upon which depends the sensible universe and the world of nature. And its life is like the best we temporarily enjoy. It must be in that state always . . . since its actuality is also pleasure . . . And thought thinks itself through participation in the object of thought . . . it actually functions when it possesses this object. Hence it is actuality rather than potentiality that is held to be the divine possession of rational thought, and its active contemplation is that which is most pleasant and best . . . and the essential actuality of God is life most good and eternal . . . and therefore life and a continuous eternal existence belong to God. (*Metaphysics*, Lambda, 1073a)

It cannot be said that these passages are the most transparent to be found in the works of Aristotle, but their overall meaning is clear. God is actual, living, and eternally contemplating his own nature, which is perfection. And it is this very same principle which provides the source of motion in this universe as we experience it. How can this be?

There must be a rational link between the nature of God and the motions of the heavens from which all terrestrial motions derive. Matter is inert and only that which is of the same nature as God could be active and so a source of motion. There must be a *primum mobile*, an outermost sphere beyond the spheres on which Aristotle thought the stars and planets had their places, through which God drives the world. Since God cannot change, there must be a hierarchy of intermediaries that share the causal efficacy of God without being God. These were the Intelligences, the idea of which had conveniently been supplied by Plotinus and the Neoplatonists. We have to have an account of how an unchanging, wholly actual God can be the source of changes in the material world, which are ultimately transitions from potentiality to actuality. For example, to serve in tennis, the player must transform the potential for motion in the ball that has been has tossed up above the base line into an actual change of location from one end of the court to the other. But God, the ultimate source of this and every other terrestrial motion, must be wholly actual.

Plotinus and Neoplatonism

As I have emphasized, Islamic philosophy was heavily in debt to Greek thought, in particular to the writings that were presumed to be by Aristotle. Looked at in hindsight it is perhaps not surprising that authors like Ibn Sīnā fused the doctrines of Neoplatonists, particularly those of Plotinus, with those of their master, Aristotle. The main works of Plotinus, the *Enneads*, were assembled and edited by Porphyry, but this text was not known as such to the early Islamic philosophers. Thinking they were drawing on Aristotle, it seems that for many important ideas they drew on Plotinus instead.

The Neoplatonists conceived the universe as the domain of a hierarchy of Intelligences, from which not only the forms of created things emerged but which also accounted for motion in the world, the problem faced by Aristotle. The doctrine of Intelligences also explained how God as Unity could have brought into being a world as Multiplicity, not only of types of things, but of individuals exemplifying those types. It purported to explain how the One could be the origin of the Many, while not ceasing to be the One.

Form and matter were the two logical "components" of all things, according to Plato. The qualities of things, which differentiated them into types, were explained by the instantiation of Forms in matter. Thus a particular spade is the shape it is and exemplifies the type of tool that it does because it realizes the Form of Spadeness. In the Platonic account a particular spade is known to a human being by the senses, but the Form of Spadeness is known by the intellect. That Form is not the actual qualities that are instantiated in the particular spade. According to Plato, it is a distinct being and resides elsewhere than in the garden shed. Plato also seems to have thought that contemplation of the Forms was the most aesthetically thrilling activity anyone could engage in. In so doing, one not only experienced beautiful things, but by intellectual apprehension, one grasped the Form of the Beautiful itself, immeasurably more wonderful than any actual beautiful thing.

The way Plotinus developed this account is nicely summarized by Schroeder (1992: 15). Form in Plato's theory is both a cause or explanation of the character of things, and an object of intrinsic value.

[Plotinus] distinguishes between two moments of use and enjoyment. When we speak of the Form as cause or explanation [of the characteristics of particular things], we are thinking of it in terms of use. When we address it as an intrinsically valuable object of intellective or spiritual vision, we are considering it in respect of enjoyment. In this scheme enjoyment has priority over use.

The hierarchy of beings that leads from the immutable divine unity to a changing mundane multiplicity begins with something other than God, thinking about God. This Intelligence is the First Emanation from God. In order to think the One (God) it must resolve the unity of the One into a plurality of attributes. But this cannot be by dividing the One. God is indivisible. The trick is that when the Intellect thinks unto itself an image of the One it must endow that image with the many attributes of God. Thus the First Intelligence is necessarily multiple, since God, though indivisible, has many attributes. This process of thinking the next higher state of becoming by the being just below it creates a hierarchy of Intelligences, becoming more and more diverse and internally complex. At the lowest level in the hierarchy of Intelligences is the Soul, analyzing and so dividing the higher Forms. It thereby creates itself as a person, the minimal Intelligence capable of transforming potentiality into actuality.

How do inferior entities arise from superior ones? Here Plotinus develops his most famous image. He seems to have intended it to be taken both literally and metaphorically. It is the image of light. With its help we can get the most illuminating insight into the nature of intelligible reality. The hierarchy of the Intelligences is a sequence of powers or activities. Plotinus distinguishes those that are inherent in substances and those that proceed from substances. In *Enneads* 6.4.22 he argues that the relation between the sequential hierarchy of powers, the Intelligences, is like the relation between the light from the Sun and that which is illuminated. Light does not depend for its existence on anything else but its source, but it is manifested in that which it illuminates. "So it is in the case of soul, considered as the activity of a prior soul, that as long as the prior soul abides, so does the subsequent activity" (quoted in Schroeder, 1991: 3).

Taking all this together we have the idea that an Intelligence, making itself into an image of a higher Intelligence, must represent to itself as a multiplicity of distinct thoughts, all the attributes of the higher being, which, in that being, are unified. So the representing Intelligence will be multiple while the represented Intelligence is still wholly one. If the world came into being in this way, and the Intelligences are also the Forms of things, or somehow incorporate them, then we can see how God as the One can be the progenitor of the world as the Many without dividing Himself, or even without conceiving the project of making a world at all. All this will happen through the dynamic nature of Intelligences, realizing themselves by analytically reflecting the attributes of those above them. But why should any of this take place?

This is the unanswerable question. Perhaps the best way to think of the doctrine of Intelligences goes like this: There are two fixed points in the pattern of Neoplatonic thinking. The first is God, the taken-for-granted center of all reality. He is unchanging, perfect, and so on. The second fixed point is the World, which is there for all to see, and it is changing, imperfect, and so on. The hierarchy of Intelligences *must* exist since we know that there is both the One (God) and the Many (the World). So we do not have to struggle to find a reason for God to create the First Intelligence whose role is to think about God. We know He must have done, since the World evidently exists. The way to cut this Gordian knot is to deny that there is a God, since we can hardly deny that there is a World. But this option was open neither to the traditionalists nor to the philosophers of Islam.

The Koranic Pronouncements

It will help to get a feel for the problem that confronted the interpreters of the Koran if we look at some of the most famous paragraphs. It is clear that a great deal is presupposed in each of the following, and that there is a great deal of latitude in their interpretation.

> ON CREATION: The Originator of the heavens and the earth! When He decreeth a thing, He saith unto it only: Be and it is. (Koran: ii, 117)

> ON WHAT THERE IS: He it is who created for you all that is in the earth. Then he turned to the heavens, and fashioned it as seven heavens. And he is the Knower of all things. (Koran: ii, 29)

> ON EVIL: Whatever of good befalleth thee (O man) it is from allah, and whatever of ill befalleth thee it is from thyself. We have sent thee (Muhammad) as messenger unto mankind and allah is sufficient as a witness. (Koran: iv, 79)

> ON SALVATION: Then whosoever doth good works and is a believer, there will be no rejection of his effort. Lo! We record (it) for him. (Koran: xxi, 94)

The role of God as creator is central to Islam, as is the idea of a finite universe. There will be a last judgment, when the moral quality of everyone's lives will be assessed. These lives have already been recorded. The first problem to which the philosophers addressed themselves was that of creation. How could the diverse and imperfect world be the creation of a unified and perfect being? It is not surprising that the philosophers availed themselves of the Neoplatonic solution to the problem.

In chapter 1 I suggested that the domain of analytical and critical philosophy can be thought of as an exploration of at least some of the presuppositions that are immanent in culturally important doctrines, theories, or practices. The work of the Islamic philosophers fits this prescription very well. The rationality of the doctrines of the Koran presupposed solutions to serious intellectual problems. Philosophers were those best equipped to solve them. That they needed solutions, and even that it was proper to bring them to the attention of everyone was by no means agreed among Muslims, then or now. The Koranic doctrines were given. Neither their rationality nor their irrationality was even to be contemplated.

THE PROBLEMS AND THEIR PHILOSOPHICAL TREATMENT

Now that we have a tentative grasp of the philosophical tools borrowed from Greece, we will turn to a detailed exposition of how the three major problems, emanation, freedom of action, and salvation were tackled by the philosophers. Traditionalists, it should be emphasized, were happy to take the Koranic pronouncements at their face value.

The most important Aristotelian of the first century of the second millennium was Ibn Sīnā. He was born in 980 in the eastern part of the Islamic domains. He spent his childhood in Bokhara. His education was based on the study of traditional texts, and on Islamic jurisprudence. At the age of 17 he reports being inspired by reading al-Fārābī. The sultan of Bokhara had a very extensive Greek library, of which the young scholar made enthusiastic use. In 998 his father died, and he was forced to earn a living. He travelled in a desultory way for some years. From 1015 to 1022 he held the demanding and hazardous post of chief minister to the ruler of Hamadhan. After further travels he settled in Isfahan in 1032, with the support of the prince of that town. He died in 1037.

The Doctrine of Emanation

The Arabic word *fayd*, literally "flowing," is used for the relationship between the One, which is the First Cause, and the Many, the material world. In the period at which we take up the story of Islamic philosophy, with the advent of Greek thought, the problem of emanation is already "on the books," so to say. However, at the turn of the millennium the treatment takes on a Neoplatonic aura, with a strong dash of Aristotelian metaphysics.

A somewhat schematic version of the doctrine of emanation is given by al-Fārābī. Just on the brink of the second millennium Ibn Sīnā presented a much better worked-out treatment, especially in his account of the reflexive self-contemplation practiced by the One. Thus Aristotle's God is well fitted, by virtue of his self-contemplation, to be the progenitor of the hierarchy of Intelligences.

The One is necessary, a unity, undifferentiated, which cannot be thought about. To be an object of thought it would have to be located in space and time, and have some differentiating properties.

> If the One is perfect . . . [Aristotle] ruled out the possibility of any intellectual commerce on the part of the Supreme Being . . . [with the world which is imperfect and other than It] . . . Despite its total independence of anything outside it . . . it apprehends, in the very act of self-apprehension, whatever has emanated from it. (Fakhry, 1983: 154)

The Islamic version of the Neoplatonic account of the One and the Many

In spelling out how contingent Multiplicity can arise out of necessary Unity the Neoplatonic Islamic philosophers made use of the Neoplatonic solution to the problem of the One and the Many by developing the idea of a hierarchy of productions, the ladder of Intelligences, modelled very closely on the hierarchy proposed by Plotinus. As emanations of the One they are not produced by causal processes, nor are they the result of a deliberate act of creation. The self-contemplation of the One by the One engenders them. This pattern is reproduced at lower levels in the order of beings, so that the first being which is created by emanation engages in self-apprehension and in the contemplation of the One. This is the first link of a chain that develops into a hierarchy of beings in true Neoplatonic style. At the level closest to the material world the human soul contemplates itself, and immediately apprehends its own identity and singularity. Human beings are self-conscious, minimal intelligences.

> The intelligence-existent must come first from the Necessary Existent, as we have asserted. In one respect another intelligence emanates from that intelligence, whereas in another respect a body emanates from the primordial bodies. If they are numerous . . . then from that intelligence another intelligence must proceed, and from the primordial body another body must emanate. Subsequent emanations continue similarly to the last level of primordial bodies . . . It has already been affirmed that the possibility of realizing the emanation of diversity and multiplicity from the one reality in this manner is fundamental to this process. (Ibn Sīnā, 1050 [1983]: 103)

The emanation doctrine allows for God to be the source of everything other than himself without jeopardizing his own completeness. We do not need to think of him as needing the world, or lacking it.

Fakhry points out that this mode of apprehension must be at the level of universal species or types. Only thus does the One avoid compromising itself with knowledge of concrete particulars. There must be a pure intellectual act by which the Forms are thought. It was not clear how God, on this theory, could apprehend any of the concrete particulars of the created, material world. This raised another problem with Koranic pronouncements of God's special care of every least thing in the material and created universe.

> The Necessary Existent is not susceptible to change, nor to multiplicity, though it knows the world and so it knows a multiplicity. But how can it do that and not admit multiplicity to its essence? The short answer is that by having "intelligent knowledge", that is a kind of knowledge that is of the form of the forms under which things are multiple. (Ibn Sīnā, 1050 [1983]: 62)

The doctrine of emanation and its dependence on the principle that from one only one can come, is nicely summed up in Fakhry (1982: 321).

> The First being gives rise to the first intellect, which in turn gives rise to the second intellect, as well as the Soul and Body of the first heaven. Unlike the First or Necessary Being, the first intellect involves an element of plurality, owing to its dual character as a being possible in itself, but necessary through its cause. This in fact is the ultimate cause

of multiplicity in a world emanating from a First Principle, which is absolutely one.

In the end the multiplicity of the world rests on the logical distinction between what is possible and what is necessary. Let us see if I can make clear how the distinction between unity and diversity is related to that between possibility and necessity.

Necessity and possibility

The distinction between necessity and possibility, between that which could not be otherwise and that which could be otherwise, is the other main conceptual distinction derived from Aristotelian philosophy. It is easy to see that this distinction fits very comfortably with such distinctions as that between unity and diversity and that between the permanent and unchanging and the ephemeral. If a certain possibility is realized then it is true that another one might have been. The apple that *is* green could have been red, and, since that is a live possibility for apples, indeed may later turn red. Every change is the actualization of a possibility.

Now comes the most difficult idea to grasp. While most existing things might not have existed, or having existed might have been different from what they were (though not too much), is there a necessary being? Such a being could not but have existed. Perhaps it is also a being which could not have been otherwise than it is? In particular, is there a being that could not have failed to exist? Aristotle seems to have thought that there was such a being. It is the God he describes in the *Metaphysics*.

Essence and existence

This question was tackled by taking up another distinction, that between essence and existence. The essence of something is the set of properties without which it would not be the thing it is. We can think of things that do not exist by thinking of the properties they would have if they did. A unicorn is a white horse-like creature with a horn in the middle of the forehead. These properties are at least part of the essence of the unicorn. A wedding ring must be circular and made of some precious metal. Wedding rings exist, unicorns do not. Yet both have essences. So essence and existence are independent in general. But if we reflect on the status of a necessary being, then Greek thought generally was inclined to hold that the essence of such a being entailed its existence. For example, if it were both necessary and perfect then not to exist would be an imperfection.

The upshot of all this is an account of how God is both necessary and One, while the universe that emanated from him is both contingent and Multiple.

The Problem of Free Action

Faith versus reason

The debates on this subject seem to have begun in a way with which we will become increasingly familiar, the clash between reason and divine authority. Some had argued that what is right and wrong is decided by reason, others that it is already fixed by the authority of the Koran. As we shall see, the schism between faith and reason is also to be found in Christianity. Similar problems emerged in both religious traditions: for example, how is human freedom *possible*? Faith declares that it must be, since God treats us as morally responsible for our actions. Reason declares it cannot be, since God foresees what each person will do in the universe he himself created. Furthermore it seems that the states of the material world, in which we live as embodied beings, are fully determined by causal laws. Our actions are realized in states of the material world. How could they be freely chosen, since that would presuppose that they might have been other than they were?

This issue is connected with the problem of evil. If God wills everything in the World, and there is evil in the World, then he must have willed that evil. The solution, according to al-Qudat (Nasr and Leaman, 1996: 413) is to reinterpret this remark into something like this: "Evil is like medicine, evil in appearance but good in reality." We do not see God's benevolence and justice, so we do not see how what appears to us to be evil must be for good.

Occasionalism

Did God create the world and leave it to evolve of its own accord? Or is he actively maintaining the flow of cause and effect into which human actions must fit? How is God involved in the world as the determination of his will? Islamic philosophers were inclined to reserve the power to act to God, leaving material things quite inert. If we take it as a principle that material things have no natural activity, then how do we account for such phenomena as the transfer of motion from a moving body that collides with one which is stationary. One solution which was popular among Islamic philosophers, and was revived in the seventeenth century in the Christian West, was "occasionalism." When a moving body strikes a stationary one, God sets the second in motion. The collision is an occasion for God to act. This account of causality reserves all causal activity to God. Similarly, when a material impulse acts on the sense organs of the human body, God creates a corresponding thought in the mind. How could there possibly be a place for human freedom to act otherwise than as the evolution of the world determined it, if the determining agent is God?

In every causal interaction God brings the effect into being. Al-Ghazālī argues (quoted in Nasr and Leaman, 1996)

> neither the existence nor the non-existence of the one is implied in the affirmation, negation, existence and non-existence of the other . . . Nor burning contact with fire, nor light sunrise . . . For the connexion of these things is based on a prior power of God to create them in a successive order. (from the *Incoherence of the Philosophers*, p. 316)

This doctrine has a familiar ring for those acquainted with modern Western philosophy. It is almost word for word the regularity account offered by David Hume. Al-Ghazālī uses the same argument to establish the non-necessity of causal sequences as we perceive them. There is no logical relation between the correlated states of affairs. The one can exist without the other, without contradiction.

We experience constant conjunctions, as a matter of fact. The reason for there to be such a conjunction is in the goodness of God.

Predestination

How did Islamic philosophers escape a slide into predestination (*qadar*)? The answer is that they did not. Orthodox Islam, from the earliest days of the Mohammedan era, favored predestination rather than free will as an account of the moral life. The philosophers, sometimes in actual peril of their lives, could not reconcile the idea of sin and judgment with the thesis of predestination. How could an act be a sin if it was predestined that it will occur? It seems as if the actor has no other role than to be the passive carrier of what will happen. So far as I can ascertain this debate was never resolved. The tendency seems to have been to fall back on an assertion of divine authority, abandoning the hopeless philosophical project of resolving the impasse. For example, in the nineteenth century, M. 'Abdu (born in 1849 in Egypt) insisted that the Koran had extensively asserted the reality of free will and the actual divine governance of the universe in every detail. Instead of seeking a philosophical resolution of the impasse that this seems to entail, he also claimed that Mahomet had rejected fatalism. A true Mohammedan does not sit about waiting for what is predestined to happen. What is predestined is what he or she will decide to do. Are we any further forward from this sophism in contemporary Western thought? I do not think so.

The Problem of Salvation

Salvation by union, contact, or conjunction with God

According to Ibn Sīnā, salvation came from union with God. But, as Aristotle argues in *Metaphysics* 19, "The Necessary Existent cannot be united with something in a reciprocal union." It can be united only with itself. In self-contemplation the Necessary existent has the greatest pleasure, since this is to contemplate perfection. Union with a lesser spirit would make that impossible. Therefore if salvation *is* by union with God, he must be in contact or conjunction with something which is also the Necessary Existent. This looks like another impasse, from which philosophy can offer no escape. A human soul could not become God, nor could it rise to the status of a comparable Necessary Existent, since there can be none other than God. It seems unlikely that Ibn Sīnā could ever have gone to so far as to presuppose that the contemplative person can become God. Even if there were to be an immolation of the self, the Soul can never be God. Just as the Indian philosophers of the second millennium had to struggle to make sense of the self-immolating union of the soul with God, *and* the survival of personal identity, so too did the Islamic philosophers. Ibn Sīnā made what must surely be the only move open. In order for such a union to be possible there must be something God-like in the character of the Soul. Ibn Sīnā does say that

> the powers of intelligence stand by themselves and lack motion. They resemble, moreover, the being of the Necessary Existent . . . there is no relation between the faculty of perception and the faculty of intelligence. (Ibn Sīnā, 1050 [1983]: 73)

Ibn Sīnā offers an ingenious account of how this might be possible. The faculty of perception separates the perceiver and the perceived. In the faculty of intelligence, that which thinks and that which is thought about are united. So it is through the faculty of intelligence that union with the divine can be achieved. By perception we experience particular things in which matter and Form are united. By intelligence we contemplate the Forms alone.

However ingenious Ibn Sīnā's Aristotelian argument is, and how cleverly it links this issue with the immortality of the Soul as an Intelligence, these analyses and explanations are treated with some skepticism. This was, indeed, as we shall see, the reaction of al-Ghazālī, and many less inclined to take philosophy seriously.

TRADITIONALISTS' PHILOSOPHICAL ATTACK ON PHILOSOPHY

To understand how the problems of emanation, of free will, and of salvation drifted out of the framework of the hard-edged, analytical Aristotelian tradition into mysticism we need to look at the immensely important Sufi tradition, which is still alive in the twentieth century. It is from that tradition that the deepest problems about the route to and the nature of salvation arose. The sternest critic of the Aristotelian Neoplatonists was al-Ghazālī, but to understand how his criticisms were linked to Islam in general we will need to look at the powerful cult of Sufism. Though Sufism predates the turn of the millennium, its most historically important advocate and sometime practitioner, al-Ghazālī, sets the tone for much of what followed in the next millennium. We shall return to study his attack on the Neoplatonic/Aristotelian or

Greek-influenced philosophical stance of such as Ibn Sīnā after we have traced the outlines of the Sufist point of view.

Sufism

The key ideas and principles of the Sufi mystical tradition are easily set down, as indeed were those of the Indian mystical tradition, to which they bear more than a passing resemblance.

1. Abandon the worldly and the temporal to reduce oneself to a condition of nonbeing, an idea in the mind of God.
2. A mystic cultivates a series of stations on the journey to fellowship with God through one's own endeavour,[1] which are matched by a "series of states (*ahwal*) with which God might favour him" (Fakhry, 1983: 239).

The result of these practices is the restoration of the soul to its original union with God, a union that preexists the earthly life.

Scholars disagree on how far the Sufi tradition should be seen as indigenous to Islam. The case against turns on the question of whether the Koran countenances practices which transcend the teaching mission of Islam and respect for Islamic law, establishing a direct relation with God. Summing up the debate, Fakhry (1983: 241) points out that there is warrant in the Koran for the practices of austerity and of meditation on God. Yet some Sufis did come into conflict with Islam, for example, over celibacy. The mystical life was not compatible with marriage, and yet Mahomed was himself married, and included many detailed rules for the proper management of relations between the sexes.

Respecting the Sufi route to God, and at the same time thoroughly imbued with the spirit of the philosopher, al-Ghazālī represents the highest synthesis of the experiential and the rational in Islamic thought.

Al-Ghazālī

Many would regard al-Ghazālī as the foremost philosopher in the Islamic tradition. He was born in 1058 at Tūs in Khurāsān, once part of the Persian empire. This town was noted for its vigorous intellectual life. Orphaned as a child, he was brought up by a Sufi guardian, studying the usual syllabus of sacred texts. He studied mostly in his home town, but did occasionally venture forth, as I recounted at the head of this chapter. He became disenchanted with the dogmatism of the orthodox, while yet unwilling to commit himself wholly to the path of reason, unlike the Greek-inspired Ibn Sīnā. He advocated the Sufi principle of direct awareness of God. The pattern of his career was soon established. He was appointed to the chair of theology at the main college in Baghdad by Nizam-al-Mulk. But he suddenly abandoned the post, withdrawing to a life of meditation and private study. He was enticed back into teaching several times, slipping away again and again, twice to his home town of Tūs, where he died in 1111.

Problems with the Greek inheritance

Established as a powerful critic of the Neoplatonic/Aristotelianism of Ibn Sīnā, al-Ghazālī was also a prominent Sufi. He was particularly scornful of the Neoplatonic solution to the problem of emanation, a solution which he declared to be nothing but fantasy. However, he made great use of the powers of Aristotelian logic, writing a famous textbook on the subject.

There are three routes to knowledge, according to al-Ghazālī. Faith, *īmān*, is the lowest. In support of this level of knowledge one can do no more than cite authorities. There is that which comes from the use of reason, scientific knowledge, *'ilm*. But there is a higher form of knowledge, that which comes by immediate experience, *dhawq*. By turning away from the seductions of this world the properly prepared person can achieve unmediated experience of God.

What do we learn? That God is One. And in so doing we might be thought to have lost our identity, because we have become one with him. In what sense am I still an individual? In India Rāmānuja was tackling the same question at about the same time. A strict Aristotelian is likely to be unsympathetic to the traditional orthodox resolution common to Christianity and Islam, that individuality is not just a matter of the soul, but also of the body, resurrected at the end of time. Aristotle had argued that only the intellect is spiritual, and therefore immortal. If this is so, then immortality is impersonal, since intellectual apprehension is only of universals, not particulars.

Recollecting that Ibn Sīnā purported to have solved one aspect of the problem of emanation by declaring that God knows only universals, not particulars, and of the problem of how the human soul can unite with God, by emphasizing the universal character of the intellect, it is not surprising that this doctrine is prominent among those criticized by al-Ghazālī.

The deepest philosophical issue turned on the Koranic remark (34,3) that "nothing, however minute, escapes God's notice." Ibn Sīnā had argued for an interpretation of the idea that God knew only the universal, thus accounting for the possibility that the world could be an emanation from God, but also other than God. This seemed flatly contrary to the remark in the Koran. If God notices the most minute of matters he must notice not only universals (Forms) but also particulars, the material instantiations of Forms, not only spadeness but spades. Philosophy could not revise Koranic doctrine, which, after all, was a divine revelation through the person of Mahomet. Philosophy then must make the Koran intelligible and coherent. God's knowledge, according to al-Ghazālī, is related to particulars which are in time and space. While these relations can change, their changes do not entail that God's essence as the knower changes. How could knowledge of the changing world be held by a being which did not change? There seems to be no answer in the writings of al-Ghazālī. It must be so.

Reconciling Sufi practice with philosophical analysis

The positive philosophy of al-Ghazālī is rooted in the technique of reflexive attention, gaining knowledge of the self. "Knowledge of self is the key to knowledge of God," he says (al-Ghazālī: ca. 1105 [1958]: 5). How do we know that it is the angelic qualities that constitute man's essence? It is because the essence of a creature is whatever is highest in it. The Prophet had said "He who knows himself knows God," echoing the remark above, but how? The argument runs as follows:

> When a man considers himself he knows that there was a time when he was non-existent, as it is written in the Koran "Does it not occur to man that there was a time when he was nothing" . . . Whatever degree of perfection he may have arrived at, he did not make himself. (al-Ghazālī, ca. 1100 [1983]: 15)

The issue of how one knows God loomed large in al-Ghazālī's writings. The use of reason, as it had been advocated by philosophers such as Ibn Sīnā, seemed to al-Ghazālī not only to obscure the way to God but actually to lead to heresy. How was one to enter into genuine communion and yet adhere to the tenets of Islam?

In an important and influential passage he reverses the direction of the search for God. Rather than finding him by the use of reason we are found by him. Quoted by E. L. Daniel in the preface to al-Ghazālī (ca. 1100 [1983]), *The Deliverance from Error*, we have the following:

> Whoever claims that theology, abstract proofs, and systematic classification are the foundation of belief is an innovator. Rather is belief a light which God bestows on the hearts of His creatures as the gift and bounty from Him, sometimes through an explainable conviction from within, sometimes because of a dream in sleep, sometimes by seeing the state of bliss of a pious man and the transmission of his light through association and conversation with him, sometimes through one's own state of bliss.

The eternity of the world

There remained a further troubling aspect of Aristotelianism, the vexed question of the eternity of the world. Though Aristotle does not claim to have settled the matter, he argues that there is no proof one way or the other. Ibn Sīnā had come up with an ingenious solution, but it raised the even more fundamental problem of the status of particulars, individual beings, with respect to God's knowledge of the world. The world is a product of divine action. It is thereby linked to God, and hence, without beginning and end. However, there is a difference between a temporally finite world of particulars and the eternity of God. The world partakes of eternity only in the divine sense. To al-Ghazālī, this logic-chopping only served to discredit the authority of philosophers to pronounce on matters of religion (Urvoy, 1991: 99).

The mystical turn

Sufis hoped for direct knowledge of God, and as a complement, they aimed for a way of life conducive to fulfilling that hope. This was one of the most basic sources of conflict between them and the Mullahs, the priesthood. The Sufis claimed that they alone had the answer to the problem of achieving union with God, and that it came from the authority of the sacred texts. It was these two aspects of Sufism, taken together, that al-Ghazālī saw as the grounds for his own efforts to provide a rigorous ground for Sufism in the Koran and associated literature. Thus Sufi knowledge of God was unmediated (*dhawq*) and they were the very men who lived the most virtuous of lives. They could not be accused of backsliding from the strict tenets of Islam.

Al-Ghazālī's doctrine of salvation is mystical. Union with God can be achieved by the route advocated by the Sufis. The reconciliation with Koranic Law is through the idea of the virtuous life, without which the meditative methods of approach to union would be ineffective, since God must reach out to meet those who seek him. But this is presented in contrast to the Neoplatonism of al-Fārābi and Ibn Sīnā. For them progress toward becoming one with the divine must be through the intellect as one of the intelligible substances, which, looked at from the opposite angle, are the stages of emanation. Thus for the Neoplatonist "Aristotelians" there is a fundamental unity between emanation and salvation.

THE JEWISH CONTRIBUTION TO
MEDIEVAL PHILOSOPHY

Unlike Christianity and Islam, Judaism's period of intense philosophical self-scrutiny was not prolonged. However, in the twelfth century it did produce one of the great philosophers of the medieval period, Moses Maimonides (1135–1204). Almost single-handedly he undertook the task of reconciling Judaic faith and reason with the tools of Aristotelian philosophy. The work of Maimonides touches on all the major themes that emerged in both Islamic and Christian philosophy as the problems of finding a rational interpretation and basis for divine revelations were tackled.

Jewish philosophy has always been closely tied to Christianity and Islam. The problem Maimonides tackled was the same problem that was tackled by Islamic philosophers, in more or less the same era of the second millennium, namely how to reconcile the preeminence given to the intellect by the great Greek philosophers with the authoritative deliverances of the holy books. This problem has been stated with great exactitude by Bokser (1950: 1).

> Moses ben Maimon . . . was the mediator between two seemingly incompatible world views – the Greek and the rabbinic. Out of ancient Greece there had come the claim of the intellect to sole competence in leading a man to the truth about himself and the world . . . all this was negated by the world view of rabbinical Judaism which warned man that reason was but a frail reed to lean on, that only in divinely revealed Scripture was he to find a dependable truth, and that by conformity to divine law alone would he find true happiness.

Maimonides' origins were Spanish. He was born in the vigorous and beautiful city of Córdoba. Dynastic wars in the Islamic world spelled trouble for Jews. In the face of threats of persecution his family travelled along the Mediterranean shore of Africa to Egypt, where they finally settled. Trained as a physician, he had a meteoric career. He become the personal physician to the Sultan Saladin himself. Somehow he found time for his philosophical studies, which culminated in one of the great works of medieval thought, his *Guide for the Perplexed*. This major work was begun in 1185 and finished about 1200. Interestingly it was written in Arabic, but soon translated into the "philosophical" language of the West, Latin.

Though Maimonides wrote several commentaries on sacred texts, and an influential work on Jewish law, we shall focus on his effort to bring together Aristotelian philosophy with the Jewish tradition. The way he did this can be read as a kind of summary or exemplar of how, in both Islam and Christianity, Aristotelian philosophical concepts were used in working out the rational foundations of religious belief. Not surprisingly, his work excited much the same sort of response among Jews as had the works of Ibn Sīnā amongst the orthodox of Islam. It presumed to tread where no mere mortal should, on the sacred ground of divine revelation. It is not surprising to find the issue of bodily resurrection as one of the issues about which Maimonides was in trouble with the more orthodox among his coreligionists. Did he or did he not believe in it? He was forced in the end to write a separate treatise to defend himself against the charge that he did not.

The controversy flared up again after his death. It even led to a great burning of his books in France. Such is often the fate of those who set up the power of reason against the force of tradition and authority. However, there is usually a historical reversal of fortune. Maimonides is certainly held to be the most important Jewish philosopher and his great book one of the most perceptive philosophical works to come out of the tradition that includes Islam, Judaism, and Christianity, and their flirtation with the rationality of the Greeks.

Reason and its place in human life

Maimonides argues that reason is an endowment that is peculiar to human beings. Man is "only distinguished from the rest of the animal creation by the consciousness that he is a living being possessed of intellect."[2] Reason is necessary for practical life, since "the food which man requires for his subsistence demands much work and preparation, which can only be accomplished by reflection and plan." But reason is capable of higher levels of activity. And in this higher mode it is the source of science, established knowledge of the world of nature. Reason "analyzes and divides the component parts of things. It forms abstract ideas of them . . . It distinguishes what is the property of the genus from that which is peculiar to the individual, and it determines which properties are essential."

However, there is yet another level at which reason can achieve knowledge, and that is of the nature of God. But the result of coming to have such knowledge is love and awe. "At the time when he [the philosopher] reflects on His works, and His wonderful and stupendous creations, and from them perceives His wisdom which is incomparable and undoubted, he immediately loves, praises, glorifies and yearns with an ardent longing to know the great God." And, at the same time, knowing him overwhelms the mere human with awe. It was by following in the steps of Aristotle that all this could be accomplished.

How could this very positive and even aggressive attitude to the power of reason be reconciled with the traditional authority of scripture and those who interpreted it? The answer is really very simple. The education of a philosopher is hard and long. Most people are not capable of it, nor inclined to undertake it. Reason cannot possibly be the universal guide to knowledge and love of God. That is where the rabbinical tradition plays its part. By a quite other route it reaches the same terminus, but that route can be followed by anyone, under the guidance of those who are versed in scripture.

The limits of philosophy: plausibility and proof

Two vexed questions perhaps lie outside the domain of philosophy. The first is the question of the eternity or finitude of the universe. Reason cannot determine what is the true temporal status of the universe. "Therefore, when the mind endeavors to contemplate what is beyond, it is unable to do so for the matter is too high for it." Aristotle held to the eternity view, but he could never establish this as a final truth.

On the matter of the moral life, the very same considerations apply. Reason can support the plausibility of the Aristotelian mean, but it cannot establish it, nor indeed is the notion easily applied by ordinary people, who may have great difficulty determining where the mean between different attitudes, emotional responses, and even virtues might be. Finally, since reason works on what is given empirically, an ethics of reason would be at best a kind of critical compilation of the common opinions of people. Something more authoritative is required, and that is the sacred writings and the rabbinical tradition of their interpretation.

How can we prove the existence of God by reason? According to Maimonides, the answer lies in theoretical physics! Motion is not self-generating. There is motion, and so there must be a Final Cause of such motion, which is not itself in motion. This could only be God. However, there is a dangerous edge to this proof, as Bokser points out (Bokser, 1950: 26). One way of sustaining the analysis is by way of the assumption of the eternity of the universe, and thus of its motion. This must require an eternal First Mover. However, Maimonides knew how inflammatory the idea of an infinite universe was to the orthodox, and he carefully qualifies it as a hypothesis only.

On the issue of God's nature, Maimonides objected strongly to the anthropomorphism of popular and traditional conceptions of God. In just the same line of thinking as his Christian and Islamic contemporaries, Maimonides arrived at the same conclusion: God is incorporeal and unitary and depends on nothing but himself. God is not "in space," nor is he subject to time. Nor can we use any of the usual epithets such as power and wisdom to describe God. God's essence and his existence were the same, so that "God exists without possessing the attribute of existence." The nescience of this position is subtle. We can know nothing of God, and so, when we attribute such properties as omniscience, we do not know what that word means in this context. What properties we do assign to God can have only the meaning of negations, ruling out some way in which God is not.

We can hardly be surprised that the work of Maimonides brought a specifically Jewish tradition of philosophical reflection on religion very nearly to an end. With hardly a word changed we could be reading one of the great philosophers of either of the other traditions. Judaic philosophy entered into the mainstream of European thought. The influence of the *Guide* on St Thomas Aquinas is well known, and it can be felt in all the great philosophers of the medieval Latin West.

Maimonides belongs in the tradition in which Aristotelian philosophy was recruited in the interests of the exegesis of a religion enshrined in a sacred text, the Talmud. Jewish philosophy did not perish. Its fate was to be absorbed into the pattern of Western thought.

THE REVIVAL OF THE ARISTOTELIAN INFLUENCE

I have set out the story of Islamic philosophy in terms of the three themes of *emanation*, the movement from God to the World, of *free will*, human beings in relation to God in the World, and of *salvation*, the movement from the World to God. But behind these debates lies a deeper rift in Islamic thought. What is the relation between philosophy and the sacred or authoritarian texts? Clearly Ibn Sīnā, for example, saw the role of Greek philosophy as a tool for the interpretation of the Koran and the *Traditions of Mahomet*. Metaphors could be untangled, anthropomorphic images such as "God sitting on his throne" could be rendered abstract, and so on. Against this attitude were ranged the literalists who were happy to take the Koran as it appeared to be, as the repository of unvarnished truth, and so not in need of any interpretation. Philosophical truth and revealed truth must, according to such as Ibn Sīnā, form a single web. Revealed truth always trumped the dictates of reason, according to the literalists.

Ibn Rushd and the Return to the Aristotelian Texts

Into this controversy came the greatest of Islamic Aristotelians, the Spaniard, Ibn Rushd (1126–98) or, as he is known in the Latin tradition, Averroes. He was born of a very well established family in Córdoba in 1126. He had an excellent education, not only in the Muslim classics, but also in philosophy, general Arabic literature, and in science. The situation of philosophy and philosophers at that time in Andalus was somewhat equivocal. During the previous regime the authorities had discouraged all but legal thought. With the overthrow of that regime by the Alhomades, by 1168, Abū Ya'quūb, the second in that succession, encouraged philosophy. Indeed it was he who commissioned Ibn Rushd to write the commentaries on Aristotle for which he became so well known. Ibn Rushd spent ten years in Seville working on the commentaries. In 1181 he took the post of *qādi* or governor of Córdoba, which he declared to be a great distraction from his real work. However, his later years were clouded by the persecution of philosophy and philosophers instituted by the third ruler in the Alhomadian succession, Abū Ibn Yūsuf. Ibn Rushd died in 1198.

His philosophical work was an exercise in balance. As Fakhry puts it (1983: 277), "Ibn Rushd is fully committed to the infallibility of the Koran . . . but he is also equally committed to the postulate of the unity of truth." What he does is to return to the texts of Aristotle, to find there the "correct" interpretation of that philosopher, which, when applied to the problems of understanding the Koran, will yield the "correct" interpretation of the sacred works as well. What must go is the Neoplatonic twist given to Aristotelian philosophy by al-Fārābi and Ibn Sīnā.

Famous for his commentaries on Aristotle, he is important for our purposes for his intervention in the debate about the relation between philosophy and scripture.

According to Ibn Rushd, divine creation takes place like any other form of creation, by the bringing together of matter and form. What is potential becomes actual. The Intelligences that power the heavens are generated from God by self-contemplation, and though they are not God, they must represent and therefore share at least some of His attributes.

At a deeper level yet, Ibn Rushd criticized Ibn Sīnā's separation of essence and existence. The thesis that the former is prior to the latter cannot be sustained. The real existence of something is necessary to the conceiving of its essence in actuality. Analyzing the essence of something as an intellectual exercise tells us nothing, since it can be done without any assumptions of existence.

To give the flavor of his meticulous exegesis of Aristotelian texts I will begin with a passage in which he lays out the characteristics of the two kinds of substances, noneternal and eternal:

> . . . he [Aristotle] begins this book [*Metaphysics* Lambda] with the principles of the non-eternal substance . . . After that, he begins to explain the principles of the eternal substance . . . Its being substance, first form and first end; then he enquires into this immovable substance, whether it is one or many, and if they are many, then what is the one to which they ascend, and what is the hierarchy of this multiplicity in relation to it? (Ibn Rushd, ca. 1140 [1984]: 75 [])

Here are the familiar themes of unity and diversity, and of the hierarchy that the Neoplatonists identified, with good Aristotelian support, as the Intelligences. In the next passage we have Ibn Rushd's formulation of a sketch of the doctrine of the higher Intelligences. The underlying presupposition, of course, is that the heavenly bodies must be self-moving since there is no visible cause of their motion. They must move in ways analogous to the way in which the other kind of self-moving being moves, namely humans.

> These celestial bodies have souls and of the powers of the world, they have only intellect and the faculty of desire . . . that imparts to them local motion. (Ibn Rushd [1984]: [1594])

Now to the all-important matter of the nature of God.

> If God's pleasure in apprehending his own essence is equal to the pleasure we feel when our intellect apprehends its own essence, that is in the instant in which it is freed from potentiality, and if that which belongs to us for a short while belongs to God eternally, that is very wonderful. (Ibn Rushd, [1984]: [1618])

And in so far as it is greater than our pleasure, so much the more wonderful. The likeness to God in the mundane world that appears in this discussion of the power of the human intellect must be heavily qualified. The highest happiness must be the intellectual apprehension of the intelligibles. God is permanently in that state. We can reach it occasionally when we think of our own essence. But we must be careful not to assume that this "like" means "the same."

In a brief but telling criticism of the Christian interpretation of the Trinity, Ibn Rushd remarks that they confuse things which are conceptually distinct with things that are ontologically distinct. True, perhaps, that God is manifested in more than one way, and hence requires more than one distinct concept to express those manifestations. But that does not show that the being of God is anything else but a unity.

The three problems with the Greek inheritance

Ibn Rushd was faced with three bones of contention in his advocacy of Aristotelian philosophy as the support of Islam. How was the principle that God knows only universals, and not particulars, to be reconciled with Koranic pronouncements on God's attention to every individual and their acts? How was the Aristotelian argument against the finitude of the universe in time to be reconciled with the Koranic doctrine of a final moment of judgment when the world will end? Finally, how can the doctrine of the resurrection of the body be reconciled with the immateriality of the soul? Ibn Rushd never resolved these problems. Nor, be it said, did anyone else.

THE INFLUENCE OF ISLAM ON THE LATIN WEST

The influence of Islamic thought on the Latin West came about largely through the use of Arab and Moorish authors as the prime source for the doctrines of Aristotle during the early Middle Ages. In so far as the Islamic authors had given their own "spin" to Aristotle, so some of this appears in the authors they influenced. The two most important, whose influence I shall briefly sketch, were the two leading Muslim Aristotelians, Ibn Sīnā (Avicenna) and Ibn Rushd (Averroes).

The Aristotelians

Ibn Sīnā's commentary on Aristotle's *Metaphysics* set out a view about God and His creation in terms of the necessity of God's being and the mere possibility of everything else. Essence and existence were distinct except in the case of God. The passage from potentiality to actuality was contingent. Thus existence (that there is something) is to be distinguished from essence (the sort of thing it is). Existence is an accident. This position was discussed and generally criticized by medieval authors, of whom Aquinas is typical and certainly the most influential. The critics argued that essence and existence are related as potency and act, so that existence cannot be an accident, as if it were just another property that a being could have or lack. Ibn Rushd also criticized Ibn Sīnā on this issue.

We have seen how meticulous were the expositions of Aristotle's philosophical doctrines and analyses that Ibn Rushd had carried out. His works served as a major source of Aristotelian scholarship in both Paris and Oxford from about 1220, and continued to play a major role until the end of the Middle Ages (Marenbon, 1996). At the same time he also suffered the anathema of being associated with a controversial view on the nature of the question of the "unity of the potential intellect." This curious debate was distinguished as much by the vituperative tone of the protagonists as the outré character of the issue. Bearing in mind that the world is brought into being by intellect, the material intellect is at a low level in the hierarchy of beings, such that it can be realized in particular individuals by instantiation in matter. It is also that which is active in individual human beings as a Form. So how can there be individual minds? What is the status of the potential intellect as an actual individual mind? According to the doctrine of forms, it should be a unity. The potential intellect must be one and eternal. This seems to cut right across the fundamental doctrinal point of the individuality of the human soul. "The wise find their happiness in being the subject in which wisdom actualises itself" (Nasr and Leaman,

1996: 342). This issue became the source of the violent attacks on Averroism that began to mount in the time of Aquinas. Needing a philosophical foundation for personal identity in the identity of the soul, he explicitly denied the unity of the potential intellect, the intellect that awaited realization in matter, so to say, to serve as the mind of an individual.

Ibn Rushd's influence then was equivocal. As the foremost expositor of Aristotle's philosophy and an influential commentator on the Aristotelian writings, he played an essential and positive part in the development of philosophy in the Christian West. Yet his own philosophical achievements, running counter to a crucial component in Christian dogma, were the targets of ferocious criticism.

THE LATER HISTORY OF ISLAMIC THOUGHT

I think it fair to say that nothing that has appeared in the more recent history of Islamic philosophy has the stature or influence of the writings of the four authors whose works we have become acquainted with, al-Fārābi, Ibn Sīnā, al-Ghazālī, and Ibn Rushd. Though there were considerable variations among their views on the great themes of emanation, free will, and salvation, they never doubted the necessary role of philosophy in the exegesis of revelation. At the same time there was a powerful reaction against philosophers meddling in theology. We must now turn to examine it more closely.

The Attack on the Philosophers

From the beginnings of Islamic philosophy there was a stream of anti-philosophers, traditionalists who rejected any attempt critically to interpret the sacred writings. Some simply asserted a literalist approach to the Koran and the *Traditions,* others used philosophical arguments to deflate the pretensions of the philosophers. Among the most important and influential was Ibn Taymiyah (1262–1327).

According to him, the only authorities on the interpretation of these writings are the Companions of Mahomet and their successors. The trouble has come from the methods that the philosophers have used, and in particular, from logic. There is no need to deconstruct metaphors since they are there for a purpose – the exposition of deep theological truths to ordinary people. But the main thrust of Ibn Taymiyah's polemic is against the two pillars of logical analysis, definition and syllogistic or formal reasoning.

The Aristotelian claim that non-self-evident truths are known through definitions brings the rejoinder that that claim is not itself self-evident, and would require proof. Such a proof would have to invoke yet other non-self-evident truths and so on. Furthermore definitions, he contends, can never advance our knowledge. They only express what we must already have known in order to construct a definition in the first place.

As for the vaunted Aristotelian method of demonstration, it can only yield knowledge of universals, which exist only in the mind. It cannot give us any knowledge of particulars, and so it can tell us nothing about God, the Supreme Particular. There is nothing else like God, so he does not instantiate a universal. Knowledge of God as the One comes only from revelation. There is no demonstrative knowledge of the existence or attributes of God.

It is but a short step from the literalism that accompanies the rejection of the attempts by philosophers to give a rational grounding to Islamic doctrine to the Fundamentalist movements of the end of the millennium that have emerged over the whole Islamic world.

Philosophy as Poetry: the Works of Rūmī

Jalāl al-Dīn Rūmī was born in Balkh in Persia in 1207 and died in 1273. Though he was the most famous of the Sufi poets, he was one among many who used poetry to express philosophical insights. I shall offer three Rūmī poems apropos of the three dominant themes of Islamic philosophy as it played its part in the interpretation of religion. The theme of all Sufi thought was unity. In Rūmī's images the unity between teacher and disciple presented an ideal of Platonic *mystical* love. His poetry expresses a powerful monism; behind the multiplicity and seeming confusion of the world as we perceive it, there lies a universal harmony, perceptible only through mystical experience. There is an ideal of the Perfect Man, who is in oneness with God. The poems quoted here are drawn from Rūmī (1997).

The unity theme

The Faithful are many, but their Faith is one; their bodies are numerous, but their soul is one.

Besides the understanding and soul which is in the ox and the ass, man has another intelligence and soul.

Again, in the owner of the Divine breath, there is a soul other than the human soul.

The animal soul does not possess oneness: do not seek oneness from that airy spirit.

If its owner eats bread, his neighbour is not filled; if he bear a load, his neighbour does not become laden;

Nay, but he rejoices at his neighbour's death and dies of envy when he sees his neighbour prosperous.

The souls of wolves and dogs are separate; the souls of the Lions of God are united.

I speak nominally of their souls in the plural, for that single Soul is a hundred in relation to the body,

Just as the single light of the sun in heaven is a hundred in relation to the house-courts on which it shines;

But when you remove the walls, all those scattered lights are one and the same.

When the bodily houses have no foundation remaining, the Faithful remain one soul.

In this poem the theme of the synthesis of overt multiplicity in true unity is expressed very clearly. With it goes another doctrine, the unity of the human soul, which is diversified in individual people, which, as we have seen, caused a great deal of trouble for the reputation of Averroes when it was broached in Christendom.

Freedom of action

God hath placed a ladder before us: we must climb it step by step.

You have feet: why pretend to be lame? You have hands: why conceal the fingers that grip?

> Freedom is the endeavour to thank God for his Beneficence; your
> necessitarianism denies that Beneficence.
> Thanksgiving for the power of acting freely gives you more power to
> thank him; necessitarianism takes away what God has given.
> The brigands are on the road: do not sleep until you see the gate and
> the threshold.
> If you put trust in God, trust him with your work. Sow the seed,
> then rely upon the almighty.

As I remarked earlier, the Sufis were impatient with the philosophical
impasse that made freedom impossible in a world where all was foreseen by the God who created it. Here we have the blunt assertion that
freedom is given.

Salvation as unity with God

> I died as a mineral and became a plant,
> I died as plant and rose to animal,
> I died as animal and I was Man.
> Why should I fear? When I was less by dying?
> Yet once more I shall die as Man, to soar
> With angels blest; but even from angelhood
> I must pass on: *all except God doth perish.*
> When I have sacrificed my angel-soul,
> I shall become what no mind e'er conceived,
> Oh, let me not exist! For Non-existence
> Proclaims in organ tones, "To him we shall return."

This poem is in many ways astonishing. It echoes the Hindu conception of the cycle of rebirths through different levels of the natural
world. It explicitly accepts the dissolution of self in oneness with God.
It is a paean of praise for deliverance rather than salvation.

The Attempt at a Synthesis of Islamic and Modern Western Philosophy

I propose to illustrate the flavor of the modernist trend in Islam that
appeared at the end of the second millennium by drawing from the
works of Mohammad Iqbal. Born in 1877 at Sialkot in what is now

Pakistan, then a province of British India, Mohammad Iqbal was educated at Government College, Lahore, and subsequently at Trinity College, Cambridge. He took his doctorate at the University of Munich. In the course of all this he managed to complete his studies for the English bar. He was influenced in a general way by Kantian philosophy, but more particularly by the work of Henri Bergson on the nature of time. He held various jobs on his return to India. He was a professor at Government College for a while, and then undertook an active legal career. Somewhat lacking in success in this career, he made a living from his writing. His eminence in philosophy and literature was recognized by the Raj and he was knighted in 1930. Consciously seeking a new strategy for Islamic philosophy, Iqbal published his major work under the title *The Reconstruction of Religious Thought in Islam* (Iqbal, 1934). He was drawn into politics, and has been credited with the first statement of the two-nation theory, from which the partition of Pakistan from India came. Never in good health in his later years, he died in Lahore in 1938.

His reconstructions are based on three interconnected principles:

1.   There are three fundamentally different kinds of beings that one might study; inanimate, living, and minds. The attempts that have been made to study these kinds of things are linked to three areas of experience which have given rise to three groups of sciences, the physical, the biological, and the psychological. Iqbal regarded psychology as just one among a group of mind-studies, others being, for example, theology and the striving for mystical experience. The total picture of the world that we get from all three is what Iqbal calls "religion."

2.   It is proper for an individual to be active. Blind obedience to fate taken as the will of God cannot offer any theoretical grounds for the hope of immortality, nor is the belief in predestination which is supposed to support the acceptance of *Qsmet*, or fate, supported by experience in any of the three realms.

3.   All three kinds of things that we can study are changing from what they were into something else. The world, the animate creation, *and* God are changing. Mahomet was the last prophet, not because he gave a final description of the three realms of experience, but because he recommended a method of enquiry that enables a day-to-day record of changes to be kept.

The metaphysical background to all this very radical doctrine is supplied by a theory of time. For Iqbal, though there are three arenas of experience and three root sciences, only physics has given us a theory of time. The most developed form of this theory is A. N. Whitehead's treatment, for whom "Nature is not a static fact in an a–dynamic void, but a structure of events possessing the character of continuous creative flow, which thought cuts up into isolated immobilities out of whose mutual relations arise the concepts of space and time" (Iqbal, 1934: 33). This point of view, however satisfying as a physical explanation of a certain kind of temporal experience, cannot serve as a complete philosophical theory, for it concerns only one of the three "regions of Reality." Iqbal says, "Time as a free creative movement has no meaning for the theory. It does not pass, events do not happen (on this theory), we simply meet them" (Iqbal, 1934: 37). For a complete theory we must turn to the other levels of experience.

Iqbal argues that there must be two selves making up each person, the efficient and the appreciative self. The efficient self, likened to the Kantian transcendental unity of apperception, apprehends the *succession* of impressions. The appreciative self, available only to deep introspection, makes available "appreciative time," a changeless now. This experience cannot be described because that would involve categories available only in serial time. The appreciative self is not a passive recipient of experiences, it is creative. We make not only our percepts but our moral and political ends as well.

This scheme is put to work to tackle one of the problems we have found endemic to Islamic philosophical theology: the nature of God and his relation to the creation. According to Iqbal, God must be capable of change. But this is not the serial change of one thing giving way to another, but appreciative change. We can experience God only as we serialize those aspects of his being which he holds in intimate, contemporary suspension, appreciatively. Thus in God there is always that which was, is, and will be held in appreciative suspension. For us who must experience him serially, and looked at from the point of view of our efficient selves, God is creative. But looked from the point of our appreciative selves given by deep introspection, he is complete, existing all at once. Here is another doctrine of emanation, but of a very different kind from the Neoplatonism of Ibn Sīnā. It is all contained, so to say, within the possibilities of human experience.

Prophets appear one by one, serially, but each adds to our appreciative grasp of God's being. Thus there will be successive revelations as humankind serializes its apprehension of God.

From there it is a short step to a resolution of the problem of freedom in a universe in which God has foreseen all. "No doubt," says Iqbal (1934: 75) "the emergence of egos endowed with the power of spontaneous and hence unforeseeable action, is, in a sense, a limitation of the freedom of the all-inclusive Ego. But this limitation is not externally imposed. It is born out of God's creative freedom, whereby he has chosen finite egos to be participants of his life, power and freedom."

Finally one must mention Iqbal's strikingly original account of the conditions of immortality. It is an achievement. One creates oneself at the same time as one experiences God's creation serially, while appreciatively transcending it. The study of the sciences would be a positive advantage in the creation of the immortal self, combined with the deep entry into the appreciative self, the way of mystical experience. It is no surprise to learn that Iqbal greatly admired and revered Rūmī, the man and his writings.

Conclusion

The history of Islamic philosophy can be seen as an interplay between three sources of authority – the sacred texts, the direct apprehension of God through mystical practices such as those advocated by the Sufis, and the deliverances of the use of reason as it is manifested in Greek philosophy, variously understood. There were three great problems: How is emanation of the Many from the One possible? How could there be free action in a Divinely ordered and created world? How is personal salvation possible in a throughgoing union with God? They were subjected to treatment on the basis of all three sources of authority. It seems to me that, despite the best efforts of representatives of all of these, no consensus as to the grounds of revealed doctrine has ever been achieved in Islam, except a shared acceptance of the divine origins of the Koran itself.

The questions that trouble us about the nature of the cosmos and its human inhabitants are answered by Islam in one potent statement:

"The cosmos and its inhabitants are an emanation from God." On the question of what we can know of that cosmos and how we should treat one another, Islamic philosophy equivocated among three answers: "From the text of the Book"; "From the interpretations of the Book"; and "From the meaning of the Book as it is revealed in direct apprehension of the Divine."

I turn now to the parallel story of philosophy in the medieval West. There too the authority of revealed religion was both opposed to and supported by the work of the philosophers.

NOTES

1   There were female mystics in the Islamic tradition just as there were in Christianity. We could match Rabi'ah al-'Adawiyah with Teresa of Avila.
2   All the translations in this section are from Bokser (1950: 17–23).

Philosophy in Medieval Europe

To the consternation of his noble family, Thomas, the seventh son of the Count of Aquino, decided to join the mendicant order of the Dominicans. To keep the lad away from the influence of his family, who were intent on dissuading him from joining such a socially dubious group, the Dominican General set off with him for Paris.

> His mother got news of this, took counsel with two of the young man's brothers and determined to waylay the party. The good friars were stopped at a place north of Rome; Thomas was seized and carried off on horseback to Roccasecca. The friars could not attempt a rescue – they were fortunate to escape scot-free – so Thomas was kept a close prisoner for more than a year and every means tried, short of violence, to shake his vocation. They even went so far as to introduce a young woman, dressed in the most alluring style, into his chamber. The effect was to stir the young giant, but not as they expected. On waking and seeing the girl, he snatched a brand from the fire, chased her out of the room, and then scorched the sign of the cross on the door . . . He remained on affectionate terms with his family . . . With his eldest sister, Marotta, he had long and intimate talks, and in the end, instead of her persuading him to abandon his religious habit, he inspired her to become a nun of St Benedict . . . Even his mother changed her mind . . . and helped him to escape. (D'Arcy, 1930: 35)

Eventually he reached Paris. There he had the great good fortune to be able to study with Albert the Great. We know this young man as St Thomas Aquinas, the greatest of all Christian philosophers. His massive works, the *Summa Theologiae* and the *Summa Contra Gentiles* are, indeed, the high points of Christian philosophy of medieval and perhaps of all other times.

THE CHRISTIAN TRADITION

Creating an Orthodoxy

The main theme of philosophy in medieval Europe and for the 500 years that succeeded the first millennium is simply stated: to make sense of Christian doctrine and find a rational foundation and justification for it. In the first millennium Christian thought was mainly directed toward the building of an orthodoxy. This required the establishment of a body of agreed doctrines. It also required the condemnation of the unorthodox. These complementary acts were the business of the deliberations of the various major councils of the Church. For example, at the Council of Nicea (325) the Nicene Creed was established and the teachings of Arius were discussed and condemned. The debate turned on whether Christ was of the same substance or only a similar substance to God. The conservatives won, and ever after it has been dogma that Christ was of the same substance as God; witness the phrase in the Nicene Creed, "being of one substance with the Father." The acts of censure were no less important, since they had the effect of silencing those who proposed alternatives to orthodoxy. For example, at Ephesus in 431 Nestor was condemned for teaching that Christ was of two substances, a material and a divine, united in the one person. This condemnation did not stick. At the Council of Chalcedon, a few years later, the Nestorians triumphed, when the council upheld the dual nature of Christ. Orthodoxy and heresy need one another. Historians sometimes call this period the era of the Fathers of the Church.

Though there were influential theologians with a philosophical bent during the first millennium, for instance, Origen (185–253), Boethius (480–524), and John Scotus Erigena (ca. 830–ca. 877), I think it would be generally agreed that there was only one great philosopher, St Augustine (354–430). The issue that so dominated Islamic philosophy, how to balance faith and reason, had already surfaced in the first mil-lennium among Christian thinkers. Augustine's quip, *Credo ut intelligam,* "I believe in order that I may understand," was often repeated by those who favored the path of reason over that of blind faith. The main weight of Christian philosophy, driven by the same forces as drove the Muslim philosophers, developed after the millennial moment. We find its beginnings a little later than the corresponding movement appeared in Islamic thought.

The Conundrums of Religion

From the very beginning Christianity, like Islam, was built around the juxtapositon of seemingly incompatible principles. Perhaps the most vexing, because the most directly applicable to the problems of every-day life, was this: God created the world in space and in time, and the people who inhabit it. How can it be demanded that people as creatures of God be held responsible for their own actions? These antithetical principles can already be found in this well-known passage from the Acts of the Apostles, 17: 22–31. St Paul is addressing the Athenians. He begins by praising their enthusiasm for religion. He then goes on to say:

> For as I went through the city and looked carefully at the objects of your worship, I found among them an altar with the inscription "To an unknown god." What therefore you worship as unknown, this I proclaim to you. The God who made the world and everything in it, he who is Lord of heaven and earth, does not live in shrines made by human hands, nor is he served by human hands as if he needed anything, since he himself gives to all mortals life and breath and all things . . . "In him we live and move and have our being" . . . While God has overlooked the times of human ignorance, now he commands all people everywhere to repent, because he fixed a day on which he will have the world judged in righteousness by a man he has appointed, and of this he has given assurance to all by raising him from the dead.

Here we have the two major presumptions of Christianity as a cosmic and moral system:

1. God made the world and everything that is in it, including the people. In him they live, move, and have their being.
2. Eventually everyone will be judged on the moral quality of their lives. It seems we can choose to repent if we so will.

Taken together, these two propositions seem to lead to an insoluble conundrum. If we live, move, and have our being in God, how can it be that any of his creations should be held morally accountable for what they have done? If God made them, is he not morally responsible for what they are and what they do?

That these problems can even be formulated presupposes a resolution of a deeper epistemological and metaphysical issue. What can *we* learn about the nature and existence of God? With what concepts could we try to express such knowledge if we can have it? Whatever answers we give to these questions must confront the riddle we have already seen as a central theme in Islamic philosophy. If God is a perfect, unchanging unity, the One, how can he bring about a world which is patently enormously diverse, constantly changing and imperfect, the Many? How can the world and its inhabitants have such a degree of independence one from another and both from God that the very idea of moral responsibility can make sense? So there are two problems. How can the One engender the Many? And how can people truly be free in a divinely ordained universe?

We have seen how the problem of unity in diversity was tackled by Islamic philosophers, presented with much the same seeming paradox. But for Christianity the issue was more complicated since a special place had to be found for the Trinity, God in three persons. To forge a divine unity from God the Son, God the Father, and God the Holy Spirit within a coherent account of the ontology of the divine was profoundly troubling. Jesus is not just a man, but God incarnate. The Holy Spirit is not just a messenger of the High God, a kind of diaphanous Mercury, but also God. If God is One how can he also be Three? On the one hand, these problems are theological, a matter of how they should be expounded and interpreted, given that they are believed by Christians to be true. On the other hand, they are philosophical, or at least are dependent on philosophical presuppositions upon which the rationality of Christian doctrine would depend. Philosophers can question the coherence of the principle doctrines of Christianity, one with another and within the whole frame of human discourses.

The Alliance with Aristotle

Most of the philosophical problems that arise in trying to support faith by reason were very similar to those faced by the Islamic philosophers, who had first tried to bring reason to bear on revelation. The Christian West looked to the same source for the philosophical tools to try to solve these questions: the works of Aristotle. They arrived in medieval Europe in much the same sort of sporadic way that they had reached the intellectual centers of Islam.

I shall divide the discussion in this chapter into three main sections. One will cover medieval attempts to deal with the nature and existence of God. The second will be concerned with the deepest question of human life: How is the moral accountability of human conduct possible in a world in which everything that happens is foreseen by the God who created it? Each of these main themes spins off technical philosophical problems, such as the nature of universals, and we shall pause from time to time to reflect upon the medieval treatment of them. The third section will cover the fourteenth-century reaction against the whole program of trying to ground faith in reason. It is of great philosophical interest because the grounds for the radical separation of theology and philosophy that were put forward by those who advocated the *via moderna* were philosophical. They were not a mere refusal, but rested on considerations that were subtle and profound. Just as the Muslims had al-Ghazālī, so the Christians had William of Ockham.

St Bernard of Clairvaux: The Scriptures are Enough

To get a sense of the climate from which the philosophical tradition in the Latin West took its start, the tradition we call "scholasticism," I will use the works of St Bernard of Clairvaux (1091–1153) as illustrations. His conservatism set him against the philosophers, particularly Abelard. His faith, he thought, was in no need of philosophical support or analysis. The sun and the times of the day provided him with a powerful set of images to express his mystical apprehension of God. "The dawn was the whole life of Christ on earth" and "O true noontide, fulness of warmth and light, trysting place of the sun, noontide that blots out the shadows" (St Bernard, 1990: 146) have a strong Neoplatonic ring to them.

The relation of the person to the cosmos (in the person of God) is, for St Bernard, expressible in the four stages of love: carnal (person to person), selfish (person to God for salvation's sake), love of God for the sake of God, and finally, intoxicated by love the spirit becomes nothing in itself in a full union with God. There is no place for philosophical work here. "The reason for loving God is God himself: and the measure of love due to him is immeasurable . . . Hence if one seeks for God's claim upon our love here is the chiefest: because he first loved us" (St Bernard, 1990: 17). Salvation is, for him, intimately tied in with the role of Mary in his theology. Her consent to bear the Lord Jesus is the cosmic turning point. "O Virgin," he cries, "do not delay to answer. Speak the word which all on earth, all in limbo, and even all in paradise are waiting to hear. Christ himself, the King and Lord of all, longs for your answer" (St Bernard, 1990: 25).

Bernard was above all a practical philosopher, in the sense of one who exhorts his fellow human beings to adopt a certain way of life. "It is humility, it is poverty freely accepted, obedience and joy in the Holy Spirit" (St Bernard, 1990: 100). His prescriptions do not lack detail. "A virgin ought not to laugh immoderately," he declared (St Bernard, 1633: 426).

As the manager of Cistercian monasteries, as the adviser and confidant of the rich and powerful, and as the author of widely disseminated devotional works of all sorts, we can see him as the dominant Christian of the eleventh century.

But nearly contemporary with him were two philosophers whose treatments of the great themes of philosophy within a Christian framework could hardly have been more different. It was from the works of Anselm and Abelard that philosophy in the Latin West took its themes and its methods. In what follows I have been as ruthless in my selection of authors as in the previous chapters. The great diversity and richness of medieval philosophy in the Latin West is represented by four important thinkers, Anselm, Abelard, Aquinas, and Ockham. Doubtless other choices might have been made, but to my mind these four illustrate the subtlety and power of the medieval mind in most of its dimensions.

OUR KNOWLEDGE OF GOD, HIS NATURE, AND HIS EXISTENCE

Christian faith includes a firm belief in the existence of God. But can that belief be supported by reason? Can the reasonableness of the belief be supplemented by finding a proof that God does indeed exist? During the subsequent centuries, even into the modern era, there were a great many attempts to develop such a proof, based on several different modes of argument. There were two major patterns. One was empirical. Rightly seen, the nature of the cosmos as we know it in our common experience was enough to support a belief in the existence of a Creator, and provided sufficient grounds for inferences as to the nature of the being who created it. The other pattern of argument was to infer the existence of God from a reasoned analysis of his nature. The task was to show that the concept of God, as it was understood in Christianity, entailed his existence. The most famous of these proofs was first worked out by St Anselm (1033–1109). This proof is still with us, and has reappeared in different guises throughout the second millennium.

St Anselm's Proof of the Existence of God

As the product of reflection on the concept of God, St Anselm's argument was philosophical in the second sense that we have identified throughout our studies. It was a work of analysis and critical commentary on some of the conceptual presuppositions of the Christian conception of God. Anselm's argument, presented in his *Proslogium* (Anselm, 1077–8 [1965]), is aimed at achieving two goals. The first is to demonstrate the Divine nature or essence. The second is to prove that God, *as so conceived*, must necessarily exist.

The argument is very simple. The first step involves asking whether it is possible to understand the definition of God as that than which no greater can be thought. If it is, then God has a kind of existence in the mind even of one who doubts his existence, since the doubter understands the concept. But if God is that than which no greater can be thought, it is greater to exist in reality than in the mind. So, God must exist in reality or objectively. Thus God exists necessarily. If God cannot but exist even the possibility of his non-existence is excluded. In this way God is wholly different from any other kind of being, since it is always possible that anything that does not have the absolute perfection that must be a characteristic of that which is the greatest of all might not have existed. Here is how Anselm himself expressed it:

And certainly this being so truly exists that it cannot even be thought not to exist. For something can be thought to exist that cannot be thought not to exist, and this is greater than that which can be thought not to exist. Hence, if that-than-which-a-greater cannot be thought exists it is not the same as that-than-which-a-greater-cannot-be-thought, which is absurd. Something-than-which-a-greater-cannot-be-thought exists so truly then, that it cannot even be thought not to exist. (Anselm, 1077–8 [1965]: chapter 3)

Copleston (1972: 77) remarks that some commentators have interpreted these passages more as an analysis of the concept of the Christian God than a proof of his existence. It seems to me that it is perfectly reasonable to take it both ways. The internal structure of the concept is, after all, what grounds the argument. Anselm certainly thought he could deduce the other salient attributes of God, such as his omniscience and omnipotence, from the absolute greatness or perfection that he found to be implicit in the concept.

In medieval times this elegant philosophical exercise was criticized by many. We shall return to it in St Thomas's discussions of proofs of the existence of God. It reemerges as one of the starting points of modern critical philosophy in Kant's way of setting bounds to the powers of pure reason. In the Kantian critique the proof provides the occasion for a subtle study of the presuppositions of the very concept of existence itself.

St Thomas Aquinas' Proofs of the Existence of God

Of all the philosophers whose works have come down to us from the Middle Ages, St Thomas Aquinas (1225–74) is the most important for us in trying to gain a perspective on medieval thought in Christendom. The problems he tackled were posed by the effort to understand the theology of Christianity and support it by reason. Like the declarations in the Koran, Christian dogma occupied a fixed point throughout the 500 years we are surveying. By the time of St Thomas, and partly under the influence of the Islamic Aristotelians, solutions to the problems of understanding and unifying Christian thought were beginning to be looked for in the writings of Aristotle, or rather, in the application of Aristotelian philosophy to the doctrines of Christian theology. Though some 200 years elapsed between the death of Anselm and the birth of St Thomas, the study of the theme of this section had not advanced greatly. It was Aquinas who brought to bear a deep knowledge of Aristotelian philosophy on the problem, and so set it in a new key.

However, to follow his discussion of these matters a basic philosophical distinction, dear to medieval thought, must be explored. This is the distinction between essence and existence, a distinction we have already found playing a pivotal role in Islamic philosophy. The essence of something is the set of properties that it must have to be the *kind* of thing it is. Generally individuals have essences only in so far as they exemplify types. Aquinas shared the view of many medieval philosophers that, in general, essence and existence were independent. "I can understand what a man or a phoenix is [that is, be acquainted in thought with its essence] and yet not know whether they exist in nature" (quoted in Copleston, 1972: 185). Existing is an act, and the material realization of the essence of what exists comes into being with it.

The essence/existence distinction is linked to two other important philosophical distinctions, that between potentiality and actuality, and that between matter and form. Essence is potentiality and existence as act is actuality. Matter, in itself, is potentiality. But matter and form together constitute substances, in which what was potential has become actual. Thus, to take a familiar analogy, the potter's clay is like matter in general. Take a lump of it, and it can be fashioned into an actual shape which realizes one of a huge variety of possible shapes. In the act of potting, the potter has imposed form on matter, has transformed potentiality into actuality. The potter has created a particular, an individual entity, but one which conforms to a kind or species.

Only in the case of God is there a being in which essence and existence are identical. To put this another way, the very concept or definition of what God is includes his existence. Without it he is less than he might have been, and so not God. This seems to make room for the sort of proof of God's existence advanced by Anselm. But Thomas will have none of it. If, indeed, it is the case that God's essence and existence are identical, to grasp this we humans would need to have so clear an idea of God's essence that we would see that "God exists" is a necessary truth, that is expresses part of what the concept of God means. We cannot reach this level of understanding. How are we going to prove the existence of God?

The famous "Five Ways" of proving the existence of God proposed by Aquinas are based on empirical evidence.[1] There are five rather diverse matters of fact that point inexorably toward the existence of God, so he argues. The first matter of fact is the existence of motion; the second is the existence of a hierarchy of efficient causes; the third is the existence of things that come to be and pass away, that is, of possible things; the fourth is the existence of degrees of perfection in finite things; the fifth is the existence of final causes, ends toward which things in the material world seem to tend. The pattern of argument in each case is the same. Since it is impossible, St Thomas contends, to follow out any of the sequences to infinity, there must be a last step in each of them, a step without which the preceding steps are impossible. Here we have an elegant example of philosophy as the discernment and critical discussion of presuppositions.

Take the case of motion: the sequence which leads from locally observed motions, the movements of things on the surface of the earth, to the motions which caused these motions, and so on, including the motions of the planets, must terminate in an unmoved mover. This strange "something" can only be God, that is, a being who induces motion without himself being in motion. When we see the tennis ball moving around the court we know there must be players, the motion of whose rackets imparts motion to the balls. The rackets in their turn are in motion because the players move them. In each case the thing moved had a potential to be moved, so setting it in motion is an actualization of that potentiality.

The detail of the argument is worth spelling out.

> Motion[2] is the reduction of something from potentiality to actuality ... [which can be done only] by something in a state of actuality ... whatever is moved, is moved by another ... but this cannot go on to infinity because there would then be no first mover and consequently no other mover, seeing that subsequent movers move only in so far as they are moved by the first mover ... this everyone understands to be God. (Aquinas, 1273 [1964]: Q. 2, Art. 3, p. 22)

The sequence of motions, causes, and existences are not all historical or temporal regresses, but, as we would now say, they can be laid out

as a pattern of explanation. For example, the movements of the players"
rackets are both prior to and explain the movements of the ball,
whereas the idea that something permanent must exist to make possible coming into being and passing away involves a contemporaneous
existent. We could not have the germinating, flowering, and dying off
of plants unless there were garden soil there all along to sustain the
process.

The details of each of the five ways differ. For example, in developing the argument about causes, Aquinas points out that an efficient
cause cannot be a cause of itself because it would have to be prior to
itself, which is impossible. Similarly, no ordinary moving thing can be
self-moved, so the final mover in the chain of motion must be something extraordinary, since it must move itself. The principle that is
presupposed by the first three ways is the impossibility of an infinite
regress of potentialities becoming actualized. Somewhere we must start
with something that is actual all along.

The fourth and fifth arguments are rather different in detail, but
share a basis in the prohibition of infinite sequences of potentialities.

> The fourth argument depends on the observation that among beings
> there are some more or less good, true, noble, and the like. But *more* or
> *less* are predicated of different things according as they resemble in their
> different ways something which is a maximum . . . now the maximum
> in any genus is the cause of all in that genus, as fire, the maximum of
> heat is the cause of all hot things. Therefore there must also be some-
> thing which is to all beings the cause of their being, goodness and every
> other perfection . . . and this we call God. (Aquinas, 1273 [1964]: Q. 2,
> Art. 3, p. 23)

The fifth proof is different again. Aquinas declares that natural bodies
act for an end, to get the best result.

> But they have no knowledge . . . whatever lacks knowledge cannot act
> towards an end unless directed by some being endowed with knowl-
> edge and intelligence . . . therefore some intelligent being exists by
> whom all natural beings are directed; and this being we call God.
> (Aquinas, 1273 [1964]: p. 23])

These kinds of proofs, arguing from some feature of the world to a
divine condition for or source of that feature, continued to be offered

by philosophers up until their wholesale demolition by Kant in the eighteenth-century. I believe we could find advocates of at least some of them to this day.

Unlike Anselm, St Thomas tackles the question of God's attributes after he has given his proofs of God's existence. Since his proofs are based on seeming matters of fact, we might have expected an anticipation of the seventeenth-century attempts to discern God's nature in his creation, the project of "natural religion." Instead he makes further play with his claim that human beings cannot grasp the true nature of God. We can say only what God is not, and mostly that amounts to little more than the assertion that he is neither finite nor does he change. There must be some positive attributes that we can ascribe to God, in accordance with the revealed truth of the Christian religion. But these can be ascribed only analogically. When we attribute wisdom to God, we are drawing on our understanding of the concept as applied to a person. But we have no idea what God's wisdom is. We can only be suggesting some sort of analogy. The same holds for any of the attributes that Christian theology ascribes to God, such as omniscience and omnipotence. We know what knowledge and power are in the case of human beings, but not what these words denote in the divine being. So, in the end, we really cannot say anything about the divine essence.

MORAL RESPONSIBILITY AND GOD'S OMNISCIENCE

Philosophy, as I have emphasized throughout this book, can be a matter of the advocacy of and exhortations to a certain way of life. It can also be a critical analysis of the presuppositions of ways of life, especially the concepts that are relevant to them. So moral exhortation to virtue is one thing, and the critical analysis of the very idea of virtue is another. This distinction is easily lost sight of, so I want to illustrate it yet again with another example. This story will also help to illustrate the difference between the Latin West, in which philosophy in the critical mode began to develop very early in the millennium, while nothing of the sort seems to have occurred in eastern Europe.

To see the difference between moral philosophy and arguments about moral principles we can look at the extraordinary turmoil brought about by the Bogumil movement at the beginning of the second millennium (Davies, 1997). This was a popular revisionist Christian cult that swept through the eastern parts of Europe, inspired by the radical preachings of a Bulgarian monk. There is a deep problem for Christian morality in the light of Christian theology, a problem we have already come across. If God has foreknowledge of what a person will do, could that person really have chosen that course of action freely? To choose freely, we think, it must make sense to say that a person could have done something other than what he or she chose to do. What are the presuppositions for that claim to be intelligible? If God knows that evil will be chosen, surely he could have created a world in which that possibility was never made actual in someone's real choice? How can there be evil in a world created by a beneficent God? This was the problem that animated the Bogumil cult in eastern Europe at the turn of the first millennium. But the followers of Bogumil did not develop philosophical analyses and criticisms of their orthodox opponents. They invented a new orthodoxy.

One could give Satan and evil an equal role in the cosmos with God and good. The Manicheans had gone so far as to declare that the world that we know and the human societies that inhabit it were obviously the work of an evil being. There was no paradox to be resolved if the creator was of the same moral nature as the creation. The Gnostics, a Christian sect of Egyptian origin, allowed evil an equal place with good. According to the Gnostics, God had two sons, Satan and Jesus. This world was Satan's domain which Jesus struggled to recover for God.

Jesus, as coeval with Satan, cannot be allowed the dominating role that he has in orthodoxy. The Bogumils rejected the miracles described in the Gospels. Rather than continue the practice of the mass, they turned to mantra-like recitations of the Lord's Prayer. The Cross, the symbol of orthodox Christianity *par excellence*, was, for them, the mark of the humiliation and suffering of Jesus at the hands of the evil forces of the Satanic world. It was not the symbol of the triumph of sacrifice and the promise of resurrection.

The Bogumil doctrine transformed orthodoxy when confronted with a seeming paradox. The situation in the West was quite different. Theological orthodoxy was a stable background to philosophical analysis and innovation. No Western philosopher took to preaching the rejection of the Trinity or a radical moral theology, fatalism perhaps.

I turn now to an exposition of the efforts by *philosophers* to make sense of the seeming paradoxes of a theology which emphasized human freedom and responsibility in a cosmos created by God who foresaw all that any person would do, thus emphasizing and seeming to negate human freedom in the same breath.

Augustine, Abelard, and the Primacy of Motives

The philosophical agenda for the whole of the era we are discussing was set by St Augustine, some 700 years before the turn of the first millennium. How can we resolve the problem posed by the need to subscribe to the doctrine of God's foreknowledge and the need to maintain the principle that people are responsible for their actions? St Augustine turned the focus of moral judgments from actions to motives, which is very much in accordance with Christ's own declarations concerning sinning in the mind. But now the problem of God's creative role in the world appears with renewed force. Surely the soul of one who does evil actions is an evil soul. God created it, along with everything else. How could a beneficent God create an evil soul? If he made Little Nell, he also made Hannibal Lecter.

St Augustine's proposal for solving this version of the "how could there be evil in a world that God created?" problem turned on a subtle distinction in the presuppositions of the thesis that evil actions have their source in the soul of an individual person.

> When the will turns to what is lower it becomes evil – not because that is evil to which it turns, but because the turning is itself willed. Therefore it is not an inferior thing that has made the will evil, but it is itself which has become so by wickedly and inordinately desiring an inferior thing. (Augustine, 412–26 [1950]: XII, 6)

But how is this turning away from "the higher" possible? It must be because that soul is defective, not in itself evil. It is the turning away that is evil. It is a deficiency to choose the lesser over the greater good. How can there be defective souls in the universe God has created?

St Augustine's solution strikes me as a sophism. God creates only the positive qualities in anything. A defect is a privation, a lack. It is not a positive quality. God has created just *this much* of a soul. The defective soul has these positive qualities but they are not enough to ensure the choice of the best. There would be no moral life in a world of saints endowed with perfect souls. Putting this another way: If there are to be moral beings, that is, beings for whom choices exist, there must be the possibility of choosing the lesser good.

However, whether this analysis of the sources of the capacity for evil is convincing, it does draw our attention to the psychological genesis of conduct. In turning moral philosophy toward the state of mind of the actor, St Augustine laid down the outlines of the treatment of moral philosophy that persisted throughout the Middle Ages.

Abelard (1079–1142) initiated the discussion of ethical topics in the first part of the second millennium, taking the same line as Augustine. Morality is a matter of the actor's mind, and so of personal intentions. The discussion changes in scale, from the cosmic to the personal. The philosophical conundrum is no longer the problem of how evil actions can occur in a God-created world, but how can there be evil intentions in the minds of beings God himself created?

The other related problem that involved a clash between moral theology and moral philosophy we have already noticed. If God has foreknowledge of what each human actor will choose, how can these choices be free? We shall return to consider an influential way of trying to solve this seeming paradox by St Thomas Aquinas. But we must first outline his famous discussion of Natural Law, in which he tries to account for the force of moral edicts which must express God's will, and our fallibility in formulating them. Surely if we knew God's will we would always try to realize it. As we manifestly fail to do so, there must be a gap between what we think we know of God's law and what it really is.

Aquinas and Natural Law

In developing the theory of Natural Law Aquinas made a lasting contribution to the repertoire of concepts and presuppositions upon which much of the subsequent discussion of the moral life rested. Aquinas' project was to establish the fundamental links between God's governance of the universe and human governance of everyday life. The link was the human power of reason.

The concept of "law"

The first step in following the way this project was realized will be to lay out St Thomas' general conception of "law."

Law is first of all a matter of the governance of acts by reason, since the "rule and measure of human acts is reason" (Aquinas, 1273 [1964]: I–II, 90, 1). It follows that "every law is ordained for the common good" since that is the true end of human association. Finally "promulgation is necessary for a law to obtain its force," that is, to be effective in the way people govern their acts. In short, an edict is a law if it depicts some aspect of a rational ordering of human affairs, if it is directed to the common good, and if it is promulgated by an authority which has been charged with the care of the community. According to St Thomas, God has a plan for humankind. There is a place for each person in a properly functioning social whole, which the law of the land, could it be the expression of moral truths, should express. How can it be ensured that law in the ordinary sense does express moral truth?

The "levels" of law

The ultimate source of social order is described by St Thomas as follows:

> a law is nothing else but a dictate of practical reason in the ruler who governs a perfect community. Now it is evident, granted that the world is ruled by divine providence . . . that the whole community of the universe is governed by divine reason. Wherefore, the very idea of the government of things in God the Ruler of the universe has the nature of law. And since the divine reason's conception of things is not subject to time but is eternal . . . therefore it is that this kind of law must be called eternal. (Aquinas, 1273 [1964]: I–II, 91, 1)

Here is the rub. How much can we discern of Eternal Law? Through the exercise of reason we can develop Natural Law, a law which does not require explicit edicts and statutes. Since it is the product of reason it must reflect Eternal Law, though imperfectly.

> [the rational creature] has a share of the eternal reason, whereby it has a natural inclination to its proper act and end, and this participation of

the eternal law in the rational creature is called the natural law. (Aquinas, 1273 [1964]: I–II, 91, 2)

Human law is morally well-grounded when it is derived from Natural Law.

That is all very well, but why do we need yet another level of law, divine law, as presented in the Scriptures? Should not Natural Law and the human law derived from it be enough?

St Thomas gives several reasons why divine law is needed. The one that seems most fundamental is that, because of the uncertainty of human judgment, all sorts of laws are promulgated. Which should we follow? "It was necessary for man to be directed in his proper acts by a law given by God, for it is certain that such a law cannot err." In the end there must be a reference back to divine law.

In short, divine law is that aspect of eternal law which has been revealed to human beings. Natural Law is what emerges through "participation by rational creatures in the Eternal law through their grasp of Divine law."

The content and role of Natural Law

The content of Natural Law comes down to three main principles for St Thomas. Do good and avoid evil; preserve life and avoid threats to it; seek truth and avoid ignorance. Here is how St Thomas arrives at the important but hardly surprising principle, to do good and avoid evil.

Since good has the character of an end and evil the contrary character, all those things to which a man has a natural inclination reason naturally grasps as goods, and consequently as things to be pursued, and it grasps their contraries as evils to be avoided (Aquinas, 1273 [1964]: IaIIae, Q. 94, art. 2).

But why "Natural Law"? St Thomas believed that there was, in human beings, a divinely implanted natural tendency to use reason and moral intuitions in making moral decisions. Since these had been divinely implanted, using them would tend to fulfill God's plan. But we do choose freely. So free will, if it is to be in accordance with the conception of Natural Law as reflecting an innate tendency to choose the good, cannot simply be the absence of external influences on choice. Rather it is rational self-determination. We choose our ends within a hierarchy of subordinate ends, which, taken together, tend to fulfill the overarching end of fulfilling our human nature.

This has the further consequence that not everything a human being does is properly a moral act. Moral acts are those for which it is true that "thanks to reason and will . . . human beings have dominion over their acts: free will is said to be the faculty of reason and will" (Aquinas, 1273 [1964]: IaIIae, 1.1).

The fallibility of human beings leaves open the possibility that unjust laws are sure to be promulgated from time to time. How can this be? A law is the edict of a properly constituted authority. It is always possible that feeble human reason could mistake what is just, that is, what is in accordance with Natural Law. The mandatory force of law comes from the status of the authority which promulgates it, but its moral standing comes from its coherence with divine law, those aspects of God's eternal law that human beings can grasp.

The Aristotelian connection

How does Aquinas manage to bring into coherence Aristotle's doctrine of human virtue and morality as conforming to the revealed law of God? There are two sorts of moral concepts, he proposes. There are the Aristotelian virtues, which are ultimately based on the virtue of prudence, the virtue which is enshrined in practical reason. (Aquinas, 1273 [1964]: IaIIae, 57.4). By this means we arrive at those everyday ends of action that lead toward the perfecting of the agent. Since this has all been arranged by God through the endowment of human beings with reason and will, practical reason will lead to genuine moral outcomes. Then there are theological virtues, the love of both the occasions and the means for the development of these virtues, the end of which is eternal beatitude. Human reason enables us to formulate the dictates of Natural Law as our best attempt to understand divine law. The latter has been revealed in Christianity, but is in need of interpretation.

Free action

How does Aquinas deal with the deep problem of how the notion of responsibility can have a place in a world where the future seems to be fixed, either by virtue of the operation of causal laws or by God's foreknowledge of what each human will choose to do in every situation? The solution offered by Aquinas strikes me as no more convincing than the proposals of the many others whose efforts to resolve the contradiction we have followed in other philosophical traditions. Free will is rational self-determination. By reason I know what it is right to do and by the gift of grace I am enabled to do it. This is compatible with divine foreknowledge, according to St Thomas. God is not *making* me do what I do. He has created me so that I make myself do what I do. But he *knows* what I will do. Grace is a sort of extra power that God is willing to give to the person who knows the good but is aware of human weakness, and prays for strength.

In modern ethics the issue of the possibility of choosing and acting freely is always "could I have done otherwise?" If not, then my act is not freely chosen. Logically, other courses of action are possible, thus in a sense I could have done otherwise. But in the moral world of St Thomas only one is actualized and God knows which one. God does not know or not know the future (as a human being would) since he is not a being constrained by the human sense of time. Thus God's foreknowledge is not the same as fatalism, which holds that my reasons and decisions only seem to play a role in a determined future.

Rational self-determination makes human beings vulnerable to blame for having chosen unwisely. If they have chosen correctly, that is, in accordance with God's law, but have failed to execute the choice through weakness of will, distraction by other impulses, and so on, they are equally culpable. There things remained, though the same issues surfaced again in the flourishing of philosophy as commentary and criticism in the fourteenth century.

THE GREAT DIVIDE: THE *VIA MODERNA* DISPLACES THE *VIA ANTIQUA*

The Aristotelians saw the cosmos as a web of necessary relations and inherent attributes, through which philosophers can make their way by studying the internal structures and interrelations of concepts. The project of the thirteenth century was mutually to adjust philosophy and the meaning of revealed religious truths to achieve an integration of the deliverances of reason and faith. By the fourteenth century profound doubts and powerful arguments were appearing, asserting the radical independence of theology from philosophy. This was the *via moderna*, the product of a conscious opposition to the *via antiqua*, in which reason was to be the foundation of faith. Theology and philosophy were to be set apart again. This was to be achieved by deeper and more subtle philosophical analysis than that which had heretofore been done. In this respect the Christian reaction to the enthusiasm for philosophy was different from the main thrust of Islamic objections to the project of the philosophers. With a few exceptions the traditionalists rejected philosophy completely. In Christendom the *via moderna* took theology to be concerned with necessary beings, necessary attributes, and necessary relations. But there are no such relations in the world that human beings can perceive. Philosophy deals with that world. It follows that the separation of theology and philosophy is absolute. This was William of Ockham's tack and it was highly effective.

Ockham (ca. 1285–1347) was embroiled not only in philosophical disputes but also in complex political intrigues that occupied both his attention and his time. Nevertheless he was an influential teacher and his views spread rapidly throughout the Latin world, the *via moderna* that dominated Christian philosophy through the fifteenth century. Ockham's problem was how to establish, in contrast to the necessity of the divine realm, the utter contingency of the world and the mutual independence of all the things that are in it. The key to Ockham's project lay in the long-running controversy about the nature of universals.

The Problem of Universals

We have seen how the distinction between essence and existence shaped much of the thinking of medieval philosophers about how God and his creatures were to be differentiated. The other deep metaphysical issue that has remained with us to the present day is the problem of how more than one individual being can exemplify the same type.

We have seen this problem already in Islamic philosophy and noted its origin in antiquity. This is not an independent problem, because it is tied up with the question of the nature of essences, what it is to be something of a certain type or kind.

It comes to the fore first of all in the eleventh century with the aggressive arguments of Abelard against the thesis that in every individual that belongs to a type there is a common essence, a real something that is found in each. If all the poppies in the garden are red, is that because in each there is somehow the same, the very same "redness," a universal? This universal could not be the sensory quality or hue of any individual poppy. It must be something else that explains how individual poppies, though different beings, can be of the same color. This is the realist account of universals. On the other hand, is there anything more to the way things fall into classes and groups than the fact of similarity between the properties of individuals? All that is in common between red poppies is that we use the *same word* "red" to describe each poppy. This is the nominalist account of universals. For realists, universals were neither in language nor in the mind but in the world. For nominalists, they could be no more than reflections of how certain kinds of words are used.

According to Abelard, the world consist of things, and things are individuals. But universals do have a role in our life in the world. They are words. Not *flatus vocis*, empty strings of syllables, but meaningful signs, *vox significata*. The universal in the above example is the word "red," which is universal in that it can be used of many things which are alike in respect of color. There are subtleties in Abelard's account that need not detain us. They enabled him to propose a psychological theory of how, via common mental representations, we can recognize individual things as red, and so call them "red." Here we have a strict nominalism, that is, an account according to which universals are names, not mysterious substances additional to the material stuff of the ordinary world. But this was far from the general view, which, until the fourteenth century, tended to "realism."

The realism with respect to universals that was much to the fore in the *via antiqua* has been beautifully described by Moody (in Edwards, 1967: vol. 8, 307):

> the doctrine that the human intellect discovers in the particulars apprehended by sense experience an intelligible order of abstract essences and

necessary relations ontologically prior to particular things and contingent events, and that from this order the intellect can demonstrate necessary truths concerning first causes and the being and attributes of God.

Ockham utterly denied this view in every detail. It seemed to him that the only necessity was in the nature and existence of God. All else was radically contingent. God could contemplate all that was possible, and that was a necessary feature of his nature. But he freely chose which of those possibilities he would realize as the cosmos.

> Ockham never loses sight of this basic Christian idea – so radically opposed to the necessitarian view – that there is no inherent necessity for anything in this world to be what it is. (Boehner, 1990: p. xix)

The most interesting aspect, for us, of this shift in mood was that it was also a shift in philosophical style. Ockham turned to the careful analysis of language to show how the realist account of universals was based on a profound misunderstanding of the logic of nominative and descriptive expressions. There are no universals. There are only words or signs used to describe similarities between independent things.

The Distinction between Intuitive and Abstractive Cognition

Ockham argued that there are two ways of knowing something. There are, he says, two senses of abstractive cognition. In one sense, "it means cognition abstracted from many singulars . . . nothing else but a cognition of a universal which can be abstracted from many things" (Ockham, 1334 [1991]: 414). Such a universal as a quality in the mind can be intuitively and abstractively known, that is, known as a singular state of mind and also as abstracted from many similar such states of mind. In the second meaning, abstractive cognition abstracts from everything about the singulars it is drawn from, including their existence. "The intuitive cognition of a thing is cognition that enables us to know [immediately] whether the thing exists or does not exist" (Ockham, 1334 [1991]: 414). Obviously we cannot know any contingent truth through abstractive cognition because we cannot know whether the property so abstracted is actually a property of some real thing. All the singular beings from which we abstracted it might have been destroyed.

Even intuitive cognition does not necessitate existence. God, who is all-powerful, can "produce the intuitive sense cognition of an object; hence he can produce it directly on his own account" (Ockham, 1334 [1991]: 506).

Ockham's move against those who held that universals were real beings that existed independently of the particular entities from which we gained our knowledge of them, depends on showing that all we need to account for our experience of the similarities and differences between the qualities of perceived things are signs or words by means of which we describe the properties of things. These signs or words, like "white" or "brave," do not name any mysterious "substance" that is literally the same in each of the singular beings which are white or brave. Each sheep is white, in itself, ultimately by virtue of God's creative power, which could have made them all blue. Each of the Argonauts was brave in himself, though God might have made some of them cowards. The same principle holds for similarities between introspected states of mind. Ockham spells it out very clearly. Yes, every universal is one singular thing. I have just one abstractive cognition of whiteness, though there are many white things. Every universal is of such a nature as to be a sign of, and predicated of, several things. As a mental content a universal is singular, but as a word it is not singular, since we say of each sheep that it is *white*, using the word "white" over and over again.

In another work Ockham sets out more direct arguments against the idea that universals are things outside the mind:

> If a universal were one substance existing in singular things and distinct from them [whiteness existing in but distinct from sheep], it would follow that it could exist apart from them . . . but this consequence is absurd . . . it would follow that God could not annihilate one individual of a substance, if he did not destroy the other individuals . . . [he would have] destroyed the essence of the individual, he would destroy the essence which is in it and others [and therefore destroy them all].
> (Ockham in Boehner, 1990: 36)

In short there is no preexisting order of essences that must be instantiated in whatever God brings into existence.

The Intractability of the Problem of Human Freedom

It will hardly come as a surprise to learn that the subtle blend of Aristotelianism and Christian theology devised by St Thomas met with little favor from Ockham and the other "modernists." Expressed in terms of logic, the key question of morality is how to accommodate the degree of human freedom that would be needed to sustain the idea of responsibility for one's actions with the theological commonplace that God knows the truth of all future contingents, that is to say, what any person will freely choose. How can we talk of people freely choosing what they will do, when God created the world, past, present, and future, and already knows which course of action they will follow? Surely human freedom is an illusion and responsibility an absurd imposition?

Ockham's doctrine of radical contingency applies not only to the beings that are created by God and the attributes they each have, but also to events, what happens in this world. There is no *necessity* about what will happen, what act any human being will perform. From this it follows that the moral life, the existence of which is not in question, presupposes human freedom in a rather strong sense. The power of the will to act or not to act is undetermined by anything other than itself. But the mere fact that an act is willed does not make it morally correct. It must be willed according to the requirement of right reason. However, right reason is not mere prudence. Acting prudently does not make the act right, though it is partly constitutive of moral propriety. The ultimate reason is that an act should be done for the love of God (Frepper, 1988: chapter 3). How is the radical contingency of events and the unconditioned freedom of the will to be reconciled with God's foreknowledge of what anyone will choose? Ockham's answer is not unlike al-Ghazāli's. Human beings are not equipped to understand the nature of God's foreknowledge.

> it has to be held without doubt that God knows all future contingent facts evidently and with certainty. But to explain this evidently, and to express the manner in which he knows all future contingent facts, is impossible for any intellect in this life. (Ockham in Boehner, 1990: 133)

What determines that an act be virtuous, for those like us, who cannot know the mind of God? Obviously, acting in accordance with his will must be virtuous. In this sense there are necessarily virtuous acts. But we can never know which they are. At best we act for a right reason. It is also true that there are no necessarily virtuous acts, since "every act, remaining identically the same, can indifferently be laudable or blameworthy . . . as it can successively be in accordance with a right-eous and a vicious will" (Boehner, 1990: 145). The separation of will from right reason makes room for the possibility of a vicious will.

Reflecting on Ockham's treatment of this complex question inclines me to agree with Frepper's observation that Ockham is running two theories to account for the possibility of morality. On the one hand he argues that the will is devoid of content and that the quality of an action derives from its relation to the determinations of reason. On the other hand he argues that the same act can be good or evil, depend-ing on whether it is brought into being by a good or evil will. This conception of the will is quite different from the neutrality of the will in the first theory. I do not think that there is a solution to this conun-drum. It illustrates the difficulty of the problem for us. If someone as astute as Ockham found himself drawn to two antithetical aspects of the matter, then it is surely an intractable problem. For the rest of the second millennium it has remained unsolved.

Logic in Medieval Europe

Aristotelian logic was studied and taught intensively in the Latin West. For example, a competently and succinctly presented account of Aris-totelian logic was written by William of Shyreswood in or about 1225, and there were many others. However, there were two fields of logical enquiry that were pursued in depth in the twelfth and thirteenth cen-turies, sophisms or intellectual puzzles, and the logic of modality, of possibility and necessity.

Abelard comes through to us not only as a theologian and philoso-pher but also as a logician of great skill and subtlety. Kneale and Kneale (1975: 202–24) devote more than 20 pages to a detailed exposition of Abelard's logic. I will content myself with a summary of his treat-ment of modality, the logic of necessity and possibility, to illustrate the meticulous character of medieval discussions of logical matters. The main topic of discussion concerning the logic of modal propositions was whether a modal expression qualified the sense of the whole proposition in which it appeared, or whether it qualified the link between one entity and another or between an entity and one of its properties. Abelard held that only the latter were genuinely modal, that is, they expressed a mode or manner of union between whatever was referred to by the subject and by the predicate of a proposition. Genuine modal propositions were later classified under the heading *de re*. Thus "Snow is necessarily white" is a modal proposition *de re*. Propositions which asserted something of the whole content of another proposition, such as "Necessarily snow is white," which expresses a qualification of the sense of "Snow is white," are *de dicto*.

Sophisms or verbal puzzles were very popular in the period. The paradox of the liar was one of those eagerly argued over. "All Cretans are liars," said the Cretan. This seems to be true if it is false and false if it is true. And there were many others, based on different kinds of difficulties.

Despite the effort put into logical studies by philosophers in the period from the eleventh to the fourteenth century, and the progress in subtlety and depth that was achieved, medieval logic was virtually ignored until the twentieth century.

NOTES

1   An excellent critical discussion of the Five Ways can be found in Kenny (1969).
2   *Motus*, often translated as "motion" is meant to cover all sorts of changes, not only changes in spatial position.

PART III

Philosophy in the West

Modern Philosophy I
MIND AND COSMOS

The World Shapes the Mind: Realism and Positivism

In the first 500 years of the second millennium we could say that Occidental philosophy was driven by the problems raised by religion. Philosophers struggled to make the worldviews of the three great revealed religions into a coherent and defensible account of human life and the material universe. We have seen how in Christendom this development ran roughly in parallel to but a little later than the corresponding development in Islam. Thanks to the availability of the works of Ibn Sīnā (Avicenna) and Ibn Rushd (Averroes) there can be no doubt of the profound influence that Islamic philosophy as "critique of religion" had on European thought. For 500 years philosophy and theology were intimately intertwined, even when the relevance of the one for the other was vigorously disputed.

The variety and depth of philosophy in the modern era is perhaps no greater than that of India in antiquity. Radhakrishnan and Moore's (1957) comprehensive history of Indian philosophy reveals a similar range of schools and opinions to those one finds in the West. The same can be said for the history of Chinese philosophy as it appears in the works of Fung Yu-lan (1937). However, the texture of philosophical thought is, so to say, more condensed, and the activity much more institutionalized than it had been in either of the Oriental civilizations.

As we turn our attention toward the second half of the second millennium a profound shift of focus is evident. The great themes are the same, but the intellectual media in which they are presented and the cognitive and material practices in which they are realized have changed. The last 500 years of philosophical reflections on human nature and the universe at large have been driven by new demands, without wholly eliminating the motives for philosophical reflection of earlier times. With the advent of the natural sciences, the decline of the feudal system, and the slow but steady transformation of the means of production and the social organization of the economic bases of the emerging nation-states of the West, new concepts and new problems began to emerge clearly in the sixteenth century.

However, until the mid-nineteenth century religion was still very much to the fore in European culture. It became increasingly problematic when considered in relation to the findings of the natural sciences. From the Renaissance the sciences themselves were quickly seen to raise philosophical issues and to be in need of critical examination. For example, what is presupposed in generalizing the knowledge acquired in the here and now to all places and all times? What is the status of hypotheses about aspects of the material world which, though unobservable, nevertheless seem to be real and effective in bringing about what we can observe?

During the second half of the second millennium, much of philosophy was driven by the problems that came to the fore with the advent of the natural sciences. The experimental method, as we know it, was well established by 1600, with such works as William Gilbert's *De Magnete*, a systematic experimental study of the phenomena of static electricity and magnetism. It served, with other such publications, as an exemplar of good work. Grand unifying scientifically oriented theories purporting to encompass the whole universe in space and in time had been presented by Gilbert, and famously by René Descartes in his massive *Principles of Philosophy*, published in Latin in 1644 and in French in 1647. This trend reached its apotheosis in 1687 with Isaac Newton's *Principia*. Science began to make independent claims to knowledge, challenging and displacing those based on the sacred books and other authoritative texts from which the Christian Church took its doctrine. Science began to take the place of theology as the focus of the deepest levels of philosophical reflection.

However, this did not mean that the relations between the claims of science and those of religion had been settled. We shall see the importance of the defence of religion in many aspects of the thought of the second half of the millennium. We will follow the rise of Natural Religion among English scientists in the seventeenth century. The conservative reaction to Darwin's theory of evolution and the appearance of the geological time-scale in the nineteenth can also be seen in part as an issue in the debates about the standing of religion as a comprehensive account of nature and humanity. The more or less complete displacement of religion from centre stage was a long time coming. It was not until the nineteenth century that a philosopher (Nietzsche) could announce the death of God and a poet (Thomas Hardy) write its funeral oration.

It hardly needs saying that many regretted this demise. I owe the following quotation from Thomas Carlyle's *Past and Present* (1886–93) to A. N. Wilson (1999: 69). It seems to express the matter with passion and insight.

> [We] have closed our eyes to the eternal Substance of things and opened them only to the Shews and Shams of things. We quietly believe this Universe to be intrinsically a great unintelligible PERHAPS . . . There is no longer any God for us! God's Laws are become a Greatest-Happiness Principle, a Parliamentary Expediency; the Heavens an Astronomical Time-Keeper; a butt for Herschel to shoot science at, to shoot sentimentalities at – in our old Johnson's dialect, Man has lost the soul out of him; and now begins to find the want of it! . . . There is no religion, there is no God; man has lost his soul and seeks anti-septic salt. (Book III, p. i).

Two main ways of construing the relation between people and the cosmos emerged in the last 500 years. The several versions of Empiricism were based on the principle that it is the cosmos that shapes human knowledge. The contrary views, Idealism, Rationalism, and Conventionalism, expressed various versions of the idea that the cosmos as we perceive it is, at least in part, a product of our own activities in shaping our raw experience.

It is almost a cliché to emphasize the shift from collectivistic to individualistic conceptions of human nature that came about in the fifteenth and sixteenth centuries. Political and moral philosophy became increasingly concerned with the presuppositions of the ways of defining the moral and political ends of human action in terms of human goods alone.

In presenting a sketch of the history of the second millennium it has been impossible to touch on every insight and to bring to the attention of the reader every philosopher of note. I have tried, here as elsewhere, to present some dominant themes in sufficient detail for the interplay of philosophical debate around their deep presuppositions to be followed closely. Inevitably the themes I have chosen reflect my view of what has been important in the development of our culture in the last 500 years.

THE FOUNDATIONS OF SCIENCE

Objectivity and Natural Religion

The shift of focus from the search for a rational grounding for religion to one for the rational grounding of natural science did not bring a passionate interest in religion to an end. The first attempt to meld religion and science began in the seventeenth century, with the advent of the idea that the nature and existence of the Creator could be discovered by studying his creation, the natural world. Far from being at odds as rival accounts of the world, the English scientist-philosophers of the seventeenth century looked to science to support religion. For example, Isaac Newton wrote to Richard Bentley: "I had an eye for such principles as might work with considering men for the belief of a Deity." Robert Boyle explicitly claimed that it is through the scientific study of the natural world that God's nature can be revealed to human beings.

A proof of the existence of God, based on the nature of gravity, was popular in the late seventeenth century. One version runs as follows:

[Gravity] cannot be caused by Matter acting on the Surfaces of Matter . . . but must be caused by something that continually penetrates its solid Substance. (Clarke, 1717: [1956] 83)

[Gravity] is the Power of a superior Agent . . . 'tis certain that the Author of this Power is an Immaterial or Spiritual Being. (Whiston, 1717: 45)

Newton did not openly support this argument but he had several of his own. Something, he thought, must intervene to stop the matter in the universe from collapsing, so that "this frame of things could not always subsist without a divine Power to conserve it" (from Newton's

Third Letter to Bentley). Furthermore, he thought that the solar system was not quite perfect mechanically and that God would have to put it right from time to time. This idea was famously ridiculed by Leibniz. Finally Newton thought that the amount of activity in the universe was declining and would have to be made good from somewhere. In each case the savior of the material universe is God.

Theology was based on the presupposition that God existed quite independently of human beings. He was not invented or brought into being by human activities – he was just *there*. Since God was supposed to have created the rest of the cosmos before he created human beings, it too must exist independently of those human beings, Adam and Eve and their descendants. There was a rich and complex objective realm, that is, a realm that existed outside the minds of the human race. People could, perhaps, develop ways of finding out more about it than they knew at any time. The basic thesis of Realism, that there existed an objective and independent world, was presupposed by every major seventeenth-century thinker. The question always was: How much can we get to know about the Cosmos?

In its beginnings science shared this presupposition with religion. When Descartes tried out his program of doubting all he had previously taken for granted, he set both God and the material universe outside the limits of immediate personal experiences. But he reasoned, thanks to God's benevolence, we can make headway in finding out more about the natural world. Though its existence can be doubted, its reality is guaranteed by God. Descartes' method of doubt was more a tool to assign degrees of certainty to what we thought we knew than an invitation to skepticism.

The Astronomical Debates

The beginnings of an interest in the presuppositions that underpinned scientific enquiries were stimulated by the clashes between astronomers and theologians during almost the whole of the sixteenth century. The usual story has it that the struggle between heliocentric and geocentric models of the solar system was between Galileo and the authorities of the Church. That indeed did occur, but there had been nearly a century of debate about the interpretation of astronomical theories before Galileo appeared before the Holy Office. The Copernican

heliocentric theory was published in 1543. It was by no means the
only comprehensive mathematical cosmology on offer. Here was the
problem: Which of the rival cosmologies was a correct representation
of the heavens? And how was this question to be decided? Astronomers
and philosophers of the sixteenth century took a variety of attitudes
to this situation. Each theory gave reasonably good predictions of
planetary positions, eclipses, and so on, but each was based on a very
different picture of the solar system.

In the sixteenth century there were at least five rival geometrical
models of the cosmos, the geocentric theories of Ptolemy, Aristotle,
and Tycho Brahe, and the heliocentric theories of Copernicus and
Kepler, from each of which the observed motions of the heavenly
bodies could be recovered by calculations. Which was the correct one,
if any? The arguments offered in support of each of these theories
reveal a range of presuppositions about the nature of scientific enquiry
that are still with us.

Christopher Clavius (1570) pointed out that the rival cosmologies
could not be sorted out by testing their predictions against the known
motions of the planets, since each gave more or less the same answers.
This situation has occurred several times in the history of science, and
the Clavian comment has been revived more than once. In the twentieth century the point has been called the "underdetermination of
theory by data." Given that infinitely many theories can be constructed
from which the relevant observations can be deduced, the evidential
force of a successful prediction gives no more support to one theory
than to any of the others.

Astronomers turned philosophers on this issue. Between them they
came up with three stances from which to evaluate theories. Interestingly, these interpretations prefigured the main accounts of science that
appeared in the nineteenth century and which have lingered on into
the twentieth. The three interpretations were as follows.

The first emphasizes our capacity for making predictions. On this
interpretation theories had no implications for the real state of the
cosmos. This interpretation was prominent in a preface inserted into
the first edition of Copernicus' *De Revolutionibus*. Osiander, who had
taken charge of printing the book, seems to have thought that a pragmatic interpretation would deflect any conservative criticism of the
theory. Copernicus himself apparently did not share this attitude to

theories and was said to have been put out when he discovered the insertion. Of course, Osiander was well aware that heliocentrism was likely to raise hackles among the authorities, so his motive was indeed benign, if somewhat over-cautious. Osiander's interpretation is reminiscent of modern *positivism*.

The second is illustrated in Ursus' defense of the strange hybrid model devised by Tycho Brahe, in which the planets orbited the sun which orbited the earth. Ursus argued for the necessity of pictorial models for psychological purposes, but suggested that they be treated as fictions, likely stories. While each had to be successful as a machine for predicting the state of the heavenly bodies, there was no point in asking which was the true picture of the cosmos. The alternative models only seemed to be rival pictures of the cosmos. They had the status of alternative fictions, stories which facilitated thought. This point of view is reminiscent of modern *conventionalism*.

Another group of philosophically minded astronomers insisted that the question to be taken seriously was whether the heliocentric and geocentric theories were rival representations of the real layout and structure of the heavens, and should be judged as such. Kepler argued for the superior representative realism of his heliocentric theory over its rivals. Melanchthon defended a realist interpretation of the Ptolemaic geocentric system. Both agreed that there was a real cosmic structure and that astronomers should be trying to represent it. Here we have an example of a point of view that prefigures *scientific realism*.

There the matter rested. Imperceptibly the scientific community, indeed the whole world, adopted heliocentrism. The philosophical problems of the legitimacy of the realist interpretation of theories faded from view. It was rekindled in the period we nowadays call "the Enlightenment," when reason was supposed to displace superstition in all matters. Modern versions of positivism take their start from the critical philosophy of David Hume, to which we shall return.

The positivist and the realist interpretations are examples of *empiricism*, although one focuses on prediction and the other on the representation of physical reality. In both it is assumed that the beliefs of the scientists who develop these theories are derived predominantly from their observations and experiences. Thought is shaped by the world.

THE RISE OF REALISM

The Independence of Mind and World

The story of modern philosophy begins in the Renaissance. However, the origin of many of its main themes must be credited to René Descartes. Born in 1596 at La Haye in the Loire region, he was educated by the Jesuits. How his intellectual rebellion was stimulated we do not know, but he soon declared himself willing to accept only those truths that he could clearly and distinctly apprehend by reflection on his own state of mind or by the study of the material world. He found a career as a military engineer eventually with the Bavarian army. With time on his hands during a protracted campaign in the Netherlands, he began a systematic examination of his taken-for-granted beliefs. This led him to his lifelong project of establishing knowledge on the basis only of ideas which were clear and distinct. Descartes' achievements in mathematics, and his work in the natural sciences, brought him international renown. One invitation proved fatal. When visiting Queen Christina of Sweden he met his death. She was not only an enthusiastic Cartesian but was in the habit of rising at a very early hour. This and the Swedish climate was too much for the great philosopher, and he died of pneumonia in Stockholm in 1650.

If the Mind is to be shaped by the World, if beliefs are to be accounted for by what is perceived to be in the world, it must be the case that the World and Minds exist independently of one another, though they are in intimate communion. Though both mind and matter are known to us by the exercise of mental powers, nevertheless, in a deep sense, they have nothing in common. Descartes gives a very clear account of the radical distinction between the mental and the material.

> There are certain accidents [properties of a substance] which we call "corporeal", such as size, shape, motion . . . and we use the term "body" to refer to the substance in which they inhere . . . There are other accidents which we call "acts of thought" such as understanding, willing, imagining . . . and so on: these all fall under the common concept of thought or perception or consciousness, and we call the substance in

which they inhere a "thinking thing" or a "mind." (Descartes, 1647 [1984]: 121–2)

This distinction was presupposed by most philosophers of the sixteenth and seventeenth centuries. Mental states, such as feelings and beliefs, are utterly different in character from material states, such as shape and motion. So we can say that the leading presupposition of the scientific spirit was something like this:

> There is more to the world than ordinary unaided observation reveals, and that the concepts and rules of thumb of everyday life can comprehend. Observing and experimenting is a better way to find out more about the world than the study of authorities. However, new concepts will be needed to comprehend it, as its nature becomes more clearly revealed. We will need a way of thinking about and representing what is now imperceptible, but which scientific research leads us to think must be the real sources of what we can observe.

In many ways this new point of view had a good deal in common with the theologically oriented worldview that it eventually displaced. God existed independently of human minds, but by the exercise of reason we could know something of him. According to the realist interpretation of science, the cosmos existed independently of human minds. By the use of scientific method people could gain some knowledge of it. The differences between science and theology lay in how that was to be accomplished, since experimenting played no role in theology, mystical experience excepted, of course.

Bacon's New Instrument

Born in 1561, Francis Bacon was educated at Cambridge and Gray's Inn, and called to the bar in 1582. He was much involved in the convoluted politics of the time. He entered Parliament in 1584, and thereafter sought "preferment" assiduously. For many years he depended on the patronage of the Earl of Essex. Many have seen his taking a leading role in the prosecution and conviction of Essex for treason as a self-serving act of betrayal. Be that as it may, his subsequent rise to the high office of Attorney General owed a great deal to royal patronage. He served both Elizabeth and James I, the Stuart king who succeeded her. Falling out of favor, he lost his position in the government in 1621 and retired to the country. However, in the course of a life heavily engaged in public affairs he found the time to write extensively and influentially on the nature and possibilities of the natural sciences. Practicing what he preached proved fatal. He caught cold while experimenting with the use of snow to test the power of cold to preserve meat, and died in 1626.

The first comprehensive and systematic discussion of scientific method in the millennium is to be found in Bacon's *Novum Organon* of 1620. Medieval philosophers commented widely on the status of empirical methods of discovery, but they left no extended and systematic treatise on the matter. Bacon tackled one of the central questions. What is presupposed in drawing general knowledge from experiments and observations, limited to the here and how? By what method could one *establish* a law of nature on the basis of experiments and observations? How could one reason *reliably* from particular facts to general laws?

Bacon's methodology is derived from his opinion that some properties of material things are more fundamental, more "real" than others. The experimental method is a technique for finding out which properties are the "most real." They could be picked out by finding the properties most widely evident in the experimental study of correlations among the observable properties of things. Not only must these properties figure in explanations of natural phenomena, but they will also be the basis of technology. Bacon argued that by manipulating the most real properties of things one can bring about changes in the less real attributes of the material world.

There are several important distinctions among kinds of properties or "natures." There are both visible and latent or hidden configurations of parts in any material thing. The systematic analysis of the observable properties of things leads to a distinction between simple and complex natures or properties. For example, Bacon thought that the properties commonly observed in material things were complex "natures," a combination of simpler properties. The job of the scientist (a word not yet in use in Bacon's time) was to discover which simple natures are the "most real." For example, he thought that "motion" was a more real simple nature than heat. So the phenomena of heat would be explained by imperceptible motions, that is, the changing latent configurations of parts too minute to be observed.

Bacon distinguished "Physics," the study of material and efficient causes, from Metaphysics, the study of the inner natures of things. He pointed out that we could observe that fire was the efficient cause of the hardening of clay *and of the melting of wax*. So observable relations between qualities, as revealed by the methods of Physics, were plainly superficial. There must be a deeper knowledge to be found, in terms of which seeming contradictions would be resolved. Metaphysics would be a study of the true but hidden natures of material things, the arrangements and motions of the invisible parts. This is clearly a version of scientific Realism.

We build up our hypotheses about the "forms" of natural phenomena, that is, what they really are, by finding by experiment what combination of most real simple natures grounds the phenomenon in question. Bacon makes quite clear that this notion of "form" is to do the work that Platonic forms were supposed to do, that is, explain the natures of particular material things. But Plato's forms were abstracted from and transcendent to matter. Bacon's, as the inner structures of bodies, are in the very heart of material things. Once we know the form of a phenomenon, say color or heat, we can develop ways of manipulating it in the interests of human beings. We know what properties we must work on to bring about the changes we want. If the form of heat is motion, then manipulations which change the quantity of motion in a body will change its temperature. "But whosoever knoweth any form, knoweth the utmost possibility of super-inducing that nature upon any variety of matter" (Bacon, 1605: ii, 5). The more we can speed up the particles the hotter a thing will be.

Bacon's method involved two phases of experimentation and observation. In the first phase the investigator made a catalogue of the correlations that could be discovered between the phenomenon of interest and other natures or properties. Thus heat is found with light, with friction, with fermentation, and so on. To find which of these correlations displays the most real simple nature or form of the phenomenon in question one must look for instances of "absence in proximity," cases in which the correlative property is present but the phenomenon in question does not occur. Thus there is light in the winter without heat, so the form of heat cannot be luminiferous. Running through the experimental program in search of counter-instances, absences in proximity, we find that the only surviving correlation is between heat and various forms of motion. From this we conclude that the form of heat is "a motion, expansive and constrained, acting in its strife upon the inner parts of bodies."

We see that Bacon cheerfully generalized his experimental results beyond the bounds of the here and now. He states his hypotheses about what are the most real simple natures quite generally. Furthermore he describes the forms (that is, the *unobservable* inner structures of things) as if they were plainly before his eyes. He does not notice that he has passed by two great philosophical problems, problems which became the focus of centuries of subsequent discussion and debate. What is presupposed when we blithely generalize the results of our experiments done in the here and now to all times and places? What grounds do we have for accepting any hypothesis about unobserved processes, when we cannot check its viability by the only standard acceptable to the newly forged sciences, observation and experiment? These problems have returned again and again to haunt the advocate of scientific Realism. They are still with us today, at the turn of the millennium.

Alternative Metaphysical Foundations for Realism

Two rather different conceptions of the *nature* of the material world crystallized out around the turn of the sixteenth century. Was the cosmos corpuscularian, a moving mass of ever more minute particles? Or was it dynamic, an ever-changing interplay of forces?

The corpuscularian philosophy

From the latter part of the sixteenth century various English philosophers had been bringing ancient Greek atomism to the attention of the public. One medium for this was the translation of the Latin poem of Lucretius, *De Rerum Natura*, an exposition of atomism that owed a great deal to Greek sources. The Realist version of Empiricism that developed in England was predominantly a form of material atomism, though the dynamicist metaphysics never lacked advocates. The first systematic attempt to set out the philosophical foundations of the atomistic point of view was made by John Locke. Like many of his contemporaries, he was wary of committing himself to the strict presuppositions of atomism, particularly the principle that there were indivisible parts of matter. For that reason such terms as "corpuscle" were used, to leave questions of real indivisibility aside. Corpuscles were the smallest parts of material things for practical purposes. But they could be divided in thought. We could imagine smaller parts. It would be impossible to prove that no technique for further dividing them would ever be found.

The corpuscularian philosophy was based on the principle that the imperceptible aspects of the material world, postulated to account for the results of observation and experiment, were identical with some, but not all, of the characteristics of the world as it is perceived by a normal human being. These were the primary qualities. John Locke listed them as "bulk, figure [shape], texture [structural arrangements] and motion." They were not only perceptible in everything, but they were also the qualities of the imperceptible parts of material things. Other perceptible qualities, such as color and taste, were not duplicated in any simple way in the underlying character of colored and tasty things. They were to be explained as the ways that the arrangements and shapes of the imperceptible corpuscles affected the human sense organs. These were the secondary qualities.

The dynamicist philosophy

William Gilbert pioneered a very different metaphysics for the natural world. While the corpuscularians, such as Galileo, used mechanics as their model for a universal science, Gilbert based his cosmology on magnetism. Magnets acted at a distance. They seemed to be surrounded by a region in which iron objects were constrained to adopt quite definite orientations to the adjacent magnetic poles, despite there being no obvious mechanical connection between the magnet and the compass. Gilbert used the phrase "orbis virtutis" or "sphere of power" to describe the underlying reality which shaped material things magnetically. The idea of natural powers, forces, tendencies, and dispositions had been a central concept of Aristotelian physics. All change, for Aristotle, was the transformation of what was potential into what was actual. Both the potential and actual states were equally real, equally aspects of an independent nature. These concepts, particularly as Gilbert developed them in his magnetic cosmology (Gilbert, 1600), are the ancestors of our contemporary concepts of "charges" and their "fields." With its emphasis on forces and on natural agents, we could call this philosophy "dynamism."

Dynamism was very different from corpuscularianism. It made use of different exemplars of reality and a different logic. Corpuscles were described in the indicative. Their properties were occurrent, possessed then and there. Powers and dispositions were ascribed hypothetically to what would happen if certain conditions were to be fulfilled. A thing or substance generally did not always manifest the dispositions ascribed to it. Gasoline is flammable when it is not yet burning!

A scientific realist could either be a corpuscularian or a dynamist. In both cases one presupposed an unobservable substrate which acted upon the human senses to engender the common experience of everyday objects and events. The empiricism of the seventeenth century was predominantly Realist. Distinctions were made in the status of beliefs. For example, Locke distinguished between "opinions," the tentative results of scientific research, and "knowledge," such as the necessary truths of geometry, which have their ultimate sources in definitions.

Locke: ideas and qualities

John Locke will appear and reappear in these pages. Perhaps more than most of the intellectual giants of the period, he had a life remarkable for its range of activities and its extraordinary reversals of fortune. Locke was born in 1632 and educated at Christ Church, Oxford, where, after profound disillusionment with the prevailing Aristotelianism, he nevertheless settled into the equivalent of a college fellowship. He lost it in 1684 in the political shufflings of the times. In Oxford he was much involved with the experimentalists, particularly Robert Boyle, through whom he came to know Newton and his circle. Attaching himself to the Earl of Shaftesbury, he held government offices until the 1680s. He spent two long periods abroad, first in the south of France and then in political exile in Holland. His involvement with science bore fruit in his *Essay concerning Human Understanding* (1690). His experience of government and the aftermath of the English revolution, which had been fought in part around the philosophical doctrine of the divine right of kings, was the basis for his extensive writings on the foundations of society. He died in 1704, in the home of the friends with whom he had spent his last years.

Locke took it for granted that human experience was confined to ideas, the contents of the mind. Ideas were, for him, mental entities that were experienced and attended to by the person whose mind contained them. Second-order ideas or ideas of reflection could be formed about first-order ideas of sensation. Though, according to Locke, we cannot be aware of material things, only of our ideas of them, we need to allow him some latitude to use the concept of "ideas of material things" before we can discuss how he formulated his fundamental categories. Allowing him this latitude, for expository purposes only, makes possible his grand distinction between ideas and qualities, between mental entities and the states of material things that cause them. The shape of a thing causes an idea of a shape in us, while the vibrations of the minute parts of a thing cause the idea of warmth in us. In some cases the engendered ideas resemble the material qualities which engender them, but in some cases ideas are engendered which are altogether unlike the corresponding material qualities which cause them. Perceived shapes are ideas of the first sort, while felt warmth is an idea of the second sort.

Since all we could be aware of, according to Locke, are ideas, we must start our investigations of the acquisition of knowledge of the natural world with them. Thus we have ideas of primary qualities, those which resemble their engendering qualities, and ideas of secondary qualities, those which do not. While the idea of motion resembles the material quality which engenders it, namely motion of some material thing against a stable background of other things, the idea of sweet does not resemble the quality which causes it. That would be an arrangement of invisible corpuscles. Secondary qualities, as referred to by quality words like "sweet," are nothing but powers to cause a person to experience a sweet taste, a Lockean idea. But these powers are grounded in states of the material stuff, clusters of the primary qualities that are the real essences of material things. The power to cause the sensation of warmth is grounded in the motion of molecules. The qualities we use to classify things, their nominal essences, are likely to be a mix of the primary and the secondary. Gold, for example, is picked out from other metals by its yellow color and its density. The former is an idea of a secondary quality and the latter an idea of a primary quality.

Though this is presented to us as if it were the upshot of an investigation in the psychology of perception, we can see very easily that that interpretation cannot be right. Since we experience only ideas, we could never find out by experience that ideas and qualities were related in the way Locke describes. We could never have an experience of qualities independent of ideas, since Locke thinks that all our experience is of ideas. So it looks as if his doctrine of primary and secondary qualities, and the corresponding cleavage of ideas into two corresponding groups, is quite inadequate as a philosophy of science. Such a philosophy should bring together a solution to the problem of how we can have knowledge of the material world with a metaphysics for that world.

John Locke presented himself as the under-labourer for Newtonian science, providing the rational grounding for a mechanistic account of the material world. What is the status of scientific knowledge in Locke's scheme?

> In these matters we can go no further than particular experience informs us of matter of fact, and by analogy to guess what effects like bodies are, upon other trials, like to produce. But to a perfect science of natural bodies (not to mention spiritual beings), we are, I think, so far from being capable of any such thing that I conclude it lost labour to seek it. (Locke, 1690 [1974]: II, 1640)

According to Locke, the only propositions that are guaranteed to be universal and true, indeed necessarily true, are those which express relations between ideas, rather than between ideas and states of affairs. Only these should we properly call *science*. Physics and other natural sciences can give us only *opinion*, useful though that will be in the practical affairs of everyday life.

It is curious to find that the English empiricists, though their philosophy was one of the sources of positivism, were also among the strongest defenders of material atomism, a real but unseen world of invisible corpuscles. The most consistent empiricist of all was Robert Boyle. He made a serious effort to establish the metaphysical thesis that matter was corpuscularian on the basis of experiments, through which he thought that he could manipulate the invisible constituents of material stuff.

Boyle's experimental metaphysics

Possessed of a substantial income, Robert Boyle became a leader of the group of enthusiasts, vigorously pursuing systematic research on a wide range of chemical and physical topics. He was born in Ireland in 1627, and educated on the continent. While at school in Switzerland he had a religious experience which shaped his life. Out walking, he was caught in a storm. Arriving back at his lodgings, he reflected on why he had been spared from being struck by the lightning. There must be a divine purpose in it. He was meant to devote his life to defending Christianity, but above all through science. He spent many years in Oxford, working with great success with his assistant Robert Hooke. He moved to London in 1668, and was much involved with the early years of the Royal Society. His interest in the East India Company seems to have been more for its potential as a missionary institution than for its commercial possibilities. Apart from a stream of scientific and philosophical publications he wrote extensively on religious matters. He died in 1691.

In his *Origins of Forms and Qualities* (1666) Robert Boyle offers an interesting argument for the reality of the mechanical corpuscles which he and many other philosopher-scientists of the period took to be the unobservable basis of the physical world. The argument makes essential use of the idea of indirect manipulation of what cannot be observed by acting upon what can be. Boyle was well aware that the doctrine of primary and secondary qualities, which he shared with John Locke, meant that the "textures" (molecular level structures), responsible for the observed qualities of bodies were beyond the limits of perception, at least with the equipment available at that time. From this Locke had drawn his pessimistic conclusion, that though we knew there must be real essences we can never do more than make conjectures about what they might be, because they can never be perceived. Boyle argued that it was possible to manipulate material corpuscles at the molecular level indirectly to bring about observable changes in the stuff one had acted upon. Indeed he showed that there were manipulations which, by changing the shapes or the textures of material stuff, could be used to bring about changes in color, taste, and so on. A green emerald, reduced to powder, is white. So, he concluded, qualities such as color and taste must be effects on human sensibility of the unobserved corpuscular

constituents of matter. Looking at the argument from a slightly different perspective, we can interpret it as a demonstration that arrangements of corpuscles are the real unobserved states of matter that cause
people to see things as colored or feel them as cold or warm.

By citing many instances of changes in secondary qualities (the
powers to cause us to have sensations of taste, color, felt temperature,
medicinal efficacy, etc.) brought about by the manipulations that should
change only primary qualities, Boyle offers an empirical, experimental
defence for the corpuscularian metaphysics.

REALISM IN RETREAT

Some Logical Criticisms

The acceptance of the corpuscularian philosophy relies on passing over
two deep logical problems unnoticed by Bacon. Even at so early a
moment in the growing claims of science as the only legitimate source
of knowledge about the material world, two of the perennial philosophical problems involved in making good that claim had already
emerged. I will call them the "problem of scope" and the "problem of
depth" respectively.

What is the *scope* of scientific laws? How far can local discoveries
about natural phenomena be generalized to the whole universe, in time
and in space?

What is the *depth* of scientific theories? How far can we take the
imaginative work of scientists in constructing theories about natural
phenomena that go beyond what can be reached by the senses, whether
they are aided or unaided by instrumentation?

In this section we will look at some of the ways these problems
have been dealt with in relation to the principles of logic.

The "problem of scope" arises when we reflect on the grounds for
belief in universal laws, given the limitations of our ability to sample
phenomena in wider regions of space and epochs of time than the
here and now. The law of gravity works to a good approximation on
the surface of the earth and, we now know, in other nearby places, but
we reason in cosmology as if it worked everywhere. Kepler was the

first cosmologist to propose a *universal* law of gravity. He even wrote a short science-fiction tale, the *Somnium*, illustrating what the effect of the moon's gravity would be for its imaginary inhabitants. The factual observations and experiments involved in these investigations fell far short of evidence that could establish belief in the universal applicability of the laws in question.

The "problem of depth" strikes philosophers when they reflect on the meaning and acceptability of theories, which refer to entities, processes, structures beyond our powers of perception. Such theories purport to be explanations of the phenomena we can observe. The imagined patterns of planetary orbits offered rival explanations of the observed behavior of stars and planets. Which, if any, was the true picture?

In the background of every philosopher, until the twentieth century, was the presupposition that the forms and the limits of rationality were to be found in the principles of Aristotelian logic. The issues raised by the problems of scope and depth were framed for most of the second half of the millennium in terms of the technicalities of Aristotelian logic.

The problem of scope

Turning to formal logic, we find the necessary principles covering "all" and "some" inferences already clearly formulated by Aristotle.

1.   If we believe "All ducks are aquatic" is true, we can validly infer that "Some ducks are aquatic" is true. If we believe that "No birds can swim" is true, then we can validly infer that "Some birds cannot swim" is also true.

2.   If we believe "Some dogs are friendly" is true, we can validly infer that "No dogs are friendly" is false. If we believe that "Some birds do not have wings" is true, we can validly infer that "All birds have wings" is false.

However, there is no logical law which would certify the inference of a general proposition, such as "All diamonds are transparent," from any number of propositions about particular diamonds. From the point of view of logic, we are able to say for sure only that "Some diamonds are transparent." Evidence is always local in space and time, but the laws of nature are supposed to be completely general, holding without exception in all regions of space and at all times. How are they to be supported, given the limited scope of any evidence?

This conundrum has been called "the problem of induction." There seems to be an unbridgeable gap between the conclusions that logic would allow and the beliefs we come to informally.

The problem of depth

The problem of depth concerns the interpretation of the concepts employed in many kinds of theoretical explanations. Many seem to point to real unobservable states of affairs. How can we find out whether theoretical propositions using these concepts are true or false?

We can see the logical source of this puzzle in the "syllogism." A syllogism is based on two premises, a major and a minor. The major usually expresses some very general proposition of the form "All A are B" or "No S are T." The minor premise could be another general proposition, but in the sciences it often expresses the results of observation and experiment in the form "Some X are Y" or "Some X are not Y." Aristotle laid down the basic principles of validity for syllogisms. More ways of analyzing patterns of correct reasoning are now available, but simple syllogistic reasoning is enough for our purposes.

Compare these two examples.

All ducks are female birds
All female birds lay eggs
therefore
All ducks lay eggs.

All ducks are made of stone
All things made of stone lay eggs
therefore
All ducks lay eggs.

Both syllogisms are valid. We have recovered a true statement from both. We have no trouble rejecting the second argument, on the grounds that its premises are *both* false. But in the case of the rival scientific theories that purport to describe unobserved or unobservable entities and processes, all we have to go on are the observations which have been reproduced in the conclusion. We cannot test the truth of the theoretical propositions independently, since by hypothesis, these propositions are about unobservable states of affairs, if they are about anything at all. So our observations do not enable us to decide between rival theories, each of which reproduces the known observations. Impasse! This has been called "the underdetermination of theories by data."

Take the two problems together, induction and underdetermination, and science seems to be on shaky ground indeed. There have been a great number of attempts to solve or to resolve these problems. They remain sources of dissatisfaction among philosophers to this day.

Some Philosophical Criticisms

Locke's realist philosophy depends heavily on the viability of the distinction between ideas and qualities, between what is in the mind and what is in the world. His version of empiricism is just the claim that qualities in things cause ideas in the mind. His corpuscularian metaphysics depends on the distinction between ideas of primary and ideas of secondary qualities, based on the principle of resemblance. The most telling criticism against Locke's realist empiricism was mounted by Berkeley against the fundamental presupposition of corpuscularianism, that primary and secondary *qualities of things* in the world incite "*ideas* of primary and secondary qualities" in the mind.

Berkeley's philosophy of "ideas"

One of the most radical and interesting philosophers of the eighteenth century was George Berkeley. Born in Ireland in 1685, he studied at Trinity College, Dublin, taking holy orders as an Anglican. His scientific studies were first fixed on the problems of perception, for example, how was distance vision accomplished? His philosophical interests stemmed from these researches. All we are justified in believing really exists must be what we can perceive, he declared. He set off for London in 1713, and, like many intellectuals of the time, attached himself to a series of patrons. He spent several years as a chaplain to wealthy families, travelling extensively in Italy and France. In 1728 he went to America to set up a college. This was meant to be in Bermuda, but

he actually spent several years in Rhode Island. The project failed for
want of financial support and he returned to England in 1731. His
project may have failed, but he is still celebrated in the Californian university town that bears his name. As Bishop of Cloyne he became
involved in the perennial question of Irish society: justice for the Irish.
He retired to Oxford, where he died in 1753.

Eschewing the idea that we could know God's nature and plan for
the world just by reflection, Berkeley shared some of the views of some
of the advocates of Natural Religion. We should be able to come to
know the rules by which God created the world by discovering the
laws of nature by the methods of the sciences.

Berkeley's famous principle, "To be is to be perceived," is based on
a critical examination of some of the presuppositions of Locke's
account of ideas and qualities. Ideas were in the mind and qualities in
matter. Ideas of primary qualities resembled the corresponding qualities, whereas ideas of secondary qualities did not. A quality like "being
colored white" was a power to induce a white sensation in a person.
These powers were grounded in clusters of primary qualities inhering
in matter, unobservable material stuff. Berkeley's arguments are of great
elegance. The first step is to show, by example, that Locke's way of distinguishing ideas of primary from ideas of secondary qualities is wholly
inadequate. The distinction between ideas and qualities, which depends
on it, must be abandoned. The second step is to point out that ideas
are inert. And there is no unobservable matter to play the active role
that Locke assigns to it, causing people's ideas. The world as we perceive it must consist of ideas. It does not consist of supposedly mind-
independent qualities (Berkeley, 1719).

Samuel Johnson, displaying a thorough misapprehension of
Berkeley's philosophy, is said to have kicked a stone, declaring "I refute
you thus!" Johnson could no more kick the material substratum of the
stone than he could see or taste it. In kicking it, he displayed the
primary qualities of the stone as ideas in his own and Boswell's pattern
of experiences.

Berkeley insisted that there is agency in the universe, but it is an
attribute only of spiritual beings. In so far as people have autonomy,
they are agents. Drawing this consequence set Berkeley in opposition
to the materialist psychologies that had begun to appear in the early
eighteenth century, psychologies which weakened the authority of

moral principles. We will follow the rise of materialism when we turn to the development of materialist conceptions of human nature.

Science is of importance, since it enables human beings to grasp God's rules for creating and sustaining the universe. But it cannot have any more real content than correlations and concomitances of kinds of ideas, and the analogies these bear to one another. There is no material substance "behind" what we perceive, nor do any of the ideas or qualities we perceive have any powers to bring anything about.

Hume's attack on natural agency and material substance

David Hume was born in Edinburgh in 1711. His education was erratic, and eventually, at the age of 23, he went to France, to La Flèche. There he settled down to write one of the great works of philosophy in English, his *Treatise of Human Nature*. Its quality was not recognized on publication, and Hume famously commented that it "had fallen still-born from the press." After several false starts, Hume became the librarian of the Advocates' Library in Edinburgh. He turned to writing a vast *History of England* (1754–62) which secured not only his reputation but his career. He became secretary to the British Ambassador in Paris, and there enjoyed a measure of literary fame. He pursued a political and diplomatic career for many years. He died in 1776, stoically enduring cancer, and refusing any deathbed reconciliation with religion.

It seems that the strength of our beliefs about the material world drawn from scientific research far exceed what would be strictly justified by logic alone. How should the gap between what logic would allow and good sense demands we believe be filled? Are the metaphysical presuppositions of the Realists justified?

Hume based his philosophical analyses on a simple principle. He asked himself what were the sources of the two leading ideas of the corpuscularians and of the dynamicists. Where do we get the idea of a material substance behind all the appearances of things? What is the source of the hypothesis that there is a cluster of causal powers producing the impressions of those appearances? According to Hume, the meaning of an idea is the impression from which it was derived. If our beliefs can be explained psychologically, that is, by showing that the impressions from which the leading ideas are derived are psychological phenomena, then we are relieved from the task of justifying their role as pointers to a realm of beings which we must believe exist but which we cannot perceive.

Here is what Hume said in his last writings on the subject, *An Enquiry Concerning Human Understanding*

> But when one species of event has always, in all instances, been conjoined with another, we make no longer any scruple of foretelling one upon the appearance of the other, and of employing that reasoning, which alone can assure us of any matter of fact or existence. We then call the one object, Cause; the other, Effect. We suppose that there is some connexion between them; some power in the one, by which it infallibly produces the other, and operates with the greatest certainty and strongest necessity . . . But there is nothing in a number of instances . . . except only, that after a repetition of similar instances, the mind is carried by habit, upon the appearance of one event to expect its usual attendant, and to believe that it will exist. This connexion, therefore, which we feel in the mind, this customary transition of the imagination from one object to its usual attendant, is the sentiment or impression from which we form the idea of power or necessary connexion. (Hume, 1777 [1963]: Section VII, Part II, p. 59)

In this famous passage Hume argues that the seeming necessity of causal relations and of causal inferences is no more than a habit of mind to expect the same effect to occur when the same cause occurs. The idea of "causal power" has no real-world reference. Its use is not a matter of logic, but of psychology. The idea of causal efficacy is brought into being by long experience of regular patterns of events.

In a similar vein, Hume attacks the explanatory and quality-sustaining role of the concept of "substance" in philosophy.

> The idea of a substance . . . is nothing but a collection of simple ideas, that are united by the imagination, and have a particular name assigned to them, by which we are able to recall, either to ourselves or others, that collection . . . the particular qualities that form a substance, are commonly referred to an unknown something, in which they are supposed to inhere. (Hume, 1739 [1965]: Part 1, Section VI)

Not only is the idea of power to be assigned a psychological origin, so too is the idea of substance. So both alternatives for a metaphysics of nature that presupposes a reality distinct from human beings and their thoughts are brought into question.

Hume's method of argument is really very simple. To find the genuine content of any idea, we must refer it to the impression from which we derived it. In the two cases in question, causal power and material substance, Hume tries to show that the originating impression is of a psychological phenomenon, not a state of worldly affairs. Neither the concept of "active power" nor that of "unobserved substance" have the meanings we think they have. It was those meanings that gave them a place in the Realist philosophy. Take them away and that philosophy is deprived of its most important concepts.

This looked like the death knell of scientific realism. There are no grounds for imaging real but imperceptible corpuscular (molecular) structures to explain what one has observed. Nor is there any meaning to be given to such dynamicist notions as efficacy, causal activity, power, natural necessity, and so on.

Hume's criticisms of dynamism had little effect on the metaphysical foundations of the natural sciences. Though Kant made much of his debt to Hume, he did not follow Hume's rejection of the reality of causal powers. Indeed Kant worked out a thoroughgoing dynamicist theory of matter in his *Metaphysical Foundations of Natural Science* of 1788. There is no Lockean matter, nor are there any primary qualities. All qualities are secondary, that is, nothing but powers to affect other bodies and the human senses. Unlike Locke, Kant took his attractive and repulsive forces to be fundamental, not in need of grounding in clusters of primary qualities.

The question of the reality of causal powers is still a live issue in philosophy. However, the stringency of Hume's philosophy did have an influence on one important development, the rise of positivism.

THE RISE OF POSITIVISM

Positivism can be thought of as a retreat from speculation to certainty. It is a philosophical stance driven by a minimalist impulse, attitude, or frame of mind, which expresses itself in a variety of philosophical theses and arguments. Always ready to wield Ockham's Razor against the proliferation of kinds of entities beyond necessity, positivists could be said to hold that it is better to accept less than perhaps one could, for fear of believing more than perhaps one should. There are several sources in the eighteenth and nineteenth centuries for the positivism that became popular in the first half of the twentieth century.

Though both Berkeley and Hume have been hailed as ancestors of positivism, British empiricism never developed the extreme anti-theory stance that it had on the continent. In France positivism began with reflections on the conditions necessary for the possibility of a science of society. In Germany and Austria it was initiated in conscious opposition to Hegelian thought, and developed as a philosophy which aimed at generalizing the apparent power and rationality of the natural sciences to all fields of human endeavor. Positivism was seen by many as the very heart of modernism, a form of life "founded on scientific knowledge of the world and rational knowledge of value, which places the highest premium on individual human life and freedom, and believes that such freedom and rationality will lead to social progress" (Cahoone, 1996: 12).

Metaphysical Positivism

French positivism grew out of the critical philosophies and anticlerical sentiments of the eighteenth century. Though positivists, in their reliance on the senses as the exclusive sources of knowledge, held rather diverse views on how moral and political principles were to be created to replace those which their criticisms of religion would have eliminated, most acknowledged the existence of irresolvable mysteries, *inconnaissables*, and all recognized the difficulties of constructing a plausible and satisfying positivist ethics.

The central figure in French positivism was the difficult and irascible Auguste Comte. He was born in 1798 at Montpellier. His education at the École Polytechnique in Paris was terminated by his expulsion. In 1818, while scratching a living as a tutor, he met Saint-Simon, with whom he began a long association, ending, as did many of his personal relationships, in an irresolvable quarrel. His marriage in 1825 was short-lived, as was his attempt to popularize his system in lectures. He was virtually unemployable. In the last years of his life he was supported by English friends, particularly John Stuart Mill. He died in 1857. He was fortunate in the friendship of Mill and Harriet Martineau. The former did much to make his work known and the latter produced the English translation of his major work by which he is still best known outside France.

Comte built his philosophy on the idea of a three-phase development of ways of understanding. Rather than describe these phases or styles as historical stages, he preferred to call them states or attitudes of mind, since he saw around him examples of people thinking in all three of the main ways he discusses. In the "theological state of mind" a person looks for explanations in terms of the "continuous and arbitrary actions of supernatural agents" (Comte, 1830–42 [1853]: 5). The next, more advanced state of mind, is only a modification of the first. Supernatural agents are replaced by "abstract forces . . . capable of giving rise by themselves to all the phenomena observed." In the third or positive state, the human mind "endeavours now to discover by a well-combined use of reasoning and observation, the actual *laws* of phenomena . . . that is to say, their invariable relations of succession and likeness."

In a striking passage (Comte, 1853, I: 23) he slips from a repudiation of the search for first or final causes to a rejection of any interest in causes at all: "we do not pretend to explain the real causes of phenomena, as this would merely throw the difficulty further back." All that Newton's Law of Gravity can do is to show us a great variety of phenomena as "only a single fact looked at from different points of view . . . the weight of a body at the earth's surface" (p. 26). So stringent was Comte's empiricism that he famously and unwisely chose the chemical composition of the stars as a prime example of unattainable knowledge.

The laws of society ought to be discoverable by exactly the same methods used to discover the laws of material nature. It should be possible to devise a scientific sociology. By the four methods of observation, experiment, comparison, and history we ought to be able to arrive at laws of society without positing any unobservable causes. But these could be discovered only by those whose "state of mind" has passed from the theological through the metaphysical to the positive, seeking only correlations among social phenomena. Since not everyone can aspire to this degree of perfection, Comte advocated the fabrication of a suitable religion to take the place of the superstitious faiths of the time.

However, it is by no means clear how adopting the positive attitude of mind leads to a system of morality. How can one be a positivist and yet provide an "objective, authoritative ethical system?" If we are confined to phenomena, what actually happens, how can we make the passage to declarations of what ought to happen? Progress, according to the threefold scheme of "states of mind," must pass from the theological to the positive. This is enough, so Comte asserted, to engender a new social morality. In the positive state of mind the true decency and generosity of human nature will come to dominate social relations, hitherto overlaid by superstitious beliefs in invisible forces. This is the "law of progress." Sociology is like a medicine for the ills of the state, letting natural health shine through. Since the main bar to progress is the persistence of primitive attitudes of mind, the cure is at hand – change the attitudes. Comte respected the role that religion had had in supporting morality. To take advantage of it, he published a catechism for those who would "take instruction" in the new religion. Not surprisingly, few took it up!

Logical Positivism

In the story of German philosophy in the nineteenth century we have a grand opposition between claims to knowledge based on scientific research, positive science, and what were seen as not much short of mystery-mongering claims to knowledge based on neo-Kantian philosophical speculation. Here we have German positivism in conflict with German idealism. We will follow the story of German idealism in a later chapter.

Mach and sensationalism

Of all the positivistically inclined writers of the nineteenth century, there is no doubt that Ernst Mach was the most influential on subsequent generations of philosophers and scientists. Three of his works, *The Science of Mechanics* (1893), *The Analysis of Sensations* (6th edition, 1906), and *Popular Scientific Lectures* (1894) were widely read, quickly translated, and often quoted in the decades that followed. Mach was born in 1838 in Moravia. He studied at the University of Vienna. Thereafter he pursued a traditional academic career. He was successively a professor in Graz, Prague, and finally Vienna, to where he returned in 1895. Most of his work in physics concerned the behavior of gases, including supersonic velocities, whence we have the Mach number that tells us how fast our Concorde is flying. Mach's antitheoretical stance was perhaps exaggerated. It seems that his apparent hostility to Relativity theory was an invention by his brother, Leopold, in an attempt to recruit Mach to the ranks of Austrian antisemitism. He died in 1916, with his great work in electromagnetism unfinished. Many of the most characteristic theses of the Logical Positivists of the Vienna Circle, that twentieth-century fount of positivism that influenced the whole Western world, can be found explicitly formulated in Mach's writings.

Mach's positivism did not emerge from philosophical reflections on problems of knowledge, but from his long-running program to rework the foundations of physics in such a way as to eliminate the unobservable domain from the ontology of the natural sciences, and particularly to eliminate any traces of reference to absolutes. He described his project very clearly.

> My definition [of "mass"] is the outcome of an endeavour to establish the interdependence of phenomena and to remove all metaphysical obscurity, without accomplishing on this account less than other definitions have done. (Mach, 1883: 267)

His method was simple. He set out to show that all concepts in physics that purported to refer to unobservable properties, entities, or relations, including "quantity of electricity" and "temperature," could be defined in terms of observable properties of material set-ups, such as the mutual accelerations of visible and tangible bodies. Newtonian mass, as the quantity of matter in a body, was not only an absolute, but also, in Mach's terms, metaphysical since unobservable. It is a mistake, so he claimed, to substitute a "mechanical mythology" for the "old . . . metaphysical scheme." "The atom must remain a tool for representing phenomena, like the functions of mathematics" (Mach, 1894: 205).

Summing up his point of view, Mach claimed that the laws of nature were nothing but devices for "the communication of scientific knowledge, that is a mimetic reproduction of facts in thought, the object of which is to replace and save the trouble of new experience" (Mach, 1894: 192).

But what were the phenomena, the facts? Examining a "province of facts," "we discover the simple permanent elements of the mosaic" (Mach, 1894: 194). According to Mach, the only positive knowledge one can have is knowledge of one's own sensations. How does this escape a charge of solipsism, of creating a world of which he is the sole occupant? Well aware of this danger, he tried to find a place for the world of material things.

> In mentally separating a body from the changeable environment in which it moves what we really do is to extricate a group of sensations on which our thoughts are fastened and which is of relatively greater stability than the others, from the stream of our sensations . . . It would be better to say that bodies or things are compendious mental symbols for groups of sensations – symbols that do not exist outside of thought. (Mach, 1894: 200)

I have to confess that I do not understand how this move could have helped Mach to escape from the solipsist trap!

The Vienna Circle

In the early 1920s, a group of Austrian and German philosophers, physicists, and mathematicians began to hold regular meetings under the chairmanship of Moritz Schlick, (1882–1936), one of the few philosophers deliberately murdered by a disgruntled student. Their avowed purpose was to develop a form of philosophy that was not only compatible with the natural sciences but shared many of their methods and ideals. The group called themselves the "Vienna Circle." They were explicitly and strongly anti-Hegelian, seeing themselves in opposition to the prevailing Hegelian orthodoxy of the German-speaking universities.

In order to accomplish their aim of constructing a "scientific" style of philosophy, they believed that their first task was the elimination of metaphysics. They took metaphysics to be any type of speculation which was not grounded in empirical data. Admiring Mach's positivistic views, they tended to assume that sensations or, at any rate, private experiences, provided the kind of unqualified grounding upon which all legitimate claims to knowledge should be based.

Every observer fills in his own content . . . thereby giving his symbols a unique meaning, and filling in the structure with content as a child may colour drawings of which only the outlines are given. (Schlick, 1932, quoted in Passmore, 1957: 376)

The positivists' technique for the elimination of metaphysics was simple. Only if a method of verification could be described for a proposition was that proposition meaningful. All of religion and much of Hegelian philosophy failed the test.

Wherever there is a meaningful problem one can in theory always give the path that leads to its solution. For it becomes evident that giving this path coincides with the indication of its meaning . . . The act of verification in which the path to a solution finally ends is always of the same sort: it is the occurrence of a definite fact that is confirmed . . . by means of immediate experience. (Schlick, 1959: 56)

Ethics was problematic. How could a moral maxim be verified? In the end the Circle came to think of moral discourse as a matter of the expression of preferences, which indeed could be grounded in the sensory data of pleasure and pain.

The verification principle for meaningfulness was soon being discussed and adopted by many philosophers outside the Circle. Was it a criterion for meaningfulness, or was it a formula for discovering the meaning of a proposition? Was the meaning of a proposition no more and no less than the appropriate *method* for verifying it? The Circle was widely believed to be advocating the latter version of the verification principle.

Since the members of the group were convinced that the only legitimate way of analyzing the structure of discourses was by the use of the principles of formal logic, they began to call their position "logical positivism." It was more or less under that title that it was brought to the English-speaking world by A. J. Ayer (1910–92), in a best-selling little book *Language, Truth and Logic* (Ayer, 1936). Though it was a somewhat stripped-down version of the views of the members of the Vienna Circle, it provided a wholesome antidote to much that was popular in Western philosophy at the time. The persecution of Jews and liberals by the Nazi regime of the 1930s led to a migration of many of the members of the Vienna Circle to the United States. There logical positivism met the native pragmatism, already much taken with the idea of logic as the prime tool of philosophical analysis.

Positivism Meets Pragmatism

The story of the influence of positivism in the United States must begin with the "pragmatic" principle upon which American pragmatism was based. Though C. S. Peirce (1839–1914) is usually credited with the deepest ideas in the pragmatist movement, it is to his benefactor and mentor William James (1842–1910) that we owe the most plausible exposition of the pragmatist relationship between truth and practice. The truth of a proposition is determined by its role in a procedure, which, in turn, is assessed for success or failure relative to the task in hand, which is itself referred to a larger framework, the long-range interests of humanity as a whole. This formulation allowed James to incorporate religious statements within the realm of the meaningful, since they had a place in practices of everyday life. Peirce had tied truth simply to agreement or consensus, which was far too relativist for James.

The Vienna Circle doctrine, that only in its method of verification did a proposition display its meaning, came close enough to the pragmatists' account of truth to encourage the refugees from Vienna to feel at home in the American scene. At the same time one or two of the younger American philosophers, particularly W. V. Quine (b.1908) at Harvard, had come to know of Russell's "mathematical philosophy." They were enthusiastic about the use of the latest developments in logic as tools for expelling nonsense from philosophy. For instance, Quine (1953) became well known for using a logical criterion for determining the scope of existence claims. Logical positivists like Rudolph Carnap (1891–1970) fitted easily into such an atmosphere.

Conclusion

The idea that it is the World that shapes the Mind has lent itself to two rather different philosophies. If the World is present to human beings only through the sensations they receive through their organs of perception, then it is difficult to see how a strict empiricist could countenance the reckless extension of claims to knowledge to encompass imperceptible regions of the universe, be they distant in space and time, or out of scale, too minute or too enormous to be taken in by a human being. We have seen how empiricism split into two schools, the realists and the positivists. Realists believed that the methods of science could penetrate beyond the bounds of sense, to give us reliable knowledge of imperceptible regions of the world. The bases for explanations of observable phenomena were to be found there. The dance of imperceptible molecules explained the observable behavior of gases, liquids, and solids. For the advocates of Natural Religion, God himself could be revealed by the application of the scientific method. Positivists were reluctant to countenance any steps beyond what could be perceived. Concepts which seemed to refer to imperceptibles, such as atoms or forces or gods, were at best devices to help us think. In no circumstances were they to be taken literally.

The schism amongst empiricists came only in the eighteenth century. However, the astronomical debates of the sixteenth century clearly foreshadowed the distinctions in the forms of knowledge on which the two schools of empiricism were based. Is the matter settled now that the millennial moment is on us? I have to say that it is not. Perhaps the choice between Positivism and Realism is not a matter of reason after all, but expresses temperamental differences that go very deep.

9

Mind and Cosmos:
Rationalism and
Conventionalism

The development of the startling and seemingly wildly paradoxical idea
that the world is shaped by the structure of the human mind takes its
start, I believe, from a somewhat less dramatic thought. We have seen
how the devotees of Natural Religion thought they could discern
God's hand in the material universe. Suppose, however, there were to
be a direct follow up from those medieval philosophers who thought
that, at least in some limited way, we human beings could form conceptions of the nature and being of God just by reflecting on the
properties that a divine creator must necessarily possess. Descartes
and Leibniz both, to differing degrees, made use of this idea. Human
beings could go some way to getting definite knowledge of how the
material universe must be, by reflecting on the necessary nature of the
God who created it. According to this view of the matter, the world
and the mind of man still exist independently of one another, but
human beings do not have to *examine* the world to discover its leading
characteristics. Reflection will suffice.

This line of thought developed into something rather different.
Kant, and a long line of philosophers who picked up his point of view,
proposed that the very being of the world, as we human beings knew
it, was shaped by the activity of the human mind. Kant thought that
the shaping was accomplished by innate features of the human mind,
realizing the logical conditions for any sentient being, human or otherwise, to have experience at all. These conditions could be thought of
as rules for synthesizing the common features of the perceived world
out of the flux of sensations. In the same "moment," so to speak, the
contents of the mind as distinctive and ordered thoughts, as these are
experienced by a self-attentive human being, are also synthesized by
imposing rules on the flux.

Starting with the insight that Kant expressed in his aphorism, "Thoughts without content are empty, intuitions without concepts are blind," that experience is an intimate fusion of cognition and sensation, conventionalists generalized and weakened the Kantian point of view.

The world is revealed to human beings, only in so far as the conventions of language, mathematics, and other symbolic systems make it possible for us to abstract something definite from the otherwise indeterminate world available to the five senses. While the rationalists presupposed that the principles immanent in the material world were necessary, conventionalists presupposed that such principles were not only culturally contingent and relative, but also ultimately arbitrary.

THE RATIONALIST ACCOUNT
OF KNOWLEDGE

Descartes and God's Immutability

In several places in his writings Descartes makes use of hypotheses about the Divine Nature to attempt to prove certain very general laws of the material world. In the case of the laws of mechanics, God's immutability is the grounding principle. When a body collides with a body "weaker" that itself, according to Descartes, it loses a quantity of motion equal to that which it imparts to the other body. Descartes' proof of this part of his general law of the conservation of total motion, runs as follows:

> the law is proved from the immutability of the workings of God, by means of which the world is continually preserved through an action identical with its original act of creation . . . when he created the world in the beginning God did not only impart various motions to different parts of the world, but also produced all the reciprocal impulses and transfers of motion between the parts. Thus, since God preserves the world by the selfsame action and in accordance with the selfsame laws as when he created it, the motion which he preserves is not something permanently fixed in given pieces of matter, but something which is mutually transferred when collisions occur. (Descartes, 1647 [1985]: 243)

Since he preserves the world by the same laws as he created it, and he does not change, motion must not only be an inherent and constant property of pieces of matter, but must pass from one to another in such a way that the total motion is always the same. If that were not so God would have changed.

Leibniz carried this line of thought a step further.

Leibniz and Necessary Worlds

Gottfried Leibniz was born in 1646 in Leipzig, into an academic family. He completed his formal education at the age of 20. He did not follow an academic career, but, like Hume, made his life as a civil servant in various capacities. His first post was in the court of the Elector of Mainz. Already, as a young man, Leibniz was demonstrating an extraordinary mastery of both mathematical and philosophical thought On a diplomatic mission to Paris he met the leading French philosophers and scientists. He followed this up with a visit to England. Through his travels on official business he was well acquainted with the international community of scientists. A rivalry very soon developed with Newton. There was the vexed but ultimately trivial question of who had invented the calculus. More substantially, they differed on matters of religion. There were consequential issues in the philosophy of physics, such as the reality of absolute time and space, which divided them still further. Later in life Leibniz took service as the librarian to the Duke of Brunswick, devoting himself to the rather mundane task of building up the resources of the library. He combined his courtly duties with a great number of projects, including that of persuading Frederick I to set up an Academy of Sciences in Germany. This was probably inspired by what he had learned of the Royal Society in London. He died in 1716, leaving most of his voluminous writings unpublished.

Leibniz's approach to the ancient question of the relation of God and the material universe was firmly anti-empirical. He believed that the universe was God's creation. The character of the material world must reflect the nature of its creator. God could operate in no other way than in accordance with the laws of logic. Reflection on the principles of logic should enable a human being to work out in a general way what God's world must be like. And this is just what

Leibniz attempted to do in his semipopular work, the *Theodicy* of 1710 [1953].

How can we work from a hierarchy of laws of logic to arrive at the specification of this world as the only possible world, in a universe in which God is more logician than mechanic? We start with the idea of a plethora of possible worlds, and proceed, step by step, to reduce them to just one. Each step involves the application of a progressively stronger logical principle.

The first cut in the plethora of possible worlds comes by applying the Law of Noncontradiction, "Nothing can be both A and not-A at the same time." This principle rules out all contradictory worlds. These would be worlds in which, if they existed, there would be beings which, at the same moment, exemplified and did not exemplify some property. This is, of course, a play on words, since we cannot even imagine such a world.

The second cut in the range of the remaining, noncontradictory possible worlds is provided by the Law of Sufficient Reason. This serves to eliminate all worlds for which there is no sufficient reason why they should be so and not otherwise. For example, according to Leibniz, the world is not embedded in an absolute manifold of space and time. In a completely uniform space and time, as would have existed before the material world was created, there would have been no reason to create the world in one place or at one time rather than another. There would have been no difference between one place and another. The space and time of our world cannot be absolute without violating the law of sufficient reason.

The third cut in the range of all noncontradictory, reason-supported possible worlds is provided by the Law of the Identity of Indiscernibles. This law states that if there seem to be two beings which share all their properties, then there really is only one such being. Or, to put the principle around the other way: Every being must differ in some respect from every other. There are considerable problems in interpreting this principle. Without going into the matter too closely, it does seem to eliminate all worlds which differ only numerically, that is, worlds which are independent and separate beings, but have exactly similar properties. Each possible world must be different from every other.

The fourth and final cut in the range of all noncontradictory, reason-supported, nonidentical possible worlds is provided by the Law of Maximum Compossibility. This law is based on the principle that if

God could have created something, he would have done so. Thus, the world as created must contain the maximum range of beings and states that can exist together. This principle would eliminate all worlds in which less than the maximum diversity of mutually possible states exists. There is, according to Leibniz, only one such world, and that is this world. Advertising this conclusion with the phrase "the best of all possible worlds," Leibniz laid himself open to Voltaire's ridicule. In *Candide* (1759) Leibniz appears as the absurd Dr Pangloss, who pops up whenever Candide suffers another disaster, to reassure him that this is indeed the best of all possible worlds.

To this day the phrase leads to misunderstandings. Leibniz means that this world is logically the best, that is, the richest in terms of possible coexistents. The question of its moral quality is impossible to resolve by human beings, since God's plan is inscrutable. Seeming evils must somehow, in a God-created universe, really be goods, if we could only see things rightly.

The project of deducing the nature of the material world from necessary or self-evident first principles has had a perennial fascination. We have seen how Leibniz was anticipated in a rather slapdash way by Descartes (1647). Whereas Descartes based his deductions of the laws of mechanics on God's immutability, in modern times the physicist and cosmologist, Sir Arthur Eddington (1935) made a new and vigorous attempt to carry out the program from certain general properties of a mathematical system, "group theory." Group theory is a method of specifying all the possible transformations that a given structure can undergo. Eddington tried to use this way of expressing the constraints on any system to deduce the defining features of the material world.

It is one thing to try to work out the main characteristics of an independent world by reflecting on the conditions necessary for it to exist. It is quite another to believe that when we perceive the world we are constructing it or reconstructing it according to principles that are either in our minds or in the mind of God. What if the world, as we perceive it, is in important respects our own creation? Kant shifted the *a priori* principles of world design from the mind of God to the minds of human beings. Necessarily possessed of a common inheritance, since the rules for synthesizing worlds reflect the logical conditions for there to be experience of any kind, people construct a common world.

CONVENTIONALISM: THE MIND
SHAPES THE WORLD

Conventionalists give priority to concepts over the senses in the genesis of the world, as it is given in experience. Unlike Descartes and Leibniz, who located the conditions that shaped the world in the necessary nature of God, Conventionalists see these conditions as human. In one way Kant is a conventionalist. The *a priori* organizing principles, though rooted in the logical conditions for the possibility of experience, are realized by human beings in their coming to know the world. In another way he is a rationalist in that he believed that the *a priori* conceptual system which is exemplified in the world is necessary and unique, derived from the logical limits on the forms of all possible judgements.

Conventionalists share the Kantian priority of concepts to determinate experience. However, they treat the system of concepts actually in use as the result of a choice among several possible sets of conventions. For example, the nature of space, as we experience it in the arrangement of material things, is expressed in a system of concepts that are in accordance with the principles of Euclidian geometry. Mathematicians have found other consistent geometries in which our experience of space might have been ordered. In fact one of these alternatives, Riemannian geometry, has become the preferred way of thinking about spatial relations in physics. To take another example: we divide people up into age groups in a certain way, adults, adolescents, and children, with further finer distinctions available when needed. The historian, Philippe Aries (1962) showed that our categories are by no means universal, even in the history of our own culture. This might incline one to think that they are conventions. They are not forced on us by "the facts." Nor do they seem to be universal features of the human mind, expressing some of the logical conditions of the possibility of experience. Having been chosen from among other possibilities, their application brings about the facts as we now perceive them by providing the means for partitioning and grouping what we perceive. But that way of shaping the world could have been different.

The force of the conventionalist attitude to the genesis of facts can be illustrated rather nicely with a simple analogy, the technique of the bacterial stain. Different features of the fine structure of bacterial cells can be brought to light by the choice of different stains. Each structure so revealed is a real structure, but not all the internal structures can be seen at once. What we see depends on the stain we choose. What can be observed and identified as an instance of some kind of object, property, relation, structure, or process is a function of the concepts with which we can describe it and the instruments which bring forth the phenomena. Thus science is, as Whilliam Whewell (1860) long ago pointed out, a cycle between observation (facts) and concepts (ideas). And I would add instruments to the given repertoire of the means for making nature display some of her attributes. Science is the result of a continuous interaction between the world and people. People use various tools, instruments, and concepts to approach it. What the world shows is what is made available to people by the use of those tools.

The conventionalist point of view was made popular a century ago by Henri Poincaré (1905). Though it has changed in some ways, it is still very much with us. In its most general form it involves the claim that what is observable is a function of the conceptual system employed to identify and describe the phenomena in question. A chemist could not pick out examples of *double decomposition* unless familiar with the concept. According to the conventionalist point of view, we do not first observe a phenomenon and then find out that it is a case of oxidation. We define "oxidation" within a framework of concepts, some of which are given their meaning by theory. Then we can identify the phenomenon. Concepts are *a priori*, their meanings established prior to experience. Moreover, concepts can be readjusted to fit circumstances. Concepts are assessed, corrected, and assimilated into already existing bodies of knowledge.

Kant and the Synthetic a *priori*

Kant's views partake of rationalism in that he assumes that there is only one system of concepts realized in human experience. They partake of conventionalism in that that system in application determines the actual form of human experience.

Immanuel Kant was born in Königsberg in 1724. The beneficiary of an excellent but strict Protestant education, he spent his life in the city of his birth, lecturing and writing. The orderliness of his life was legendary. It was said that the citizens would set their clocks by the timing of his daily walk. He had family connections with the British Isles, and was well informed on political and philosophical developments in Britain and France. His liberalism in politics and religion led to some troubles with the authorities, but he outlived them. He died in 1804 in the very city in which he was born. It is worth remarking on the contrast between the extraordinary richness of his intellectual life and the breadth of his writings, and the extreme provincial dullness of his surroundings.

While Locke thought of the contents of the mind as ultimately determined by the active powers of matter, Kant's innovative philosophy inaugurated a very different way of thinking about the relation between mental activity and the world as we perceive it. Leibniz and Descartes had built their form of *a priorism* on the idea that by thinking about the necessary attributes of God we could know something about the world before we examined it in any way. For Kant, the *world* as we perceive it is the product of the work we do in shaping the flux of sensations. We do this without conscious thought, according to certain *a priori* rules. In this way, we synthesize an empirical world of things, causes, events, and so on. We live in a common world because we share rules for synthesizing worlds by the same synthetic activity that shapes our thoughts and feelings into individual minds. The key to the form of this activity is the *unity* of the world and of each individual mind.

In his *Critique of Pure Reason* of 1781, followed by a much revised second edition in 1787, Kant developed his astonishing and subtle account of the formation of minds and worlds. His writings are difficult partly because of the subtlety and complexity of his thought and partly because of the very precise terminology that he develops for his purposes. In what follows I have tried to present the main outlines of his philosophy in a relatively simple way, without distorting the depth of the insights he offers the attentive reader.

The project of philosophy is to bring to light what is implicit in all our knowledge and experience. Kant explains what he means by "experience" as follows: "Experience is the sum of all cognitions wherein objects are given to us." Here is the source of the problems that he intends to unravel.

But though all our knowledge begins with experience, it does not follow that it all arises out of experience. For it may well be that even our empirical knowledge is made up of what we receive through impressions and of what our own faculty of knowledge (sensible impressions serving merely as the occasion) supplies from itself. If our faculty of knowledge makes any such addition, it may be that we are not in a position to distinguish it from the raw material, until with long practice of attention we have become skilled in separating it. (Kant, 1787 [1996]: B1)

Kant's project is to find the "additions" imparted by the synthesis to the realm of experience – both outer, the world as we perceive it, and our minds, as we know them by reflection.

He distinguishes between "intuition," by which he means the direct apprehension of something, and "understanding" which is the power we have to manage concepts in thought. In commenting on this distinction he gave us the well known aphorism:

Thoughts without content are empty, intuitions without concepts are blind. (Kant, 1787 [1996]: B75)

We also need to grasp what Kant means by his distinction between what is pure and what is empirical.

Intuition and concepts . . . constitute the elements of all our cognition . . . [they] are empirical if they contain sensations; they are pure if no sensation is mixed in with the presentation. (Kant, 1787 [1996]: 106)

The understanding cannot intuit anything, and the senses cannot think anything . . . Only from their union can cognition arise. (Kant, 1787 [1996]: 107)

How are we to abstract the "additions" we have made from our concrete acts of thinking and perceiving? This requires two steps. The first step, the "Transcendental Aesthetic," goes as follows:

Segregate from sensibility everything that belongs to sensation, so that nothing will remain . . . but the mere form of appearances . . . [this yields] two pure forms – space and time. (Kant, 1787 [1996]: 74–75)

Now we can see what has been added to mere sensations to create a world of objects laid out in space and time, complementary to our minds, in which thoughts and feelings are experienced sequentially as the order of time.

However, the world displays a much more detailed structure than that. There are permanent objects and causal sequences to be seen everywhere. So there must be another phase, and a second step in the process of bringing our "additions" to light. Kant calls this step "Transcendental Logic."

> In a transcendental logic we isolate the understanding [just as we isolated sensibility in step 1] and we select from our cognition merely the part of thought that has its origins solely in the understanding. The use of this pure cognition rests on the condition . . . that objects to which it can be applied are given to us in intuition. (Kant, 1787 [1996]: 115)

Here is what we get.

> If we abstract from all content of a judgement as such and pay attention only to the mere form of understanding in it then we find that the function of thought in judgement can be brought under four headings. (Kant, 1787 [1996]: 123)

The analytical phase of this work yields a matching pattern of four sets of three concepts. These will appear in the objects of intuition, what we perceive, since these objects are the products of a synthesis, by which the understanding shapes the manifold of sensations into the world as we perceive it, and about which we can make judgments.

This synthesizing activity of the understanding yields both a unified consciousness in the person and, complementary to the knowing mind, there is just one world. The last Kantian term we need to grasp is his use of the word translated as "transcendental." Something is transcendental if it is necessary for experience but not given in experience. We do not intuit, that is, directly apprehend space and time, only things and events ordered in certain ways. Similarly, we do not apprehend causality as such, but events ordered in such a way that one is a condition for the other. We do not apprehend our selves, our egos, but we experience our minds as unified. This is the synthetic unity of apperception, by which Kant means the unified structure of representations as mine. I can always preface any of my intuitions with "I think." All of these aspects are transcendental. The job of the philosopher is bring them out in such a way that we can think them, as pure concepts of the understanding.

How are the *a priori* categories and the experience I have of a determinate and ordered world related? Kant argues that there must be something intermediate, which is "homogeneous with the category . . . and with the appearance" (Kant, 1787 [1996]: B177). He calls such intermediaries "schemata." These are rules of synthesis, by which the world is put together as an orderly appearance. To each of the schemata there corresponds a general proposition, such as the principle that "All alterations take place in conformity with the law of the connection of cause and effect" (Kant, 1787 [1996]: B235). This is the propositional expression of the schema of cause, which is one of the categories of "relation." Causal relations are those which can be expressed in the form: "If so and so, then such and such."

Propositions expressing schematisms are synthetic *a priori*. They cannot but be true of the world as we experience it, but we could not come to know them unless we experienced such a world. This is why human beings find themselves in an intelligible world. It has been put together by the use of schematisms that correspond to the possible forms of judgment. Synthetic *a priori* propositions must determine the basic forms in which all empirical knowledge, that is, all science, must be expressed.

The system of judgments, categories, concepts, and schemata is involved in creating the empirical world we perceive and the structure and contents of the mind of the perceiver. But this system is not arbitrary. It is not just a convention. Kant thought that it was the only system that there could possibly be. The pattern of forms of judgment, he thought, could not have been otherwise. He finds the logical conditions of all possible experience in the closed set of forms that judgments could take. This is a presupposition of his approach that has been much discussed and criticized. Why should there be just *twelve* forms of judgment?

Though much of the detail of Kant's extraordinary achievement in laying bare the presuppositions of our way of being has been relegated to history, the general outlook that we find in this thrilling analysis has been followed up by many other philosophers.

The English Interpretation of Kant

Whewell and the idea–fact cycle

The most impressive and thoroughgoing attempt at refining the rationalist point of view, pushing it more toward conventionalism, was undertaken by William Whewell (1794–1866). Sometimes spoken of as the "English Kant," he weakened the Kantian *a priori* character of the intellectual content of science to allow for its modification and growth as our knowledge of the natural world increased. He based his work firmly in studies of the history of specific branches of science, tracing out the interplay between "ideas" and "facts." He showed that there was a cyclical development between the poles of several equivalent pairs of oppositions. There are cycles between "ideas" and "facts," "theories" and "observations," and so on. We can pick out facts only if we have some concepts to do it with, and so such facts will necessarily display such concepts. If I use the concept of "apple" to select a fruit, it must display the attributes that are definitive of the "apple" concept. But Whewell's historical studies had convinced him of the mutability of both terms of the seeming opposition. As our concepts changed and developed so too would the facts that were available to us change and develop. However, these changes were constrained by what he called the "leading idea" that defined a science. On the other hand there were often quite new and surprising results of observation and experiment. These needed to be accommodated in the body of the science in question. To do this, the ideas of the science, its theories, would have to be modified. And thus modified they made possible the apprehension of new facts. Thus we find, in the sciences as they have actually developed, a cyclical process of mutual transformation and adjustment between thought and experience (Whewell, 1860 [1970]).

Whewell claimed that a scientist makes a discovery when he finds that he can add an organizing idea to a multitude of sensations without strain. Kepler added the organizing idea of an ellipse to a multitude of astronomical observations. Whewell called this process the "colligation" of facts. Sometimes the existing stock of ideas already contains the necessary organizing idea, sometimes the stock of ideas must be refined and elaborated. Whewell called this the "explication of the conceptions." He argued that the relations among ideas must be necessary, but it is contingent whether they will serve any useful role in the colligation of facts. The patterns of relations among ideas, and so the ideas themselves can be adjusted under the pressure of facts. Of course, these facts are the result of the application of earlier ideas to our sensations. The final step in Whewell's analysis of the genesis of scientific knowledge was the introduction of the important principle of consilience. The support that a hypothesis gets is enhanced when it is found to fit well with another hypothesis, whether or not there is any increase in the amount of supporting evidence. Whewell saw consilience as the means by which theory could grow and develop against a fairly static background of supporting evidence.

Poincaré and Conventionalism

One of the great mathematical physicists of all time, Henri Poincaré was born in 1854. He enjoyed a conventional and successful academic career. Membership of the Académie Française in 1908 gave him freedom from the routine of the classroom to develop his highly original approach to mathematical physics, anticipating the relativistic revolution in many important respects. Realizing that the principles of geometry were not laws of nature but conventions, he turned to philosophy of science, partly to dissociate himself from a radical relativism that had its advocates in France. He died "full of honors" in 1912.

The key to Poincaré's version of conventionalism was his thesis that the principles of geometry and chronometry were conventions, used by us to create the spatial and temporal ordering of experience. Space and time, as relational systems, are abstracted from the full richness of experience:

> it is not nature which imposes them on us, it is we who impose them on nature because we find them convenient . . . Is mathematical analysis then, whose principal object is the study of these empty frames, only a vain play of the mind? It can give the physicist only a convenient language . . . without this language most of the intimate analogies of things would have remained forever unknown to us. (Poincaré, 1903 [1958]: 13)

However, Poincaré insisted that we should not exaggerate the role of convention in science, as if the whole of what it revealed about the universe was a free creation of the human mind.

In discussing the extreme relativism of Edward Le Roy, Poincaré tackles the question of whether conventionalism requires us to say that the scientist creates the fact. He makes two distinctions of importance. There are brute facts which are transformed into scientific facts by being expressed in one of the languages of science. But these languages are not just conventions. Unlike social conventions, for example, they can be true or false. Facts are often the expression of classifications, but "This convention being given, if I am asked: Is such a fact true? I shall always know what to answer, and my answer will be imposed on me by the witness of my senses" (Poincaré, 1903 [1958]: 118).

In short, conventions are not merely like the rules of languages; they *are* the rules of languages. If we take each set of conventions to be the basis of a theory, then rival theories are essentially rival languages, differing in the way French or German differ. The propositions may look different, but the facts are the same, whatever language is used. The objectivity of the world is what is common to all human beings and other sentient creatures. This can be no more than the elementary sensory givens of perception, with all the specific forms of ordering abstracted.

PARADIGMS AND THE SOCIOLOGY OF KNOWLEDGE

How far can we take the Constructionist Idea?

Experiments bring phenomena to light while our judgments as to what these phenomena should be taken to be are based on the repertoire of concepts we have to hand. An experiment is needed to make bromine appear as a dark reddish liquid. We need the periodic table of the elements to describe it as an element and as a halogen.

Thought and experience can always be made to match. In a long process of mutual adjustment each transforms the other. It is easy to slip from this insight into the false but exciting claim that we are not really exploring the fit between our theories and an independent material reality. What we perceive is created by our concepts. For example, Hacking says:

> When [we have brought matters into consilience] . . . we have not read
> the truth off the World. There usually were not some pre-existing
> phenomena that experiment reported. It made them. There was not
> some previously organized correspondence between theory and reality
> that was confirmed. (Hacking, 1992: 58)

Hacking's remarks about experiments in the first half of the quotation
are surely right. However, the correct conclusion is not that there is
no previously organized correspondence between theory and reality to
be confirmed or disconfirmed. Conventionalism is not idealism, the
doctrine that the stuff of the world is thought.

This leads us to the postmodern position that the discourses of the
sciences are just one genre among an indefinite number of possible
kinds of stories that could be told about the plants, animals, minerals,
the astronomical environment of the earth, the nature of human
cognition, and so on. Science is privileged neither as a royal road to
reality, nor as a uniquely powerful way of categorizing, recognizing,
and ordering phenomena. Positivism supports the first clause and
conventionalism the second.

Why is it thought that no distinctions of authenticity or truth can
be drawn between a multiplicity of narratives by reference to how ade-
quately they present the topics they address? This radical claim comes
in part from a thesis drawn from the writings of Thomas Kuhn. In an
extravagant moment he claimed that a new and complete world-for-
us is created by the acceptance and use of each distinct way of looking
at and understanding the world. There is no end to the possible story-
lines with which we can make sense of our material environment and
the behavior of other people. Any attempt to use the world as a
resource in deciding between story-lines is pointless since that would
require that there should be access to the world independent of story-
lines. There is, it is claimed, no such access. The world no more constrains scientific narratives as to their authenticity than the printed text
of a poem or novel constrains the readings of those who engage with
it. Each narrative generates a "world" that is in general accordance
with it.

> The word doesn't reflect or represent the world; the word contains the
> world and not the other way round. Therefore, texts are self-referential
> – they refer only to themselves, not to anything outside themselves.

There is no such thing as the real world . . . All that's left is a succession of misleading signs, a parade of words beyond the power of humanity to control them. (Lehman, quoted in Murphy, 1997: 136)

This seems to be a rather strong form of idealism. Can we preserve the insights of conventionalism without going the whole way with the postmodernist?

The Relativity of Knowledge to Paradigms

In the decade around the 1960s there began a vigorous and even acrimonious debate on the subject of scientific progress. Among the many contributors to the debate two have left a lasting mark. T. S. Kuhn's arguments for the irrationality of what we take to be the great breakthroughs in scientific progress were complemented by attacks on the reduction of scientific methodology to the application of simple logical schemata. The most violent and, perhaps for that reason, one of the most influential was mounted by P. K. Feyerabend (1975). These authors thought that there was a gap between the reasonable degree of belief in facts and theories which were based on the logical analysis of scientific discourse and practice, and the actual beliefs held by working scientists. If logic was not enough to account for science, something else must be at work. What was it?

The problem of progress

It is now more than forty years since T. S. Kuhn (1922–96) published his influential book on the nature of scientific progress. He was not the first to realize that the science of any period was made intelligible as to both content and method by the existence of a taken-for-granted set of beliefs and practices. Metaphysical and methodological presuppositions are intimately interwoven. But he gave this point of view a new impetus by forging a link with the social aspects of scientific communities. He called these background clusters of ideas, exemplars, and techniques "paradigms" (Kuhn, 1957). In later writings he preferred the expression "disciplinary matrix" to avoid some of the ambiguity of the original expression. As well as the metaphysics and methodology that define a disciplinary matrix or paradigm, there is also a favored exemplar of good method, a paradigm in another sense, that is, a model of good work.

With the help of paradigms Kuhn was able to offer a dramatic and, to many, a shocking, reinterpretation of the very idea of scientific progress. The achievements of those who initiated paradigm shifts "was sufficiently unprecedented to attract an enduring group of adherents . . . it was sufficiently open-ended to leave all sorts of problems . . . to resolve" (Kuhn, 1996: 11).

According to Kuhn, a scientific revolution, such as the shift from a geocentric to a heliocentric picture of the universe, was not a rational development driven by overwhelming empirical evidence against the old picture and for the new. It was not the result of the application of an irresistible logical schema. Rather it was a kind of revelation, a shift of perspective, a paradigm change, in which all that had been taken for granted in the previous epoch was abandoned, and new meanings, methods, and so on were created. The scientific situation before the paradigm change and after it were, he said, incommensurable. He meant by this that there was no possibility of a comparison between the situations before and after with respect either to their meanings or to their empirical groundings. The world of the new paradigm was a dif- ferent world from that of the old. "In so far as their recourse to that world [the real, unchanging, independent material world] is through what they see and do we may want to say that after a revolution, sci- entists are responding to a different world" (Kuhn, 1996: 111). Strictly speaking, adherents of each successive paradigm could not understand one another. This was dramatic stuff indeed.

Progress is not to be thought of as a linear progression, accumulat- ing ever more well substantiated truths about the natural world, but as a succession of incommensurable world pictures. The transition from one paradigm to another is driven by all sorts of forces, social, per- sonal, and intellectual. There is no paradigm completely independent of these forces. A paradigm is both the possession of a scientific com- munity and its defining characteristic. In joining a community one is indoctrinated into the way of thinking of that community, and so the local paradigm becomes one's own cast of mind.

By a close study of Galileo's work and influence, Feyerabend (1975) was able to show that the power of Galileo's new mechanics to win over the physicists of the day could not possibly be explained as the application of logic as the means for deriving and assessing hypotheses. Galileo's arguments were neither inductions of generalizations from an assemblage of particular facts, nor were they eliminations of rival hypotheses about the nature and causes of motion by finding counter-instances.

If a hypothesis has a false consequence we can use deductive logic to infer that the hypothesis is false. For example, if we think that malaria is caused by noxious vapors then sleeping under a net should have no effect on the incidence of the disease. But it does have such a effect, hence the vapours hypothesis must be false. Galileo's *Discourses Concerning Two New Sciences* (1638) not only did not, but could not have worked on the minds of its readers like that.

> Galileo replaces one natural interpretation by a very different and as yet (1630) at least partly unnatural interpretation. How does he proceed? How does he manage to introduce absurd and counter-inductive asser-tions, such as the assertion that the earth moves, and yet get a just and attentive hearing? . . . Galileo's utterances are indeed arguments in appearance only. For Galileo uses propaganda. He uses psychological tricks in additional to what intellectual reasons he has to offer . . . Galileo "reminds" us that there are situations in which the non-operative character of shared motion is just as evident and as firmly believed as the idea of the operative character of all motion is in other circumstances. (Feyerabend, 1975: 81)

Feyerabend argues very convincingly that the force of the new approach came from getting people to accept a new way of thinking of what was "natural" and what needed to be given a special explana-tion. In Galileo's time, thanks to his influence, it came to seem quite natural for something to keep on moving unless an outside force stopped it. It came to seem natural for something to fall toward the center of the earth, without any extra driving force. A horseman at full gallop can throw up his spear and catch it again. Why? Because the spear partakes of two independent motions, the horizontal motion of the horse, and the vertical motion of the upward throw. It was these and other telling examples that carried the force of conviction, by changing the reader's perception of what need to be explained and what did not. This resort to what is natural for each era in science is very like the role of Kuhn's disciplinary matrix.

It hardly needs saying now how these intuitions, unqualified by any further refinements, led straight to a strong form of relativism. What counts as scientific knowledge, what counts as a problem and its solution, what counts as an anomaly, and so on, are determinate only relative to a paradigm.

If the world as it is manifested to us depends on the paradigm we adopt, and that in turn depends on the community in which we have grown up, then the sociology of scientific knowledge has a more profound place in our understanding of science than merely delineating the conditions under which such matters as the distribution of research grants are to be understood.

The Strong Program

In the 1970s, in several places, a new discipline, the sociology of science, began to make itself felt. The analysis of the patterns of reasoning that had been used to try to explain the genesis and relative quality of scientific claims to knowledge began to seem too detached from the reality of the human institutions in which these claims were made. The full consequences of the relativism of Kuhn and Feyerabend were drawn by the sociologists of the Edinburgh School, particularly David Bloor and Barry Barnes.

There are three relativist features of the interpretation of the sciences according to Barnes and Bloor (1996: 22).

1. The observation that beliefs on a certain topic vary.
2. The conviction that which of these beliefs is found acceptable in a given context depends on or is relative to the circumstances of the users.
3. Regardless of their truth and falsity the credibility of all beliefs is problematic. There are local and specific causes of credibility.

It has been argued that the sociological account is obviously incomplete. Though I may explain why Darwin believed that fossils were survivals from the remote past and Fitzroy did not, by reference to upbringing, class affiliations, and so on, none of these considerations explains whether either man ought to have believed what he did. Perhaps there are trans-historical, trans-cultural standards of correct reasoning with the help of which we could discuss whether or not what someone actually believed is what, in the circumstances, he or she *ought* to have believed. Barnes and Bloor, and others, have pointed out that we can always ask about the origins of standards of correct reasoning. Where do they come from? There seem to be no standards for the assessment of standards. "For the relativist there is no sense attached to the idea that some standards or beliefs are really rational as distinct from merely locally accepted as such" (Barnes and Bloor, 1996: 27).

In what sense could there be scientific progress? Within each paradigm we can identify development, but how can we adjudicate between the successive paradigms, if these moves are classed as "developments" only relative to paradigms? For a final adjudication of these matters we must surely wait for the third millennium. For a judicious review of the current state of the debate see Ian Hacking, *The Social Construction of What?* (1999).

Since the middle part of the nineteenth century logic has been seen by many philosophers as a close ally or even a proper part of the scientific attitude to the world. It is appropriate, then, to include a brief sketch of its recent development at this point in the story of philosophy in the second half of the second millennium.

Logic in the Modern Era

The brief glimpse we have had of the study of logic in medieval times revealed some refinements and extensions of Aristotelian insights and forms. Still, for many centuries, logic was taken to be the systematic study of the principles of right reasoning. However, in the modern era, the idea of an analysis of cognitive processes to reveal their formal character began to take on a new breadth. Perhaps the whole of our language-borne thought could be expressed in a formal system, with symbols of determinate meaning replacing the language that had been developed for the business of everyday. Logic might become a kind of *science* of language.

Leibniz was not the only enthusiast for such a project, but his conception of "universal character" was well known. The creation of a symbolic system that would express in clear and unambiguous ways what it was that a person was thinking seemed a highly desirable project. Leibniz knew of the Chinese way of writing down language, using a system in which concepts rather than sounds are represented symbolically. His own scheme was not a success.

Frege's Begriffschruft

The idea of a "concept script" was revived towards the end of the nineteenth century by Gottlob Frege (1848–1925). Mathematical representations of the logic of Aristotle had begun to be developed, for example, by George Boole (1815–64). Frege took the idea a great deal further, particularly by developing the rules of quantifiers in a clear way (Frege, 1879 [1952]). Propositional logic is concerned only with the relations between whole propositions in patterns that reflect relations between truth and falsity, Quantifiers provide the possibility of a fine-grained analysis of the internal structure of propositions, similar to but more general than the Aristotelian scheme. For example, the existential quantifier, "There is an x such that x is . . ." and the universal quantifier "For all x, x is . . . ," together with propositional logic, allow the development a powerful formal system. Frege made some attempt to apply these ideas to philosophical problems, particularly those raised by mathematics.

Russell's analytical use of logic

From the point of view of the history of philosophy, it was Bertrand Russell's use of the formal systems of logic for purposes other than merely expressing the structure of arguments that marks a major step in philosophical method. Like Frege, Russell believed that if only one could reveal the true logical form of seemingly paradoxical and philosophically problematic propositions, the difficulties would simply melt away. This view was also behind the remarkable logical work of Ludwig Wittgenstein's early years. His cryptically written but powerful work, *Tractatus Logico-Philosophicus* (1922), was intended to resolve philosophical problems once and for all by the development of an entirely clear and final formal language. Though he himself realized that the project was misconceived, the idea of resolving philosophical problems by displaying logical forms has remained very much part. of the techniques of analytical philosophy. I will illustrate the method with a single but telling example, the resolution of the problem of the truth values of propositions that refer to imaginary, that is, nonexistent entities. This is part of Russell's famous "theory of descriptions" (Russell, 1919).

How are we to express the status of such a proposition as "The King of France is bald" when there is no one who is King of France? Is it false? Well, how could we know? In a perfect and uniform language it would desirable if every meaningful proposition could be assigned to one or the other "truth" category, true or false. Russell's strategy was to try to bring out the logical form of propositions of this sort in general (Russell, 1905).

Using the apparatus of logic we could express the form of the troublesome proposition something like this:

There is a King of France *and* there is not more than one King of France *and* there is nothing which is King of France and not bald.

The first clause is certainly false if there is no King of France. Since any compound proposition created by conjunction is false if any of the conjuncts are false, the whole proposition is false.

Russell gave this analysis a strong philosophical twist. He argued that the fundamental way that a person came into contact with the world was by simple and direct sensory experience. What was then apprehended could be picked out by a "logically proper name" such as "this" or "that," independently of our identifying any of the properties of the being in question. All other ways of referring to things were in one way or another descriptions, including proper names.

The deep point that this seemingly trivial issue about the grammar of names touches on is the seeming fallibility of all referring expressions of the ordinary sort, names and definite descriptions, to guarantee that their putative referent exists. However, Russell thought that anything which could be picked out by a logically proper name existed so indisputably that a remark like "This exists" is not only redundant but hollow.

Whether one is prepared to follow Russell into these waters, and whether one finds his subtleties convincing is not to the point here. It is, I believe, a splendid example of the method of logical analysis in search of the underlying forms.

Russell had very ambitious plans for his program of revealing the inner structures of all cognition as logical forms. His greatest project, which he undertook with A. N. Whitehead, was to try to show that the whole of mathematics could be rendered in the formalism and with the concepts of logic. This great work was published as *Principia Mathematica* in 1910–13.

How far have these ideas and ambitions survived? I think it fair to say that the project of reducing mathematics to logic is generally thought to have been a failure. There are profoundly paradoxical consequences that have emerged from the attempts, not only by Russell, but by other logicians and mathematicians, for instance, David Hilbert (1899). The larger project, of using logic to resolve all philosophical problems by creating an entirely clear and unambiguous formal expression of our thought has also been under fire. Wittgenstein, in particular, developed a very different kind of analysis, displaying the multiple forms of language in a nonformal way, as a method for escaping from the puzzles on which philosophical problems ultimately rest (Wittgenstein, 1953). The school of philosophy that flourished in Oxford in the fifties and sixties of the last century was also based on more informal methods of revelatory analysis than the stringent forms of logic (Hacker, 1996).

Conclusion

The case for a modest conventionalism as the most plausible account of how our knowledge of the cosmos is created seems overwhelming. The task for philosophers has been to establish a balance between the extremes of positivism and relativism. Though Kant's analysis is deep and subtle, it is surely going too far to claim that the whole structure of experience is a human product. Nor is the suggestion that there are many story-lines with which we can make sense of our experience, and between which we cannot adjudicate, any more convincing. Whewell seems to me to have got it about right. There is an evolving cycle of influences between perception and conception, observation and theory. Perhaps we might revive his judicious compromise for the third millennium.

The Unity of Mind and World: Idealism, Phenomenalism, and Phenomenology

Philosophy is hardly notorious as a hazardous trade. Few philosophers have met a violent death. Moritz Schlick was "gunned down" by a disgruntled student in 1936. This tragic events cannot be put down to the fact that this man was a philosopher. On the other hand, philosophical theories cannot serve as a protection from the assassin's bullets either. This thought might turn our minds to a curious confrontation between philosophy and reality that took place in Florence on April 15, 1944.

With Benedetto Croce, Giovanni Gentile was the most prominent Italian philosopher of the interwar years. He rose to prominence under Mussolini. Gentile was able to find in his version of idealism a philosophical foundation for the fascist state that was then emerging in Italy. He became Minister of Education. However, the point of this story is drawn from his general philosophy.

He worked out a more extreme form of idealism than either Hegel or Bradley. His position has been summed up in the following: "The act of thinking upon which all subjective consciousness depends, becomes the pure act by which the whole world of ordinary reality is created." The thought and the thing are one and the same. This is an example of solipsism, the most extreme form of subjective idealism. The world and the subject's experience of the world coincide.

Here is the paradox. Gentile died on that date in Florence, at the hands of a band of partisans. They were disgruntled with his support for the puppet fascist republic of Sal 6. It is said that he was walking down a lane, quite unsuspecting, when he was shot in the back of the head. By what "pure act" was the assassin's bullet given reality in the solipsistic world of Giovanni Gentile? (See Devine, 1975: 205). Or should we say that he was assassinated in the "world" of the partisan gunman, but simply vanished in his own?

The Legacy of Kant

Kant's philosophy has been among the sources for two rather different subsequent developments in the history of philosophy. The emphasis on the role of *a priori* rules in the syntheses of the world out of the flux of sensations, rules expressed in synthetic *a priori* propositions, must surely have been among the sources of conventionalism, as I have suggested in chapter 9. However, it seemed to some philosophers that the noumenal realm, the sources of sensations and the locus of agency, were empty and gratuitous additions to a philosophy that could do without them. Thus the Kantian constructivist philosophy served as a major source of idealism, the thesis that the world is of the same nature as the mind. The Kantian account of the origin of the empirical world and of the contents of consciousness in the synthetic activity of the mind is specific to individuals. We inhabit a common world because we share the forms of judgment and so the matching system of categories, concepts, and schemata.

It is a short step from there to the claim that the world, as we perceive it, is a creation of the human mind. This astonishing claim took two forms, one of which comes from Kantian philosophy and the other from the empiricism of Locke and Berkeley. *Sensationalism* or *phenomenalism* was based on the Lockean principle that human beings could be aware only of ideas, the contents of the mind. What we experience as perceptions must be clusters of sensations, not the coexisting properties of the things that we suppose cause these sensations. *Idealism* was based on the Kantian principle that the forms of experience were imposed by the synthesizing powers of the mind. The perceived world and the mind that shaped it were of the same character.

THE RISE OF IDEALISM

It may, at first hearing, appear strange to declare that the world is dependent on the mind. It may appear even stranger that a prominent school of philosophers hold that world and mind are of the same essential character. Matter and thought seem as different as anything could be. Surely the world is material and our perceptions and knowledge of it are mental. However, the contrary opinion was widely held in the nineteenth century. We shall turn now to follow the way idealism developed from its late eighteenth-century origins in Germany to its last moments in England at the beginning of the twentieth century.

The German Interpretation of Kant

The Kantian philosophy strongly suggested that priority should be given to the mind, to thought. Both J. G. Fichte (1762–1814) and F. W. J. Schelling (1775–1854) developed a philosophical cosmology on the basis of a belief that moral and cognitive aspects of human life could not be reduced to cause–effect relations. According to Kant, these are products of the synthesizing power of the mind exercised on sensations. Sensations are aspects of consciousness. What we take to be material things can exist only by virtue of their relations to human sensibility, that is, as experienced by someone. On the other hand, the mind is in no need of relations to sustain it. In a sense, it is absolute. The idea is something like this: A sensation must exist in relation to a mind, since it is nothing but an experience. The mind need have no particular experience to exist. It is not related to anything. To put this in another way: what is really real must be unconditioned. It cannot depend on anything else, for if it did *that* would be the ultimate reality. For Fichte and Schelling the individual human mind had this character of unconditional independence. Hegel took a further step, generalizing the basic idealist principle. He proposed that there must be a wholly unconditioned mind-like being, *Geist* or Spirit, which comes to be more and more itself as history unfolds. Roughly *Geist* is the consciousness of the whole human race. It is, if you like, what is *really* real!

Hegel and the Historical Realization of Logic

The influence of G. F. W. Hegel on nineteenth-century German thought was profound. In many ways that influence can still be discerned in philosophy in the twentieth century, through its role in the genesis of Marx's system. Hegel was born in 1770 in Stuttgart. He began his education in the theology faculty at Tübingen. His first university post was in Jena, as a *Privatdozent*. This was the usual "entry-level" job in the German academic system. One survived on the fees that students paid to attend one's lectures. The Napoleonic wars interfered in his career and for nearly a decade he earned his living as a schoolmaster. In 1816 he was appointed a professor in Heidelberg, and then shortly afterwards in Berlin. Struck first of all by admiration for Napoleon and the politics of liberty, as were Beethoven and many other Germans, he eventually turned to the authoritarian model of Prussia for his political ideals. He died of cholera in 1831.

In this section I have relied almost wholly on secondary sources. I confess to finding the works of Hegel himself very difficult to grasp. Two authors have provided a particularly helpful guide for the perplexed: namely, Michael Inwood (1983) and Charles Taylor (1979). Hegel's basic thesis is that spirit or *Geist* brings itself into the fullness of being in history. This development can be understood as initiated by the fracturing of a primitive unity between *Mann* and the universe. This results in an opposition between what Taylor calls "expressive unity" and "rational autonomy." Expressive unity is seen in the way the singularity of individual consciousness is manifested in the language used by an embodied person. A person just speaks or acts. Rational autonomy is the capacity to choose according to reason. A person reflects on what might be said or done The task of human development is to find a way of synthesizing these diverse trends. The contrast might be put something like this: "I want . . ." is a simple expression of desire, while "I should . . ." is the product of reflection on desire in the light of a moral or prudential principle.

Synthesis of seeming opposites is possible because any opposition presupposes an identity. Only that which once was a unity could stand in opposition to itself. Otherwise the seeming opposites would have nothing whatever to do with one another. Or we could say that once opposition appears it presupposes an identity. As Taylor (1979: 15) puts it: "the relation of each term to its opposite is a peculiarly intimate one. It is not related to an other, but to *its* other, and this hidden identity will necessarily reassert itself in a recovery of unity."

The world as spirit is evolving from a fracture of its primitive unity through progressive oppositions which eventually will culminate in a higher unity. These oppositions are overcome, one after another, by the synthesis of their seemingly contradictory poles. This is Hegelian dialectic. The most fundamental opposition is that between consciousness, an attribute of all higher organic beings, and self-consciousness, a wholly human capacity. The contrast is between that which is unreflective and that which is reflective. This opposition arises in history by virtue of the existence of humanity, the only species in which self-consciousness has evolved. The historical development of the human race occurs through the transcendence of opposition after opposition by a synthesis of each successive opposition. From primitive unity, which has been fractured by the evolution of self-consciousness, history moves on to the higher unity of the fully developed mind of *Mann*, in which consciousness and self-consciousness are finally synthesized. Among the progressive sequence of oppositions that must be overcome is that between the determinism of the material nature of the embodied person, and the freedom of rational choice enjoyed by the mature human agent.

The development of the human race from unity to opposition to unity again, is also the development of the universe as the expression of *Geist*. The World Spirit, like all that is mental, must be embodied. It finds its material substrate in the human race itself. Hegel was not a pantheist. God is not embodied in the whole material universe, but realized materially in the organic being of humanity.

The much-vaunted opposition between Hegelian pretensions and the established findings of science played a very important part in the "political" development of German universities in the nineteenth century. Rejection of Hegelian claims to set philosophy above science was among the most important sources of the logical positivism of the Vienna Circle. For them, not only was philosophy not in a superior position to the natural sciences, but philosophy should be carried on as if it were a science. Hegel's type of analysis was anathema to them.

Inwood (1983: 66–8) makes clear that Hegel, though critical of particular scientific theories, was not inclined to reject the science of his time. He did, however, criticize a too facile empiricism. Since the laws of nature are presumably necessary truths it should be possible to deduce them *a priori*. Enquiries driven by "Why?" questions generally lead to a hierarchy of explanations. Do such hierarchies open out to infinity? For every "Why?" question another can be asked of the answer to the first. Hegel hoped for explanations that do not generate further

"Why?" questions. The principles of such explanations must express how things must necessarily be. Only then would a ladder of explanations come to an end in a principled way.

But there is a deeper problem. . . . "The core or essence of the world is pure thought or thought-determinations and the sciences progressively disclose them to us" (Inwood, 1983: 67). Again, if scientific concepts are pure thought we should be able to extract what is implicit in them without recourse to empirical studies. If we cannot do this, Hegel seems to think that we have not refined the relevant concepts enough. The work of refinement is a task for philosophers.

Inwood points out that Hegel first saw empiricism as a kind of freedom. It released one from the dictates of established authority. Later he came to see it as an impairment to the autonomy of the human spirit. In Hegel's words, "this sensuous material is and remains for empiricism something given, this is a doctrine of unfreedom, for freedom consists just in my having nothing absolutely other than myself over against me" (quoted in Inwood, 1983: 67). In so far as the state of the world is a given with which I must cope, it is a constraint on my freedom.

The upshot seems to be this: the world is not a fixed and final entity which natural scientists can explore at their leisure. It is a developing "something," which is material but also spiritual. *Geist* is thought, but it must be embodied to be. The sciences can serve only to disclose this development, which must be happening via the dialectical synthesis of oppositions. The world they disclose is realizing itself in the human race as it becomes self-conscious. In the course of that dialectic progression the development of the natural sciences comes about. They too must be subject to the developmental logic of the synthesis of oppositions and to the necessities of thought.

Idealism in England

German idealism thrills, in part because it is notoriously obscurely presented. The version of idealism that developed in England has the virtue and the vulnerability of relative clarity. There are several main theses to be found in the writings of F. H. Bradley (1846–1924), the leading idealist author in the England of his time. Knowledge was possible only if the following three conditions were satisfied:

1. There are, in principle, two kinds of relations. Internal relations are constitutive of the beings they relate, and external relations, which are independent of the natures of those things which they relate. According to the idealists, all relations are internal. Perception is an internal relation between a mental state and a perceived object. So the perceived object is partly or wholly constituted mentally.

> It is assumed on general grounds that all relations are "internal," and then, since knowing and its object are related, it is concluded that knowing must make a difference to its object, thus overthrowing realist epistemology [which is based on the independence of knower and thing known]. (Ewing, 1934)

2. The correspondence theory of truth, that a proposition is true if it corresponds with the facts, presupposes that propositions and states of affairs are wholly independent. But according to condition 1 they are not. The only defensible account of truth is coherence, that propositions and facts are of the same kind, namely mental entities, and therefore are logically related. There will be a vast network of internally related propositions which gradually develop as the mind of Man evolves. True propositions are those which slot neatly into this network, all of which cohere with one another. This follows more or less directly if we are ready to accept the principle that perception is an internal relation between perceiver and what is perceived. Facts and thoughts mutually constitute one another.

3. Universals, like redness, are not independently existing Platonic forms, nor are they, as Ockham tried to show, merely words that help us to think about groups of similar things. They exist concretely in the entities that exhibit them. They are neither abstract entities nor concepts expressed in words.

Finally, and most importantly, Bradley set out to show that the ordinary view of the world as an independent realm of self-existing material things, confronted by minds of a wholly alien character, was self-contradictory. This follows if we conjoin the independence thesis with presuppositions 1 to 3. There must, therefore, be an Absolute in which there are no contradictions. The Absolute is realized in the totality of ordinary minds. It is not some supra mind of which individual minds are independent products. For the religiously inclined the

Absolute would be God. We progressively attain a grasp of this wholly harmonious possibility of experience, which is the Absolute Mind realizing itself in the human race. This is clearly a development of the Hegelian principle of the evolution of *Geist* realizing itself in the history of human kind.

It seems to me not too fanciful to find an echo of the fundamental principle of classical Indian philosophy, that the individual self, *Atman*, and the universal ground of being, *Brahman*, are one. I do not know to what extent Bradley was acquainted with Oriental thought. I think it unlikely that he knew nothing of it.

The ultimate fate of idealism might have seemed to have been settled by the 1930s. It had been the target of powerful critical attacks by the Cambridge philosophers, Russell and Moore. It had been excoriated as an irrational bar to the progress of science and science-inspired philosophy by the positivists of the Vienna Circle. Though it was still taught in the universities of India and New Zealand in the 1950s it was surely dead as a source of inspiration and of satisfying solutions to philosophical problems.

PHENOMENALISM

The topic of this chapter could have been presented as an exploration of the thesis that personal, subjective experience is the true object of human knowledge. The job of the philosopher is to bring out and examine presuppositions that are inherent in framing a common human life in the light of the insight that everyone is, in a sense, a prisoner of his or her own consciousness. Phenomenalism is the name of a point of view, initiated by the Lockean theory of ideas and the critical development of that theory by Berkeley, which has surfaced again and again in European philosophy.

From the point of view of phenomenalism, the philosopher's job is to analyze the realm of what we perceive into its most elementary sensory units. This should allow us to identify the principles that are involved in the organizing of those units into objects of perception. This has obvious affinities with the Kantian point of view. The flux of sensations is synthesized according to rule into an empirical world and the subjective experience of a human individual. Material things do not appear as the causes of our perceptions. They are held to be constructions out of elementary sensations.

Phenomenology tackles the same question, namely what is involved in creating the world as we experience it? The phenomenologists tried to develop a technique by means of which the marks of objectivity, of the passage of time, and so on, which are present but taken for granted in conscious experience, can be brought into focus.

Phenomenalism looks first for the elementary units and only then for the principles of order. Phenomenology looks first for the marks that present things, events, and so on to us in a certain way, and leaves the elementary sensations to emerge as a kind of residue. The most influential modern version of phenomenalism has been the "sense datum" theory.

The Sense Datum Theory

Among the perennial puzzles that philosophers address is how we can know anything of a world that exists independently of ourselves. Bertrand Russell, in the early period of his philosophical development, was a keen advocate of the importance of the concept of "sense datum" in giving accounts of human knowledge.

Bertrand Russell was born in Monmouthshire in 1872. Brought up austerely by his grandmother, his formal education began at Trinity College, Cambridge. His interests spanned mathematics and philosophy from an early age, and his work displayed a conviction that these disciplines were intimately related. Returning to Cambridge as a Fellow of Trinity, he began his great collaborative work, *Principia Mathematica*, with A. N. Whitehead. This was followed by a string of books in which the problems of philosophy were subjected to a rigorous examination in the light of the mathematical logic he had developed. Uncompromising in his moral stances, he went to gaol for his opposition to the First World War. It could be said that the rest of his long life was devoted to one radical cause or another. His concern with education led to his founding a school based on principles of free expression. Later he became a leading figure in the opposition to nuclear weapons. His private life was complicated by marital problems and the financial strains of earning a living outside the comfortable shelter of the

academic establishment. His last years were passed in seclusion in North
Wales. He died in 1970. His once towering reputation has faded in
recent years, partly due to the shift away from the optimistic cer-
tainties of a faith in the power of logic to resolve the problems of
philosophy.

Russell distinguished two kinds of knowing, by acquaintance and by
description. Sense data, the elementary contents of consciousness, were
known by acquaintance. One could not be in any doubt, he thought,
as to the sensation one was experiencing. One might not be seeing
the autumnal maple leaf, but surely one was indubitably experiencing
a red patch in one's visual field. There was also knowledge by description. Our knowledge of the material things that caused the sense data
to exist was inferential. We could describe things and other people, but
we could not "know" them directly.

> The reason I call my doctrine *logical* atomism is because the atoms I
> wish to arrive at as the last residue of analysis are logical atoms, not
> physical atoms. Some of them will be what I call "particulars" such
> things as little patches of colour or sounds – momentary things – some
> of them will be [universals] predicates or relations and so on. (Russell,
> 1975: 179)

How did the elementary sense data form up into representations of
things and people? Material things, says Russell, are logical constructions out of sense data. What exactly did Russell mean by this
pregnant phrase?

> The logical status of Piccadilly [as a series of classes of material entities]
> . . . series and classes are of the nature of logical fictions . . . [this] will
> dissolve Piccadilly into a [logical] fiction. (Russell, 1975: 191)

The idea is really quite simple. Material things are made up of classes
of more elementary beings, for example, sense data. Since, according to
Russell, classes are logical fictions, so must material objects be. Why
did he think that a class was a logical fiction? This takes us back to
our discussions of the status of universals. A class is a group of entities
that are taken together by us, by virtue of the similarity between them
in a respect interesting to us. There is no "class" existing in some higher
state which the individuals come under. Classes are useful fictions.

From our vantage point we see affinities with Locke's doctrine of ideas, with Berkeley's criticism of the distinction between ideas of primary qualities and ideas of secondary qualities, and with the synthesizing activities of the human mind that are at the heart of Kant's point of view.

A generation of philosophers struggled to make sense of the theory, and to resolve some of its more problematic aspects. For example, are sense data on the surfaces of things, or are they nothing but the contents of consciousness? I think it fair to say they got nowhere, however ingenious were some of the attempts at solving the problems. The sense datum theory has gone from the philosophical agenda, though there are signs of its return in a new guise. Some philosophers have begun to write about "qualia," elementary sensations (Chalmers, 1996). Its disappearance can be explained partly through sheer attrition, but partly through the ridicule to which the presuppositions of the whole programme were subjected by J. L. Austin (1962). However, I would not be surprised if it played a prominent part in the philosophical debates of the third millennium.

PHENOMENOLOGY

Husserl's Analytical Techniques

Another way of examining the presuppositions of perception as a source of knowledge must be credited to Edmund Husserl (1859–1938). He invented a way of doing philosophy that has been very influential and has adherents to this day. This is *phenomenology*. Husserl abandoned his youthful enthusiasm for the reduction of logic to psychology. His program could be thought of as a kind of "experimental" working out of the Kantian theory of synthesis, with which we are now very familiar. Husserl thought that it should be possible to extricate the *a priori* logical principles that are immanent in the way the material world and other people are presented to us, by examining our essentially private conscious experience.

The idea is simple, but the execution difficult and problematic. One scrutinizes one's conscious states to bring to light the various features of *them* that differentiate the experience we have of material things, people, and other aspects of the world that we are familiar with. This process should leave behind sensations unattached to extrapersonal reality.

Since we are interested in schools, themes, and trends, I will not follow Husserl's intellectual development, but go straight to the most influential aspect of his thought, *transcendental phenomenology*. In explaining this it will be necessary to cope with some very irritating terminological innovations. I hope that the thrust of Husserl's philosophy can be brought out by making his terminology clear and accessible.

The problem to which Husserl devotes himself is simply put: Conscious experience points beyond itself in all sorts of ways. How is what is immanent in consciousness related to what is transcendent to it? "How can cognition reach beyond itself? How can it reach to a being that is not to be found within the confines of consciousness itself?" (Husserl, 1964: 3).

> Cognition in all its manifestations is a psychic act . . . it is the cognition of a cognizing subject. The object cognized stands over against cognition . . . How can knowledge transcend itself and reach its object reliably? . . . yet the perceiving is simply a mental act of mine. (Husserl, 1950 [1960]: 15)

This question is more complex than it looks. Not only are such things as material objects transcendent to conscious experience, but Husserl thought that universals were too. Universals are presupposed in all thought since they are the basis of the human capacity to recognize this or that thing as a being of a certain sort. Universals, referred to by such abstract nouns as "redness," are not just oblique ways of referring to the linguistic practice of using the same word, "red," to describe each member of a group of similar things. The most troubling issue for Husserl is the status of the self. Is it immanent in consciousness, or is it transcendent to it?

Husserl contrasts the natural attitude of mind toward experience, taking the world and our cognitive powers for granted, and the philosophical attitude which subjects experience to analytical scrutiny. The philosophical attitude requires a different stance to experience from that typical of the natural attitude. To express this special stance Husserl thought he needed a novel terminology. The first terms it seems advisable to try to get hold of are *noetic, noematic,* and *doxetic.*

The noetic investigation of the contents of the mind is a study of those forms of consciousness in which objectivities are presented experientially. We see a tree as a tree, a thing in the park. By "bracketing" the fact that we know that it is a tree, we may be able to discern how the objectivity of a tree as a thing in the park is presented in consciousness. A noematic investigation is a study of the objectivities themselves, as they are re-presented in reflection. Experiencing a tree and reflecting on the tree as experienced are two different acts. In the one the focus is on the tree, in the other on the way the tree has been experienced. The contents of these acts are different. This pattern must be hierarchical, since we can obviously continue this procedure by reflecting on the experience of reflecting on the experience of seeing the tree.

Whatever serves as the unanalyzed ground of any such hierarchy is doxetic. When we reflect on what it was about the experience of a tree that presented it as a thing in the park, and bracket that aspect of the experience, that is, set it aside, we are left with the simplest sensations of shape, color, and so on. We reach the noematic level in one direction and the doxetic in the other.

The second group of terms to grapple with includes "epoché," which is closely related to the idea of phenomenological reduction. In order to grasp how objectivities present themselves in consciousness as such, I must "bracket" the fact that I unreflectingly take them as objective. The phenomenological reduction abstracts the marks of each taken-for-granted "reading" of experience. After a sequence of reductions, these marks are wholly bracketed, and the pure doxetic phenomena remain. At the same time we become aware of the logical principles immanent in the ordinary experience of trees.

> Thus to each psychic lived process there corresponds through the device of phenomenological reduction a pure phenomenon which exhibits its intrinsic (immanent) essence (taken individually) as an absolute datum. (Husserl, 1964: 35)

> Even if I should put in question the ego and the world and the ego's mental life as such, still my simply "seeing" a reflection of what is given in the apperception of the relevant mental process, yields the

phenomenon of this apperception . . . [this] is an absolutely given, pure
phenomenon in the phenomenological sense, renouncing anything transcendent . . . Thus to each psychic lived process there corresponds
through the device of the phenomenological reduction a pure phenomenon, which exhibits its intrinsic (immanent) essence . . . as an
absolute datum. (Husserl, 1964: 34–5)

Thus the philosopher's task is accomplished by the revelation of the
essences of all cognitive acts. (Husserl, 1964: 53)

What of the self? In his earlier works Husserl drew from his reductions the fairly traditional conclusion that the Ego, the self as the perceiving and acting core of personhood, was a "non-constituted
transcendence." There were, as it were, signs of its presence in certain
structures of reduced experience, hinting at the existence of an "I-pole"
that could never be in consciousness. There was no way that the agent
carrying out a phenomenological reduction could bring the perceiving self to light as an object of consciousness and so a fit item
for phenomenological reduction. In a move that some have thought
was an abandonment of the spirit of phenomenology, Husserl later
began to try to give an account of the Ego in terms of certain properties that he thought could be discerned in reflection on "the self."
It was not to be left as an "empty pole of identity." The Ego acquires
properties because it is that which is at work in constituting the features of experience that are made visible by reduction. Husserl even
went so far as to identify his concept of the Ego with the Leibnizean
monad, which, in a sense, contains the whole world, in that it reflects
the whole world from its own point of view. Phenomenology comes
very close to solipsism if it is identified with ontologies like that of
Leibniz. Leibniz was forced to introduce the extremely implausible
thesis of a preestablished harmony between the unfolding of the inner
natures of each and every monad in order to reconstitute an ordinary
world.

The patient reader who has followed me through these steps may
have already spotted a feature of Husserl's phenomenology that led
to a schism in the development of this tradition. All these moves take
one more and more into the condition of solipsism, that is, of the
coincidence of individual consciousness with the whole world that
is contained within it. How would it be possible to reconstitute the

intersubjective world of everyday life from the results of bracketing every assumption about the independent existence of things and people?

Alfred Schutz, who can have only a brief mention here, suggested a way of revamping phenomenology to bypass this problem. Instead of bracketing out intersubjectivity, the other people and the material things one deals with jointly in one's social world, he argued that we should proceed in just the opposite way. The world is given to us as intersubjective. Phenomenology should begin by bracketing out our individuality, each and everyone's particular point of view. We should use the phenomenological reduction to identify the marks of the person in the transpersonal intersubjectivity with which the social world is given (Schutz, 1967). It is not surprising that Schutz is the only philosopher whose brand of phenomenology has been taken seriously in the social sciences.

Heidegger's Project: to Discover the "Being of Being"

However difficult it has proved to get a grip on Husserl's version of phenomenology, it has not proved impossible to follow, I hope. One can get a general idea of what he is up to. It is not so different from the project that Kant undertook, to bring to light the synthetic *a priori* bases of common experience. In a history of the philosophy of the twentieth century, Husserl's influence on many others both within and outside the ranks of academic philosophers has been immense.

Among his pupils the best known must surely be Martin Heidegger. His work became well known during the 1930s. We can get some idea of what he was about if we see him as undertaking a grand generalization of Husserl's project. What concept must be presupposed in every experience? Being. How shall we characterize it? We cannot explain it in terms of anything else, since it must be the ultimate explainer.

There is a problem for an author who wants to make the core of Heidegger's philosophy available to the general reader. The writings of Martin Heidegger are thought by some to be so impenetrable as to be literally nonsense.

> When using words in what seem totally arbitrary ways, when welding words into uncouth chains of hyphenation, Heidegger claims that he is, in fact, returning to the well-springs of language, that he is realising the authentic intentions of human discourse. (Steiner, 1978: 15)

Heidegger is so well-known, and so frequently ranked among the great philosophers of our era, that we must make an effort to discern at least the outlines of what his message might be. In what follows I am indebted to Steiner's excellent (1978) exegesis of Heidegger's writings. It enables us to pick and choose our readings among a wide and difficult body of writing.

There are two basic ideas that seem to animate Heidegger's thought. The first is simply that Being is the topic for philosophical examination. What it is for something to exist at all is both assumed as a postulate in every undertaking, and ripe for examination. The second main idea is that to examine something philosophically is, above all, an etymological enterprise. Whatever cognitive tools we have now at our disposal are what they are by virtue of their history. The history of the linguistic tools for philosophizng reaches back to the root language of all philosophizing, Ancient Greek. I use the term "philosophizing" to pick up the Heideggerian intimation that to do philosophy is to be engaged in an undertaking, a project.

The root problem to which philosophizing is to be addressed is to give an account of Being. This has to be a general account. As Heidegger puts it, "all being [ordinary existence as one among many existents] is in Being [existence in general]."

> As far as content goes, phenomenology is the science of being of beings – ontology. In our elucidation of the tasks of ontology the necessity arose for a fundamental ontology which would have as its theme that being which is ontologically and ontically distinctive, namely, Da-sein.[1] This must be done in such a way that our ontology confronts the cardinal problem, the question of being in general. (Heidegger, 1953 [1996]: 33)

The account, whatever it is, must be couched in language. It is only language that stands apart from that which it is used to describe.

"What is the character of everything that exists, and which distinguishes it from nothing?" is the general question that Heidegger seems to be addressing. If this is the problem, why is its very formulation seemingly so empty? If cosmological physics is not the way to give an answer, what possible answer could there be?

Heidegger seems to take this sort of riposte to his project as a symptom of a kind of cultural pathology rather than a *reductio ad absurdum* of his program. His diagnosis of the illness of the modern world is that something has gone wrong in the course of history. We have "forgotten Being." How did that come about?

To understand this "forgetting" and to put our finger on the source of the corruption of the modern intellect, Heidegger makes great use of the term *Da-sein*, roughly "being there," where "there" is the world. We are "thrown into the world." By which he means, I think, that we find ourselves enmeshed in an already existing and linguistically ordered reality, in which there are other beings like myself. Everyone is a product of history. The existence of other people, each a historical product, each having been thrown into a prestructured world, opens up the possibility of forgetting Being.

> Da-sein has, in the first instance, fallen away from itself as an authentic potentiality for being its own self. It has fallen into the "world." "Fallenness" into the "world" means an absorption in being-with-one-another, in so far as the latter is guided by idle talk, hunger for novelty and ambiguity . . . on no account . . . do the terms "authentic" and "inauthentic" signify "really not," as if in this mode of existence Da-sein was altogether to lose its being. (Heidegger as quoted in Steiner, 1978: 94)

And here we enter into a region of Heidegger's thought that seems to me to have been very attractive to some of my acquaintances who have taken Heidegger seriously. According to him technology, as an end in itself, is one of the culprits, as are various kinds of nihilism. These mark a decline of civilization on a grand scale. But the above quotation seems to suggest something altogether more mundane. It seems that Heidegger also has in mind the ordinary flow and commerce of everyday life. Just living the ordinary round is a distraction of the proper focus of humanity.

Could the heart of civilization be recovered? Heidegger recommends a return to the earliest forms of philosophy before Plato and Aristotle. We should also turn our attention away from the products of our technological civilization to such arts as poetry. One can easily see this advice as a turning away from the mood of the Enlightenment and the history of modern psychology. Heidegger thinks we have been following a story-line which is dominated by the existence of science, both as a prime topic for philosophical reflection and as a model for that reflection. Starting in the seventeenth century, the dominant mood of our civilization has been formed by an admiration for science and its presumed modes of rationality.

The phenomenological aspect of Heidegger's project is the close attention he calls on us to pay to how the very existence of things is presented to us. He took his start self-consciously from Husserl's phenomenology. The techniques of bracketing should allow an attentive analyst to discern the features that distinguish the various form of being, from which the character of existence in general, Being, might be discerned.

However implausible we might find the problem of Being, it is the case that Heidegger's writings are full of observations and insights that are not without value. For instance, his emphasis on the historical character of language has found echoes in some recent linguistics. His distrust of the Enlightenment is a feature of some postmodernism. A dislike of technology is also an important theme of some of the writings of environmentalists.

Conclusion

The most obvious way that the world presents itself to the conscious person is just in the subjective contents of that consciousness. That there is a material world, as the source of the experience, is at best a speculation. Perhaps the mental is all that there is. We can take this on a grand scale in the Hegelian cosmic vision. Or we can take it more minutely in the analyses of the fine details of the contents of consciousness. Should we start with assumptions about sense data and try to find the logical principles that weld them into objects and events? Or should we start with Husserl's painstaking analyses of the contents of consciousness by bracketing commonsense assumptions to try to reveal the principles of structure at the outset?

At the end of the day, there is not much to be said in favor of idealism as a grand cosmic vision. At the very least, there are limits to the ways we can implement our belief systems. Obstacles seem to arise from something other than our states of mind. We must concede, with the positivists and realists, that Mind and World are independent. We must also concede to the conventionalists that the aspects of the world that are available to us are determined in part by the sort of perceptual systems we have, the sorts of apparatus we have managed to invent and the sorts of concepts we have developed to describe, explain, and classify the phenomena brought into being by our activities.

NOTES

1   Heidegger uses this spelling to give the concept an active flavor.

PART IV

Philosophy in the West

Modern Philosophy II
PERSONS AND THEIR RELATIONS

— 11 —

Human Nature

On a chilly winter day, probably in 1617, a French military engineer, by name René Descartes, serving with the Bavarian army in a campaign in the Netherlands, took refuge by a warm and inviting stove, some say in a bakery. Being of a reflective turn of mind, the man began to muse on how sure he could be of anything going on outside the room. Indeed it struck him that he could not even be sure that there was a room around him, or that he had a body. The only matter of which he could be quite certain was that, even when dreaming, he was thinking something. Even to doubt that he was thinking was to think. If that was the case he was above all a *thinking thing*.

The Paradoxical Being: The Person

The deepest source of the urge to philosophical reflection must surely be the conundrum of human nature. What sort of beings are we? Higher than the brutes, yet lower than the angels? The apex of the long thrust of organic evolution? Information-processing mechanisms? In trying to answer these questions philosophers have brought to light some of the presuppositions of the human form of life, in its practical, its moral, and its social aspects. That we are embodied and so partake of the material world is as obvious as the complementary fact that we seem to have capacities and attributes that are as different from the attributes we share with material things as they could possibly be.

Which has priority in delineating the concept of a person? We tend to pick out individual people, for instance, in a police line-up, mostly by bodily appearances. Yet each person has a sense of his or her own identity that does not need verifying by looking in the mirror or otherwise checking on bodily attributes. It is evidently related to the mysterious fact of consciousness and and more especially to self-consciousness.

In what follows in this chapter it will become evident that many of the philosophers we will study have taken for granted a rather mundane kind of material thing as an exemplar. If our typical material thing is something like a stone, we may indeed find it hard to imagine how it could have mental and moral attributes. Nor is it any easier to imagine how it could have the living attributes of plants and animals. How can a material thing be the seat of consciousness? But, of course, we do not know what are the limits to the possible properties of material beings. Maybe a capacity to think and feel is among them.

Nevertheless, the scene for much philosophizing about human nature in the last 500 years of the second millennium has been based on the assumption that the mental and material attributes of persons are utterly different. People have some of the same properties as material things, some of the same properties as animals, and some properties which seem to be uniquely human. How is this possible? Descartes settled the form of this problem at the beginning of the seventeenth century. His explanation for the diversity of human attributes was based on the idea that a person was a compound of two quite different substances. There was a mental substance, the mind, to which mental attributes were ascribed, and a material substance, the body, which collected all the material properties of a person.

The Cartesian legacy

We will begin this survey with Descartes' version of the person. Philosophers have rejected it, modified it, or taken it up in various ways, but they have never been able to ignore it. We will then turn to a survey of the ways that philosophers have tackled the problem of personal identity. By what criteria are people identified and individuated by others? What is my individuality and identity to myself? Or to put the matter in another way, how is the third-person view I have of other people and they have of me to be integrated with the first-person view I have of myself? I certainly do not have to check whether

I am the same person today as I was yesterday. Does it make any sense to suppose that I might be wrong about whether or not I am the same person? Finally we will look briefly at the problem of the limits of what one can know of oneself and of others.

The history of philosophical accounts of the self, the core of personhood, can be seen in outline in the views of five well-known philosophers. Descartes declared the self to be an entity, an immaterial substance. Hume pointed out that this alleged entity, the self, could not be observed by inward scrutiny. In introspection all one would ever find in the "inner realm" would be a bundle of thoughts and feelings. The "I" which searches could never bring itself under scrutiny. The next step was taken by Kant. He agreed with Hume that the self can never encounter itself. But he found two transcendental unifying centers, outside the realm of experience, outside the scope of the empirical or perceptible "self." We know that our thoughts and feelings are unified in the one mind, and we know that we have the power to follow the dictates of reason in making decisions. The final step was taken by Wittgenstein (1953) and by Strawson (1956). They both point out that the being that Descartes hid away in the depths of subjectivity, that Hume could not find by looking inwards for it, and that Kant placed outside the realm of any possible experience, was actually right in front of our eyes. It was the public, embodied, language-using person. It is neither buried in the inner core of personal being nor elevated into the realm of the transcendental.

THE NATURE OF A PERSON

There seem to have been two main attempts in post-Renaissance Europe to develop an account of the nature of human beings as persons. Dualists based their analysis upon a presupposition of an irreducible difference between the mental and the material aspects of persons. Monists based their analyses on the presupposition that whatever appearances there may be to the contrary, a person consists of only one kind of stuff and has only one kind of attribute.

Dualism: Mentalism

According to the dualists, a person is a union of two radically different types of entity, one a material body and the other an immaterial mind. Some, like Descartes (1641), have held that mental phenomena are attributes of a mental substance. While our bodies are all fashioned out of the same material stuff, each individual mind is a unique "thinking thing," an ego. For some philosophers it doubled as the soul. Others, like Locke (1690) and Hume (1739), held that mental phenomena are immaterial entities that, taken together, constitute the mind. For them, the mind was a "bundle" of perceptions and feelings. Both versions are dualistic. There are both bodies and minds.

Since we are aware not only of the messages of the senses but also of at least some of our feelings, desires, and ideas, each person must not only be a center of consciousness but also of self-consciousness. But how is it possible for immaterial mind and material body to interact, as it seems they obviously do? How can a physical stimulation of a sense organ lead to a sensation? How can a decision lead to an action in the material world?

Descartes' dualism of substances

Descartes came to the view that mind and body are different *substances* in the course of reflecting on whether any of his beliefs were so secure that they could not be doubted. He begins with a reminder of the method by which he will reach the sure ground of indubitable belief.

> To begin with, I will go back over all the things which I previously took to be perceived by the senses, and reckoned to be true; and I will go over my reasons for thinking this. Next I will set out my reasons for subsequently calling these things into doubt. And finally I will consider what I should now believe about them. (Descartes, 1641 [1985]: 51)

> there is nothing so far removed from us as to be beyond our reach, or so hidden that we cannot discover it, provided only we abstain from accepting the false for the true, and always preserve in our thoughts the order necessary for the deduction of one truth from another. (Descartes, 1644 [1985]: 16)

But what could serve as a premise for the deduction of secure knowledge about oneself? It must be both thinkable and indubitable.

Borrowing from earlier sources, Descartes gave us the most famous of all philosophical arguments: *cogito ergo sum*, "I think therefore I am." Its role is to serve as the source of a sure ground for belief. Doubt, which seems to undermine belief, can actually be recruited to support it. If someone is doubting that he or she is thinking, then, since doubting is a species of thinking, that person *is* thinking. So the existence of thinking is indubitable. So far so good. But where is the person in this?

His argument, so often quoted and parodied, is supposed to prove that a thinking *thing* exists, namely a mind, soul, or ego, a mental substance that is truly Descartes (Descartes, 1641 [1985]: 19). The argument is very simple: "I think therefore I am" (Descartes, 1644 [1985]: 194).

While the name "Descartes" refers to the whole ensemble, body and mind, Descartes takes for granted that the pronoun "I" refers to the ego, the really real Descartes, the immaterial entity that is the mind part of the composite person, René Descartes.

Criticisms of Cartesian dualism

There are some obvious difficulties with the move from the indubitability of the existence of acts of thinking to the conclusion that there must be at least one immaterial thinking thing. At most we know thinkings must exist, not that there must a substance, an entity that is doing the thinking. The circularity of the argument is clearer in French than in Latin.

Je pense

donc

Je suis.

Far from proving the existence of a Cartesian ego, an immaterial substance that it is the real me, the argument is circular. "*Je*," the word that denotes the core of Descartes' very self, the Cartesian ego, appears in the premise of the argument and in the conclusion. It cannot therefore have been deduced from an indubitable premise.

The only valid argument that the doubting paradox supports is this:

> Doubting exists
> therefore
> Thinking exists.

One might well reject the idea that personhood is rooted in an immaterial entity while still holding that thinking, feeling, and willing are immaterial processes. Rejecting the Cartesian ego as the basis of what it is to be a person does not mean that we must accept materialism.

What lies behind the presupposition that whatever is mental must belong to an utterly different substance from that which is material? Descartes took for granted that the mental attributes of a person are immaterial. If these are the attributes of a mental substance, as a mind it is indivisible and, being indivisible, must be immortal. The body is made up of parts and these can be dispersed. The body is mortal.

There is a more radical difficulty for mind/body dualism. How are these apparently utterly different substances related? That they *are* related is indubitable. The bodily organs of sense supply the mind with sensations that are not at the whim of the person, while the mind makes the relevant parts of the body move in ways that the person intends. So mind and body must interact. How could such an interaction occur? It seems impossible for something immaterial and something material to influence one another.

Spinoza's dualism of aspects

To understand the gamut of philosophical accounts purporting to elucidate the mind–body problem once and for all, we need to bear in mind the distinction between substances and their properties. We might be convinced that a person consisted of only one kind of substance, and yet we might still want to say that whatever the substance constituting a person, be it material or mental, that substance has two or more kinds of irreducible properties. States of consciousness seem to be utterly different kinds of properties from physical states of the body. So we arrive at another kind of dualist position, a dualism of properties and processes. Among the best worked-out versions of this point of view, extended to a cosmic scale, is the philosophy of Spinoza.

Baruch de Spinoza was born in 1632 in Amsterdam. His parents were refugees from an outburst of antisemitism in Spain. When quite young he broke away from Judaism. Though he was well-versed in Christian thought he was never baptized. He changed his name to Benedict de Spinoza as part of his apostasy. In disfavor with the Jewish community and later with the Christian establishment, both Catholic and Protestant, he lived humbly. The last years of his life were spent in The Hague as a lens-grinder. The target of such marked hostility from both communities was due to his passionate resistance to the dictates of authority, be they religious or political. He died in 1677, covertly admired by many, but to enjoy only a posthumous fame.

In the search for an adequate image of the person, Spinoza embedded his dual-aspect view in a much larger cosmic frame, in which matter and spirit were the two modes under which God manifested himself in the universe. Spinoza declared that "the object of the idea constituting the human mind is the body, in other words a certain mode of extension which already exists" (1677: Proposition XIII). He remarks in a note that "we thus comprehend not only that the human mind is united to the human body, but also the nature of the union between mind and body," since both are modes of the one substance which is God. Thought is an attribute of God and so too is extension, the essential characteristic of anything material. To put this simply, according to Spinoza there is just one substance, but it is manifested both as a thinking thing and as a material thing. There is no question of how the interactions between mind and body and body and mind are to be explained. There are no such interactions. The relations between modes are not causal. We could think of them as two ways in which the same "stuff" appears.

In Proposition VII of Part II of the *Ethics*, Spinoza introduces a crucial thesis for his resolution of the mind/body problem, namely that the order and connection of ideas is the same as the order and connection of things. This is simply because both are aspects of the same reality, that which Spinoza calls "God." There is a kind of preestablished harmony. There is only one "unfolding" manifesting itself in the two modes: thought (mind) and extension (matter).

Monism: Materialism

Traditionally materialists have tried to solve the problem of how mind and body can interact by "materializing" the mental. If it could be shown that the phenomena taken to be mental were really material after all, caused by material stimuli in the sensory systems, then there would be no problem. A person is nothing but a particular living body.

One might think that experiment and observation could settle this matter. Philosophers can still take it to be their business because the mental and material aspects of a person will always *seem* to be radically different. At the very best empirical research can show only that there are systematic and exceptionless correlations between material and mental states. We have well established vocabularies for describing states of both kinds. On the face of it mental concepts and material concepts seem radically different. Whether such correlations lead to materialism or idealism or some other resolution will have to be decided by conceptual analysis. Can we show that one set of concepts can be reduced to the other? Are there reasons for thinking that such a reduction is impossible? That is work for philosophers.

Materialism comes in weak and strong forms. According to the weak form the mechanisms of thought and action are wholly material, that is there is only one kind of substance involved, but we must remain agnostic about whether the mental and material states of a person are mutually reducible to each other. Mental states might be non-material emergent states of material mechanisms. In the strong version not only are the mechanisms material, but, it is claimed, mental states are really material states of the brain and central nervous system.

A weak materialism

Even J. O. de La Mettrie, in *L'Homme machine* (1748), notorious in the eighteenth century for his stance against the identification of the mind as the Christian soul, made no attempt to argue that mental states and processes were actually physical states and processes.

He offers a great variety of examples to show that in general "The various states of the soul are always correlated with those of the body" (La Mettrie, 1748). This is offered as an empirical thesis, a matter of fact, but it is also intended to serve as an absolute presupposition for a scientific research program. La Mettrie is careful to draw back from any claims about the essence of human kind. "Man [in the species sense] is a Machine so organized that it is impossible to arrive at a clear idea of it, and consequently at a definition." At best we can arrive at the highest state of probability for the presupposition on which the rationality of a materialist research project depends, namely that every mental state is correlated with a material state.

The correlation between physiological and mental states is clearly causal, but in a very narrow sense. "Our feeble understanding," he says, "derived from very crude observations, cannot show us the relations that obtain between cause and effect." Physiology cannot explain *how* consciousness arises from matter, it demonstrates only *that* it does. The scientific program of neuropsychology was to be based on taking the observable correlations between mental states and material states of a human being to be without exception.

The most important thesis that La Mettrie put forward concerned the activity of the human organism. Though he claimed to be taking the Animal/Machine concept from Descartes and extending it to human beings, he did not leave it unmodified. He gives a dynamic interpretation to the material mechanism. Organisms have active powers. "Living bodies have all that is needed for self-movement, feeling, thought . . . and to conduct themselves, in a word, in the physical and the moral world" (La Mettrie, 1748). Like Locke, he thought that matter could have mental powers, but unlike Locke, who drew back from asserting it as his settled opinion, he affirmed it. This aligns him with Joseph Priestley (1777) who argued vigorously for the idea of a common material basis for both physical and cognitive powers.

I have chosen to illustrate the modest form of materialism in the work of one of its founders, writing in the eighteenth century. At that time one could hardly say that materialism, weak or strong, was the "official doctrine" of well-informed people. Throughout the nineteenth century philosophers generally struggled with the problem of making sense of dualism. It is not till the explosion of neurophysiological discoveries in the twentieth century that a strong form of materialism began to take over as the dominant conception of the nature of persons. The biological revolution of the nineteenth century, effectively denying that human beings were the beneficiaries of a special act of divine creation, prepared the way for the radical reductionism of our time. From its inception, Darwin's (1859) account of the origin of human beings through a process of *natural* selection in a wholly material world was taken to be a challenge to the religious version of dualism. How could souls suddenly appear in the unbroken sequence of material beings, transformed by the selection of minute mutations?

Two strong materialisms

The dominant materialism of our own time is strongly reductionist. I will illustrate it with two popular lines of argument. If it could be shown that all that has hitherto been expressed by the use of mental concepts could be expressed with material concepts only, then the realm of the mental becomes redundant in a material world. The other popular stance is based on the success of the neurosciences, especially when allied with the project of creating artificial intelligence, in explaining human cognitive and practical abilities. Both lines of argument have been taken to lend support to a strong materialism. Both suffer from serious weaknesses.

ELIMINATING MENTAL CONCEPTS   If it could be shown that all mental concepts could be replaced by material concepts, without loss of content, the mind/body problem would evaporate in a very fundamental way. The logical subject on which the reformed vocabulary would be predicated could be nothing other than a material thing, the body. If we have words only for physical states then we can talk only about material things. This program of vocabulary reform has been called "eliminative materialism."

How could one show that a vocabulary was so radically defective that it ought to be replaced by a different set of words? In the 1950s several philosophers of science, notably Norwood Russell Hanson (1958), pointed out that there is no sharp division between the meanings of words used in explanations and of words used in descriptions. The latter always incorporate theoretical concepts. For example, when the word "hot" is used in the description of a calorific phenomenon, people literate in science understand it as having a complex meaning. It is partly phenomenological, referring to how something would feel, and partly theoretical, referring to the kinetic theory of molecules in motion, which explains why one thing is hot and another cold. In the eighteenth century scientists thought of heat as an invisible fluid, but the same principle of meaning applied. Calling something "hot" would have suggested to a well-educated person of the time the presence of a goodly amount of caloric. The word "hot" is *never* used by scientists and educated laypersons just for describing how something feels.

In an attempt to discredit the psychological vocabulary of one vernacular, namely English, Paul Churchland (1984) argued that it must be faulty since it incorporated the concepts of "folk psychology." According to eliminative materialists, mentalistic words like "belief" and "memory" are used by ordinary people to refer to mental entities. The presupposition that there are such entities is taken to be the basis of an informal or "folk" psychology. But, according to the eliminativists, there are no such mental entities. Folk psychology is a false psychological theory. The mentalistic vocabulary of the vernacular is laden with misleading presuppositions.

According to the eliminativists, there is a developing and true theory of cognition. It is based on neurophysiology, and presupposes nothing other than states and processes of the brain and central nervous system. We should eliminate everyday expressions like "pain," which presuppose the existence of feelings, mental entities, in favour of "firing in the c-fibres," an expression which presupposes only material entities. The phrase "the sound of the flute" should be eliminated in favor of descriptions of the form of sound waves propagated by flutes, together with the terminology for describing the processes that occur in the nervous system of the listener when bombarded with vibrating air molecules.

There is no mind/body problem, because, it is alleged, there is no scientifically acceptable vocabulary for referring to and describing the "mind" side of the problematic pair.

There are any number of problems with this proposal. Such a purging of the vocabulary jumps the gun. There is little ground for the thesis that the psychology implicit in English is based on an ontology of mental *entities*. Already in the eighteenth century Thomas Reid based his account of human cognition on an ontology of mental powers.

> Power is not an object of our external senses, nor even an object of consciousness. There are some things of which we have a direct, and others of which we have only a relative conception, power belongs to the latter class . . . power is a quality, and cannot exist without a subject to which it belongs. We cannot conclude the want of a power from its not being exerted; nor from the exertion of a less degree of power, can we conclude that there is no greater degree of power. (Reid, 1788: chapter 1)

In recent years both Gilbert Ryle (1947) and Wittgenstein (1953) have shown that much of the psychological vocabulary of the English and

German vernaculars seems to work with dispositional concepts rather than concepts for mental entities. To say that someone believes something is more likely to be understood as an assertion about what that person would say or do than a hypothesis about an alleged mental entity, "a belief." To take another example: "intelligence" is not the name for some mental property that varies in quantity from one person to another, in the way that the material property of weight varies. To call someone clever, smart, ingenious, and so on is to ascribe certain skills and capacities to that person. In the same way, character and personality traits are also dispositions to say or do things rather than states of mind. "Tender-hearted" *means* "if presented with the sufferings of someone else, will be sympathetic," while "brutal" means, among other things "when dealing with other people will tend to act cruelly and inconsiderately."

The problem of the irreducibility of the mental seems to be with us still. I have no doubt that it will be as persistent in the third millennium as it has proved to be in the second.

MENTAL MACHINES   There is a second version of strong materialism that does not depend on dubious claims about the meanings of our mentalistic vocabulary. There is a long history of attempts to devise machines that will simulate the performances of human beings. Mechanical toys that could imitate all sorts of human actions, such as playing musical instruments, walking, and so on, were popular in the seventeenth and eighteenth centuries. It is a short step to imagining that a mechanism could be constructed that would perform cognitive as well as practical activities. In each century the most sophisticated mechanisms of the time became the basis for models of the brain. In the seventeenth century the models were hydraulic, fluids in tubes. In the nineteenth century mechanical devices were favoured. Charles Babbage designed the first machine that would have simulated mental operations, such as arithmetical calculations, had it ever been built. In the twentieth century the telephone exchange took over as a popular model, once it was realized that the brain and nervous system were conduits for electrical impulses.

For many enthusiasts the ultimate mind machine appeared after the Second World War – the electronic computer, soon to be capable of simulating a wide range of cognitive functions previously performed only by human beings. Alan Turing not only invented the modern computing machine but put in train the long-running philosophical debate about the relation between thinking and its material basis, sparked off by reflection on the amazing capacities of some of these machines (Turing, 1950).

He proposed a simple test to prove that it made sense to declare that a machine could think. Imagine two conversations taking place, perhaps by telephone, one between an investigator and another human being, and the other between the investigator and a suitably programmed computer. The investigator does not know which conversation is with a person and which with a machine. Turing argued that if the investigator could not tell from how the conversations went with which being he was conversing, we would be obliged to say that the machine could think.

The basis of this form of materialism is a simple analogy:

$$\text{Brain : Thinking :: Machine : Computing.}$$

If sufficiently sophisticated machines can simulate a great range of cognitive skills, not only must they be said to think, but also brains, carrying out the same tasks, must be thought of as computers. The mind is not an entity. The realm of the mental is the performance of computations using the available programs, be it in a computing machine or in a brain. "L'homme machine" has been given a new lease of life in the computational metaphor, in the popular equation of thinking/brain with computing/computer.

The enthusiasm with which the computational model of mind was received was extraordinary. "Computer scientists" vied to create programs which would simulate more and more sophisticated cognitive processes. Philosophers made extravagant claims about the final reduction of the mental to the material. But two kinds of difficulties soon surfaced. On the technical side, the ability to create successful simulations of even so simple a cognitive process as classifying seemed to elude the engineers. On the philosophical side, two aspects of human mentality seemed to find no place in the machine picture. These were intentionality, the way a symbol has meaning for a human being, and consciousness, awareness of one's environment and of one's own states (Searle, 1983). Innovations in computing, particularly neural nets and connectionism, have given new life to the basic analogy. However, even an enthusiast for the program of artificial intelligence in its very latest dress must confess that the reductionist inferences drawn from the limited success of the practical ambitions of the engineers have come to look less and less plausible.

The literature spawned by this debate is truly vast. Rather than cite a library of relevant and fascinating books, I would suggest that the interested reader begin to follow the twists and turns of the debate through the excellent overview in Jack Copeland's *Artificial Intelligence* (1992), recently reprinted. What shall we say at the millennial moment? As a former enthusiast for the computational metaphor I am inclined to think that the "minds and machines" debate will fade away. The vigorous advocacy of rather simplistic materialisms that has marked the last two decades of the second millennium seems to be over. There has been no resolution. How a certain organized group of molecules can "secrete" thoughts and feelings is as far from resolution as ever.

Noumenal Selves

In each of these attempts the search for the source of personhood has been confined to the realm of what we might perceive. Suppose our failures to find the source of personhood are due to the fact that it is real but imperceptible. Kant's solution was to acknowledge an empirical self, our selves as we know them, and a transcendental self – an aspect of personal being that we know must exist but of which we could have no direct experience.

We come at the imperceptible self from two directions. It is evident that each human mind is an organized whole, a unity. It is also evident that people can act contrary to the forces and impulses that bear upon them.

Kant uses the expression "apperception" for the intuition that a thought, a feeling, a mental act is mine. However, there is no intuition, no overall view of that unity, in which it presents itself to me as an intuition. That too would have to be part of the unified field that is *my* mind. The unity of apperception must be transcendental. It is presupposed in all I think and do, since I represent my mental life to myself as mine, but it is not perceptible as such.

Kant distinguishes between the phenomenal world, the realm of causality, and the noumenal world, the realm of reason. The empirical self, the personhood each of us experiences in self-reflection, does not seem capable of free action. "This [inner] sense represents to consciousness even our own selves only as we appear to ourselves, not as we are in ourselves" (Kant, 1787 [1996]: B153). "I cannot determine my existence as a self-active being; all that I can do is to represent to myself the spontaneity of my thought . . . my existence is still only determinable sensibly, that is as the existence of an appearance. But it is owing to this spontaneity that I entitle myself an *intelligence*" (Kant, 1787 [1996]: B158, footnote b). To be an intelligence is to be moved by reason rather than by causes. I find that I have the freedom to act unconditionally, moved only by reason. This appears to me as spontaneity, an event without a cause. I know I can so act, that I can weigh up reasons and choose my course of action rationally, regardless of the causal forces acting upon me. Yet I have no experiential, empirical knowledge of myself as I am but merely as I appear to myself.

According to Kant the core of selfhood, that which perceives and that which acts, is beyond the realm of what can be given to me in intuition. But I know that there is such a unity and such a power. It is transcendental.

The Irreducibility of Discourses

The philosophical study of the nature of the self has shifted in recent years toward an investigation of the linguistic means by which selfhood is expressed. This reflects a profound insight. Human individuality is not a consequence of each of us possessing a hidden, substantial, Cartesian soul, nor being an imperceptible transcendental agent. It is there for all to see and interact with – the human being as a publicly recognized person. Philosophy of selfhood has taken a linguistic turn. Instead of trying to imagine how mind and body might interact we analyze the kinds of predicates that are used to describe persons. We study the devices we use to refer to ourselves and to beings like us. If the core of the self is the irreducible public person, then that should be evident in the presuppositoins of the meaningfulness of the grammar of personal pronouns

The failure of the reductionist program might well persuade one to acknowledge that there are *irreducible* sets of person-descriptive predicates, in use in human affairs. One set is used for describing the body and its states. Simple body predicates such as "weight" and "height" are not exclusive to human beings. They can be used to describe any material thing. Another set of predicates can be used only of organisms. While we can discuss the mortality of frogs and even of bacteria, it makes no sense to say that a stone is alive or dead. A third set is used for describing the mental life of conscious beings. Mental predicates, for the most part, can be used only of human beings, though some can also be used of animals. A dog can be said to be alert. Elephants never forget. A fourth set can be used only of self-conscious beings. Only people can feel guilty, realize a mistake has been made, and so on. There is only one way of describing a stone. There are two ways of describing a plant or a micro-organism. There are three ways of describing a higher animal. There are four ways of describing human beings as persons. The person is the basic particular of human life (Strawson, 1956). All four ways of describing a person are required to do justice to the facts of human life.

A person must be embodied in order for it to be possible for that person to be reidentified as one and the same person on different occasions. For the most part this involves the use of material predicates. These are used to ascribe publicly observable properties, among which are those by which successive bodily appearances are recognized as those of the same person. In hard cases mental predicates are sometimes involved when a person tries to establish an identity by recalling events from the distant past.

The uses of the word "I"

People have proper names or some equivalent unique appellation, such as a Social Security Number. However, these appellations hardly express the heart of the sense one has of oneself as a unique and singular being. The job seems to be reserved to pronouns. "I" seems to be *the* "self" word. Does it refer to a person in the way that a proper name refers to someone? Perhaps "I" is a peculiar kind of proper name, one that changes its referent from user to user. When we look closely at the grammar of the first person we will see that words like "I," "me," and "mine" do not function as names. Their referential role is subtler. The word "I" does refer or point to someone, namely the person speaking. But it does much more than that.

One can come to know to whom "he" or "she" refers by tracking back or forward through a sequence of pronouns until one reaches an

ordinary referring expression like a proper name or a definite description. "Cleopatra put *her* hand in the basket of asps and so *she* died."
The first person functions in another way. The use of "I" expresses
something to do with the current speaker. But it is not an alternative
to the person's proper name. Wittgenstein (1953: 410) likened "I" to
words like "here" and "now." "Here" is not the name of a place, like
"Champaign-Urbana." "Now" is not the name of a time like "January
1, 2000." All three, and lots of others, are indexicals. "Here" indexes the
content of a statement with the spatial location of the speaker, while
"now" does the same for time of utterance.

What role does "I" play? It serves to index the content of what is
said with various properties of the person who is speaking. The English
"I" indexes the content of what is said with the spatial location of the
speaker and the social force of what is said with the speaker's moral
standing. For example, in a statement like "I can see the way out" the
first-person pronoun informs the listener from which point in space
the way out can be seen, namely where the speaker's body is. In "I can
just reach the top shelf," the pronoun locates the action where the
speaker is standing. In a statement like "I'll answer the door," it not
only informs the listener which person will do the job, but also
commits the person who spoke to carry it out. In "I will get the
laundry in" the pronoun is used to take responsibility, to make a
promise, and so on. It shows who is responsible. The indexical roles of
the first person invoke attributes of the embodied *person* as embodied
speaker, namely spatiotemporal location and moral standing. In no case
does "I" name or refer to an inner core of being, a Cartesian ego.

Wittgenstein pointed out that I cannot be mistaken about being
myself, that is, the same person I was yesterday, while I can be mistaken about whether I have previously met someone to whom I am
introduced. In using "I" I cannot misname myself. The self, then, whatever it is, is not an inner "thing."

In this grammar we find a clue to some aspects of the self, the sense
one has of one's singularity and uniqueness as a person. While the loca-
tive role of "I" seems to be universal in that all languages we know of
use the first person for this purpose, the commitment role varies
widely. It depends on the degree to which there are institutions of
verbal commitment recognized in a society, and on the degree to which
acts of commitment are personal or collective. The person is indeed
the ultimate unit of analysis to which all these predicates are ascribed.

It is the publicly observable, embodied being, to which all sorts of mental and moral attributes are ascribed.

Here again, at the end of the second millennium we find the linguistic turn in a particularly striking form. The presuppositions on which so much of our lives rest seem in the end to be linguistic.

PERSONAL IDENTITY

Individuality and Identity

What is it to be one and the same person? This question is more complex than it looks, since it involves two issues: *individuality*, that which makes one person unique and different from every other; and *identity*, that which makes a person the same person yesterday and tomorrow. Presupposed by the questions raised by the problem of understanding, and applying the concepts of identity and individuality of human beings, is some account of what it is to have a sense of self, of being a unique individual.

The Sense of Self

The philosophical problems posed by the presuppositions of the ways we manage the concept of a person were clearly seen and differentiated by John Locke. There is the problem of personal identity. By what criteria do we decide that the being before us is the *same person* as we have met before? This matter is determined, Locke thought, by reference to the identity and continuity of a human body. It consists in "nothing but a participation of the same continued life by constantly fleeting particles of matter, in succession vitally united to the same organised body" (Locke, 1690: Book II, chapter 27, Section 16).

There is a quite different sort of presupposition to our use of the concept of a person of ourselves. What is the form and content of the sense a person has of being him- or herself? Locke realizes very well that this is not a matter of criteria by which one might determine the question of one's own personhood. His discussion is an analysis of the sense of selfhood, of being a person. It is, he argues, to be conscious of, that is, to have ideas of one's past and one's present and to anticipate one's future. Selfhood is a matter of a certain structure and content of consciousness. It is not to realize that one is a Cartesian ego. It is to have a certain kind of experience, a certain kind and organization of ideas. Since "consciousness always accompanies thinking, and it is that, that makes everyone to be what he calls self, and thereby distinguishes himself from all other thinking things . . . and in so far as this consciousness can be extended backwards to any past action and thought, so far reaches the identity of that person" (Locke, ibid). This is what it is to *be* a self, a person. The sense one has of one's own personal identity is determined by continuity of consciousness. Just as the mind is a conscious unity at any one time, so the self is a unity of consciousness through time. The psychological basis of the sense of self must be memory. Continuity of consciousness through time is not a criterion for judging whether or not one is one and the same person. There could not be any such criterion.

Locke proposed a thought experiment that illustrates the difference between being the same man and being a person or self. The soul of a prince and the soul of a cobbler exchange bodies. Since the soul carries the consciousness of the prince, the hybrid being composed of the royal soul and the artisan's body would be the same self or person as the prince, but not, Locke thinks, the same man. "The body too goes to the making of the man" (Section 15). The "sense of self" of the hybrid being just is the awareness it has of a certain order and range of ideas of which that being is conscious.

In Britain the philosophical discussion of the presuppositions of the concept of selfhood followed Locke's position, mostly to reject it. Joseph Butler (1736) and Thomas Reid (1788) both argued against the coherence of the principle that memory determined selfhood. They realized that the concept of "memory" presupposed the continuity of self. To take some idea as a person's remembrance, it must be taken to be a recollection of something that happened to that person. The reach of what is remembered consciously cannot be the basis of the sense of self. Reid offered a simple counter-example. An old man remembers incidents in his younger life, but not what he did as a child. When young he remembered having stolen some apples as a boy. If reach of memory determined selfhood, that human being must be host to two persons. And that is absurd.

Hume, for his part, denied the very notion of "the self" *as an entity*. All that one could be acquainted with was the flux of one's own mental states. One could not discern any entity from an impression of which one could derive an idea of a permanent self that would explain the coherence and continuity of one's ideas. The reason was typically empiricist. Memory, Hume remarks (1739 [1962]: 311), "does not so much *produce* as *discover* personal identity" which is nothing but a pattern of coincident and sequential relations between mental states. Hume asks (p. 301): From what impression do we get the idea of a self? Such an impression would have to be the same throughout one's life, because it would be the impression of a permanent "thing" to which all one's fleeting experiences belonged. Search as one might, there is no such impression. The mind is a flow of ever new ideas. The self is a convenient fiction. All we have is a sequence of impressions and the ideas derived from them. Consciousness consists of nothing but a bundle of fleeting mental states. But who is it that is conscious of them all?

At this point we can turn back to the insights of Wittgenstein and Strawson. The person whose uniqueness and sense of identity puzzled us is there for all to see. It is the many-faceted embodied being the character of which is presupposed in everything we do. Our problem is already disposed of. The presuppositions of the possibility of personal identity are nothing other than the conditions for the use of proper names and personal pronouns.

There the matter seems to stand at the turn of the millennium. Have we really condensed an ocean of metaphysics into a drop of grammar?

KNOWING PEOPLE

What is presupposed in any claim to know the personal attributes and current states of mind of a person? What can I know of my own thoughts and feelings, dispositions, and powers? And what can I know of the mental lives of other people?

In the seventeenth and eighteenth centuries the scope and quality of self-knowledge never seems to have been put in question. Descartes, Locke, and Hume all seem to have taken for granted that reflection on one's own thoughts and feelings is a source of sure and certain knowledge. Though Kant queried naive assumptions about the source of that knowledge, he does not seem have doubted that one does know one's own mind. Doubts about the grounds for claims to know the mind of someone else come to the fore somewhat later.

So far we have been examining the history of philosophical reflection on the presuppositions of everyday ways of knowing about human beings and understanding them. In the nineteenth century the idea of a *science* of human mental life began to emerge. Through the practice of chemistry one can know about the nature and potentialities of material stuff. Is there a corresponding science by means of which we could get to know about the properties of mind? The earliest efforts were based on an analogue of Newtonian atomism, applied to the Lockean conception of the mind as a container of ideas. Just as natural scientists looked for the laws of association and interaction among material atoms, so psychologists should look for patterns of association between types of ideas, the mental atoms. Generally the associationists were satisfied with personal introspection to provide the data.

However, at the end of nineteenth century a growing uneasiness with such optimistic presuppositions begins to show itself. Sigmund Freud devised a striking version of an old idea: that there is more in the mind than we can tell. More disturbing was the questioning of how far could one know what reasons one had oneself for what one did.

Freud and Understanding Oneself

There can be no doubt about the vast influence that the writings of Sigmund Freud have exerted on Western conceptions of the person and of the lives that people live. Freud was born in Moravia in 1856. He studied medicine in Vienna, and then, drawn to neurology, with J. M. Charcot in Paris. The psychopathology of hysteria became his dominant interest. How could one account for neuroses and, having accounted for them, cure them? He became convinced that the sources of psychopathology were to be found in the forgotten experiences of early childhood, especially sexual experiences. From this came his radical hypothesis of a duality of mind, a conscious arena of thoughts and feelings and an unconscious realm, in which inaccessible memories linked up into distorted associations that manifested themselves in thoughts and actions of a seemingly quite different kind. The person was the playground of three kinds of "forces": the Id, primitive impulses, the Ego, rational cognition, and the Superego, the constraints of society. He believed that the unconscious showed itself in the content of dreams and in undirected talk about the past. Freud's works have been collected in a standard edition, but the reader wanting to get an authentic overview should consult Freud's own (1933) summary of his theory and practice. Driven out of Vienna by the Nazis, he settled in England, dying in London in 1939.

His biography encapsulates his philosophy. Originally his realms of mind were given a neurophysiological interpretation, but this seems to have been lost as the theory became more and more mentalistic. The key insight from the point of view of the history of philosophy is the limitations which Freud identified in the possibility of self-knowledge. Everyone, not just the neurotic patient, has an inaccessible unconsciousness, affecting everything that one thinks, feels, and does. Access to the unconscious requires outside assistance, best of all by the practitioner of psychoanalysis.

Criticism of the Freudian picture of the person has focused both on the general theory and on the treatment procedures that Freud devised. On the one hand the psychological assumptions, particularly the alleged dominance of the sexual impulses and their role in human development, have been largely rejected. At the same time grave doubts have been cast on the efficacy of Freud's techniques for the treatment of neurotic symptoms. The talking cure has been supplanted by more and more chemotherapy, in line with the growing conviction that it is in the brain's capacities to function "properly" that the foundations of thinking must be sought.

Philosophers have been critical of the ontology, of the doubling up of mind. Does it make sense to suppose that there are cognitive mental processes of which a person is unaware? How could there be an unfelt emotion? Could not a much less extravagant account be based on the idea of neural traces, rather than unconscious mental states? From time to time Freud seems to have interpreted his theory this way himself.

Recently the problem of making sense of the concept of self-deception has been prominent in discussions of the Freudian mind. Criticism of the Freudian stance on repression has been focused on the implausible idea that the self-deceiving person is split into two "semi-persons," the one who deceives and the one who is deceived.

Has the Freudian account of persons and their lives been decisively refuted? One can hardly say that, but it is true to say that it has faded from its once prominent place in Western self-understanding. There is much that one does not know about oneself. However, the idea that that material is stored in a kind of doppelgänger of the conscious mind has come to seem more and more implausible.

Freud based his psychotherapy on the principle that the psychoanalyst has an important role in promoting the patient's self-understanding by providing interpretations of the content of dreams, slips of the tongue, and other unintentional disclosures. The psychoanalyst may have better understanding of the mind of the patient than the patient has. However, the whole enterprise rests on the presupposition that through their conversation the analyst does have access to the thoughts and feelings of another human being. What does that presuppose?

Knowing the Minds of Others

When Descartes, brooding by the fire, could find no surety in anything that his senses told him, he initiated a problem of such long standing that it might almost be definitive of philosophy itself. Even if I do have some confidence in what I learn about the material world by perception, yet the thoughts and feelings of other people must surely remain forever problematic. Not only do I have no surety in what I think someone else is feeling, but I cannot even be sure that the being in question is conscious, or to put it very dramatically, has a mind at all.

It is an easy slide from common-sense doubts about the extent of my knowledge of the thoughts and feelings of another person to a full-blown skepticism about what I can really know of the thoughts and feelings of another. How do I know that the character of how others experience the world and their own minds is anything like my experience of these matters? How can I be sure that other human beings have a mental life at all?

It is not far from that doubt to solipsism, the idea that the domain of a common world breaks up into individual islands bounded by the limits of our own consciousnesses – not one world to which we all have partial access, but as many worlds as there are people. This train of thought can go further. How can I justify my belief that there are any other consciousnesses at all if my experience of other people is just their appearances in my subjective realm? This is full-blown solipsism, where the world is reduced to my world.

The problem of "other minds" has several facets. One concerns the meaning of the words we use to describe our private thoughts and feelings. The skeptic wonders how I can know what those words mean to anyone else, since they seem to refer to states of affairs known only to that other. Wittgenstein addresses this problem in a key section of his *Philosophical Investigations*. That there is a problem of other minds depends on a yet more general presupposition, that behind public displays of cognitive skills lies a hidden realm of private cognition where the real thinking occurs. This presupposition was the main target of Ryle's *The Concept of Mind*.

Wittgenstein's treatment of the problem of "other minds"

Wittgenstein's ideas and aphorisms have appeared from time to time in these studies. At this millennial moment there is a growing realization of his enormous importance as a philosopher.

Ludwig Wittgenstein was born in Vienna in 1889, the youngest son in the large family of Karl Wittgenstein, a prominent and cultivated Austrian industrialist. Ludwig was educated privately until the age of 14. Among his fellow pupils at his first school was a certain Adolph Hitler. His further education was largely technical. He worked on aeronautical problems in Manchester but soon moved to Cambridge and the tuition and society of Bertrand Russell. Their relationship was intimate and stormy. Enlisting in the Austrian army in the First World War, Wittgenstein spent the last months as a prisoner of war in Italy, where he finished his *Tractatus Logico-Philosophicus*. Convinced that this work had brought the long history of philosophy to an end, he spent a decade in various professions, including working as a schoolmaster and an architect. He returned to Cambridge in 1930, having realized that his claim to have brought philosophy to an end was premature. Apart from the war years, he remained there until 1947. His personal influence was immense, despite his reclusive habits. He often withdrew altogether from human company to his cottage in Norway. In the later part of his life he spent time in a remote part of western Ireland. Almost all his work has been published posthumously. He died in 1951. He has been very well served by a remarkable biography, *The Duty of Genius*, by Ray Monk (1996).

In his youth Wittgenstein was greatly impressed by the writings of the newspaper columnist, Karl Krausz. Disgusted by the hypocrisy of the Viennese at the *fin de siècle*, Krausz developed a technique of social criticism as a critique of language. By simply juxtaposing a plain description of some aspect of Viennese life with the sort of things that people said about it, he showed rather than described the corruption of life through a display of the corruption of language.

Wittgenstein's technique in philosophy was rooted in the same intuition. Seemingly intractable problems may have their roots in presuppositions about the grammar of the language involved that, once clearly revealed, will allow us to escape the linguistic trap that sets the problem. In the case of knowledge of the thoughts and feelings of other people, perhaps by paying close attention to how some mistaken or confused presupposition about language is involved in the seemingly intractable problem about how I can have any secure knowledge of your private thoughts and feelings, the impasse can be overcome.

This clears the way for a rather different way of thinking about the problem of other minds, by turning it into a question about how one gets to know the meanings of words for private experiences. This is one very fruitful aspect of Wittgenstein's famous "Private Language Argument."

The Private Language Argument

Would it be possible to build a language by attending only to my own private states of consciousness, such as my bodily feelings, and attaching words to them by some kind of inward pointing? That this was possible seemed to be a presupposition of some of Russell's ideas about language and meaning. The Private Language Argument is designed to show that there can be no such language, the words of which gained their meaning by private acts of attending to private states of mind.

In the first phase of the argument, Wittgenstein continues his campaign against treating the meanings of words as the objects they denote. He is concerned to show that no one could teach or learn words for private feelings if the only method of teaching and learning was by pointing to an exemplar to which both teacher and pupil could attend. The pupil cannot perceive what the teacher is inwardly pointing to when using the word "itch," while the teacher cannot tell whether the pupil is attending to a sensation of the right sort. How are the meanings of such words learned? Wittgenstein's solution is to suggest that there are natural expressions (Wittgenstein, 1953: 242) of certain private experiences, particularly sensations of pain and the like, for which verbal substitutes can be picked up informally or by being deliberately taught.

> How does a human being learn the meaning of the names for sensations? . . . Here is one possibility: words are connected with the primitive, the natural, expression of the sensations and used in their place. A child hurts himself and he cries; then adults talk to him and teach him exclamations and later sentences. They teach the child new pain-behaviour. (Wittgenstein, 1953: 244)

So the verbal expressions will have the same "grammar" as the natural expressions. Words, so used, do not describe feelings, but express them. The tendency to groan is part of what it is to be in pain, neither more nor less important that the unpleasant feeling itself.

The mistaken idea that mental words are learned by a teacher pointing to an example presupposes not only a certain view about meanings, namely that they are the objects denoted by the words, but also that bodily feelings and other "mental states" are private *objects*. If there are no private mental objects then the attempt to adapt the baptismal account of meaning to explain how we could learn them is hopelessly astray. There are other ways of learning the uses of words than by pointing to shared exemplars, for example, by attending to public expressions of private experiences.

Some commentators have thought that this account of meaning committed Wittgenstein to behaviorism, as if our newly learned psychological vocabulary referred to the expressions and not the feelings expressed. This is yet another misunderstanding that comes from the denotational account of meaning. Wittgenstein deals with this mis-understanding in debate with his imaginary interlocutor in a famous paragraph:

> But you will surely admit that there is a difference between pain-behaviour accompanied by pain and pain-behaviour without any pain? Admit it? What greater difference could there be? And you again and again reach the conclusion that the sensation itself is a nothing. Not at all. It is not a something [a being of the same general kind as material things], but not a nothing either. (Wittgenstein, 1953: 304)

Why does Wittgenstein make this distinction? What is it that is most revealing about the concept of "material thing"? It is surely the cri-teria by which we apply the word "same" to them, that is, how we individuate and identify one and the same thing, or two different things that are alike in some way. Are the rules for applying the word "same" to feelings and other states of mind the same as those for applying it to material things?

How are we to understand such claims as "I had the same feeling yesterday" and "I felt the same as you did when I heard about the acci-dent"? It can only be by comparison of public expressions, allowing for all kinds of personal variants in how people behave. The wholistic principle, that the tendency to express a state of mind in a certain way is part of what it is to be in that state of mind, ensures that in normal circumstances, sameness of expression is a good guide to sameness of feeling.

There really is no "problem of other minds." There are a number of criss-crossing and overlaying rules for the use of words like "itch," "same," and so on, that, once brought out clearly, leave no further room for puzzlement. Of course, this argument too is built upon certain foundations, in particular that there are aspects of the human form of life that are "natural," that is, part of what it is to be a human being. This ensures that we can acquire a common vocabulary. That we do acquire a common vocabulary in its turn presupposes the idea that there are natural expressions, wholistically bound into a unity with the feelings they express.

Ryle's criticism of the myth of the "ghost in the machine"

In his influential work, *The Concept of Mind* (1947), Gilbert Ryle (1900–76) set about demolishing the whole Cartesian way of dealing with the mental aspects of human life, and so with Descartes' picture of the person. He accused Descartes and those who followed the same line of thought of the commission of a serious fallacy, a category mistake. In distinguishing between the human body and the human mind, Descartes treated both as if they were of the same category, namely substances. Ryle's project was to show from a study of the way we used our everyday mentalistic vocabulary that the material body and the mental aspects of human life belonged to different categories.

The secret, he thought, was to distinguish between two kinds of properties, occurrent and dispositional. An occurrent property was something like perceived shape, which was attributed to something then and there, as it was perceived. A dispositional property was possessed by something even when it was not being displayed or exercised. The fallacy, Ryle thought, was to interpret mental or cognitive attributes of people as if they referred to mysterious, inner, mental processes, accompanying all mental and physical activities public and private.

Ryle was no behaviorist. Far from denying the reality of private experience, he extended his analysis to that too. To say that someone is doing something intelligently is not to refer to an inner process that accompanies what is being done. It is to indicate how the task is being done, be that task privately or publicly performed. To say that someone knows something, either propositional or practical, is to ascribe to that person a disposition to carry through a task successfully, or to recall a fact, and so on.

It is easy to see that, if Ryle is generally right, the problem of other minds as it has been traditionally conceived in the Cartesian tradition simply disappears. Of course people can lie about what they think and feel, they can conceal their emotions and their opinions. However, these skills only make sense within a framework of concepts in which it makes sense to say that people can tell the truth and open their hearts and so on, *and be understood*. We are perfectly able to ascribe mental attributes to other people without having to guess how possessing or exercising that attribute might seem to them.

DUALISM AND DESTINY

Despite the shift during the last century and a half from seeing a person as an embodied soul to picturing a human being as an advanced organism unique only in its cognitive powers, there is a persistent Occidental tendency to think in dualisms. We have seen materialism and idealism come – powerful monistic attempts at grounding our ways of thinking and being – and we have seen them go. The same dualistic tendency is evident in Oriental philosophy too. How the ultimate fate of a person is conceived depends on the particular variety of dualism presupposed by a culture.

The Ubiquity of Conceptual Dualisms in Philosophies of the Person

In retrospect and from a global perspective, we look back on a thousand years of three very different and persisting traditions as to the particular kind of dualism that underlies the working ideas and practices that express the nature of a person in each tradition. However, at a certain level of abstraction all three traditions build on a dualism between the person as a distinct and identifiable individual and the universal or extrapersonal matrix in which that human individual and others of the same sort live. *Brahman* is universal as the deep nature of the cosmos, while *Atman* is the individual realisation of the cosmic nature in a person. Among other things which crystallized around *li*, its ancient meaning of a universal system of conventions and practices constitutive of social propriety persisted. *Ch'i*, by contrast, is constitutive of people as individuals. In Occidental philosophy Descartes expresses clearly the deep presupposition of Islam, Judaism, and Christianity alike, that while there is only one material stuff, divided into individual bodies, each mind/soul is a single and unique substance. There is only one matter but many minds. What is that second substance?

Somewhat less evident in the long perspective is another fundamental distinction that seems to be clearly discernible in Indian and Occidental thought. Both traditions bring out the presupposition of a common metaphysical ground in the distinction between what is material and what is immaterial in persons. In the Occidental tradition it commonly maps onto the distinction between body and mind, the one material and the other immaterial. Indian philosophy builds the material/immaterial distinction into the foundational presuppositions of the deep distinction between what is real, the immaterial, and what is illusion, *māyā*, the world as we perceive it, material and perishable. Our contemporary dualism is different again. The "second substance" is meaning and the world of symbolic activity that supervenes on the materiality of signs.

At the millennial moment there is a striking polarity between various forms of biological reductionism and linguistically oriented psychologies and even sociologies. Psychobiologists have worked toward a general materialism as a deliberately contrived foundation for concepts of personhood through vigorous attempts to assimilate psychology to biology directly. The role of genes in the genesis of behavior has been complemented by computational models of mind that are interpreted as abstract representations of brain structures and processes. We even find the curious neologism "mind-brain" used quite widely.

Linguistically oriented social constructionists, while acknowledging brains as the tools of thought, have worked toward a dualism of sorts. The uses of symbols are taken to be subject to rules and criteria of correctness which seem utterly unlike the causal processes mediated by material mechanisms that characterize the biological way of viewing persons. I am inclined to think that the dualism of symbolic task and material tool, on which the social constructionist position is based, does reflect the presuppositions of modern conceptions of and practices concerned with persons. I expect it to become the principle linking material brains and their immaterial cognitive products in the centuries to come.

Of one thing only am I fairly sure. I do not believe that there is any prospect of a new dual *substance* way of thinking about persons returning. Cartesianism is dead. It is not what is presupposed in any concept of the person in the social and material worlds that are currently in play, be it in the law, medicine, the arts, and so on.

The Ultimate Destiny of a Person

Beliefs about the ultimate fate of people, in the context of the knowledge of the inescapability of the death and dissolution of the body, seem to be related far less to the psychologies of the three great traditions than to the metaphysical schemes presupposed by each. In the Occidental tradition the soul, being immaterial, necessarily survives the dissolution of the material body. The problems that might arise for someone seeking evidence for this belief are set to one side very simply. Immaterial beings are imperceptible. So the fact that the dead, as souls, are not visible, audible, or tangible should not be brought up as counter-evidence to the belief in immortality. Ghosts, shimmering in the dark and rattling their chains, come from a very different tradition, which, at times, becomes entangled with the pure immaterialism of the Cartesian metaphysics. The second substance, for instance, as it is portrayed in the forms of Aeneas' dead comrades in the Underworld in Virgil's *Aeneid*, is material, though of a more refined and diaphanous character than the rougher stuff of flesh. Even in Cartesian thought the immaterialist character of the mind has often gone along with a kind of refined materialism in the hypothesis that much mental activity takes place by the movement of "animal spirits."

Indian thought, as we have seen, is rooted in the presupposition of a cosmic monism, of which *Atman* is but an aspect. Whether the ultimate fate of a person is endless rebirth, or the achievement of *nirvāna*, or, as in the philosophy of Rāmānuja, fusion with *Brahman* while maintaining a sense of self, the metaphysical basis of all of these versions of the fate of the enlightened and unenlightened alike is the same. There is no metaphysical issue to be debated. To put it crudely, to be a Hindu or a Buddhist just is to buy the whole package.

There is an interesting similarity between a strand of Chinese thought on the ultimate destiny of persons, and what one could call ideas about the "secular survival of personhood" that are all around us at the millennial moment. Chinese thought, as we have sampled it, and setting aside the imported Buddhist philosophy in China and Japan, saw personal survival not in the continuity of individual consciousness, but in the presence of remembrances of the dead in the thoughts and practices of their descendants. Having a reputation, not being forgotten by everyone, was thought. by some, to be highly desirable. Rituals of remembrance maintained the place of the person in the community. I do not think it too fanciful to see a somewhat similar point of view emerging as the genetic basis of organic life becomes more and more established as *the* presupposition of twenty-first-century culture. The very idea of surviving as a clone, though the latest examples of mammalian cloning seem to show how fanciful the pre-

sumption of perfect bodily identity is, reflects the idea of surviving in
one's descendants.

Of course, this idea has always been part of European culture, particularly in the upper classes, but genetics has given it a "scientific"
grounding. Being remembered has become not just a matter of granite
headstones, and having a place in a world of information technology,
in bibliographies, anthologies, and records of all kinds, however humble.
The genes inherited by one's descendants are a kind of perennial record
of what it was to be oneself. This seems to be a view of postmortem
survival that is close kin to some of the views expressed in Confucian
and Taoist thought. Since there does not seem to be much sign of a
serious revival of a broadly defended Cartesianism, at least in the West,
I expect the third millennium to see the combination of genetic and
cultural "survival" to become more and more firmly established in the
world at large.

Conclusion

The philosophical investigation of the concept of "person" has been
enormously influenced by the mind/body problem that emerged
from Descartes' privileging of private over public knowledge. It appears
on the one hand as the problem of how two quite different kinds of
entities could interact, and on the other as the problem of assigning
priority between bodily continuity or consciousness and memory as
the basis for judgments of personal identity. Materialists have tried to
assimilate everything mental to the material aspects of human organisms. None of the reductionist programmes has been totally successful.

Whichever way these matters are settled, it remains true that what
other people think and feel is often private. If there is to be a science
of human life, there must be some way of supporting the viability of
claims to know something about the subjective states of other people.
Without that, psychology could be nothing more than an impover-
ished behaviorism. Sociology could be no more that a statistical survey
of the observable patterns of institutional and economic behavior, and
anthropology a repertoire of travelers' tales. It has begun to look very
much as if the seemingly intractable problems involved in making sense
of the presuppositions of our strongly individualistic Western sense of
personhood can be dissolved by paying close attention to the ways

personhood is manifested and expressed. We can study these by attend-ing to our ways of taking or repudiating personal responsibility and of expressing personal identity.

Human life is lived in the light not only of what people are dis-posed to do as a matter of fact, but also in the light of what it is sup-posed in any given social milieu that they should do. We must turn from the history of attempts to ground our knowledge of one another's thoughts, feelings, and beliefs, acknowledging the dual character of human beings, to a survey of the ways that philosophers have tried to provide a sound, rational basis for judgments of right and wrong, good and evil, virtuous or vicious actions and characters. What are the presuppositions of the possibility of fruitful and enriching human associations on both a large and a small scale?

Relations among Persons I
Moral Philosophy

Having surveyed the most important metaphysical issues that have clustered round the concept of a person, I now turn to the complementary question: What is presupposed in the very idea that there are norms and standards in accordance with which people should behave? This is the province of moral and political philosophy.

The transition from a worldview dominated by religion to one dominated by science changes not only our general metaphysics, but also the direction in which we seek support for moral and political concepts and judgments. While the doctrine of Natural Law as the human version of God's Law made for a coherent moral/political climate in medieval times, the new orientation toward humanism reopened all the questions once seemingly settled by revealed religion. How do we defend various prescriptions for the good life and how do we justify emphasizing this or that catalogue of human virtues? Is this a matter for empirical enquiry into the facts of human life? Or is it possible that the outlines of an answer can be arrived at by pure reason? Both alternatives have had their advocates.

Above all one must keep in mind that after the Renaissance "discovery" of humanism, the individual comes to stand at the centre of patterns of knowledge and morality. Duties give way to rights and authority gives way to reason in the moral and political philosophies of the second half of the millennium. The apotheosis of this trend was the great European movement we call the Enlightenment.

With the recentering of philosophy on the individual, the old problem of how freedom of action is possible retained a central place in the ruminations of philosophers. Leibniz took it to be the familiar problem of how there can be a personal responsibility in a universe created and wholly foreseen in all its history by an omniscient God. It reappears in naturalistic guise. How can there be human freedom in a universe in which every bodily event has a material basis predetermined by the processes of nature? At the same time the question of the grounds of political authority stood in need of analysis. What are the presuppositions of the duty one has to obey the constituted authorities in a secular state? Under what circumstances does such an authority lose its right to rule? And so on.

Alisdair MacIntyre describes the contrast between medieval and modern contexts of moral and political philosophy as follows:

> in the Middle Ages social ties and political ties have a unity, just as they did for the Greeks, even if the unity of feudalism and the unity of the *polis* [the Greek city-state] were quite different. [In the modern world] a man is related to the state not via a web of social relations binding superiors and inferiors in all sorts of ways, but just as subject. A man is related to the economic order not via a well-defined status in a set of linked associations and guilds, but just as one who has the legal power to make contracts . . . what emerges is a new identity for the moral agent. (MacIntyre, 1966: 124)

Philosophers now have to reconcile not only freedom with causality, but freedom with secular authority, and the dictates of self-interest with the demands of the interests of others. The end of feudalism as the basis of political authority and the decline of the influence of the Catholic Church as the one arbiter of faith and morals made room for the appearance throughout the social world and its self-reflective discourses of the moral and political individual. Such a being had a claim to liberty, to freely choose a way of living, and a right to the pursuit of self-interest. How could morality, the rules of propriety in personal relations, have authority among beings of this sort? How could there be a constituted authority whose right to reign would be affirmed and accepted by such free individuals and on what grounds? If the sovereign power required the consent of the citizens to be authorized to act, how was that to be obtained? Was the solution to that problem a presupposition of any form of orderly association among free men?

In this chapter we will follow some of the ways that moral philosophers sought to develop a grounding for moral authority in an increasingly secular society.

FOUNDATIONS OF MORALITY

To some extent the distinction between moral and political philosophy is artificial. Both involve the search for the grounds of principles of right and wrong conduct that are effective or seem to be effective in bringing about an orderly and satisfying form of life. While political philosophy focuses on the relations between authorities and citizens, moral philosophy focuses on the relations between individuals.

The Moral Sense

By what criteria are we to assess the moral quality of human conduct? In the prevailing seventeenth- and eighteenth-century climate of empiricism, it is not surprising to find among British philosophers an emphasis on psychological aspects of the assessment of conduct and character. According to Hume, the principles of moral philosophy should come from a "cautious observation of human life" (Hume, 1739–40 [1962]: 44) rather than the exercise of reason on basic and necessary principles. His argument is brief and telling:

> Since morals . . . have an influence on the actions and affections, it follows, that they cannot be derived from reason; and that because reason alone . . . can never have any such influence. Morals excite passions, and produce or prevent actions. Reason of itself is utterly impotent in this particular. The rules of morality, therefore, are not conclusions of our reason. (Hume, 1739–40 [1962]: 192–3)

One might be tempted to think that moral philosophy should give way to anthropology, to reports of what people in fact find pleasing. But this was not Hume's conclusion. The second stage of his treatment of the foundations of morality is the demonstration that moral principles are not reports of matters of fact. If one knows nothing else about Hume's moral philosophy one knows that he declared that we cannot derive an "ought" from an "is."

The source of morality, Hume thinks, must be a moral sense, by which we experience the effects of the character of virtuous and vicious actions. "To have the sense of virtue, is nothing but to *feel* a satisfaction of a particular kind from the contemplation of a character ... We do not infer a character to be virtuous because it pleases; but in feeling that it pleases after such a particular manner, we in effect feel that it is virtuous" (Hume, 1739–40 [1962]: 205). In short, the concepts of a virtuous character and a pleasing character are the same. Ultimately the whole edifice of morality depends on pain and pleasure. But what gives us pleasure in a *morally* relevant way? This comes from the utility of what is done and the sympathy we have for others. We ought to do what is useful to others.

How can there be Universal Moral Principles?

Reflecting on Hume's analysis of the grounds of moral judgments suggests that it fails to provide a ground for universal moral judgments. It might well be that one group of people have a different conception of what is virtuous, that is, useful and pleasing, from that held by another. How could we arrive at the very criterion of what would anywhere and any time be a *moral* judgment? This was the problem Kant set out to solve. As we shall see, it emphasizes the individual as the site of morality even more radically than Hume's psychologically oriented account of the basis of moral judgments.

For Kant, as we saw in discussing his account of the self, every human action must be considered in relation to two "orders," the phenomenal world which is strictly governed by causal laws, and the intelligible world, governed by reason. Considered in the phenomenal world, human beings are bound by causality and they cannot act freely, that is, choose courses of action independently of the material and psychological forces that act upon them. But considered in the intelligible world, the world in which reason reigns, people are free. This freedom is manifested to us in our intuitions of spontaneity of some of our thought and action. Thus we are at once phenomenal organisms and noumenal agents.

Kant wants to find that which is unconditionally good. Actions done for the sake of pleasure or even for some useful end are directed to something extrinsic to the act itself. There seems to be only one candidate for an unconditioned principle of action: to do one's duty for the sake of doing one's duty.

This allows him to distinguish between categorical, unconditional imperatives, and hypothetical imperatives which express the rules for the performance of the actions that are valued according to the value of the desired and desirable results that are to be achieved. There are rules of skill for which technical knowledge is required, and prudential rules, which ensure that our actions are in our own interests. Neither kind of hypothetical imperative goes to the heart of the matter. Only a categorical imperative, a principle of action that is independent of particular situations and personal motives, could be the ultimate moral law. Kant's exposition of the nature of the categorical imperative is one of the great moments in the history of philosophy.

The categorical imperative appears in two versions in Kant's writings. The first formulation runs as follows:

> Act only on that maxim through which you can at the same time will that it should become a universal law. (Kant, 1785 [1964]: 52/421)

Kant calls this the "supreme principle of right." It requires us to respect everyone's right to act in accordance with the moral law, that is, autonomously, without any kind of coercion. What makes this imperative categorical, that is, unconditioned? It is unconditioned because "if [an action] is thought of as good in itself, and hence as necessary, [it is the product of] a will which of itself conforms to reason as the principle of this will" (Kant, 1785 [1969]: 36). Conforming to reason is simply avoiding contradiction. Morally wrong actions will lead to self-contradictions.

The second formulation of the categorical imperative looks very different from the first.

> Act in such a way that you always treat humanity, whether in your own person or in the person of any other, never simply as a means, but always at the same time as an end. (Kant, 1785 [1964]: 66–7/429)

This version is tied in with the other outstanding aspect of Kant's moral philosophy, the emphasis on our capacity to act freely, independently of extrinsic forces. This version of the categorical imperative defines the "Kingdom of Ends," an idealized social order in which all people are treated as free and responsible agents.

A rational being belongs to the realm of ends as member when he gives universal laws in it while also himself subject to these laws. He belongs to it as sovereign when he, as legislating, is subject to the will of no other. (Kant, 1785 [1969]: 59)

It is not difficult to see that these two versions express the same idea, that what marks off the moral from every other kind of judgment is the attention to and preservation of persons, as autonomous agents. It is also evident that so bare a principle as "adopt as moral laws only those maxims that respect the autonomy of all concerned" could not serve as a source of any particular moral rules.

Given some putative moral system, the categorical imperative enables us to filter the genuine moral laws from all other maxims. What makes a judgment or a rule moral is not its content but its form. "It concerns not the material of the action and its intended result but the form and principle from which it results" (Kant, 1785 [1969]: 38). Kant tests conduct against the categorical imperative by showing that a morally defective rule, such as a recommendation to lie, is contrary to reason since the maxim "Always lie" contradicts itself. Adopting it would destroy the distinction between truth and lies and so render it empty.

Such an austere philosophy could hardly be expected to form the basis of more popular philosophical approaches to morality. Some content is needed that can be supported by philosophical arguments, shown to be conceptually linked to some important value that defines the good life. Three major schools of moral philosophy appeared in the subsequent centuries, each offering a general account of the content of moral judgments.

THE CONTENT OF MORAL JUDGMENTS

Ethics developed into three major schools of thought. There were those who looked for the grounds of moral rightness in the consequences of actions, the utilitarians. There were those who looked for these grounds in the intrinsic character of moral actions, which are known by a kind of direct moral intuition. The third major school of ethics has developed as a branch of analytical philosophy, based on a close examination of the formal properties of moral judgments. These are the "prescriptivists." Other ways of dealing with the presuppositions of moral discourse have been proposed. For the purposes of our overview of a millennium I shall take the three here mentioned as indicative of the way moral philosophy has been practiced in the last century of the second millennium.

The Utilitarians

The idea that actions should be judged only by reference to their consequences is not only still a popular view, but it appeared very shortly after the beginning of the nineteenth century, mainly in the first fully industrialized nation, the United Kingdom. It was also of importance in that it was defended by one of the most skilled and influential philosophers of that century, John Stuart Mill. The thesis that morality resides in the consequences of actions was proposed in the previous generation, by both Hume (1740) and by Jeremy Bentham (1789), but it took on greater philosophical sophistication with the writings of Mill.

John Stuart Mill was born in 1806, the son of the philosopher and economist James Mill. The child was subject to an educational regime of notorious severity, starting Greek at the age of three. His living was secured by the patronage of his father, and he spent his active life as a civil servant in the India Office. James Mill intended his son to assume the leadership of the political movement founded by Bentham. The avowed aim was to replace intuition and emotion in the management of life by reason. The younger Mill suffered a "crisis" of faith, and turned away from the strict letter of utilitarianism to a richer sense of the depth and importance of cultural matters. His life was further transformed by his relationship with Harriet Martineau Taylor, whom he married after her husband's death. Their collaboration was evident in much of his later work. Mill was a courageous polemicist, not least in his attack on the treatment of women in Victorian times. He died in 1873.

What sort of consequences are relevant to the moral assessment of the actions that bring them about? Clearly the happiness of all concerned. Pleasures are the source of happiness, so the actions most to be commended are those which bring about the most pleasure and the least pain. Two major problems are evident in this seemingly simple and commonsensical proposal. Some pleasures seem more valuable than others, so how can they be ranked? Bentham proposed a purely quantitative measure. This is the source of the notorious aphorism: "Quantity of pleasure being equal, pushpin [a game] is as good as poetry" (Bentham, 1789: II, 253).

Can we harness the individual's desire for happiness to the project of bringing about the greatest happiness for all? Perhaps the sum of all the individual happinesses just is the happiness of all. More fundamentally we can ask why we should maximize pleasure, even knowing full well that most people do. How do we get from the "is" to the "ought"? Mill confronted and tried to solve these problems. He began by simply asserting that this is what the rightness of actions is. Thus, he says:

> Utility, or the Greatest Happiness Principle, holds that actions are right in proportion as they tend to promote happiness, wrong as they tend to produce the reverse of happiness. By happiness is intended pleasure, and the absence of pain; by unhappiness, pain and the privation of pleasure. (Mill, 1861 [1998]: 55)

In justification he offers only an anthropological fact about human beings. "This firm foundation," he says, "is . . . the social feelings of mankind; the desire to be in unity with our fellow creatures" (Mill, 1861 [1998]: 77).

Not all pleasures are of equal worth, at least to any individual. There are higher and lower pleasures. "Better to be Socrates dissatisfied than a fool satisfied." Now the question is: Who is to judge? According to Mill, only those who have experienced both kinds of pleasure are qualified and they will come to an unequivocal answer, which will define the higher pleasures:

> it is an unquestionable fact that those who are equally acquainted with, and equally capable of appreciating and enjoying both, do give a marked preference to the manner of existence which employs the higher faculties. (Mill, 1861 [1998]: 56)

There is a strong whiff of elitism about this refinement of the utilitarian stance. It amounts to an abandonment of the key utilitarian move, which was to find a single concept with which to define the content of moral judgments and rules. The criterion of worth is no longer pleasure and pain but the relative sophistication of the faculties involved in coming to experience them.

What is the relation between my pursuit of my own individual happiness and the cultivation of the greatest happiness of the greatest number? Does the former automatically achieve the latter? Mill's move here is to assert that the pleasure another feels is a source of happiness for me, so indeed the transition from individual goals to group goals *is* automatic. As a psychological generalization the principle is plainly false.

Mill's attempt to sustain the principle that people ought to pursue pleasure is notoriously fallacious, since he seems to be deriving it from the alleged factual generalization that everyone actually does desire pleasure. But the inference from what everyone does want to what everyone should want is clearly fallacious. Anyway it is simply not true that everyone desires pleasure, unless one dilutes the concept so far as to make anything that anyone desires a pleasure. The austerities of the monastic life derive some of their value just from the fact that they are not enjoyable in the ordinary sense. If the concept of pleasure is extended to cover hair shirts and kneeling on cold stone floors at all hours of the night, then it is not doing any work in specifying a universal goal for morally worthy actions.

There is an obvious objection to the whole program of utilitarianism. Virtue and vice seem to be desired and shunned respectively in themselves, and not by virtue of anything else to which they may be conducive. Mill's argument at this point looks decidedly slippery.

> They are desired and desirable in and for themselves; besides being means, they are part of the end. Virtue, according to the utilitarian doctrine, is not naturally and originally part of the end, but is capable of becoming so; and is desired and cherished, not as a means to happiness, but as part of their happiness [that is, of those who have learned to cherish virtue]. (Mill, 1861 [1998]: 83)

It is important to realize that Mill is not defining the good as the pleasurable. Rather he is offering a criterion, namely being pleasurable, as a way of recognizing the good. The good is the general benefit of mankind [*sic*] since what is pleasurable is of the highest utility.

Between the views of Kant and Mill there could hardly be a greater gulf. Both site the focus of morality in the individual. For Kant it is the individual's cognitive powers that are the source of the most binding of moral principles. For Mill it is the individual's capacity for feeling that is the source of the deepest moral intuitions as to what is good.

The Intuitionists

According to the intuitionists, the moral quality of an act is a property of that act which can be grasped intuitively, like any other property. However, unlike natural properties like color and shape, moral attributes are non-natural properties.[1] The chief proponent of this view has surely been G. E. Moore. He published his *Principia Ethica* in 1903. In that book and elsewhere he presented two major principles.

The first defined the nature of moral attributes. He claimed that there is such a thing as the intrinsic goodness of actions, their consequences, experiences, works of art, and so on. The second principle sets goodness at the foundation of ethical thought. Intrinsic goodness is indefinable. The concept behaves in certain respects like a color concept, for instance, "yellow." We can learn what "yellow" means only by being shown an example. There could be no verbal definition of "yellow."

From these two simple but contestable principles, he arrived at the formulation of his best-known contribution to ethics, the naturalistic fallacy. If good is an intrinsic, non-natural, and indefinable property of a wide variety of things, then there is no set of natural properties that express its meaning. To propose any set whatever as defining the concept of goodness is to commit the naturalistic fallacy.

The argument he offers for this famous dictum goes like this:

> Suppose we propose that some natural property "P" is the meaning of "good." It makes perfectly sense to ask "Is P good?" For example, if I propose that "happiness" is what "good" means, then it makes perfect sense ask "Is happiness good?" However, if we carry through the substitution of "good" in these queries we arrive at the plainly nonsensical pseudo-question, "Is happiness happy?"

There are two further consequences of this doctrine. Moore was generally unwilling to link goodness and obligation logically. Though he thought that one had a duty to create a world in which the property of goodness was instantiated in things and actions, the two concepts so linked were not synonymous. To say that something is good is not to say that it ought to be created or maintained or protected.

Secondly the attribution of goodness to whatever a person is attending to is not dependent on any affective state of that person, such as liking it, dreading it, or discerning what it tastes like. To include any of these matters in the judgment is to commit the naturalistic fallacy.

It can hardly be said that Moore's account of the presuppositions of moral discourse met with much agreement. However, it served as s stalking horse for critics who learned a great deal about the foundations of ethics by criticizing it. For example, Hancock (1983) points out that there are difficulties in making sense of the idea of ethical knowledge, if we can know ethical propositions of Moore's sort are true only by direct intuition. What if my intuition is not in accord with yours? In the case of natural properties we can consult a publicly agreed sample. It is not clear how this might work in the ethical realm where disagreement is endemic.

More seriously the very concept of a "non-natural and simple" property that is supposed to carry all the weight of human morality seems naive. A moral dispute could hardly be more than the kind of disagreement that might occur when two people look at a new acquisition in the local art gallery.

Prescriptivist Ethics

The rightness of actions does not seem to be properly explained by their power to please the most sophisticated members of a society. Nor does the adjuration "Do your duty" seem all that helpful when it does not tell me what it is that I should be doing to do it. Being told to intuit a non-natural property has not seemed all that helpful to the project of understanding the role of argument in moral matters. In the second half of the twentieth century some philosophers began to look closely at the logical form of ethical statements. Perhaps the superficial appearance of ascribing properties to actions concealed a deeper "grammar." If the formal structure of moral discourse could be displayed, perhaps it would dispel the errors and endless indeterminate debates that seemed to plague the history of moral philosophy. What do we use moral statements for? It may be that when carefully analyzed there is no trace of the logical form of statements which are typically used to ascribe properties to something.

Among several authors to make this move was R. M. Hare. What is the logical form of the kind of statements that typically occupy the attention of moral philosophers? Hare opens his book uncompromisingly.

> The reason why actions are in a peculiar way revelatory of moral principles is that the function of moral principles is to guide conduct. The language of morals is one sort of prescriptive language. (Hare, 1952: 1)

There are imperatives which overtly and directly prescribe a course of action. "Do this!" And there are value judgments, such as "This is a good avocado." On a prescriptivist reading, this could be a way of saying "I advise you to eat it!" It may look like a description of the avocado, but it serves a prescriptive function.

The first step in establishing that there is a different logical form to be discovered that distinguishes prescriptive language from descriptive is to show that the former cannot be reduced to the latter. The gross logical form of both kinds of statements includes a phrase expressing the content, say "you shutting the door" (the phrastic), and a phrase expressing the force of the utterance. It might be "Do it" in the case of the imperative, and "Yes" in the case of a description. Assent by the person addressed in each case has very different consequences. By this and other means Hare sets about showing that imperatives have a different form from descriptive statements.

The final move in the argument is to show that value judgments are indirect or oblique imperatives. To say something is good is to advise someone, or even urge someone to do it, eat it, choose it, and so on.

> The primary function of the word "good" is to commend . . . When we commend or condemn anything, it is always in order, at least indirectly, to guide choices, our own or other people's now or in the future. (Hare, 1952: 127)

The other morally important word "ought" is clearly prescriptive.

Once again, as in Kant's versions of the categorical imperative, moral philosophy seems to lack content.

EXISTENTIALISM

From the end of the Second World War until the late 1970s another strand of moral philosophy appeared which has to be woven into the tapestry of this history. It is particularly associated with Jean-Paul Sartre (1905–80). Its sources are diverse, but chief among them the writings of Søren Kiekegaard (1813–55) must surely be numbered.

The moral philosophies we have encountered so far in this survey of the second half of the second millennium have been concerned with the identification of and justification for making use of certain kinds of reasons for making choices and acting upon them, so that these acts are morally accountable. When asked "Why?" eighteenth-century philosophers tended to answer "Because it produces pleasure." Nineteenth-century British philosophers tended to answer "Because it brings the greatest happiness of the greatest number." Kant could sternly offer only "Because it is my duty." Why should any of these answers satisfy us? What reasons could we give for them? We seem to have a naturalistic thesis, "Because that is how human nature is constituted." We might try making a rationalist claim like that of Kant, that the only answer that would be acceptable would point to a kind of judgment which is not conditional on something non-moral. The existentialists turned their attention away from the content of morality to focus on the moment of personal commitment to a way of life.

Kierkegaard and the Origins of Existentialism

In a number of works, but particularly in *Either/Or*, Kierkegaard examined the foundations of moral commitment. Whatever reasons might be found for choosing this or that way of life cannot be endlessly supported by chains of other reasons. At some point we just choose. One commits oneself to a basic principle, doctrine, or way of life, without further reason.

> What is it then, that I distinguish in either/or? It is good or evil? No, I would only bring you up to the point where the choice between the evil or the good acquires significance for you. (Kierkegaard, 1843 [1944]: 172)
>
> My either/or does not in the first instance denote the choice between good and evil; it denotes the choice whereby one chooses good *and* evil/or excludes them. (p. 173)

The key point for the moral life is that having chosen the ethical life, "the original choice is present in every subsequent choice" (Kierkegaard, 1843 [1944]: 223). Life will then be built around choices between good and evil.

There are, broadly speaking, two possible life forms between which one can choose. Kierkegaard presents each in the words of an imagined protagonist. The ethical form of life is recommended by a judge, and the aesthetic by an anonymous adherent of a more "laid-back" way. To choose the former is to choose to adopt the distinction between good and evil. To choose the latter is to choose some other dichotomy for managing one's life.

In choosing between an aesthetical and an ethical life, choosing the latter is to choose to be bound by duty in general, from which particular choices in favor of duty will follow. This requires attention to one's own character, motives, and desires. "He who chooses himself ethically has himself as his task" (Kierkegaard, 1843 [1944]: 262). On the other hand "the aesthetic individual . . . regards some things as belonging to him accidentally, other things as belonging to him essentially. The distinction is however extremely relative, and it is merely for lack of energy an aesthetic individual maintains this distinction" (p. 264). There is nothing in the life of an individual who chooses the aesthetic way like the core of dutifulness that accrues to one who lives ethically.

The crucial point is that whatever distinction there is between good and evil comes from the choice to live a certain way. Choice is not determined by reasons, though they can be given. To count this or that as a reason presupposes that a choice has already been made. In the end there must be choices made simply and directly. For Kierkegaard, in the moral life, these reduce to that between living ethically, bound by duty, and living aesthetically, bound by feeling. To live ethically is, in the end, to live the Christian life.

Sartre and Existentialism in France

Jean-Paul Sartre dominated French intellectual life in the decades immediately after the Second World War. He was born in 1905 in Paris and for the early part of his life followed a conventional career as a university teacher. However, in the course of the war he found his métier not only in active service in the Resistance, but in the aftermath as a journalist, novelist, and playwright. It was in these forms that his version of existentialism first became well-known. His great work, *Being and Nothingness*, was written during the war, but appeared in English translation only in 1958. Throughout his life he took up radical stances against oppression by the powerful, often at great personal cost to himself. His detestation of the "establishment" led to his declining the Nobel prize for literature in 1964. He died in 1980.

Sartre's version of the doctrine of the radical power of choice in ethical and political matters is not offered in the defense of religious faith, as was Kierkegaard's. There are two main distinctions upon which "existentialism," the Sartrean point of view, rests. One has to do with the nature of human beings, the other with the authenticity of a life.

Human beings are conscious of their own existence and of what they do. Thus a human being is *Être-pour-soi*, a being for itself, while a thing lacking consciousness is *Être-en-soi*, a being in itself. But there is something paradoxical about what it is to be a "being-for-itself":

> In fact the *self* cannot be apprehended as a real existent; the subject cannot *be* self, for coincidence with self . . . causes the self to disappear. But neither can it *not* be itself since the self is an indication of the subject himself. (Sartre, 1943 [1958]: 76)

One cannot pay attention to oneself. The "I" that seeks itself cannot be the "I" that is found. Nevertheless, though I could not apprehend myself, I do know such matters as what I conceive myself as lacking.

But how does this create *freedom*? First of all, freedom is tied in with possibility, what I might do, and that is tied in with a perceived *lack*. "The possible is the something which the For-itself lacks in order to be itself" (Sartre, 1943 [1958]: 102).

Above all a being-for-itself is aware of possibility as lack, and thus meets the basic condition of freedom, that it can choose, that is, make good the lack. This is both thrilling and terrifying. It is terrifying because, once we grasp this aspect of being human, we realize that the future is ours to make. It is not something in the face of which we must simply settle down to passive acceptance. However, Sartre points out that most people most of the time resist the very idea that they have this radical freedom and hence radical responsibility for their own lives.

There is a further step, which might strike the reader as somewhat esoteric. Does freedom have an essence, necessary and sufficient attributes for some power to be "freedom"? Sartre remarks that acts do have essences. We can say what are the necessary and sufficient conditions for some group of workers to be on strike. "But, if we wish to reach the constitutive power, we must abandon any hope of finding it an essence" (Sartre, 1943 [1958]: 431). And this is because freedom is beyond the realm of causes. If I am aware of all these causes and motives there is something which is me which is not any of them.

> Indeed the sole fact that I am conscious of the causes which inspire my action, these causes are already transcendent objects for my consciousness; they are outside . . . I escape them by my very existence. I am condemned to exist forever beyond my essence, beyond the causes and motive of my act. I am condemned to be free . . . we are not free to cease to be free. (Sartre, 1943 [1958]: 439)

This move strikes one as very similar to Kant's way of introducing the distinction between the empirical and the transcendental self. If we are indeed all free in this radical way, why isn't the human world full of free spirits, making their own lives? Why are so many people simply living lives that have been, so to say, provided for them?

Sartre's answer invokes his other major concept, *mauvaise foi*, bad faith. He uses this to characterize a certain common kind of life. This is a life lived according to an existing and unexamined pattern of moral precepts and criteria. People leading such a life see themselves as confined in it, unable even to conceive of other possibilities, and certainly unable to choose one.

> To be sure, the one who practices bad faith is hiding a displeasing truth or presenting as truth a displeasing untruth. Bad faith then has in appearance the structure of falsehood. Only what changes everything is the fact that in bad faith it is from myself that I am hiding the truth. (Sartre, 1943 [1958]: 49)

But what is it that is deeply morally relevant that I conceal from myself? It is that I have the radical freedom to adopt whatever mode of life is open to me in the conditions of the contemporary state of the world. To exist authentically is to be aware of the possibility of radical choice, choice unconditioned by the existing moral order and social practices that ordinarily shape a life. I do not know whether Sartre's original motivation in developing his moral philosophy was political. However, it very quickly became so. He seemed to many to have demonstrated that new political commitments were always possible, particularly to the political Left. Indeed, he marched with the students in the events of 1968, when the French state seemed for a few days to be in danger of toppling.

The influence of existentialism was once very great. It played an important part in early feminist claims highlighting the arbitrariness of patriarchal forms of social order. In the era of the Third Way and the benign governance of the Hidden Hand of economic rationality, the idea that one has the possibility of a radical choice as to one's form of life seems little more than a romantic myth.

Recent Extensions of the Traditional Ethical Topics

In the rather internalist history of moral and political philosophy that I have just sketched certain issues seem scarcely ever to have found explicit voices. Two of these sprang to the fore as the second millennium ended.

Do the same moral and political concepts and the same principles of justice, rights, and so on apply to all human beings equally? Feminism arose in the second millennium, over and over again, through challenges to the traditional negative answer to the question. What would a society that eschewed all moral and political distinctions based on gender be like? Only in very recent times has this issue found a truly audible voice.

Can the same concepts be applied to nonhuman entities? Environmentalism arose in the second millennium, beginning in the seventeenth century, through the insistence by a growing number of authors and activists that the relationship of people to the natural world was not just practical but also moral. What is the moral relationship between human beings and the environment of plants and animals in which they must live? What is presupposed in answering the question at all? However, the close philosophical examination of the presuppositions of human practices in relation to the environment has emerged only recently.

Feminism

The ultimate presupposition of the attitude of a taken-for-granted male superiority in all social and intellectual matters is simply the belief that the natures of men and women differ fundamentally and *naturally*. There is then no remedy for female inferiority. Education, for example, was thought to be damaging to women's child-bearing powers. The frivolousness of the female character militated against any role in serious politics. Men ruled and women obeyed. This principle engendered the main features of the traditional moral order. There were mutual obligations of care on the one hand and of service on the other.

It is important to be clear about the difference between the issues of matter of fact, false beliefs about the relative capacities and vulnerabilities of men and women, and conceptual issues, the philosophical presuppositions of traditional moral orders. These are not independent but they are rooted in different kinds of debate. For example, the citation of the achievements of brilliant and successful women as counter-examples to the general thesis of feminine inferiority is a different kind of argument from a challenge to the binary oppositions that must be presupposed in any claim of morally and politically relevant difference.

The main philosophical issue, it seems to me, has been the standing of the binary oppositions which have been presupposed in traditional practices. In this context the obvious candidate for examination has been that between "man" and "woman." This opposition is traditionally assumed to be sharply polarized, so that a human being belongs to one or the other of these categories. Since the biological opposition between "male" and "female" is more or less strictly polarized, the mapping of the social and psychological categories "man"/"woman" onto that opposition seemed both natural and inevitable. But that is not the end of the matter. There are other mappings which are crucial to the maintenance of the alleged superiority of men. For instance "man"/"woman" has been mapped onto "culture"/"nature." And from there it is a short step to "rational"/"emotional," an opposition that has played a large part in the maintenance of the thesis of feminine inferiority.

We can recognize three ways that these mappings have been challenged. The most radical has been to challenge the viability of *all* binary oppositions. This has been the route followed by many authors, such as Hélère Cixous (1987), attacking the grounding principle of the structuralist movement in cultural studies generally. A less radical argument leaves the opposition "man"/"woman" intact while denying that the politically and morally oppressive dichotomies, such as "rational"/"emotional" divide up people into categories in the same way (Richards, 1982). A third style of argument is based on a denial of the essentialist implications of the whole business of drawing distinctions. There are, it is alleged, no such things as the essential differences between men and women. If there are no essences then the observable differences must be cultural artifacts and could be different (Davies, 1999).

In a great many ways the social distinctions between the roles of men and women have been either abolished or eroded. How far these developments are to be put down to political forces shaped by philosophical analyses of tendentious conceptual distinctions is not easy to adjudicate. There are other forces at work, particularly in the economic substructures of Western or Westernized societies. What cannot be denied is the audibility of the philosophically animated feminist voice.

Environmentalism

The "green" movements of recent decades have been very widely publicized. Arguments for environmentally friendly policies have been presented as largely utilitarian, based on claims as to what would be in the rational self-interest of citizens at large. Closely tied in with the advocacy of practical policies have been philosophical discussions of the presuppositions of the relation of people to their world.

These have been concerned with two main issues, the rights of non-human creatures to a certain kind of life, and the duties of human beings to care for their natural surroundings and resources.

The defining and defense of animal rights as a philosophical issue has been mainly built upon an argument from analogy. It has been claimed that there are sufficient similarities between higher animals and human beings that some of the morally relevant mental capacities, for instance, to feel pain and be overwhelmed by terror, exist in animals as much as in people. It follows that those moral maxims that apply to human beings in virtue of those capacities and vulnerabilities apply to animals too (Singer, 1976).

Duty to the environment has been grounded in the idea of "stewardship," at least since the eighteenth century. Underlying the overt exhortations to care for the world has been a presupposition based on the distinction between powers and vulnerabilities. Those with power have a duty to succour those who are vulnerable. Human beings have amply demonstrated their power to affect the environment, therefore they have the duty to protect and restore it. In short, people have a duty to act as planetary doctors (Lovelock, 1987). Practical issues of the scope of this caring and the possibilities of making matters worse have been much in the public eye, but are irrelevant to the philosophical issues as to where duties lie, even if it is the negative one of trying to minimize damage.

MORAL RELATIVISM

So far in this chapter I have been describing arguments and positions in moral and political philosophy that have been presupposed by their authors and indeed those who have taken them up, to be of universal application. Happiness, duty, the rational advantage of making a social contract, and so on, have been assumed to be more or less the same for everyone. At just the moment that a world political and economic order seems to be slowly and painfully emerging so has a vociferous advocacy of the relativity of moral principles to local cultures, and the rejection of the very idea of moral universals. Where did this idea start?

Anthropology and Moral Relativism

During the 1940s the realization that there were many seemingly viable moral systems, other than the Christianity that the colonial regimes had taken for granted, began to filter through into Western philosophy as a ground for moral relativism. The beginnings of this interpretation of the discoveries of anthropologists are usually credited to Franz Boas. His discussion of these matters is very subtle, and deserves to be set out in some detail.[2]

Boas argues that the question of cultural relativism has to be tackled indirectly, through reflection on what it would take to establish that there are cultural universals. He begins by pointing out that cultural diversity can be explained in various ways: there are "external conditions or internal causes which influence [people's] minds" (Boas, 1896 [1940]: 272). If we are to treat these explanations as showing merely superficial variations on universal aspects of the human organism or the human mind, we must establish that there are the relevant universals. The assumption of universalists is that "if an ethnological phenomenon has developed independently in a number of places its development has been the same everywhere . . . this leads to the generalisation that the sameness of ethnological phenomena found in diverse regions is proof that the human mind is always the same everywhere" (p. 273). Thus diversity would be a superficial variation on a fixed foundation.

However, he argues, there is a flaw in the reasoning. Identity of phenomena is no proof of identity of origins. "The same phenomenon may develop in a multitude of ways." There is no logical basis for the "conclusion that there is one grand system according to which mankind has developed everywhere" (p. 275). Boas emphasizes the importance of specific historical connections in the development of specific cultures. We must study ethnological phenomena, not in isolation, but in the whole specific cultural setting. The best presumption when we find "an analogy of single traits of culture among distant peoples . . . is that they have arisen independently" since they must be considered to be embedded in complex and unique cultural matrices (p. 277).

It is worth remarking that for Boas the issue was empirical. It was an open question whether the presumption of independent origins would prove to be justified. It is up to the universalist to provide empirical evidence for the hypothesis of ubiquitous traits.

A resolution of the inconclusive debate between universalists and relativists in the human sciences, inspired or at least initiated by anthropological explorations, has been proposed, with his usual panache and subtlety by Clifford Geertz (1989). He draws a distinction between two conclusions that might be drawn from the anthropological literature. There is no doubt that anthropologists have described many diverse human customs and practices. He cites, at random, "ghost marriage, ritual destruction of property, initiatory fellatio, royal immolation and . . . nonchalant adolescent sex" as examples of ways of acting alien to our way of life.

What should we say? The wrong thing is to conclude that there are no cultural universals. It should never have been any anthropologist's intention to prove such a thing. Indeed, Boas had already shown that any such proof would be invalid. The correct thing to conclude is that we should not uncritically take it for granted that *our* local cultural forms and practices are the universal ones, to be looked for beneath the "strange versions" that have appeared elsewhere. Wittgenstein (1979) made the same point in his critical remarks against James Frazer's treatment of alien cultural practices as bad or primitive science. They were not science at all, so they could not be good or bad science.

Anthropological fieldwork establishes neither radical relativism nor radical universalism. It should be read rather as a "repositioning of horizons and the decentering of perspectives" (Geertz, 1989: 31) comparable to the Copernican revolution in astronomy.

The Postmodernist Attack on the Possibility of Moral Universals

The same relativist argument that purports to debunk empirical criteria of truth-to-nature as the basis of confidence in science-generated knowledge has been applied to political and moral issues as well. Arguments against the viability of the idea of an essential human nature are treated by postmodernists as arguments for moral relativism. They are supposed to dispose of any claims for trans-situational, trans-cultural moral criteria.

> The more basic problem these [Aristotelian and Kantian ethics] and similar attempts to ground ethics in an account of intrinsic or essential human nature is our strong postmodernist suspicion that there is no such thing . . . there is no historical essence that is both universally found and yet is also determinate and substantial enough to generate or justify . . . a definite ethical theory. (Shusterman, 1990: 119)

To do justice to the postmodernist localization and hence relativization of morality I shall summarize the best short argument in the literature on this matter, an argument developed in various places by Richard Rorty, but elegantly expressed in a recent essay (Rorty, 1989). It has all the characteristics of the best postmodernist advocacy, an air of sweet reasonableness that leads to a conclusion that one would say was morally dubious at best. Rorty, a man of high moral principle himself, escapes our moral censure only by abandoning a central principle of the postmodern position, and indeed subverting his own argument, as we shall see.

His discussion begins with a distinction between two ways of making sense of people's lives. One is "by telling the story of their contribution to a community," the other "is to describe themselves as standing in an immediate relation to some non-human reality" (Rorty, 1989: 35). The one finds a basis in *solidarity*, the other in *objectivity*. Realists wish to reduce solidarity to objectivity, by developing procedures by which human beings can form representations of nonhuman reality, that are not merely social. Pragmatists wish to reduce objectivity to solidarity. For pragmatists, "the desire for objectivity is not the desire to escape the limitations of one's community but simply the desire for as much intersubjective agreement as possible" (p. 37).

Now comes the fatal compromise. Rorty agrees with the inheritor of the values of the Enlightenment that we should both adopt and seek to justify "toleration, free enquiry and the quest for undistorted communication . . . [for the pragmatist this] can only take the form of a comparison between societies which exemplify these habits and those which do not, leading up to the suggestion that nobody who has experienced both would prefer the latter" (p. 43).

There is a glaring flaw in this important move, the vital move of the whole defense of moral relativism. Even if one granted that one could pick out exemplifications of tolerance, free enquiry, and relatively undistorted communication, why should one prefer them? According to Rorty anyone who has tried others will choose them. This is how Mill tried to justify basing morality on the higher pleasures. But the choice someone makes might depend on all sorts of factors. What if someone, say Pol Pot, insisted that intolerance, the dictatorship of the proletariat, and censorship in the interest of the party struck him as preferable, *having tried liberal democracy*?

Rorty admits to falling across the dilemma between ethnocentrism and relativism, and opts for ethnocentrism, that is, for societies which exemplify *his* three good things. But this option is just what leads to the vicious consequences of moral relativism. Now we have no criterion for preferring his three good things to other triads of social goods, such as "Duty to God," "Respect for one's betters," and "Woman's place is in the home"; or why not "One Folk, One Land, One Führer."

Geertz (1989) rightly castigates those who would find cultural universals in genetics and the biological endowment, since this is surely too coarse-grained to touch the parts of life that only philosophy can reach. It seems to me that we are ending the millennium with a problem that was thrown up with the advent of an alternative vision of the cosmos to the theological one. Where can we find a moral grounding that will be binding on all human beings?

The Recovery of Morality

Many, not only philosophers, have felt the need to reestablish some universal moral principles. In their absence it is not easy to override the extreme relativist interpretation of local variations in moral sensibility. If these are allowed equal standing with all others, it is hard to see how anyone who was not a member of the Khmer Rouge could condemn the killing fields nor an opponent of the Nazis the holocaust. After all, if you are a postmodernist you must admit that, as ways of living, they seemed right to the people who carried them out. Rorty's upper-class, eastern American establishment mores do strike me as morally superior to the principle of ethnic cleansing. But that is because I share the morals of his tribe, belonging to one that has the same historical origins. But that is not good enough to override the moral intuitions of members of the SS. The postmodernist plea that the voices of the underprivileged or otherwise silenced members of our society should be heard, and their moral intuitions respected, is entirely worthy. But it can, if generalized, easily turn into a doctrine of moral permissiveness. It could lead straight to the conclusion that, since the moralities of the proponents of the Final Solution, or of the methods of social transformation by massacre adopted by the Khmer Rouge, are "other" than those advocated by the liberal, Western Enlightenment, they are voices that *must* be heard. According to strong relativism our disgust and abhorrence of such moralities has no force beyond the confines of our culture. The denial of any universal ground for morality can lead someone of sensibility and moral decency like Rorty to such a disturbing statement as this:

> what counts as being a decent human being is relative to historical circumstances, a matter of transient consensus about what attitudes are normal and what practices are just and unjust. (Rorty, 1989: 43)

Rorty proposes that "something behind history" such as an origin in a general trans-historical conception of human decency, is to be replaced by a "sense of human solidarity." On what might this be based? Fellow feeling? And how would such a sense distinguish the fellow feeling of the guilty thrill of sadistic solidarity with those who organized the vanishing of the *desaparacidos* in Argentina or Northen Ireland, from the solidarity one might feel with the victims of the Kossovo massacres? This is thin moral gruel indeed. We need something more robust than that. Fellow feeling is a poor criterion for attaining moral value.

Morality in the Conditions for the Possibility of Language

In recent years several philosophers have based a case for the existence of at least some moral universals on an analysis of the conditions for the possibility of language (Lukes, 1975; Habermas, 1984–7; Holiday, 1988). The counter-argument to relativism is based on a paradox. The conditions under which arguments in favor of moral relativism can be understood must include the conditions for the possibility of the existence of a language with which those arguments can be expressed. If those conditions include moral conditions, then they must be tacitly accepted by anyone who uses language, and expects to be understood. To argue or even to speak against there being any universal moral principles is to presuppose at least some.

The next step is to show that there are at least some moral conditions among the conditions that language should be possible. Holiday (1988) offers three such necessary conditions.

1. There must be a general acceptance of the power of ritual to fix the conventions on which the possibility of linguistic communication depends. Meanings cannot be established by force. Each person in the community of speakers and listeners must be willing to be bound by the conventions in force in that community.

2. There must be a mutuality of respect, a kind of distributive justice, in giving all persons the right to make meaningful statements. If the members of one group make statements which they expect another group to understand, they cannot deny that statements made by that group have meaning for them.

3. There must be a social institution of truth telling. Even if there were a great deal of lying and deception, in the absence of the institution of truth-telling the distinction "true/false" would lapse. All statements would then have the same status as efforts at communication, namely none.

The point is that these are not merely pragmatic conditions for the efficacy of communication, such as clarity and loudness. They concern relations between people, which boil down to mutual respect and sincerity. In other words, they incorporate minimal conditions for the preservation of persons. As such they are among the roots of a *universal* morality.

This is not the only route to moral universals. Others have turned on such matters as the species-wide sensitivity to suffering. But to me the demonstration of the paradox of asserting a position that undermines its own conditions of assertibility is a particularly satisfying way of showing how a philosophical thesis can fail.

Conclusion

The split between collectivist and individualist morality that appeared
in the Renaissance was followed by 300 years of moral philosophy
that sought the grounds of moral imperatives in individualistic forms
of thought and experience. Individual feelings and individual exercises
of reason were the two basic sources of moral intuitions. Even though
it was assumed that these attributes of individuals were universal in
humankind, the step to a society was always problematic. This problem
will set the agenda for the next chapter. We will find that both Vico
and Marx offered ways of understanding the transition from one social
form to another, but neither gave an account of the genesis of
institutions from the intentions and actions of individuals. The social
contract, popular in the seventeenth century, was not so much an
explanatory theory as a metaphor used to express the consensual nature
of political obligation.

The ultimate version of the pleasure/pain basis for moral choice,
Mill's utilitarianism, had all sorts of weaknesses, but the paramount one
was the implausibility of an arithmetic of pleasure by which the good
of groups of people could be defined. Kant's Kingdom of Ends generated universal moral laws, but only in so far as they applied to all
individuals, taken one by one. The idea of the moral constraints on a
predominantly social being played no part. Individual consciousness and
rationality was primary and social orders merely products.

Hegel and Marx offered something very different. For them individual morality was secondary in that it could do no more than express
the social relations that were primary in any form of life. It has taken
nearly another 200 years for the primacy of social forms in the genesis
of cognitive capacities and moral intuitions of individuals to once again
become a dominant idea, to be seen everywhere in the many ways in
which the social constructionist point of view has appeared at the end
of the second millennium. Ironically just at the time that the beginnings of the postmodernist movement began to appear in France, it
was in that country that the most radically individualistic moral philosophy made its appearance, existentialism. The truly moral moment
was the commitment by an individual act of choice to some way of
life. And, as Kierkegaard put it, once that choice has been made, the
form of all other moments of choice is already decided.

Recent moral philosophy in the West is much more in the Kantian vein than either collectivist or existentialist ways of understanding the nature of the good. It has become a search for the characteristic logical form of moral judgments and rules. The method is analytical and the topic the logical form of moral judgments. We have looked at one of the many studies of the language of moral judgments, as prescriptions. Of course this led to a lack of interest in the content of moral principles which has recently been reversed.

The focus of the most interesting recent discussions of content have been in feminist critiques of the moral basis of society, and in environmentalism. Philosophical challenges to taken-for-granted presuppositions have raised important issues such as the viability of binary oppositions, the role of essentialism in political and moral thinking, and the importance of the distribution of powers and vulnerabilities in the world and its various inhabitants.

Take away the authority of the Church as the mundane expression of God's moral authority, and the diversity of the moral orders we find at different times and different places, serving as the foundations of the normative systems of human forms of association, seems very striking. The problem for moral philosophy is to find a way of acknowledging this, yet resisting the slide into moral relativism. We need something that all societies must have in order to provide a source for some minimal moral practices which can serve as a standard for international action against the evils that seem to be ever ready to reappear. The role of language in forming and maintaining all human forms of life offers itself as the most plausible universal source of morality.

It makes sense to make moral assessments of what people do only if it also makes sense to ascribe to them responsibility for their actions. That, in turn, presupposes that it makes sense to assume that someone who did a blameworthy or praiseworthy action could have done something else in exactly those circumstances. In the end what we do is "up to us." Yet how could any of this make sense if we can also show that our actions could not have been other than they were? We have seen the importance of the problem for Indian, Islamic, and Christian philosophers. For those who center their conception of the universe on a creative and omniscient God there seems to be a paradox in supposing that a divine goodness is compatible with divine foreknowledge of everything that will happen. For materialists the seemingly deterministic flow of events, including those that involve parts of the human body, seems incompatible with the presupposition upon which all moral intuitions rest, that there are circumstances in which a human actor could have done otherwise.

At the end of the second millennium it does not seem to me that philosophers are very much further forward on this matter than they were one or even two thousand years ago. People have a very strong intuition that they can and do act against the grain of events, and yet reflection on the nature of the cosmos, and even on the workings of "mental machinery," suggests that the intuition is an illusion. It does seem to me that at this moment we are seeing the deterministic point of view overtaking the moralistic. For example increasingly moral failings are being put down to an ever-expanding realm of illnesses. Instead of castigating someone for extravagance a diagnosis of "shopping addiction" is entered and treatment, no doubt by a specialist, is advised.

The philosophers we have studied have been surprisingly uniform in coming to the despairing conclusion that the clash of the intuition of the possibility of freedom and any of the various ways in which the future has been thought to be constrained is insoluble. Even the linguistic turn has left us with a "two-story" story presented with something of the attitude of William of Ockham – don't waste time in worrying about reconciling them. There just are two ways of describing what people do, even if there is just one thing that people are, namely material organisms. Neither can displace the other. Both are needed to make sense of the whole gamut of human life.

NOTES

1   For an excellent account of intuitionism in general see Warnock (1979: chapter 3).
2   I am very grateful to Matti Bunzl of the University of Illinois for scholarly advice on the position of Franz Boas.

Relations among Persons II
Political Philosophy

Wittgenstein once embarrassed and alarmed his friends by insisting that they meet at a café, where he read them his "confessions." Biographers are not forthcoming about the content. However, we have the confessions of Jean-Jacques Rousseau in plenty. He too had the idea of giving readings from them. Rousseau was an unstable man, unfaithful to his friends and lovers, and slack in fulfilling his commitments. He forced his life-long mistress, Thérèse, to dispose of their five children in orphanages. When one of the families with whom he stayed was packing up their possessions, a ribbon was missing. It soon emerged that he had it. When accused of stealing it, he insisted that one of the serving girls had given it to him. Despite her sad protestations he maintained the false accusation, and in the end both were dismissed (Dobinson, 1969). Yet this was the man who wrote so well on the moral foundations of the state, and tried to devise a regime of education that would build the noblest characters. It has been said that only those who see the moral weakness in themselves have a profound insight into the human heart. This aphorism would fit Rousseau rather well. There are others too, whose lives and doctrines seem far apart. Locke, the friend of liberty, was notoriously secretive. Is there such an inversion between character and opinions as a general rule? I think not. The lives of the philosophers whose political philosophies I will be discussing in this chapter do not seem to me to reveal a common pattern. Philosophical insights are not necessarily the product of deep self-understanding.

Philosophical Foundations
of the State

The modern era poses to the political philosopher, above all, the problem of reconciling personal liberty with the constraints of political obligation. What must be presupposed for a well-grounded reconciliation to be possible? The first steps to a distinctively modern approach to moral and political philosophy involved the idea of natural rights, those that accrued to an individual just by virtue of being human. They were thus independent of edicts of governments or the dictates of social custom. They are the very grounding of the idea of freedom. We shall see three root-ideas locked into a pattern of concepts, freedom from all but the most minimal constraints, individuals as the ultimate source of political authority and a moral groundwork of inalienable rights. It is well to bear in mind how sharply this pattern contrasts with that of feudal society, in which prescriptions of duties in a highly structured collective largely defined the moral life.

The Myth of the Social Contract

If there are natural rights pertaining to individuals then civil society and its moral atmosphere must come to exist, at least in principle, by a voluntary act on the part of an individual who belongs to it. Whether there ever were such voluntary acts setting up a social contract conferring powers on a civil authority is not the point. The very idea of authority as a creation by individuals who make a social contract highlights the difference between moral and political systems, the principles of which derive from an authority that transcends any individual obliged by them and those which reflect the play of instinct and reason in individuals.

Locke's version of the contract story

Locke (1690) made use of the concept of the social contract to present an account of the nature of political obligation among free individuals. His account of the metaphor of the contract runs as follows:

every Man, that hath any Possession, or Enjoyment, of any part of the Dominions of any Government, doth thereby give his *tacit Consent*, and is so far forth obliged to Obedience to the Laws of that Government, during such Enjoyment, as anyone under it. (Locke, 1690: Section 119)

Locke thought that propositions expressing moral "laws" were necessarily true, since they did not describe matters of fact, but relations among ideas. For example the concept of "good" is internally related to that of "whatever causes pleasure." So moral sanctions can only be the reward of pleasure and the infliction of pain. These psychological states are personal and individual, and the "contract" is an expression of enlightened self-interest. By joining with others I protect myself from them. This idea had already had a famous expression in Hobbes's *Leviathan* of 1651:

[the agreement to create civil government] is more than Consent or Concord; it is a real Unity of them all, in one and the same Person [the Sovereign], made by Covenant of every man with every man . . . [This creates a Commonwealth, the essence of which is] One Person, of whose Acts a great Multitude, by mutual Covenants one with another, have made themselves everyone the Author, to the end he may use the strength and means of them all, as he shall think expedient, for their Peace and Common Defence. (Hobbes, 1651 [1914]: Part 2, 17)

The alternative is anarchy and chaos, that war of everyone against everyone that is the brute state of nature. It is worth remarking that Hobbes thought he had experienced just such a state of anarchy during the English Civil War, which ran on through the second quarter of the seventeenth century.

Philosophers and others have asked whether Hobbes, Locke, and other authors who based the existence of the state and the authority of the sovereign on a social contract, be it individual in a monarchy or collective as in a representative democracy, meant it to refer to a real moment in the prehistory of all societies. It seems to me that most authors of the period used the idea of the social contract as a metaphor for a presupposition of the possibility of a civil society. Such a society is possible because the members tacitly consent to the authority of the sovereign. Rational people would do so for their own benefit, if the matter were ever to come to a moment for conscious decision.

Natural Law in the sense Aquinas gave to this phrase, that is, the human attempt to express the divine law, has no place in the political philosophy of the second half of the millennium. In one way or another, the ground and source of civil laws and moral maxims must be found in something *human*.[1] A secular version of natural law theory, based on the principle that law arises as human reason reflects on the conditions necessary for a flourishing life, has been promoted in recent years by John Finnis (1980).

Rousseau and the General Will

The idea of a collective ground for the governance of a state was in vogue not only in England. It had one of its most powerful expressions in the political writings of Jean-Jacques Rousseau. Born in Geneva in 1712, his early years were a catalogue of disasters and sexual adventures. Capturing the affections of a Catholic enthusiast, Madame de Warens, he found a home with her for a while. During that time he picked up certain musical skills, with which he earned a precarious living when he eventually made his way to Paris in 1741. His acquaintance with Voltaire and Diderot bore fruit in the patronage of Madame d'Epinay. That did not last and he was soon on the road again. He settled first in Luxembourg, where he wrote the *Social Contract*, first published in 1764. In the same year his work on education, *Émile*, was published. After various short-lived migrations he reached England in 1766, and the patronage of Hume. It seems that during this time his mental state began to deteriorate. His justified suspicions of the threat of persecution from the authorities, outraged by his political writings, turned to paranoia. Once again he fell out with his patrons and he returned to France in 1770 to eke out a meagre living in Paris. He died in 1778. The radical philosophers of the French "Enlightenment," such as Saint-Simon (1760–1825) were greatly influenced by Rousseau's political writings, and in a sense one could say he provided some of the theoretical grounds for the Revolution.

In his famous work, *Social Contract* (1764) Rousseau presented a quite detailed prescription for the basis of collective political institutions. The "General Will," however that is to be ascertained, must have priority over the wills and wishes of individuals if a civil society is to be stable and prosper. *The* problem for political philosophy is to show how the constraints of a collective can be reconciled with the radical freedom of the individual members of that collective. The solution is the creation of a certain kind of legislative *institution*.

Of course political freedom is not anarchy, doing whatever you feel like doing at the moment. It can only mean obedience to the laws we make for ourselves. The question is how this making is to be achieved. Like the English philosophers of the previous century, Rousseau thought that it must be achieved by the forging of a social contract. But he drew a stronger consequence from it than did his English predecessors.

> Hence, in order that the social pact shall not be an empty formula, it is tacitly implied in that commitment – which can alone give force to all others – that whoever refuses to obey the general will shall be constrained to do so by the whole body, which means nothing other than that he shall be forced to be free. (Rousseau, 1764: Book I, chapter 7, p. 64)

I shall follow Plamenatz (1963: 395–411) in extracting some of the principles that Rousseau lays down for the processes of contractual and consenting civil government. They are all counsels of perfection, or perhaps well suited to very small societies, unlike our massive contemporary supranational states. Nevertheless, in an important way some of the moral motivations that are evident in Rousseau's prescriptions have become part of the unexamined presuppositions of the Western conception of the ideals of civil society.

These principles follow one from another. They rest on a simple but powerful presupposition for the possibility of a political association of free citizens. To live an orderly and secure life we must be bound by law and consent to it. That is possible only if we have a hand in making that law. "Obedience to a law one prescribes for oneself is freedom," says Rousseau. Spelled out in more detail, the legislative process by which the general will is realized in the laws of a community involves certain requirements:

1. People taking part in legislative decision-making must do so as members of the whole collective and not as representatives of particular interests and associations. "Thus, if the general will is to be clearly expressed, it is imperative that there should be no sectional associations in the state, and that every citizen should make up his own mind for himself" (Rousseau, 1764: Book II, chapter 3).

2. The covenant brings about the existence of the society as a political entity. "Each one of us puts into the community his person and all his powers under the supreme direction of the general will; and as a body we incorporate every member as an indivisible part of the whole" (Rousseau, 1764: Book I, chapter 6, p. 61).

3. The key to legislation is the ascertaining of the general will. The will of all is merely the aggregate of individual desires, while the general will "studies only the common interest." How can we be sure that the deliberations of a group do result in the expression of the general will? Rousseau realized that the proper workings of society require public enlightenment and the willingness of citizens to subordinate their private desires to the common good. Both, he says, need guidance. But who is to be charged with that task?

As for morality, Rousseau seems to have thought that it would take care of itself. Just by taking part in the governance of the state, the citizen acquired the civic virtues, which were the basis of the moral life.

It is not difficult to see in the writings of those philosophers, who thought of the source of political obligation and the rights of sovereigns to rule in the consent of the citizens, the ancestry of much that we take for granted in contemporary political life. However, the idea of the genesis of the general will in the collective acts of a citizenry of individuals did not go unchallenged. The Hegelian philosophy of the dialectical development of the World Spirit developed into a very different conception of the state and of citizenship.

THE EVOLUTION OF STATES

Two differing responses to the hypothesis of the social contract as the source of political order and political obligation, the right of the state to our obedience, followed very quickly on the popular views of Locke. As we have seen, Rousseau tackled the question of the psychological plausibility of the social conditions expressed in the metaphor of the contract. At more or less the same time Vico was proposing a very different account, in which little trace of rational intentions on the part of the architects of states could be found.

Vico and the Role of Unintended Consequences

The question of how a group of individuals can come to have a collective identity troubled Giambattista Vico (1668–1744). Unlike his distinguished predecessor, Niccolò Machiavelli, he did not see the collective as the product of the power and will of the sovereign. He remarks that

> It is true that men have themselves made this world of nations . . . But this world, without doubt, has issued from a mind often diverse, at times quite contrary, and always superior to the particular ends that men had proposed to themselves; which narrow ends, made means to serve wider ends, it has always employed to preserve the human race upon this earth. (Vico, 1725: 1108)

How is this possible? What can account for the transition from anarchy to the institutions of the state? There is no need for a social contract to bring the conditions of order into being in Vico's view. Social order comes to be because the conditions for its emergence are already in existence.

> Yet chance did not divert them nor fate force them out of this natural order. For at the point when the commonwealths were to spring forth, the matter was all prepared and ready to receive the form, and there came forth the commonwealths composed of body and mind. The prepared materials were these men's own religions, their own languages, their own lands, their own nuptuals, their own names, their own arms . . . and because these things were their own they were completely free and therefore constitutive of true commonwealths . . . The fathers at this juncture, by uniting themselves in an order, came to produce the sovereign civil power, just as in the state of nature they had held the family powers. (Vico, 1725: 630)

By bringing about the birth of families, each with its own language and rules of life, providence had at the same time brought into being the natural law to be used in the management of commonwealths.

The Problematic Status of Collectives

Vico's account of the genesis of the state neatly avoids the issue of how individuals can jointly constitute a collective entity the properties of which are not just aggregates of the properties of individuals. He denies individual intentions a role and at the same time traces the means of maintaining institutions back to simpler institutions. In essence Vico assumes the native character of institutions. They are just there. The utilitarians, whose moral philosophy we have surveyed in the previous chapter, had no difficulty with collectives of human beings, for the complementary reason to Vico. The properties of groups just were aggregates of the attributes of the individual members. The happiness of all was the arithmetical sum of the happinesses of each. Mill and his mentors and disciples presupposed that only individuals and their states of mind and body were real.

In the twentieth century the issue has surfaced again. Are the collective aspects of human societies just patterns of the unintended consequences of individual actions according to individual intentions? If they are, then there seems to be a rather important consequence for sociology as a putative science. Explanations of mass phenomena must be sought not in other mass phenomena, but in the intentions of individual actors. This proposal has been called "methodological individualism" (Popper, 1957).

Rawls and the Doctrine of "Fair Procedure"

The most recent attempt to give an account of the state as the product of joint rational action has come from John Rawls (1971). This is, once again, a social contract account. People are imagined to get together to make an agreement as how they shall be governed in order that certain social and moral goods should be preserved. At the heart of Rawls' analysis is the idea of a "fair procedure." The means of distribution of rewards need not necessarily result in equal shares for all. But it must reflect what is fair. Justice, says Rawls, *is* fairness.

How is this commonplace good to be achieved? Adopting a highly original form of the "original position," the mythical starting point for the rational management of the creative consensus, Rawls requires that those who make the contractual act should be ignorant of all social and cognitive qualities of the others engaging in contracting into the state. There is therefore no place for expressions either of resentment or condescension in the consensual act.

According to Rawls, inequity in the distribution of rewards can be justified in a situation where the contract has ensured basic rights for all, by some such criterion as service to the disadvantaged and underprivileged.

The ethnocentricity of the Rawlsian account of justice is quite striking. The contract ensures basic rights, but does not enjoin basic duties. Here it falls short of the demands that Rousseau's contract places on the citizen. That service to the underprivileged should define the level of reward also seems very American.

As I remarked at the outset of this survey, our understanding of political and, to a lesser extent, moral philosophy seems to require at least a glance toward an externalist account. The original positions of Hobbes and Rawls, and the goods brought into being by the contractual act, seem to differ by just the way that the social situation of the English Civil War and that of the enlightened liberal democracy of post Second World War America differ.

THE HISTORICAL CONDITIONING OF SOCIAL NORMS

In following the development of ethical thought in the modern era we have been charting a series of views that are centered round the individual human being. The core of the moral life, according to this tradition, is to be found either in individual experience, be it of pleasures and pains or other affective states, or in the exercise of reason, legislating rules for oneself that must be rules for others. All this is in keeping with the Cartesian tradition that lies at the heart of philosophy in the modern era. But this tradition did not go unchallenged. An alternative way of conceiving of morality, a way which made social relations paramount, took its start from the writings of Hegel. It achieved its most potent form in the attempt by Karl Marx to apply it to real social reforms. In a quite fundamental way this route to the understanding of the genesis of morals meant that moral and political philosophy were one and the same. The problem discussed in the first section of this chapter, how to conceive the relation between individuals and the institutions of which they are members, reappears in the philosophies of Hegel and Marx. How people should treat one another is dependent on the larger social and historical frame of action.

Hegel and the Evolving World Spirit

The key idea is that morality is not some fixed and universal code, derivable from the ubiquitous and necessary attributes of human nature in general. It appears in different forms during the passage of history. We have already seen how Hegel pictured the history of humankind as a development from a state in which a primitive, taken-for-granted social order gradually developed into the self-consciousness of modern humanity, in which the embodied world spirit or *Geist* finds its ultimate realization. This is not only a development of cognitive powers but also a development of moral sensibility.

Primitive human social orders are not self-conscious. People simply fulfill their given roles. But the seeds of change are already sown. The dialectic begins when individuals become conscious of themselves as persons in contrast to their given roles. This happens as these societies become more complex. At this point criticism is born. And here is the paradox that drives the historical transformations of social orders or forms of life. A form of life may suggest possibilities of living to its members that cannot be fulfilled within that very form of life. The effort to fulfill them necessarily transforms that form of life into something else. This is the dialectic of history. At each stage there will be certain norms definitive of the current social order which express and determine the moral standards of the time. So at each transition they will change.

The most potent image that expresses Hegel's conception of this dynamic is the mutually deforming relation of master and serf. It is not hard to see the origins of some characteristic ideas of Marx in this image. The master as the self-conscious and dominant member of the pair treats the serf as a thing, thus denying the serf the possibility of development. Paradoxically this also denies to the master the possibility of further development, since his only alter ego is the thing-like serf. How can this deadlock be broken? Hegel tried to demonstrate that neither the social order of the Roman Empire nor its successor, the Christian Church, really transcended the master – serf relationship.

Every social order includes not only opportunities for action but also limits to action. Gradually, as a society becomes self-conscious these limits make themselves felt. People set about overcoming them. This is the pursuit of freedom, as it is conceivable from within each social order. Freedom is different for each social order since the limitations on human action fix the meaning of freedom at each epoch. At the same time they fix the domain of responsibility and thus the morality of the time. At each transition the domain of responsibility becomes wider. The scope of self-conscious understanding of the opportunities for and limitations on action that become available to human actors changes the domain of the possible. This pattern of development, Hegel thought, must eventually culminate in a perfect state.

Since morality is only to be made sense of within a given social order, the idea that had animated the philosophers of the modern era, that morality is centered on some trans-historical and perhaps necessary aspect of *individual* cognition, must be mistaken. It is to be found neither in individual self-perception nor in the individual, rational, self-legislating will of the Kingdom of Ends.

Marx and the Material Dialectic

The last step in the relativizing of morality to the local social order, before postmodernism, is surely Marx's revisions of the philosophy of Hegel. The leitmotif of Marx's life work has been well summed up by MacIntyre (1966: 211).

> Like Hegel, Marx envisages freedom in terms of the overcoming of the limitations and constraints of one social order by bringing another, less limited social order into being. Unlike Hegel, he does not see those limitations and constraints as primarily the limitations and constraints of a given conceptual scheme. What constitutes a social order, what constitutes both its possibilities and its limitations, is the dominant form of work by which its material sustenance is produced.

Though technology determines the basic form of work at any time, there are social relations of production by means of which that form is actually realized. These necessarily involve distinctions in function that become fixed as classes, with conflicting interests. So in the nineteenth century there were capitalists and workers. The people who live in any actual social formation have a conceptual scheme by which they make sense of it. Generally such a scheme both explains and conceals the true nature of the social order.

Karl Marx was born in Trier in Germany in 1818. He studied law but took up journalism as a profession, editing newspapers and publishing political tracts. His radical views led to one crisis after another. In 1843 he moved to Paris, and then Brussels. Expelled from there largely because of his role in the publication of the Communist Manifesto with Frederick Engels, he finally settled in London in 1849. Supported for the necessities of life by Engels, he famously spent his days in the British Museum acquiring a vast knowledge of economic matters, both theoretical and practical. These studies were the basis of his most famous book, *Capital*. A firebrand in print, Marx was a man of gentle charm in daily life. He died in 1883. His grave in Highgate cemetery has become a place of pilgrimage.

For Marx, the principles of morality are strictly local, the maxims and precepts of a class. The differences in the moral basis of the life of the bourgeoisie and that of the workers, as these are perceived by the members of these very classes, does not explain or account for the relations between the classes. That is determined by the social requirements to realize the existing modes of production (Marx, 1867). It follows that there are no trans-historical moral principles to which an appeal can be made in judging the moral standards prevailing at any time. If people in the dependent class are not getting what a certain mode of production makes available to those in the dominant class, they will set about getting them. And so the underlying contradiction between classes can emerge as revolution. Transition to a new social order, which abolishes the distinction that created the constraints of the old, will usher in a new moral order along with the new social order. This can be none other than the social requirements for implementing new means of production.

In some respects Marx's presuppositions regarding the source and status of social orders are not unlike those of Vico. One succeeds another, and Marx's theory purports to explain the transition. But the metaphysical problem of how a collective could have properties that are more than or different from those of any of its members does not find either a formulation or a solution in Marx's writings. It remains on the agenda to this day.

PHILOSOPHICAL FOUNDATIONS OF REPRESENTATIVE GOVERNMENT

Democratic forms of government have emerged at many epochs and in many places. The Viking form of representative government survives to this day in Iceland. In the course of the eighteenth and early nineteenth centuries the British monarchy evolved into the exemplary democracy we see today. Though in comparison with the democracies of Britain and Scandinavia, American democracy seems limited in scope, hardly touching the authoritarian style of the small-scale institutions of everyday life, at the level of the nation it represents the only example of a liberal democracy designed by a group of highly educated men, with the express intention of safeguarding political liberty. Though inspired by the political writings of John Locke, the philosophical foundations were laid anew by James Wilson, Thomas Jefferson, Alexander Hamilton, John Adams, and others. For the purposes of this chapter I have chosen James Wilson's writings to show the distinctly character of the political philosophy that was brought to the service of justifying the American Constitution.

Inventing the Republic

Writing after the event James Wilson (1742–98) attempted to provide a thorough philosophical grounding for the kind of representative democracy that he and his fellow constitutionalists had brought to fruition, though not without acrimony. As set out in his lectures on the Constitution (Wilson, 1896) delivered in 1790–1, Wilson sought a necessary grounding for the American Constitution and a guarantee of its moral role in the life of the citizen.

The natural origin of society

Wilson bases his derivation of the broad lineaments of the American Constitution on two theses about the nature of human beings, part anthropological and part theological. The first thesis sets out the natural "social intellectual" powers of the members of humankind.

> The Author of our existence intended us to be social beings: and has, for that end, given us social intellectual powers. They are original parts of our constitution and their exertions are no less natural than the exertion of those powers which are solitary and selfish. (Wilson, 1896: vol. 1, 258)

The second treats our moral capacities similarly. He goes on to remark, in the same vein, that "our moral perceptions, as well as other powers of our understanding indicate, in the strongest possible manner, our destination for society" (p. 261).

From this basis in the natural powers of human kind, intellectual and moral, we derive the actual bases of civil society. "Deeply laid in human nature, we now behold the basis of one of the principal pillars of private municipal law; that which enforces the obligation of promises, agreements and covenants" (p. 261). Thus we need no legal sanction to keep agreements. Rather the possibility of municipal law rests on the natural propensity to do so. By the same token, he declares that "the moral sense restrains us from harming the innocent." These are the "two great principles which prepare us for society." There is, it seems, no need for a contract. "We have all the emotions," he says (p. 263) "which are necessary in order that society may be formed and maintained." In short, "To a state of society, then we are invited from every quarter. It is natural; it is necessary; it is pleasing; it is preferable for us."

The expression of these sentiments and tendencies is the law: "this law, natural or revealed, made for men or for nations, flows from the same source: it is the law of God" (Wilson, 1930: 256). There is an obvious difficulty in Wilson's evocation of "natural law." Unlike the medieval treatments of natural law theory that link the mundane and the divine by invoking reason to link human conceptions of natural law with God's law, Wilson offers an empirical survey, so to say, of common perceptions of human nature. Nor does the derivation of the rule of law echo the Aristotelian theory of the *polis* as fitting citizens for the rule of law. The theological basis seems to be redundant.

The sources of representative democracy

We are still some way from representative democracy. Like many of the others who took part in the founding of the American republic, Wilson commends the Constitution for a feature which many of its foreign observers consider its weakest point, the principle of division of powers between legislature, executive, and judicial branches of government. There is not the same distrust of democracy that one finds in the patrician attitude of Alexander Hamilton. Indeed, Wilson goes on to introduce in outline a contract theory, overlaying his theological/ anthropological account.

> In the social compact, each individual engages with the whole collectivity and the whole engages with each individual. These engagements are obligatory, because they are mutual. The individuals who are not party to them are not members of the society. (Wilson, 1896: vol. 1, 272).

By what means is the general will to become known? By the voice of the majority "which must be deemed the voice of the whole." Wilson grounds this doctrine in the empirical assertion that the greater number are less likely to be mistaken than the lesser number. Without the Rousseauesque addition the democratic component of his ideal form of government would lack a grounding. But it is easy to see that this is an independent premise.

There is a variety of considerations of very different logical levels offered in Wilson's account. The discussion of the social compact provides us with an analysis of what it is to be a member of a society, though the means of engagement between the collective and the individual level is left indeterminate. The main argument for bringing everyone into the political arena is anthropological, that as a matter of fact we are endowed with certain powers and emotional propensities that "invite us into a state." In the early part of the argument Wilson presents the human character as naturally virtuous. However, by page 352 of the printed version of his lectures we find a different beast emerging, the bad propensities of human beings which need to be curbed. Law is now presented as a constraint, rather than an opportunity. There speaks a Justice of the Supreme Court!

The End of History

If the end of moral philosophy is to be found in the necessary conditions for the possibility of language, as some philosophers have recently argued, where would one look for the end of philosophical reflections on the presuppositions of the very idea of the state and society?

In 1992 Francis Fukuyama published his *The End of History and the Last Man*, elaborating on the theme that he had broached first of all in an article (Fukuyama, 1989). This work seemed to announce the end of political debate and so of political philosophy. In the article he had based his conclusion on a strong psychological presupposition, that the two universal and basic human needs were the need for liberty and the need for equality. Only liberal democracy, he argued, could satisfy both at once. The point was philosophical: not that since, as a matter of fact, the last authoritarian moral and political system had collapsed, such systems could now never reappear. Rather the argument was directed to showing that the concept of liberal democracy could not be superseded by any form of the governance of society that would meet the needs derived from the psychological presuppositions.

The book reshapes the argument to include the thesis that technology plus the free market will satisfy material needs indefinitely, ending want in principle. The psychological universal is revised, to become the need each person has for recognition by others. This has been pointed out by many sociologists and social psychologists, for instance, Erving Goffman (1967), for example, as the search for honor. Only liberal democracy can satisfy this need for everyone. The alliance of an economy of markets and a liberal democratic form of state organization represents the best shape that the human form of life could take. Whether the emergent form of this alliance that has appeared in the West, the Third Way, is permanent or stable is a matter of fact, which Fukuyama's philosophical argument does not address.

There are very strong psychological presuppositions required by the argument. Fukuyama himself observes that desire for status and the instinctive deference one feels and/or displays toward others might be of equal psychological power. The argument is incomplete (Sim, 1999), but certainly suggestive.

In China the direction of influence was from the forms of social life to the psychological attributes of people, the opposite direction from that presupposed in Occidental political philosophy. Both Wilson and Fukuyama, exemplifying Western presuppositions of the relation between human nature and civil society, try to demonstrate how liberal democracy emerges as a form that meets the demands of given or natural human characteristics Chinese philosophers, especially those belonging to the dominant Confucian and neo-Confucian schools, presupposed a concept of the person as above all a social actor. The metaphysical-psychological concepts of *ch'i* and *li* developed out of socially important aspects of the role of the person as citizen and family member. Among all the things which crystallized around *li* its ancient meaning persisted. It referred to a universal system of conventions and practices constitutive of social propriety. *Ch'i* is constitutive of people as individuals. It is not too fanciful to think of Taoism as sharing something of the same idea but turning it on its head – advising withdrawal rather than engagement in the practical business of administration. The desirable psychological state of *wu-wei* could be looked on as the psychic version of withdrawal from the realm of political activity.

Chinese moral philosophy moves in the same direction. The Confucian virtues are social. Mencius extracted four native impulses to action from the rich complexity of human psychology. All four are interpersonal and social. They are manifested as pity, shame, reverence, and a sense of right and wrong. With education these are transformed into the four virtues. *jen*, platonic love; *y*, a capacity to recognize one's inadequacy in any social activity; *li*, a proper sense of social behavior; *chih*, the power to recognize correct and incorrect behavior. The social focus of the virtues is very clear. It is also clear that in Confucian thought, virtue arises out of universal native tendencies only through education. We can see this in the presuppositions of Mao's "cultural revolution" as clearly as it appears in Confucius' opening of a school. In a word, in Chinese thought moral transformation is not through repentance and absolution but through a confession of error and a program of reeducation. In Oriental political philosophy, in which morality and political propriety are not sharply separated, society creates people. In the political philosophy of the Occident, at least since the seventeenth century, it has been presupposed in the search for the foundations of liberal democracy that people create society.

Conclusion

The agenda for political philosophy was set in the Renaissance – how to set up a secular state in which political obligation could be well grounded. Machiavelli's solution, an authoritarian reign by a wily prince, could not survive into the atmosphere of northwestern Europe. From the mid-seventeenth century the search for a rational grounding of political authority in the citizens themselves began. I have chosen a very restricted selection from among the many who contributed to the project. "Natural law" took on an anthropological flavor, as the mundane conditions for a flourishing life began to appear among the premises of philosophical arguments. That the link with theology was persistent into the supposedly secular enlightenment is quite evident in the writings of James Wilson. In one way, Fukuyama's "derivation" of a political philosophy is very unlike that of James Wilson and John Locke. Nowhere does he invoke God. Instead natural science is the touchstone of his version of "natural law." Perhaps the end of the second millennium did mark the end of political philosophy in a certain sense.

The last century of the second millennium could also perhaps be seen as a kind of test for the attempt to apply the Hegelian conception of historical change in practice. The Communist regimes that followed the Second World War advertised themselves as realizing the material dialectic. The less authoritarian socialist experiments in some of the northwestern European democracies nevertheless set up bureaucracies that became entrenched behind paper ramparts. Perhaps the Third Way is the end of not just a century but millennia in which the urge to govern has been in conflict with the demand for liberty. Perhaps Fukuyama is right, and that both come from sources so deep in our natures that political philosophy will always be the management of a compromise.

NOTES

1   Oddly, it was the more extreme English Protestants who instigated the revolution against Stuart despotism. Yet, a conception of the godly governance of the minutiae of life did not preclude a philosophical search for a rational basis for civil society.

Bibliography
References and Further Reading

General Reading

Edwards, P. (1967) *The Encyclopedia of Philosophy*. 8 vols. London: Macmillan.
Kenny, A. J. P. (1999) *A Brief History of Western Philosophy*. Oxford: Blackwell.
Kneale, W. C. and Kneale, M. (1962) *The Development of Logic* Oxford: Clarendon Press.
Law, S. (2000) *The Philosophy Files*. London: Orion Dolphin.
Passmore, J. (1957) *A Hundred Years of Philosophy*. London: Duckworth.
Scharfstein, B.-A. (1978) *Philosophy East/Philosophy West*. Oxford: Blackwell.
Scruton, R. (1996) *An Intelligent Person's Guide to Philosophy*. London: Duckworth.
Smart, N. (1999) *World Philosophies*. London: Routledge.
Wilson, A. N. (1999) *God's Funeral*. New York: W.W. Norton.

Chapter 1: What is Philosophy?

Blumberg, A. E. (1967) "Logic, Modern." In P. Edwards, *The Encyclopedia of Philosophy*, vol. 5, 13–28.
Collingwood, R. G. (1940) *An Essay on Metaphysics*. Oxford: Clarendon Press.
Flew, A. G. N. (1965) *Essays in Logic and Language*. Garden City, NY: Anchor.
Hamlyn, D. (1967) "Epistemology: History of." In P. Edwards, *The Encyclopedia of Philosophy*, vol. 3, 8–38.
Kant, I. (1787) [1996] *Critique of Pure Reason*, trans. W. S. Pluhar. Indianapolis: Hackett.
Leibniz, G. (1710) [1951] *Theodicy*, trans. A Farrer. London: Routledge and Kegan Paul.
Nielsen, K. and Abelson, R. (1967) "Ethics: History of." In P. Edwards, *The Encyclopedia of Philosophy*, vol. 3, 81–116.
Prior, A. N. (1967) "Logic, History of." In P. Edwards, *The Encyclopedia of Philosophy*, vol. 4, 509.

Reid, T. (1788) [1969] *Essays on the Intellectual Powers of Man* [*The Human Mind*]. Cambridge, MA: MIT Press.

Shweder, R. (1998) *Welcome to Middle Age! (and other Cultural Fictions)*. Chicago: Chicago University Press.

Walsh, W. H. (1967) "Metaphysics." In P. Edwards, *The Encyclopedia of Philosophy*, vol. 5, 301.

Wilson, A. N. (1999) *God's Funeral*. New York: W.W. Norton.

Wittgenstein, L. (1922) [1991] *Tractatus Logico-Philosophicus*, trans. D. F. Pears and B. McGuiness. London and New York: Routledge.

——(1956) *Remarks on the Foundations of Mathematics*, trans. G. E. M. Anscombe, R. Rhees, and G. H. Von Wright. Oxford: Blackwell.

——(1969) *On Certainty*. Oxford: Blackwell.

Chapters 2 and 3: Indian Philosophy

Aurobindo, S. (1918) [1990] *The Life Divine*. Pondicherry: Aurobindo Ashram.

Dasgupta, S. (1940) *A History of Indian Philosophy*. Cambridge: Cambridge University Press, vol. 4.

Frauwallner, E. (1973) *History of Indian Philosophy*. Delhi: Motilal Banarsidass.

Kalupahana, D. J. (1976) *Buddhist Philosophy: A Historical Analysis*. Honolulu: University of Hawaii Press.

Lakashamma, G. (1990) *The Impact of Rāmānuja's Teaching on Life and Conditions of Society*. Delhi: Sundeep Prakasha.

Ling, T. (1973) *The Buddha*. London: Temple Smith.

Nan Huia-chin (1995) *The Story of Chinese Zen*, trans. T. Cleary. Boston: Charles E. Tuttle.

Prabhavanda, Swami (1963) *The Spiritual Heritage of India*. Garden City, NY: Doubleday.

Puligandla, R. (1975) *Fundamentals of Indian Philosophy*. Nashville: Abingdon Press.

Radhakrishnan, S. (1927) *The Hindu View of Life*. London: George Allen.

Radhakrishnan, S. and Moore, C. A. (eds) (1957) *A Source Book in Indian Philosophy*. Princeton: Princeton University Press.

Smith, V. A. (1924) *The Oxford History of India*. Oxford: Clarendon Press.

Vidnyabhusana, S. C. (1971) *A History of Indian Logic*. Delhi: Motilal Bananidass.

Chapters 4 and 5: Chinese and Japanese Philosophy

Chen Ku-ying (1977) *Lao Tsŭ: Text, Notes, and Comments*. San Francisco: China Materials Center.

Chuang Tsŭ [1927] *Tao te Ching: The Writings of Chuang Tsŭ*, trans. J. Legge. In *The Writings of Kwange*. Taipei: Ch'eng Wen.

Cohen, A. A. (1964) *The Communism of Mao Tse-tung*. Chicago: Chicago University Press.

Confucius (ca. 500 B.C.) [1998] *The Analects*, trans. D. Hinton, Washington, DC: Counterpoint.

Creel, H. G. (1969) *Chinese Thought from Confucius to Mao Tse-tung*. Chicago: University of Chicago Press.

——(1982) *What is Taoism?* Chicago: University of Chicago Press.

Eberhard, W. (1964) *A History of China*. London: Routledge and Kegan Paul.

Fung Yu-lan (1937) *A History of Chinese Philosophy*, trans. D. Bodde. 2 vols. London: George Allen and Unwin.

Ho, F. M. (1992) *The Reception of Confucius in Japan*. Totowa, NJ: Optima Press.

Humphreys, C. (1955) *Buddhism*. Harmondsworth: Penguin.

I Ching, trans. C. F. Bayan (1950) Princeton: Princeton University Press.

Lao Tsŭ (600 B.C.) [1937] *Tao Tê Ching [The Sayings of Lao Tsŭ]*, trans. L. Giles. London: John Murray.

Mao Tse-tung (1961) *Mao Tse-tung*. Peking: Foreign Languages Press, vol I.

Persig, R. M. (1975) *Zen and the Art of Motorcycle Maintenance*. New York: Bantam.

Richards, I. A. (1932) *Mencius on the Mind*. London: Kegan Paul.

Suzuki, D. (1958) *Zen and Japanese Culture*. Princeton: Bollingen.

Waley, A. (1939) *Three Ways of Thought in Ancient China*. London: George Allen & Unwin.

Watts, A. (1936) *The Spirit of Zen*. London: John Murray.

Wing-tsit Chin (1963) *A Source Book in Chinese Philosophy*. Princeton: Princeton University Press, and London: Oxford University Press.

Chapter 6: Islamic Philosophy

Al-Ghazālī, A. H. M. (ca. 1100) [1983] *The Alchemy of Happiness*, trans. C. Field. Armonk, NY: Sharpe.

——(ca. 1105) [1958] *The Incoherence of the Philosophers*, trans. S. A. Kamali. Lahore: Anarkali Press.

Aristotle (ca. 395 B.C.) [1993] *Metaphysics*, trans. C. Kirwan. Oxford: Clarendon Press.

Bokser B. Z. (1950) *The Legacy of Maimonides*. New York: Philosophical Library.

Fakhry, M. (1983) *A History of Islamic Philosophy*. London: Longman.

The Holy Koran, trans. M. M. Pickthall (1977) Rabita: Muslim World League.

Hourani, G. F. (1976) *Averroes*. London: Luzac.

Ibn Sīnā (Avicenna) (ca. 1020) [1973] *Metaphysica*, trans. P. Morwedge. New York: Columbia University Press.

Ibn Rushd (ca. 1180) [1984] *Metaphysics*, trans. C. Genquand. Leiden: Brill.
——(ca. 1193) [1967] *Averroes on the Harmony of Religion and Philosophy*, trans. G. Hourani. London: Luzac.
Iqbal, M. (1934) *The Reconstruction of Religious Thought in Islam*. Oxford: Oxford University Press.
Maimonides, M. (ca. 1200) [1961] *A Guide for the Perplexed*, trans. M. Friedlander. New York: Dover.
Nasr, S. H. and Leaman, O. (1996) *History of Islamic Philosophy, Part II*. 2 vols. London: Routledge.
Plotinus (ca. 253–270) [1969] *Enneads*, trans. S. McKenna. London: Faber.
Rumi, al-D. (1997) *The Essential Rumi*, trans. C. Banks. San Francisco: Harper.
Schroeder, F. M. (1992) *Form and Transformation: A Study in the Philosophy of Plotinus*. Montreal and Kingston: McGill-Queens University Press.
Urvoy, D. (1991) *Ibn Rushd (Averroes)*, trans. O. Stewart. London and New York: Routledge.

Chapter 7: Philosophy in Medieval Europe

Anselm, St (1077–8) [1965] *Proslogium*, trans. M. J. Charlesworth. Oxford: Oxford University Press.
Aquinas, St Thomas (1273) [1964] *Summa Theologiae*, trans. T. Gibbs. Garden City, NY: Doubleday.
——(ca. 1263) [1975] *Summa Contra Gentiles*, trans. A. C. Pegis, Notre Dame: Notre Dame University Press.
Augustine, St (412–426) [1950] *The City of God*, trans. M. Dodds. New York: Hafner.
Bernard, St (of Clairvaux) (ca. 1130) [1633] *The Rule of Good Life*, trans. A. Balt, London: Downey.
——(ca. 1130) [1990] *Love without Measure*, ed. P. Diemer. London: Darton, Longman and Todd.
Boehner, P. (1990) *Ockham: Philosophical Writings*. Indianapolis: Hackett.
Copleston, F. C. (1972) *A History of Medieval Philosophy*. London: Methuen.
D'Arcy, M. C. (1930) *St. Thomas Aquinas*. Boston: Little Brown.
Davies, N. (1997) *Europe*. Oxford: Oxford University Press.
Frepper, L. (1988) *The Basis of Morality according to William Ockham*. Chicago: Franciscan Press.
Kenny, A. J. P. (1969) *Five Ways*. London: Routledge and Kegan Paul.
Lisske, A. J. (1996) *Aquinas's Theory of Natural Law*. Oxford: Clarendon Press.
Marenbon, P. (1997) *The Philosophy of Peter Abelard*. Cambridge: Cambridge University Press.
McInerny, R. (1993) *The Cambridge Companion to Aquinas*, ed. N. Kretzmann and E. Stump. Cambridge: Cambridge University Press, chapter 7.

Moody, E. A. (1967) "William of Ockham." In P. Edwards, *The Encyclopedia of Philosophy*, vol. 8, 306–17.

Ockham, William of (1328) [1974] *Summa Logicae*, ed. P. Boerner, G. Gal, and S. Brown. New York: St Bonaventure.

——(1324) [1991] *Quodlibetal Questions*, trans. A. J. Freddoso. New Haven and London: Yale University Press.

Chapter 8: The World Shapes the Mind: Realism and Positivism

Aries, P. A. (1962) *Centuries of Childhood*, trans. R. Baldick. New York: Kropf.

Ayer, A. J. (1936) *Language, Truth and Logic*. London: Gollancz.

——(1978) *Logical Positivism* Westport, CT: Greenwood.

Bacon, F. (1605) [1973] *The Advancement of Learning*. London: Dent.

Berkeley, G. (1719) [1985] *Principles of Human Knowledge*. London: Fontana.

Boyle, R. (1666) *On the Origins of Forms and Qualities*. Oxford: Davis.

Cahoone, L. E. (1996) *From Modernism to Postmodernism*. Cambridge, MA: Blackwell.

Carlyle, T. (1886–93) [1977] *Past and Present*. New York: New York University Press.

Carnap, R. (1950) *Testability and Meaning*. New Haven: Yale University Philosophy Club.

Clavius, C. (1570) *In Sphaeram Ioannis de Sacrobosco*. Rome: Apud Vitorum Helicanum.

Comte, A. (1853) *The Positive Philosophy of Auguste Comte*, trans. H. Martineau. London: Chapman.

.Descartes, R. (1647) [1985] *Principles of Philosophy*. In *The Philosophical Writings of Descartes*, ed. J. Cottingham, R. Stoothoff, and D. Murdoch. Cambridge: Cambridge University Press, vol. I.

Gilbert, W. (1600) [1958] *De Magnete*, trans. P. F. Mottelay. New York: Dover.

Hacking, I. (1999) *Social Construction of What?* Cambridge, MA: Harvard University Press.

Hilbert, D. (1971) *Foundations of Geometry*. La Salle, IL: Open Court.

Hume, D. (1739) [1965] *A Treatise of Human Nature*. Oxford: Clarendon Press.

——(1777) [1963] *Enquiries concerning the Human Understanding and the Principles of Morals*. Oxford: Clarendon Press.

Locke, J. (1690) [1974] *An Essay concerning Human Understanding*, ed. W. J. Yolton, London: Dent.

Mach, E. (1883) [1914] *The Analysis of Sensations*, trans. T. J. McCormack. Chicago: Open Court.

——(1894) [1918] *Popular Scientific Lectures*, trans. T. J. McCormack. La Salle, IL: Open Court.

Mill, J. S. (1872) [1996] *A System of Logic*. London: Routledge.

Newton I. (1617) [1992] "Third Letter to Bentley." In *The Correspondence of Isaac Newton*, ed. H. W. Turnbull. Cambridge: Cambridge University Press, vol. 3.

Popper, K. R. (1965) *Conjectures and Refutations*. New York: Harper and Row.

Psillos, S. (1999) *Scientific Realism*. London: Routledge.

Quine, W. V. (1953) *From a Logical Point of View*. Cambridge, MA: Harvard University Press.

Schlick, M. (1949) *Philosophy of Nature*. New York: Philosophy Library.

Whiston, W. (1717) [1983] *Astronomical Principles of Religion*. London: Heldestein, and New York: Olm.

Chapter 9: Mind and Cosmos: Rationalism and Conventionalism

Barnes, B. and Bloor, D. (1996) *Scientific Knowledge: A Sociological Analysis*. London: Athlone Press.

Descartes, R. (1647) [1985] *Principles of Philosophy*. In *The Philosophical Writings of Descartes*, ed. J. Cottingham, R. Stoothoff, and D. Murdoch. Cambridge: Cambridge University Press, vol. I.

Eddington, A. (1935) *New Pathways in Science*, Cambridge: Cambridge University Press.

Feyerabend, P. K. (1975) *Against Method*. London: Verso.

Frege, G. (1879) [1952] *Translations from the Philosophical Writings of Gottlob Frege*, ed. P. Geach and M. Black. Oxford: Clarendon Press.

Galileo Galilei (1638) [1952] *Dialogues concerning Two New Sciences*, trans. H. Crew and A. de Salvio. New York: Dover.

Goodman, N. (1978) *Ways of World Making*. Indianapolis: Hackett.

Hacker, P. (1996) *Wittgenstein's Place in Twentieth-century Analytical Philosophy*. Oxford: Blackwell.

Hacking, I. (1992) "The self-vindication of the laboratory sciences." In *Science as Practice and Culture*, ed. A Pickering. Chicago: Chicago University Press, chapter 2.

——(1999) *The Social Construction of what?* Cambridge, MA: Havard University Press.

Hilbert, D. and Ackermann, W. (1928) [1950] *Principles of Mathematical Logic*, trans. L. M. Harword, G. C. Lackie, and F. Steinhardt. New York: Chebea.

Kant, I. (1787) [1996] *Critique of Pure Reason*, trans. W. S. Pluhar Indianapolis: Hackett.

Kuhn, T. S. (1957) [1996] *The Structure of Scientific Revolutions*. 3rd edn. Chicago: Chicago University Press.

Leibniz, G. (1710) [1953] *Theodicy*, trans. A. Farrer. London: Routledge and Kegan Paul.

Murphy, N. (1997) *Anglo-American Postmodernity*. London: Routledge and Kegan Paul.

Poincaré, H. (1903) [1958] *The Value of Science*, trans. G. B. Halstead. New York: Dover.

Russell, B. A. W. (1919) *Introduction to Mathematical Philosophy*. London: Allen and Unwin.

Whewell, W. (1860) [1970] *On the Philosophy of Discovery*. London: Parker.

Whitehead, A. N. and Russell, B. A. W. (1910–13) *Principia Mathematica*. Cambridge: Cambridge University Press.

Wittgenstein, L. (1953) *Philosophical Investigations*, trans. G. E. M. Anscombe. Oxford: Blackwell.

Chapter 10: The Unity of Mind and World: Idealism, Phenomenalism, and Phenomenology

Austin, J. L. (1962) *Sense and Sensibilia*. Oxford: Clarendon Press.

Bradley, F. H. (1893) *Appearance and Reality*. Oxford: Clarendon Press.

Chalmers, D. (1996) *The Conscious Mind*. New York: Oxford University Press.

Devine, E. et al. (1975) *Thinkers of the Twentieth Century*. London: Macmillan.

Ewing, A. C. (1934) *Idealism: A Critical Survey*. London: Methuen.

Hegel, G. W. F. (1807) [1949] *The Phenomenology of Mind*, trans. J. B. Bartlie. London: Allen and Unwin.

——(1837) [1956] *The Philosophy of History*, trans. J. Silbee. New York: Witley.

Heidegger, M. (1953) [1996] *Being and Time*, trans. J. Stambaugh. Albany: SUNY Press.

Husserl, E. (1950) [1960] *Cartesian Meditations*, trans. D. Cariras. The Hague: Martinus Nijhoff.

——(1964) *The Idea of Phenomenology*, trans. W. P. Alston and G. Nakhnikian. The Hague: Martinus Nijhoff.

Inwood, M. (1983) *Hegel*. London: Routledge and Kegan Paul.

Leibniz, G. (1710) [1952] *Theodicy*, trans. A. Farrer. London: Routledge.

——(1717) [1956] *The Clarke–Leibniz Correspondence*, ed. H. G. Alexander. Manchester: Manchester University Press.

Rorty, R. (1989) *Contingency, Irony, and Solidarity*. Cambridge: Cambridge University Press.

Russell, B. A. W. (1975) *Logical Essays*, ed. R. C. Marsh. New York: Capricorn.

Sainsbury, M. (1979) *Russell*. London: Routledge and Kegan Paul.

Schutz, A. (1967) *Phenomenology of the Social World*. Evanston, IL: Northwestern University Press.

Shusterman, R. (1990) "Postmodernist ethics of taste." In G. Shapiro (ed.), *After the Future*. Albany: SUNY Press.

Steiner, G. (1978) *Heidegger*. London: Fontana Press.

Taylor, C. (1979) *Hegel and Modern Society*. Cambridge: Cambridge University Press.

Wittgenstein, L. (1953) *Philosophical Investigations*, trans. G. E. M. Anscombe. Oxford: Blackwell.

Chapter 11: Human Nature

Berkeley. G. (1734) [1985] *A Treatise concerning Principles of Human Knowledge*. London: Fontana.

Butler, J. (1736) [1886] "Of Personal Identity." In *The Analogy of Religion*. London: Bell.

Churchland, P. M. (1984) *Matter and Consciousness*. Cambridge, MA: MIT Press.

Copeland, J. (1992) [1998] *Artificial Intelligence*. Oxford: Blackwell.

Darwin. C. (1859) *The Origin of Species, or, the Preservation of Favoured Races*. London: John Murray.

Descartes, R. (1641) [1985] *Meditations on First Philosophy. The Philosophical Writings of Descartes*, ed. J. Cottingham, R. Stoothoff, and D. Murdoch. Cambridge: Cambridge University Press, vol. II.

Freud, S. (1933) *New Introductory Lectures on Psychoanalysis*. London: Hogarth Press.

Hacker, P. S. M. (1996) *Wittgenstein's Place in 20th-Century Analytical Philosophy*. Oxford; Blackwell.

Hanson, N. R. (1958) *Patterns of Discovery*. Cambridge: Cambridge University Press.

Hume, D. (1739) [1962] *A Treatise of Human Nature*. Oxford: Clarendon Press.

La Mettrie, Julien Offrray de (1748) *L'Homme machine*. Leyden: Elie Lizac.

Leibniz, G. W. (written, 1714) [1960] *The Monadology*. In *Philosophical Texts*, trans. R. Francks and R. S. Woolhouse. Oxford: Oxford University Press.

Locke, J. (1690) [1974] *An Essay Concerning Human Understanding*, ed. J. W. Yolton. London: Dent.

Monk, R. (1990) *Ludwig Wittgenstein: The Duty of Genius*. London: Cape.

Nagel, T. (1998) "Conceiving the impossible and the mind–body problem." *Philosophy*, 73, 337–52.

Priestley, J. (1777) [1975] *Disquisitions relating to Matter and Spirit*. New York: Arno Press.

Reid, T. (1788) *Essays on the Intellectual Powers of Man*. Edinburgh: John Bell.

Ryle, G. (1947) *The Concept of Mind*. London: Hutchinson.

Searle, J. R. (1983) *Intentionality: An Essay in the Philosophy of Mind*. Cambridge: Cambridge University Press.

——(1992) *The Rediscovery of the Mind* Cambridge, MA: MIT Press.

Spinoza, B. de (1677) [1930] *Ethics*, trans. W. Hale and A. H. Stirling. London: Oxford University Press.

Strawson, P. F. (1956) *Individuals*. London: Methuen.

Turing, A. (1950) "Computing Machines and Intelligence." *Mind*, 59, 433–60.

Vartanian, A. (1960) *La Mettrie's L'Homme Machine: A Study in the Origins of an Idea*. Princeton: Princeton University Press.

Williams, B. A. O. (1973) *Problems of the Self*. Cambridge: Cambridge University Press.

Wittgenstein, L. (1953) *Philosophical Investigations*, trans. G. E. M. Anscombe. Oxford: Blackwell.

Chapter 12: Relations among Persons I: Moral Philosophy

Austin, J. L. (1962) *How to do Things with Words*. Oxford: Clarendon Press.

Benthem, J. (1789) [1834] *Deontology: or, the Science of Morality*. London: Reese, Orme.

Boas, F. (1896) [1940] *Race, Language and Culture*. New York: Free Press.

Cixous, H. (1987) *The Newly Born Woman*, trans. C. Clement and S. Gilbert. Manchester: Manchester University Press.

Davies, B. (1999) *A Body of Writing*. Heemstede, the Netherlands: Alta Mira Press.

Derrida, J. (1982) *Margins of Philosophy*, trans. A. Bass. Brighton: Harvester.

Geertz, C. (1989) "Anti anti-relativism." In *Relativism: Interpretation and Confrontation*. Notre Dame: Notre Dame University Press, 12–34.

Habermas, J. (1984–87) *The Theory of Communicative Action*, trans. T. McCarthy. Boston: Beacon Press.

Hare, R. M. (1952) *The Language of Morals*. Oxford: Clarendon Press.

Holiday, A. (1988) *Moral Powers*. Hassocks: Harvester Press.

Hume, D. (1740) [1998] *An Enquiry concerning the Principles of Morals*. Oxford: Oxford University Press.

Kant, I. (1785) [1969] *Foundations of the Metaphysics of Morals*, trans. L. W. Beck. Indianapolis: Bobbs-Merrill.

Kierkegaard, S. (1843) [1944] *Either/Or*, trans. W. Lowrie. Princeton: Princeton University Press.

Lovelock, J. E. (1987) *Gaia: A New Look at Life on Earth*. Oxford: Oxford University Press.

Lukes, S. (1975) *Individualism*. Oxford: Blackwell.

MacIntyre, A. C. (1966) *A Short History of Ethics*. London: Macmillan.

Mill, J. S. (1861) [1998] *Utilitarianism*. Oxford: Oxford University Press.

Moore, G. E. (1903) *Principia Ethica*. Cambridge: Cambridge University Press.

Richards, J. R. (1982) *The Sceptical Feminist*. Harmondsworth: Penguin.

Rorty, R. (1989) *Contingency, Irony, and Solidarity*. Cambridge: Cambridge University Press.

——(1989) "Solidarity or objectivity?" In *Relativism: Interpretation and Confrontation.* Notre Dame: Notre Dame University Press, 35–50.

Sartre, J.-P. (1943) [1958] *Being and Nothingness,* trans. H. E. Barnes. London: Routledge.

Shusterman, R. (1990) "Postmodernist ethics of taste." In G. Shapiro (ed.), *After the Future* Albany: SUNY Press.

Singer, P. (1976) *Animal Rights and Human Obligations.* Princeton, NJ: Princeton University Press.

Warnock, M. (1979) *Ethics since 1900.* Oxford: Oxford University Press.

Wittgenstein, L. (1979) *Remarks on Frazer's "Golden Bough,"* trans. A. C. Miles. Atlantic Hills, NJ: Humanities Press.

——(1993) *Philosophical Occasions: 1912–1951,* ed. J. C. Klagge and A. Nordham, Indianapolis: Hackett.

Chapter 13: Relations among Persons II: Political Philosophy

Bentham, J. (1789) [1834] *Deontology; or, the Science of Morality.* London: Reese, Orme.

Finnis, J. (1980) *Natural Law and Natural Rights.* Oxford: Clarendon Press.

Fukuyama, F. (1989) "The end of History?" *National Interest* (Summer), 3–17.

——(1993) *The End of History and the Last Man* New York: Avon.

Giddens, A. (1998) *The Third Way: The Renewal of Social Democracy.* Cambridge: Polity Press.

Goffman, E. (1967) *Interaction Ritual.* New York: Anchor Books.

Hobbes, T. (1651) [1914] *Leviathan.* London: Dent.

Hegel, G. W. F. (1821) [1945] *Philosophy of Right,* trans. T. M. Knox. Oxford: Clarendon Press.

Locke, J. (1690) [1924] *Of Civil Government: Two Treatises.* London: Dent.

Marx, K. (1867) [1990] *Capital: A Critique of Political Economy.* London: Penguin.

Plamenatz, J. (1963) *Man and Society.* London: Longman.

Popper, K. (1957) *The Povertry of Historicism.* London: Routledge.

Rawls, J. (1971) *A Theory of Justice.* Cambridge, MA: Belknap Press.

Rousseau, J. J. (1764) [1968] *The Social Contract,* trans. M. Cranston. Harmondsworth: Penguin Books.

Sim, S. (1999) *Derrida and the End of History.* Cambridge: Icon Books.

Vico, G. (1725) [1948] *Scientia Nova [The New Science],* trans. T. G. Bergin and M. H. Fisch. Ithaca, NY: Cornell University Press.

Wilson, J. (1896) *Collected Works,* ed. J. D. Andrews. Chicago: Callaghan.

——(1930) *Selected Political Writings,* ed. R. G. Adams. New York: Knopf.

Index

Hegel, G. W. F., 4, 247–50, 326, 337, 338, 339
Heidegger, M., 259–62
history
end of, 344–5
and meaning of freedom, 339
psychological presuppositions, 344
role of free market, 344
and successive social forms, 337
Hobbes, T., 119
hsing (mentality), 85, 87
Hui-neng, 96–7
human nature, neo-Confucian conception, 106–7
humanism, 191, 300
Hume, D., 137, 195, 211–13, 214, 269, 286, 287
Hume's method, ideas and impressions, 213
Humphreys, C., 114
Husserl, E., 255–8, 262

I Ching, 93
"I think therefore I am," 271
criticisms of, 271–2
Ibn Rushd (Averroes), 126, 149–51, 152, 153, 189
Ibn Sīnā (Avicenna), 126, 132, 134, 138, 139, 141, 145, 148, 152, 153, 158, 189
Ibn Taymiyah, 153–4
ideal civic life, Confucian, 81
idealism, 74, 191, 262
conditions for knowledge, 251
in England, 250–2
in Germany, 247–50
ideas and qualities (Lockean), 202–4
identity, personal, 65–6, 284–6
as consciousness, 285, 286
as a man, 285
and memory, 285, 286, 298
of self, 285, 286

identity of indiscernibles, 225
immortality in Chinese thought, 93–5
materialist conception, 94, 101
imperatives, hypothetical v. categorical, 304
imperatives, indirect, 311
individual souls, Indian, 64
individualist/collectivist view of society, 191
indriyas (senses), 42
Intelligences, hierarchy of, 128–30, 149, 150
intuition, Kantian, 223, 230
intuitionism, 309–10
Inwood, M., 248, 249, 250
Iqbal, M., 156–9
Islam, in India, 35, 36, 69
Islamic influence, 152–3
Islamic philosophy, beginnings, 124
reconstruction of, 157–9
Īśvara, 34, 43, 45, 46, 62, 63, 64, 65

James, W., 220
Japanese philosophical imports, 111
jen (disinterested love), 85, 87, 107
Johnson, Samuel, 210

Kant, I., 19, 22–3, 26, 222, 226, 228–32, 244, 246, 280, 281, 303–5, 309, 312
karma, 42
Kepler, J., 194, 233
Kierkegaard, S., 3, 312–14, 326
Kingdom of Ends, 304, 326
knowledge, 6
routes to, 141, 142
Koran, 125, 136, 140, 142, 148, 157, 159
Koranic doctrines, 131, 132
Kuhn, T., 236, 237–9

La Mettrie, J. O. de, 274, 275
Lao Tsǔ, 88, 94

law
concept of, 176
eternal, 176
human, 177
"levels" of, 176
natural, 176, 177–8
reason and law, 178
laws of nature, Mach's psychological account, 217
Leibniz, G., 19, 20–1, 26, 222, 224–6, 241, 300
li (ritual or principle), 82, 103, 107, 108, 110
generalization of, 104–5, 106
Locke, J., 201, 202, 205, 229, 255, 284, 285, 287, 329, 341, 346
logic, 7–8
Buddhist, 53
Indian, 52–4
induction, limits of, 64
knowledge source, 54
as science of language, 241
logical constructions, 254
logical form, 242, 243
logical positivism, 216–20
metaphysics as speculation, 218, 219
verification principle, 219
love, from carnal to divine, 165–6
Lu Hsian-shan, 100, 107, 108

Mach, E., 216–18
Machiavelli, N., 335
Maimonides, M., 144–8
Manicheans, 173
Mao Tse-tung, 79, 117–19, 120
Martineau, H., 306
Marx, K., 326, 337, 339, 340
Marxism, 78, 116–19
master/serf relation, 338–9
materialism, Indian, 37, 58–9, 73
materialism, strong, 276–80
eliminative, 276–8